DRAWING THE PAST, VOLUME 1

DRAWING the PAST

VOLUME 1

Comics and the Historical Imagination in the United States

Edited by Dorian L. Alexander, Michael Goodrum, and Philip Smith

UNIVERSITY PRESS OF MISSISSIPPI / JACKSON

The University Press of Mississippi is the scholarly publishing agency of the Mississippi Institutions of Higher Learning: Alcorn State University, Delta State University, Jackson State University, Mississippi State University, Mississippi University for Women, Mississippi Valley State University, University of Mississippi, and University of Southern Mississippi.

www.upress.state.ms.us

The University Press of Mississippi is a member of the Association of University Presses.

Manufactured in the United States of America

First printing 2022
∞

<Library of Congress Cataloging-in-Publication Data to come>

British Library Cataloging-in-Publication Data available

CONTENTS

ACKNOWLEDGMENTS

Dorian L. Alexander would like to thank their coeditors for all their trust and mentorship over the past several years. Thanks to my grandparents for their love and continued belief that I'm doing something worthwhile and arcane with my life. And finally, to Nicole Martin, without whom I might not have ever made it this far.

Michael Goodrum would like to thank his splendid coeditors and our contributors for all their hard work. I would also like to thank UPM for their efforts on this volume. My wife, Emma, and our children, Anna and Elise, also provided their own personal brand of love and insight. More prosaically, I would like to thank Dr. Martens for their truly excellent shoes.

Philip Smith would like to thank Dorian for suggesting this project back in what feels like a lifetime ago (Wondercon in 2017 if memory serves). They and Mitch have been excellent colleagues and friends on the journey to create this book. I would also like to thank my wife, Stephanie, for her love, support, and peanut butter Oreo cheesecakes. I performed my work on this book while serving as faculty at the University of The Bahamas (this brings the count to Smith 6, Oenbring 1) and as associate chair at Savannah College of Art and Design.

DRAWING THE PAST, VOLUME 1

INTRODUCTION

DORIAN L. ALEXANDER, MICHAEL GOODRUM, AND PHILIP SMITH

The founding principle of this book is that the ways in which we represent history are crucial to the politics of today. History has always been a matter of arranging evidence into a narrative, but the public debate over the meanings we attach to a given history can, in our current age, seem particularly acute. While this book was conceived and written, paralegal and protestor Heather D. Heyer was murdered in Charlottesville three blocks from a statue of Robert E. Lee. The debate over the statue and its removal was only one aspect of a divisive moment in American politics, which came to one of its many heads in Charlottesville. One might say, in a simplistic but not inaccurate version of the events that unfolded, Heyer was on the streets that day because she believed that the statue represents one account of American history, and her killer murdered her because he believed that it represents another.

Comics, like all artistic mediums, possesses the power to mold history into shapes that serve both its prospective audience and its creator. Comics are particularly suited to this manipulation, engaged, as often as they are, in the act of mythologization. As lauded comics creator Grant Morrison intones in his philosophical treatise/autobiography *Supergods*, comic book characters often carry the spiritual canvas and moral weight of religious deities.[1] Almost immediately following the clash of historical forces in Charlottesville, *Action Comics* #987 was released to a tide of controversy. The comic features a scene where Superman, a longtime icon of "truth, justice, and the *American* way," defends a group of undocumented immigrants from an angry white man in nationalist attire.[2] The scene emphasizes Superman's identity as an immigrant, prioritizing the saccharine "melting pot" narrative of United States history superficially taught in most American high schools. This angered conservatives already leery of a Superman who had renounced his US citizenship in 2011, signaling a paradigm shift in the way the United States' historical relationship with the world would be represented in the comic.[3] The "American way" Superman enshrines was no longer a uniquely, superpowered hero, flying in to save the world from evil forces, but rather a member of the globalist community, a part of the world it might be trying to save.

It makes sense, then, that history, no stranger to the creation of hagiographies, particularly in the service of nationalism and other political ideologies, is so easily summoned to the paneled page. Comics, like statues, museums, and other easily accessed vehicles for historical narrative, make both monsters and heroes of men, while fueling the already fiercely burning and combative beliefs in personal versions of American history. The consequences of this inferno should not be ignored.

As a nation, the USA has always been fascinated by its own history. More precisely, with attempts to curate a specific history while marginalizing or obliterating others. Ronald Takaki refers to this as the "Master Narrative of American History"—the notion that American society is rooted in white migration from North European nations, a principle that is simultaneously demonstrably false and yet enshrined in generations of historical and cultural narratives.[4] Popular culture plays a vital role here in the construction of an "imagined community"; the creation of a community who, through processes of ideological investment in abstract concepts, come to believe in the concrete existence of a nation and feel a sense of their belonging to it.[5] Through misleading narratives about who "really" constitutes the nation, supported by elite political and historical utterances and accompanied by an avalanche of supporting popular culture, particular narratives and images take hold in the ideological imagination of individuals and communities. For instance, early accounts of American migration history, such as Oscar Handlin's *The Uprooted* (1951), focused on patterns of migration from Europe to the detriment of Asia and Africa, defining the legitimacy, the "American-ness," of those arriving in the US in the process.[6] As is clear from this brief account, the ways in which we understand history have a profound impact on how we live our lives and how we imagine the future.

Controversy over the removal of monuments (both Confederate monuments in America and, for example, debates around a statue of Cecil Rhodes in Oxford, England, in 2015) is one example of the ways in which art, history, and national narratives intersect, indeed, how they can intersect repeatedly on the same point of debate at different historical moments: Tony Horwitz dramatized the afterlife of the Confederacy in his Pulitzer Prize–winning book, *Confederates in the Attic: Dispatches from the Unfinished Civil War* (1998). While political and cultural narratives continue to circulate questioning predominant accounts of the Civil War and positing alternatives, and continue to command belief from significant numbers, it appears that the South will indeed rise again, if only in debates about itself, at specific moments. These discrepancies are often caught up in the drifts of popular culture. The heroes and villains of the past are not as likely to be chosen by historians as they are to be created by the public imagination. This book seeks to complicate this act of creation by collecting a diverse series of essays examining the process.

The way in which film shapes the public's perception of historical events has been explored in texts like *The Historian and Film* (1976), *The Historical Film: History and Memory in Media* (2000), and *Histories on Screen: The Past and Present in Anglo-American Cinema and Television* (2018). Nations, and national identity, are constructed through not just geopolitical boundaries but imaginary ones. Culture offers a space in which debates can inhere, but it also constructs that space by offering preferred trajectories of understanding. Films and comics play a pivotal role in this narration of the nation by offering up visual icons for identification and showing how they move through space, interacting with both the space itself and the people who inhabit it. Comics are related to film in that both have emerged as predominant forces of popular influence, and both utilize a combination of the visual and the verbal. Comics is unique, however, in its spatial construction and temporal engagement, which requires more of the reader's imaginative investment to make the form function than does film, and therefore it deserves to be interrogated on its own terms.

Before we can examine how history is represented by comics, we must acknowledge what historical representation *is*. In F. R. Ankersmit's book on the subject, historical representation is conceived as a replacement of the past itself. He argues that postmodern fretting over how narrative organization might brutalize history and the consequential resistance to thematic framing of the past has been nothing but a disservice to our ultimate understanding of the past. History, he posits, fails when it merely attempts to describe the past, for mere description is impossible. In this, History as a practice can never achieve the goal set out for it by Leopold von Ranke in his *History of the Latin and German Peoples* (1824) "to show the past as it really was."[7] History is itself a representation, a thing (albeit one usually made up of words) that replaces another thing. Comics, with their more readily recognizable "thingness," carry unique potential for readers' understanding and engagement with this act of replacement, whether they are primarily engaged in the act of historical documentation or fictional narrativization or some combination thereof. In addition is their powerfully layered capacity for metaphor. Historical metaphorics, already capable of shaping historical reality (think of Burckhardt's epoch-creating use of the metaphor *renaissance*), explodes with possibility when produced in the comics form, unfettered by imposed temporality and the use of language alone.

In part, this volume is also informed by the works of Hayden White, Nathalie Zemon Davis, and Robert Rosenstone, all of whom seek to understand the role of fiction in the practice of historiography. Collectively, these critics offer a revised understanding of our means to distinguish between credible and incredible representations of a given event, demonstrating that all attempts to represent history unavoidably encode meaning not inherent in the original object. This problem is perhaps most effectively articulated by Ira Berlin, who argues, "History is not about the past; it is about arguments we have about the past."[8] These critics gave rise to an approach to historiography that recognizes that no historical account can be considered wholly transparent.

A key event in academic interest in comics as a medium for historical narrative was the publication of Art Spiegelman's *Maus* in *RAW* magazine. James Young was one of the first scholars to examine Spiegelman's alchemy of Holocaust testimony with visual invention.[9] Joseph Witek identifies a turn toward more sustained and serious treatment of history in comics in the 1980s, positioning that as a development arising from the "heritage of fact-based comics in America" before going on to investigate "how such comic books function as narrative media and as embodiments of ideology," both of which are questions integral to this volume.[10] Spiegelman, of course, was not the first to seek to represent a historical object through comics. Depending on the definition of comics one accepts, one might make the case that for the first four centuries of its existence, history was the dominant, perhaps only, subject of the comics medium. David Kunzle argues that the earliest comics were medieval frescoes and stained-glass windows that sought to express literalist interpretation of scripture for both literate and illiterate audiences.[11] They were, in the terms of their creators and original audiences, historical narratives. Similarly, Hillary Chute has framed some of the works of Jacques Callot and Francisco Goya as comics. During the seventeenth and eighteenth centuries, true crime comics, printed using woodblocks, circulated in early broadsheets. They depicted in pictographic form crimes, captures, and executions. The use of comics as a tool for making truth claims about the past continued into the twentieth century with series such as *True Crime Comics* (1947), *Real Life Comics* (1941), *Classic Comics* (1941), *Topix Comics* (1942), and the early publications by EC, a company that began its existence as Educational Comics but found fame as Entertaining Comics as part of a debate as to whether comics could serve the purposes found in either of its names.

Charles Hatfield's *Alternative Comics* (2005) attempts to tackle the evasive question of truth in a medium that relies upon an aesthetic strategy of artifice and exaggeration. Hatfield coined the term "ironic authenticity" to describe the use of self-conscious falsification as a means to establish a compact between creator and reader. Nina Mickwitz, too, makes an important intervention in our understanding of truth claims in graphic narrative in *Documentary Comics* (2015) in which she broadens our vocabulary of aesthetic strategies used in comics reportage. These interventions provide us with a means to consider graphic memoir such as Marjane Satrapi's *Persepolis* (2000); Alison Bechdel's *Fun Home: A Family Tragicomic*; Guy Delisle's *Shenzhen* (2000), *Pyongyang: A Journey in*

North Korea (2003), *Burma Chronicles* (2007), and *Jerusalem* (2011); or Harvey Pekar's *American Splendor* (1976–2008), and comics reportage such as Joe Sacco's *Palestine* (1996), *Footnotes in Gaza* (2009), *Safe Area Goražde* (2000), and *The Fixer* (2003), or Emmanuel Guibert's *The Photographer* (2000–2006).

While comics reportage, documentary comics, and autobiography share similar tools and address similar tensions between fact and aesthetics, they remain fundamentally different from history comics in that they seek to describe events for which the artist was an eyewitness and, in many cases, an active participant. Historical comics are not drawn from memory but offer a nonliteral interpretation of an object (re)constructed in the author's mind. They are a form of mediation between sources (both primary and secondary) and the reader. As with many aspects of comics criticism, there exists a longer tradition of theorizing history comics in francophone Comics Studies than in English. French academics such as Henry Rousso have been theorizing the question of comics and history since the 1980s.[12] Michel Porret famously defined comics that take up historical subjects as a valuable means to understand the history of thought.[13] The field has, at the time of writing, had a series of important interventions by Pascal Ory and Adrien Genoudet.[14]

Genoudet, building on the work of Gil Bartholeyns, argues that we need a distinction between *histoire* ("history") and the *passé* (literally "the past").[15] *Histoire* is a question of establishing, empirically, what occurred, whereas *passé*, in the sense he proposes, is the stuff of impressions and images that summon a sense of the past. It is the translation of memory (including the memory of others) into text. *Passé* may be historically informed but contains within it the ways in which a given object has traveled through a culture and accrued meaning over time. Popular culture, including the comic book, Genoudet argues, primarily concerns *passé* rather than *histoire*. Comics, he argues, are formed from photographs and other images "which pre-exist culturally as forms of the past because we identify them as such."[16] We are taught to visualize history in specific ways (particularly in ways that emulate and are drawn directly from photography), and so the *passé* is not necessarily a means to understand the past as it occurred ("*l'origine des images du passé*"), but it is a way to understand the ways in which the past is reimagined and repurposed within a given cultural moment and by a particular creator ("*ces culture et mémoire visuelles des auteurs*"). This does not make comics invalid as a form of historical discourse, however. The artist, he argues, seeks to create a story by filling the gaps between an existent vocabulary of images; "to draw the past requires the artist to embroider around what we have *already seen*—to compose with the *invisible*."[17] This act of gap filling is potentially a means to visualize that which is otherwise lost: "these drawn characters who look at us [from the pages of a comic] are the absent, the absent of history, national memory, photographs, families."[18] They do not represent, he argues, an alternative to a "true" history or a counterfactual, but "*une autre histoire*" which exists in the absence of any definitive "truth."

Genoudet alerts us to the fact that assessing comics in terms of their relationship to "truth" is philosophically naive. When we consider the representation of history in and through comics, we can, of course, assess it in terms of the extent to which the creator presents information that is consistent with existing sources and academic consensus. There is, in other words, a simplistic level of criticism that interprets the text in terms of getting the "facts" (such as we currently understand them) "right." This level of understanding is perhaps undertheorized but is nonetheless far from trivial, particularly when we consider that mass media are consumed far more widely than the academic accounts from which they are drawn. An inaccurate yet vivid account of an event may threaten to overwrite more empirical and well-supported sources in public consciousness. The question of inaccuracy can also, as Maryanne Rhett and Bridget Keown demonstrate in this volume, alert us to rhetorical decisions made by creators and allow us to uncover the ideologies that inform a given work.

Given the state of flux in which History as a set of practices exists, there is also the very real possibility that a meticulously researched historical comic produced in 1947 will bear very little resemblance to the historical "truth" as currently accepted, in much the same way that some historiography of that era is also now, in itself, redundant. One only has to consider the shifting attitudes to the widely lauded *The Age of Jackson* (1945, Pulitzer Prize winner 1946), where Arthur Schlesinger Jr. omits Native Americans entirely and therefore leaves out one of the aspects of Jackson's presidency now seen as defining. More contemporary attitudes to Jackson, broadly indicative of scholarly consensus in the twenty-first century, can be derived from the title of the off-Broadway musical *Bloody Bloody Andrew Jackson* (first performed in 2008). In their book *Redrawing the Historical Past: History, Memory and Multiethnic Graphic Novels*, Martha J. Cutter and Cathy J. Schlund-Vials collect a variety of essays that speak to comics' place in this ongoing reconfiguration of historical narratives, specifically examining how multiethnic graphic novels affect history itself in their resistance to dominant perspectives.[19] But, this is by no means a tidy or linearly progressive process. Deliberate and self-conscious misrepresentation of history can also risk changing the meaning of the object depicted through transformation and omission—when, in *Manifest Destiny*, for example, a fictional version of Lewis and Clark encounter, and then participate in, the slaughter of a tribe of sentient bird creatures, the creative team, Chris Dingess, Matthew Roberts, and Owen Gieni, misrepresent the historical massacre of Native Americans. As Chase Magnett argues, the text becomes a case of "genocidal apologetics"; by transforming Native Americans into cannibalistic birds, the creative team present a version of history that seems to validate the violence of the colonizer, while also upholding notions of continental expansion as a progression into "virgin territory."[20]

If we stop our assessment simply with the question of "accuracy," however, we avoid engagement with some more-difficult but potentially redemptive aspects of the relationship between representation and object. It would be naive to imagine that there exists an alternative medium wherein the representation of the object is wholly transparent. The written word, the photograph, and the film are all curated and encode context and imply meaning that is not inherent in the object itself. What makes comics different is that its artificiality is overt. A central concern of the historical comic (and, indeed, to graphic memoir and reportage comics) is the fact that comics is a conceptual rather than an observational tool; when one looks at a comic, it is immediately obvious that the images therein have been drawn and thus are to be understood as mediated and nonliteral. There have been several interventions in Comics Studies that address this issue. In *Disaster Drawn*, Hillary Chute submits that "pitting visual and verbal discourses against each other, comics calls attention to their virtues and to their friction, highlighting the issue of what counts as evidence."[21] The relationship between the image and the object in comics, in other words, is always obviously figurative. Indeed, comics are not only nonliteral but *dramatically* nonliteral. Exaggeration and metaphor, as Will Eisner argues, are central components of the medium.[22] Comics can (perhaps must) be a form of what Linda Hutcheon calls historiographic metafiction—work that "incorporates [. . .] theoretical self-awareness of history and fiction as human constructs."[23] In *Ethics in the Gutter*, Kate Polak argues that comics contains various tools such as space (symbolic or literal) for readers to connect panels, tension between text and image, and fluidity of focalization, all of which invite an intimate relationship between reader and character.[24] Polak is rightly cautious about the word "empathy" when the historical subject remains unknown to us, but she argues that comics can offer a subjective account of a fictionalized experience, offering a kind of engagement quite different from other media.

In order for a comic to be understood as taking a rigorous approach to a historical object, Mickwitz argues, creators often employ authentication strategies such as the use of black-and-white; a restrained aesthetic erring toward (although never quite achieving) the literal; the absence of humor; the inclusion of footnotes, photographs, maps, infographics, and other ancillary materials; and authorial self-insertion. Ted Rall's *Snowden* (2015) and Sonny Liew's *The Art of Charlie Chan Hock Chye* (2015) are exemplars of such works, showing detailed evidence of historical research such as footnotes. Approaches that borrow from academic practice seek to augment their own truth claims through the inclusion of external reference points—the discipline of History-as-practice as well as the relevant content of that discipline—and also the textual language of comics, the "highly developed narrative grammar and vocabulary based on an inextricable combination of verbal and visual elements" that structures the texts and their relationships with readers and that which is represented.[25] Comics-as-history is therefore a hybrid form and can be linked to History-as-comics, as seen in Howard Zinn, Mike Konopacki, and Paul Buhle's *A People's History of American Empire: A Graphic Adaptation* (2008). Paul Buhle's interest in the relationship between history and comics can be traced back to his time as a postgraduate student in the 1960s and his involvement with *Radical America*, a journal linked to the Students for a Democratic Society, and the publication in 1969 of *Radical America Komiks*. Ann Marie Fleming's biography *The Magical Life of Long Tack Sam* (2007), similarly, is a collage of photographs, newspaper clippings, documents, and other materials, with four-color-style inserts that speculate on the gaps such materials leave.

History comics often adopt an aesthetic approach that mimics the documentary interview. The visual component of Art Spiegelman's *Maus*, for example, is performatively, even dramatically, metaphoric, and yet the presence of an author proxy, the inclusion of photographs and (redrawn) maps, and the self-reflexivity all communicate an earnestness that seeks to validate the text's truth claims. The same strategy is adopted in *A People's History of American Empire* through inserting Zinn himself into the narrative; *Logicomix*, a graphic biography of the philosopher Bertrand Russell, also incorporates the depiction of debates among the creative team about how to represent their subject. Comics making truth claims often also employ cruder drawings, particularly those that seem to have been made using simpler tools, to add to a perceived sense of authenticity. In the case of Marjane Satrapi's *Persepolis*, for example, simple drawings are used to imply a child's perspective. These strategies are a means to signal to an audience that the text takes a sincere approach to its subject; that it aspires to truthfulness, and has refrained from unnecessary embellishment or speculation; and, where invention is unavoidable, has clearly signposted the author's imagination at work. A good example of this can be found in Joe Ollmann's graphic introduction to *The Magic Island*, where Ollmann inserts himself as narrator, both as an external figure and one being carried along by the book's author, William B. Seabrook; in an instance where visual metaphor is employed, Ollmann cites this within the frame as a "heavy-handed metaphor . . . borrowed from editorial cartoons."[26] As Ollmann demonstrates, comics are a space where relatively accurate accounts (in Ollmann's instance, the American occupation of Haiti from 1915 to 1934 and Seabrook's visit to the island), both pictorial and narrative, can coexist with flights of fancy and allusion that augment rather than detract from the overall effect of the comic.

The perceived absence of style is itself, of course, a style. Historical comics are subject to the same fundamental problem that exists in the various media that seek to represent some form of truth, namely, the tension between journalistic and aesthetic impulses. The documentary genre found in film, prose, and comics aspires to an impossible standard of objectivity—of presenting events "as they occurred" or as they might have been experienced by one who was present at the time—and generally arrives upon an aesthetic that communicates the desire without achieving the aim. Documentary style, as we know from film, can be reproduced in nonfiction (consider, for example, mockumentaries such as *What We Do in the Shadows* [2014], and "found footage" films such as *The Blair Witch Project* [1999]).

Mickwitz suggests that the approaches to truth telling made possible through animation outlined by Paul Wells are just as possible through comics. These include: imitative (where established conventions of documentary or history are replicated as in *Snowden*), subjective (where stylistic choices are made to draw attention to the inherent subjectivity as in *Alan's War*), fantastic (where abstract ideas can be visually represented as in *Habibi*), and postmodern (where reflexivity is employed to question the relationship between the presented representation and its referent as in *Maus*).[27] It is via these approaches that Mickwitz believes comics "share an investment and engagement in negotiating and exploring the relationship between reality and representation as a social, visual, and narrative practice."[28] Mickwitz is concerned primarily with nonfiction comics, however, which are not the sole focus of this book.

Documentary style threatens to rob comics of their most potent tools—their capacity to evoke emotions. Rutherford argues, "[The] sense of conflict between journalistic and aesthetic impulses recurs constantly in the theorization of documentary, and is linked to a privileging of language that subordinates the experiential properties of image and sound."[29] Comics that represent a historical subject have the capacity to present history as experienced, of exploring an internal world that might be lost to more empirical accounts. As Brian Massumi argues, "matter-of-factness dampens intensity."[30] This has led to a profusion of imaginative works staged at all points of history, exhibiting an impressive variety of artistic styles and genres. It may be tempting to dismiss works that forgo the versimilitudinous signifiers described above as lacking in historiographical purpose, ideology, or intention. This can be recognized as a mistake, however, when one considers the consequence of Frank Miller's determinedly heteronormative vision of Spartan society in *300*, with its vaguely nationalistic and other ahistorical themes of Western enlightenment, or stumbles upon Brian K. Vaughan and Niko Henrichon's clunky, if earnest, ruminations on the United States' invasion of Iraq in *Pride of Baghdad*, a story following three lions escaped from the Baghdad Zoo, doing their best to survive the war. Abraham Kawa, author of a comic exploring the birth of Athenian democracy, asserts that not only can fictional comics have historical purpose, but fictional comics have the ability to provide a more comprehensive historical portrait. By setting an authoritative "this is how it happened" attitude to the side, fictional historiographic narratives can reveal and engage with the fractured and often contradictory perspective of historians and the primary sources they work with.[31]

The fanciful renderings of the past found in popular culture and the genre of historical fiction often incite professional ire, for they tend to be both more widely propagated and woefully inconsiderate of academic research, creating formidable potential to warp and rend accurate understanding of historical events and persons. One recent example is the debate around the authenticity of *Hamilton: An American Musical* and its engagement with the historical narrative. While the wariness of historians is not misplaced, members of other fields have heartily embraced what a little imagination can do in terms of accessibility and understanding. Where would paleontologists be without their artistic depictions of dinosaurs and what might have been? The bones of the past, historical facts and documents, can benefit from being clothed in the colorful flesh and blood of artistic license and dramatic narrative.

Comics such as *300* and *Pride of Baghdad*, even historically situated superhero stories where Batman finds himself included in the Constitutional Convention or Mystique is planning heists in 1921, provide unique ways to engage with history separate from the more introspective autographics like *Maus* and reportage comics like *Palestine*. These wholly imagined (and often fantastical) comics exacerbate the historiographic metafictional element of the medium, adding to the way in which the gutter and hand-drawn materiality call attention to the artificial nature of history. They force readers to acknowledge their distance from the historical experience being portrayed by including fictional (and impossible) characters within the narrative and better lend themselves to more complicated ethical contemplation through the utilization of multiple perspectives and focalizations. Returning to Ankersmit, "the best historical representation is the most original one, the least conventional one, the one that is least likely to be true—and that yet cannot be refuted on the basis of existing historical evidence."[32] While that final caveat might disqualify much historical fiction, the sentiment holds true regardless of whether the representation being crafted is meant to be a history or simply historically situated. That is to say, when it comes to history, stretching the limits of the imagination only serves to aid in our understanding of the past and, through that understanding, shape ourselves and our futures.

DRAWING THE PAST

The contributors to this volume cover diverse terrain to provide a map of current approaches to comics and their engagement with historical representation. As with a map, we hope that others will follow these suggested routes and use them as a means of navigating their own paths through the field, charting new territory as well as reshaping our ideas of already-explored spaces. To that end, let us consider the points of departure featured here.

The first section of the book, History and Form, explores how the existence and shape of comics as a medium influence the histories it incorporates. Comics, drafted as they often are at the behest of multifaceted corporate entities and various consumer demands, are influenced by forces that other avenues of historical representation are not. The medium's relationship with other mediums, film and television in particular, also inspires questions related to form, as does the era certain comics were written in.

Martin Flanagan considers the way in which the Marvel corporation has constructed and reimagined its own history, through its Legacy storylines, films, and paratexts. Marvel, Flanagan argues, has managed its relationship with fans by creating a sense of continuity and stability. They offer a "return" to or "renewal" of specific themes and tropes that construct and curate notions of an industrial history in dialogue with the contexts of creation and reception over decades.

Bridget Keown and Maryanne Rhett's chapter "Diana in No Man's Land: Wonder Woman and the History of World War" considers the ways in which the 2017 film *Wonder Woman* engages in dialogue with both the character's comic book past and the historical era in which it is set. Much of their argument concerns granular questions of deliberate inaccuracies as well as larger thematic problems concerning the function of World War I in collective historical memory. The film, they argue, departs from the values espoused by the original Wonder Woman, contributes to the erasure of women from narratives of World War I, and promotes a form of feminism that continues to celebrate masculine ideals and the male gaze.

Peter Bryan's "The Buckaroo of the Badlands: Carl Barks, Don Rosa, and (Re) Envisioning the West" considers the representation of the mythic Old West in the works of two Disney cartoonists, one of whom filtered the West through his personal experience of its "passing into memory," and one of whom experienced the West only through such acts of filtering. Disney comics, Bryan argues, resisted dominant representations of American history, offering a far less glamorous imagining of the American frontier than those found in film or television at the time. This chapter demonstrates how comics exist in dialogue not just with history as event and History as practice but also with other media iterations.

In "Flags of our Fathers: Imperial Decline, National Identity, and Allohistory in Marvel Comics," Lawrence Abrams and Kaleb Knoblauch examine the ways in which the decline of European empires shaped the representation of international relations in Silver and Bronze Age Marvel comics. They demonstrate that the question of neo- and postcoloniality was a recurring theme in Black Panther and Captain Britain storylines, exploring the ways in which superhero narratives can be used to engage with contemporary geopolitics.

The second section, Historical Trauma, concerns the question of trauma understood both as individual traumas that can shape the relationship between the narrator and object, and historical traumas that invite a reassessment of existing social, economic, and cultural assumptions. Scholars such as Mickwitz and Polak have written at length on the usefulness of comics as a medium for engaging with historical trauma, particularly in the way that iconicity vitalizes racial dialogues and protects victims of past of traumas.[33] This section, then, questions the usefulness of comics in the contemplation of historical trauma. The United States' relationship and/or infliction of racial trauma is given particular attention, as are the ways in which the fantastical nature of comics is used to help assuage the traumatizing anxieties that plague national identity/purpose in times of crisis by threading romanticized pasts and presents together.

Stephen Connor's "Victor Charles and Marvin the ARVN: Vietnamese and Enemy and Ally in American War Comic Books" examines the representation of the Vietnamese participants in the Vietnam War as portrayed in American war comics. Comics creators, he demonstrates, used and developed a range of visual languages and accented cadences to represent the Vietnamese, evoking racist caricature from the World War II era but also offering a rehabilitative space for the Vietnamese allies who, in the terms the story, were able to embody "American" forms of heroism. In so doing he demonstrates how visual representation and the narrative in which it operates as a coconstitutive part can exist in tension, with one reinstating, through falling back on preexisting stereotypes and cues, what the other seeks to deconstruct.

In "Magneto the Survivor: Redemption Cold War Fears and the 'Americanization of the Holocaust' in Chris Claremont's *Uncanny X-Men* (1975–1997)," Martin Lund examines the ways in which the figure of Magneto, who, in his various incarnations, has embodied different versions of the Holocaust survivor in American popular consciousness. Lund demonstrates how both Magneto and the memorialization of the Holocaust in the US exist in dialogue with contemporary concerns while always drawing on history.

Jordan Newton's chapter, "'How Would You Like to Go Back through the Ages—in Search of Yourself?': Time Travel Comics, Internationalism, and the American Century" investigates the frequent appearance of time travel as a narrative device in the early years of the Cold War. Newton draws on work that foregrounds time travel as a "laboratory" in which alternative histories and futures, and indeed presents, are interrogated and positioned alongside contemporary projections of "the American Century."

In the final section, Mythic Histories, some of the ways in which comics add to the mythology of the United States are explained. This expansion of the American mythos is a kaleidoscope of various interrelated techniques. The major players in the American canon are cast and recast as heroes or villains (sometimes contemporaneously), as are the defining characteristics of American heroism and villainy. The identity of the country itself is revealed to be a process of imagining and reimaging its ages, golden and dark. Like a cathedral, it is a construction of distinct and discordant layers, each a testament to the artistic prejudices of its architects and builders.

Max Bledstein's chapter, "Federal Bureau of Illustration: Comics Depictions of J. Edgar Hoover," considers the comic book life of the FBI's most notorious director. Series such as *Dynamic Man* and *Dale of the F.B.I.*, he argues, draw upon the visual and thematic vocabulary of the superhero genre, rendering Hoover in terms of a conservative and glamorous version of American national identity. Bledstein therefore directs our attention to the ways that comics create mythic histories of their own, which may then in turn contribute to the framework through which the individuals they represent are understood by historians.

Matthew Costello's "When Hawkman Met Tailgunner Joe: How the Justice Society of America Constructs the Fifties as a Usable Past" contrasts different visions of the 1950s as they are shown in Justice Society of America storylines. These contrasts, he demonstrates, show the mutability of the past and the ways in which our understanding of what has been are always a reflection of the contemporary moment. The 1950s is a routinely romanticized space for white conservative America, and Costello's account of how, and when, the McCarthyist climate is reproduced and re-presented offers insights into the continuing relevance of the decade in national narratives.

In "Aftershock's Rough Riders and Reification of Race Reimagined," Christina M. Knopf argues that the allohistorical incarnations of US presidents, and specifically the reimagining of Roosevelt found in the *Rough Riders* series, reinforce the primacy of a white male hegemony. Knopf's analysis of this through the phenomenon of steampunk is particularly revealing, showing how spaces that seemingly reinterpret the past also, in others, reinstate political elements of it.

Finally, Michael Fuchs and Stefan Rabitsch's chapter, "'Out There Hunting Monsters': *Manifest Destiny*, the Monstrosity of the American West, and the Gothic Character of American History," reveals how the titular comic draws attention to the problematic aspects of the Lewis and Clark expedition that are sometimes obscured by historians. In doing so, they explain, readers are forced to confront the specters haunting American expansionism. It is our hope that this work will contribute to ongoing debates around, and provide new directions in, the relationship between comics and history. It is intended to be read alongside, but independent of, its sister volume, which expands the themes explored here to comics that take history beyond the United States as their subject.

NOTES

1. Grant Morrison, *Supergods: What Masked Vigilantes, Miraculous Mutants, and a Sun God from Smallville Can Teach Us about Being Human* (New York: Spiegel and Grau, 2012).

2. Dan Jurgens, *Action Comics* #987 (DC Comics, 2017).

3. Todd Huston Warner, "Superman Shields Illegal Immigrants from White Supremacist in Latest DC Comic," Breitbart, September 13, 2017, accessed September 10, 2018, https://www.breitbart.com/big-hollywood/2017/09/13/in-new-comic-superman-beats-up-white-people-for-attacking-illegal-aliens/; David S. Goyer, "The Incident," *Action Comics* #900 (DC Comics, 2011).

4. Ronald Takaki, *A Different Mirror: A History of Multicultural America* (Boston: Little, Brown, 2009).

5. Benedict Anderson, *Imagined Communities: Reflections on the Origin and Spread of Nationalism* (London: Verso, 2006).

6. Oscar Handlin, *The Uprooted* (Philadelphia: University of Pennsylvania Press), 1951.

7. F. R. Ankersmit, *Historical Representation* (Stanford, CA: Stanford University Press).

8. Ira Berlin, *The Long Emancipation: The Demise of Slavery in the United States* (Cambridge: Harvard University Press, 2015), i.

9. James E. Young, *Writing and Rewriting the Holocaust: Narrative and the Consequences of Interpretation* (Bloomington: Indiana University Press, 1988).

10. Joseph Witek, *Comics as History: The Narrative Art of Jack Jackson, Art Spiegelman, and Harvey Pekar* (Jackson: University Press of Mississippi, 1989), 11.

11. David Kunzle, *The Early Comic Strip: Narrative Strips and Picture Stories in the European Broadsheet from c. 1450 to 1825*, History of the Comic Strip, vol. 1 (Berkeley: University of California Press, 1973).

12. Henry Rousso, "Reminisences de guerre dans la bande dessinée," *Vingtième siècle: Revue d'histoire* 3 (1984): 129–32.

13. "une source précieuse pour l'histoire des mentalities." Michel Porret, *Objectif bulles: Bande dessinée et histoire* (Geneva: Georg, 2009), 19.

14. Pascal Ory, 'L'histoire par la bande?' *Le Débat* 177 (November–December 2013) : 90–95; Adrien Genoudet, *Dessiner l'histoire: Pour une histoire visuelle* (Paris: Éditions Le Manuscrit Paris, 2015).

15. Gil Bartholeyens, "Loin de l'Histoire," *Le Debat* 177 (November–December 2013).

16. "un tel amalgame divers, d'échelles et de qualités, construit, diffuse et préexiste culturellement en tant que forms du passé parce que nous les identifions comme telles." Genoudet, *Dessiner L'histoire*, 54.

17. "dessiner le passé nécessite de broder autour de ce que l'on a *déjà vu* pour composer avec *l'invisible*," Genoudet, *Dessiner L'histoire*, 99.

18. "Ces personnages dessinés qui nous regardent ce sont les absents, les absents de l'histoire, de la mémoire nationale, des photographies, des familles." Genoudet, *Dessiner L'histoire*, 154.

19. Martha J. Cutter and Cathy J. Schlund-Vials, *Redrawing the Historical Past: History, Memory and Multiethnic Graphic Novels* (Athens: University of Georgia Press, 2018), 1, 2, and 6.

20. K. Garret and C. Magnett, "Sunday Slugfest: Manifest Destiny #18," Comics Bulletin, November 1, 2015, http://comicsbulletin.com/sunday-slugfest-manifest-destiny-18, accessed December 1, 2016; Dragos Mair, "Western Nightmares: Manifest Destiny and the Representation of Genocide in Weird Fiction," *Studies in Comics* 8, no. 2 (2017): 157–70.

21. Hillary Chute, *Disaster Drawn* (Cambridge: Harvard University Press, 2016), 7.

22. Will Eisner, *Comics and Sequential Art* (n.p.: Poorhouse Press, 1985).

23. Linda Hutcheon, 'Historiographic Metafiction: Parody and the Intertextuality of History," ed. P. O. Donnell and Robert Con Davis (Baltimore: Johns Hopkins University Press, 1989): 3–32, 5.

24. Kate Polak, *Ethics in the Gutter* (Eugene: University of Oregon Press, 2017).

25. Witek, *Comics as History*, 3.

26. Joe Ollmann, "Foreword," in *The Magic Island*, by William Seabrook (New York: Dover, 2016), xiii.

27. Paul Wells, *Understanding Animation* (London: Routledge, 1998).

28. Nina Mickwitz, *Documentary Comics: Graphic Truth-Telling in a Sceptical Age* (New York: Palgrave Macmillan, 2016).

29. Anne Rutherford, "The Poetics of a Potato Documentary That Gets under the Skin," *Metro: Media & Education Magazine*, no. 137 (Summer 2003), 126–31

30. Brian Massumi, "The Autonomy of Affect," *Cultural Critique*, special issue, The Politics of Systems and Environments, Part II, no. 31 (Autumn 1995): 83–109, 86.

31. Abraham Kawa, "Drawing from History," afterword to his *Democracy* (London: Bloomsbury, 2015), 205–6.

32. Ankersmit, *Historical Representation*, 22.

33. Polak, *Ethics in the Gutter*, 112, 120; Mickwitz, *Documentary Comics*, 116, 120, 126.

WORKS CITED

Anderson, Benedict. *Imagined Communities: Reflections on the Origin and Spread of Nationalism*. London: Verso, 2006.

Ankersmit, F. R. *Historical Representation*. Stanford, CA: Stanford University Press, 2001.

Bartholeyens, Gil. "Loin de l'Histoire," *Le Debat* 177 (November–December 2013).

Berlin, Ira. *The Long Emancipation: The Demise of Slavery in the United States*. Cambridge: Harvard University Press, 2015.

Chute, Hillary. *Disaster Drawn*. Cambridge: Harvard University Press, 2016.

Eisner, Will. *Comics and Sequential Art*. n.p.: Poorhouse Press, 1985.

Garret, K., and C. Magnett. "Sunday Slugfest: Manifest Destiny #18." *Comics Bulletin*, November 1, 2015. Accessed December 1, 2016. http://comicsbulletin.com/sunday-slugfest-manifest-destiny-18.

Genoudet, Adrien. *Dessiner l'histoire: Pour une histoire visuelle*. Paris: Éditions Le Manuscrit Paris, 2015.

Goyer, David S. "The Incident." *Action Comics* #900. DC Comics, 2011.

Handlin, Oscar. *The Uprooted*. Philadelphia: University of Pennsylvania Press, 1951.

Huston, Warner Todd. "Superman Shields Illegal Immigrants from White Supremacist in Latest DC Comic." Breitbart. September 13, 2017. Accessed September 10, 2018. https://www.breitbart.com/big-hollywood/2017/09/13/in-new-comic-superman-beats-up-white-people-for-attacking-illegal-aliens/.

Hutcheon, Linda. "Historiographic Metafiction: Parody and the Intertextuality of History," edited by Patrick O'Donnell and Robert Con Davis, 3–32. Baltimore: Johns Hopkins University Press, 1989.

Jurgens, Dan. *Action Comics* #987. DC Comics, 2017.

Kawa, Abraham. "Drawing from History." Afterword to *Democracy*, 205–6. London: Bloomsbury, 2015.

Kunzle, David. *The Early Comic Strip: Narrative Strips and Picture Stories in the European Broadsheet from c. 1450 to 1825*. History of the Comic Strip, vol. 1. Berkeley: University of California Press, 1973.

Mair, Dragos. "Western Nightmares: *Manifest Destiny* and the Representation of Genocide in Weird Fiction." *Studies in Comics* 8, no. 2 (2016): 157–70.

Massumi, Brian. "The Autonomy of Affect." *Cultural Critique*, special issue, The Politics of Systems and Environments, Part II, no. 31 (Autumn 1995): 83–109.

Mickwitz, Nina. *Documentary Comics: Graphic Truth-Telling in a Sceptical Age*. New York: Palgrave Macmillan, 2016.

Morrison, Grant. *Supergods: What Masked Vigilantes, Miraculous Mutants, and a Sun God from Smallville Can Teach Us about Being Human*. New York: Spiegel and Grau, 2012.

Ollmann, Joe. "Foreword." In *The Magic Island*. By William Seabrook. New York: Dover, 2016.

Ory, Pascal. 'L'histoire par la bande?' *Le Débat* 177 (November–December 2013): 90–95.

Polak, Kate. *Ethics in the Gutter*. Eugene: University of Oregon Press, 2017.

Porret, Michel. *Objectif bulles: Bande dessinée et histoire*. Geneva: Georg, 2009.

Rousso, Henry. "Réminisences de guerre dans la bande dessinée," *Vingtième siècle: Revue d'histoire* 3 (1984): 129–32.

Rutherford, Anne. "The Poetics of a Potato Documentary That Gets under the Skin." *Metro: Media & Education Magazine*, no. 137 (Summer 2003): 126–31.

Takaki, Ronald. *A Different Mirror: A History of Multicultural America*. Boston: Little, Brown, 2009.

Wells, Paul. *Understanding Animation*. London: Routledge, 1998.

Witek, Joseph. *Comics as History: The Narrative Art of Jack Jackson, Art Spiegelman, and Harvey Pekar*. Jackson: University Press of Mississippi, 1989.

Young, James E. *Writing and Rewriting the Holocaust: Narrative and the Consequences of Interpretation*. Bloomington: Indiana University Press, 1988.

HISTORY and FORM

CHAPTER ONE

COMING HOME TO "LEGACY"

Marvel's Problem with History

MARTIN FLANAGAN

Marvel as an organization (taken here as Marvel Entertainment, as the key subsidiary of Disney, with its film, television, and comics divisions representing the spearheads of its public engagement) is in a moment of realigning its corporate identity. With critics, notably Derek Johnson, interpreting the success of Marvel Studios in blockbuster film entertainment as clinching an apparently "inevitable" predestiny, long dormant within expressions of the corporate identity, the Marvel of today highlights the attainments of the film division with a view to making sure these do not outshine other divisions.[1] These other divisions offer strategically crucial products that, however, find mixed success: the television project is a work in progress, and the comic publishing arm—although using initiatives like the 2017 Marvel Legacy relaunch to profess its own vibrancy and maturity—transpires in difficult market conditions, as we shall see later.[2] At the heart of this nexus of successful, developing, and arguably struggling Marvels, we glimpse the company's supposed treasure: a world-beating set of IP that attracts global consumers, many of whom have weak ties (if any) to comic books.

In this climate Marvel's attempts to use film success to upgrade or clarify its identity rate far more scrutiny than ever they would a few decades hence. Public pronouncements about the film division's aims sometimes seem to qualify the role of comics. At the very least, they throw into dispute the claim that the body of comic publishing furnishes "historically significant [. . .] foundational texts" for the now fully transmedia Marvel sphere.[3] Along these lines, two years prior to Legacy's 2017 changes, the readership received a message from editor-in-chief (EIC) Axel Alonso. Appearing in a free comic allowing fans to preview a sweeping 2015 reboot, the statement ostensibly existed to stoke excitement for the changes that were coming in "All-New, All-Different Marvel." However, it started on a different tack:

> What was your first encounter with the Marvel Universe? Did you pull a comic book off a spinner rack at the five and dime like I did, or did you float out of a movie theater, your mind blown by what you saw on the Silver Screen [? . . .] If you liked that feeling, you're going to love [. . .] "All-New, All-Different Marvel."[4]

Soon, Alonso was redoubling his message, reinforcing the impression of a Marvel in difficulties over managing the old and new elements in its projected identity. In August 2017, aiming to motivate readers for another relaunch—one that promised to backtrack on some of the creative directions of "All-New, All-Different"—Alonso wrote:

> I remember walking into the five-and-dime on Clement Street [in San Francisco] with my grandmother like it was yesterday. [. . .] I'd seen the *Spider-Man* cartoon, of course, but this was my first Spider-Man comic book and it blew my mind. [. . .] Whether you bought your first comic at a five-and-dime or a specialty store, or you're taking your first steps into the Marvel Universe, MARVEL LEGACY is for you.[5]

Alonso's EIC post is now filled by the controversial C. B. Cebulski—and some of the negative press about that appointment ties into concerns about the legitimacy of Marvel's diversity commitments, as discussed later in this piece.[6] Comparing the two Alonso statements, the same qualification—that inaugural Marvel experiences for many consumers involve media expressions that do not involve comics—lingers (along with the five-and-dime store). The idea, though, that appreciating Marvel's efforts to restate its "legacy" is not philosophically incompatible for both long-standing fans *and* utterly new entrants speaks to a more challenging point for Marvel. This is the flame that Marvel Legacy wished to kindle, and we shall return to it.

If the "Legacy" term is particularly instructive, another buzzword surrounding Marvel projects in 2017 joins it to form a linguistic trail, helping us to interpret company attempts to clarify its present offering, while preserving a connection to Marvel authenticity. While Legacy's impact is in the comics line, the other concept that attached itself to Marvel in 2017 "homecoming"—was experienced in Marvel Cinematic Universe (MCU) texts. *Spider-Man: Homecoming* (directed by Jon Watts) brought the prodigal character back to the film studio containing the DNA of his 1962 creation by Stan Lee and Steve Ditko. Officially a Sony release, *Homecoming* is a coproduction of Columbia Pictures with Marvel Studios, bearing the MS fanfare sequence (notably, with adapted music) and containing input from key personnel on both sides of the camera: from studio figurehead Kevin Feige and high-profile lieutenants Victoria Alonso (head of Physical Production) and

Louis D'Esposito (studio copresident—all three occupying producer/executive producer roles on *Homecoming*), to key star Robert Downey Jr. as Iron Man.

If Marvel is in a heightened state, or even crisis, regarding the balance of old and new informing its identity, there is a sense in which these two terms measure out the gamble that venerable characters can paper over cracks in coherence. Firstly, this concerns its right and authority, *as* Marvel, to deploy, with impunity, characters that are seen as belonging to its comics universe, a freedom that was, in recent times, impeded by Disney/Marvel's difficult relationships with various Hollywood studios holding the right to filmically exploit its characters. The second area of sensitivity is in the less industrially fraught but still complex area of its comic book continuity. With William Proctor, we might say that acquiring a habit centering on either of the "Big Two" publishers (Marvel and DC Comics) can be daunting for entrants because "readers who attempt to traverse [. . . their] sprawling continuity [. . .] must possess substantial intertextual competences" to aid its navigation.[7] The stakes in simplifying this process—in reassuring new entrants that character iterations whom they have loved in Marvel movies and TV shows will populate stories bearing few demands on prior purchases or complicated lore—have risen dramatically, due to the business need to draw in new readers, while simultaneously addressing longer-term fans who have failed to accept, or drifted away completely from, initiatives like All-New All-Different. This rejection is often in the context of objections to revenue-generating tactics and gimmicks (particularly, among what might be called the hardcore, relaunches and crossovers that disrespect history as symbolically encoded in the high issue counts of established titles).[8]

Though not a sole focus of this chapter, this problem does provoke thoughts about how Marvel involves its own history in justifying new initiatives directed to both the desired new fandom and established ones. Many journalistic outlets (from trade, popular, and "legitimate"—such as UK "broadsheets"—sectors) have noted or upbraided Marvel over attempts to habituate readers to a fresh, more diverse cast in high-profile titles.[9] Here, a secondary "legacy" twist emerges, as readers' attachment to published bodies of fictional history is posited as an impediment to their "coming home" to a socially updated Marvel universe.

In 2017 the idea of "legacy" was allowed, via trade discourse and an obfuscating Marvel PR strategy, to be understood as a fault line: the reader community that had shown loyalty to Marvel for decades was being marked off from the set of new, implied-as-younger readers that would form its future consumer base.[10] The split—accurately or not—was painted as ideological in nature. Focusing on the terms "legacy" and "homecoming" (and how Marvel has deployed them), we may shed new light upon a bigger issue regarding Marvel; this is the paradoxical impulse that Derek Johnson has identified as "[t]he company's overall dilemma [, . . . that] of trying to hold on to the old and the new."[11]

UNDERSTANDING LEGACY

Legacy sought to recenter Marvel textual enterprises on a perceived standard and natural set of characters in 2017. To help us understand it, a brief examination of two high-profile comic releases, from the initial wave of Legacy titles, will be undertaken. They comprise the "one-shot" *Marvel Legacy* #1 (cover dated November 2017) and *Captain America* #695 (January 2018).[12] *Legacy* #1 aims to propel the entire narrative campaign (priming storylines to be explored in subsequent series). The fresh-start approach taken by the Captain America issue, relaunching an ongoing series, was not line-wide. *Amazing Spider-Man*'s Legacy resumption point (#789) differed because it was in the minority of titles that published, unbroken, through the *Secret Empire* event, running throughout 2017.[13] This event, hard on the heels of *Civil War II* (a 2016 event whose episodes loosely paralleled MCU events), had at its heart an unpopular remix of the history of Captain America, at one point positioning Steve Rogers as having served Nazi analogues HYDRA for decades.[14] *Captain America* #695 thus reacts by moving on from, if not wiping away, controversial recent canon; the presentation of a soul-searching Steve Rogers contextualizes *Secret Empire* but consigns its traumas to a less material level of importance.[15] Cap's slate is thus cleaned, and the restoration of the fan favorite (and, for Marvel, comparatively vintage) Mark Waid as cocredited storyteller alongside Chris Samnee accentuates the sense of classicism.[16]

The individual-issue approach taken here is appropriate, since Legacy is specifically a "relaunch," not a full reboot (it does not wholly revoke recent continuity).[17] One of the tools Legacy used to acclimatize new buyers was the three-page "primer" strip—generally a version of an origin—included in campaign-branded debut issues (*Amazing Spider-Man*, *Captain America*, *Black Panther*, and others), thereafter freely accessible online. *Captain America*'s primer, for instance, straightforwardly retells Rogers's origin, including his membership in the Avengers. Since no new elements of status quo are introduced, we can surmise that this relaunch means to purge unpopular elements associated with *Secret Empire*, leaving a residual "classic" version of Cap.[18]

The various narrative strands of *Marvel Legacy* #1 attempt to position key characters for the campaign, under the auspices of a single, oversized, and "untold" story. "Legacy" is the first word beheld in the comic (in voiceover narration). The tale introduces a (traditionally fractious) Marvel team of 1,000,000 BC, thus overtly providing the "new" (no readership of any standing has seen this team before) and the "historic" at once. Reestablishing the deep, mythic foundations of the Marvel Universe (hereafter, MU), these "Prehistoric Avengers" betray Marvel's pressing priorities: members of the character communities associated with Thor, Black Panther, Dr. Strange, and X-Men are foregrounded (with Thor and—sensationally—Black Panther both in receipt of widespread movie exposure between

October 2017 and February 2018).[19] The narration continues by meditating on the group's diverse makeup (one Black character and two women): "[Legacy is] a lot more *complicated* than it used to be. [. . .] There are so *many* of us now, in all different shapes and colors and creeds. Or maybe there always were and we just didn't notice."[20] This, itself, is a historical recapitulation, as *Marvel Legacy* approaches the self-conscious reflection for which key 1970s Marvel runs were known, particularly when "elite ideologies of privilege or the centrality of one race, creed, or lifestyle were reexamined by sometimes shocked superheroes.[21]

A displacement in time forwards the narrative to a present-day car chase. Cues suggest that the off-panel narrator is the pursued Ghost Rider; but this is misdirection. The narrator is revealed later to be Valeria Richards, daughter of Reed and Susan, the couple at the heart of Marvel's missing-in-action superfamily, the Fantastic Four. Val is both a small child physiologically and a massive intellect; however, her depiction under certain writers seems to selectively endow her with child or adult emotions. Here, her narratorial role reflects hope for the future—redolent of the Four as the inaugural superteam of the "Marvel Age," growing out of discourses of national renewal and frontier discovery.[22] However, shabbily sidelined in current continuity as the team had been, Valeria's prominence also suggests the correction of a false Marvel course.[23] Though young, she is the image of her father, Reed—once a child prodigy—in scientific acumen and invention. Yet we might balk at her emotional capacity for wisdom, expressed, as it is, almost as a diagnosis of the areas separating Marvel from large parts of its traditional customer base (she is both young and connected to authentic history). Although her parents do not feature, *Legacy*'s commitment to Valeria, Johnny Storm, and the Thing constitutes a clarification of Marvel's understanding of the FF's importance to its roots (unsurprisingly, their return followed in summer 2018).

Indeed, wrapping around all of *Legacy* #1's vignettes, whether returns to familiar MU cast members (Rogers, Jean Grey) or introductions for new readers of some of Marvel's controversially refreshed heroic identities (a woman Thor, Black Captain America, and female/Black American Iron "Man" lead the comic's action scenes), Valeria's is an extremely "meta," self-aware commentary. Hardly unusual for Marvel, this is a symptom of the comics line turning to a tactic that, with my colleagues, I have elsewhere confirmed as a major ingredient of Marvel Studios' profile: a tendency where the corporate authoring entity gives diegetic expression to its current concerns.[24] In considering the classical Hollywood studio's recourse to the tactic, J. D. Connor argues that this represented consolation for historic firms that faced bewildering change in the 1960s: "The old studio-brands craved the structures of the past in the face of a more fluid and provisional production environment; finding this impossible [. . .] they [. . .] started to represent [. . . their own histories] in screen 'metanarratives,' carving allegorical studio stories into their fictions."[25] Valeria's voiceover, and the overall atmosphere of *Legacy*

#1 accompanying her comment that "change is never easy," take Marvel's recent struggles, and even missteps, and makes them into story; further acknowledging that those phases in a publisher's existence where it syncs closely with fan desire and approval come and go in cycles: 'Cataclysm [. . .] is averted at the last possible moment, until the next one comes along.'[26]

Waid and Samnee's first Legacy issue—initiating the "Home of the Brave" arc—sees ideas of nation as requiring renewal. As many commentators have noted (we single out Jason Dittmer here), Cap's relationship to nation has never been as simple as iconography might suggest.[27] In subsequent issues Rogers traverses the landscape, questing for the inspiration to lead again. In *Secret Empire*, the name of Captain America was sullied (both within and without the diegesis).[28] Notably, then, a flashback—marking a decade before the present time where Legacy events start, and a point soon after Cap's emergence from North Atlantic waters (in sliding Marvel Time)—announces the issue's beginning.[29] The hero's condensed origin is offered—curiously, for the primer strip is a mere twenty pages away—and a Cap new to the American public fights fascists in Nebraska. Waid and Samnee mine an ongoing theme whereby the heroic legend (expanded to nation-sized dimensions) is measured against the real man; flashback ended, Rogers is thus seen returning to Burlington in the present, finding that the town has acknowledged his protection by renaming itself Captain America.[30] The fascists resurface, the fight resumes—inaugurating a new "hunt" storyline—and his salutary influence a decade before is shown on a little girl (to whom Cap explains that the strong have a responsibility to always protect the weak).

The issue's main agenda is to restate the principles and style of patriotism of Captain America (particularly, Steve Rogers's antifascism). This draws a line underneath *Secret Empire*'s "evil Steve," thus exploiting the Legacy opportunity to overwrite unpopular story developments. Issue #695 was reviewed favorably, awarded 9/10 ("Amazing") by IGN. Alex Widen at Bam! Smack! Pow! rated it a "hopeful, feel-good first issue" and—tellingly—construed its events as an "apology" for two years of the *Secret Empire* storyline.[31] A respectful depth of historical character essence, and a new beginning, were observed as having been simultaneously achieved. Summing up how this success resonated beyond targeted casual or new readers (for whom primers are presumably required), the Facebook group Issues with Comics hosted a response from a decades-long fan of Captain America:

> I want to sincerely thank Mark Waid, Chris Samnee and the rest of the team. [. . .] Thank you for creating a story that reminds me of why I love comics. Thank you for giving me the sheer enjoyment I had when reading comics as a kid [, . . . and] for doing it all in a single issue story, and thank you most of all for returning my favorite superhero to me.[32]

The nostalgic element ("reading comics as a kid") and the idea of a hero's return are striking, although Waid, a writer with publicly liberal leanings (clear from his social media), has included story elements that relate to crises in current US sociopolitical discourse. This appears to refute the way that hardcore Marvel fans are sometimes constructed (see Johnson, and later in the present essay) and challenges an idea that values in comics have unrecognizably altered since earlier phases of Marvel.[33]

Integral to these two issues' introduction to the bigger Legacy project is a sort of plea for reader understanding as Marvel rediscovers itself. The attraction of consensus via the restoration of pre-approved "classic" character identities lies behind signals sent in *Marvel Legacy* #1 (for instance, that Sam Wilson, usually the Falcon, wishes to renounce the famous shield and associated identity of Captain America), and the issue makes most sense in this light. *Captain America* #695 exhibits its "back-to-basics" classicism in the form of a refocusing on authentic elements from Marvel's past. Along with Waid's reappointment, it was largely received as making right a perceived loss of direction.

THE ROLE OF COMICS

If parts of Axel Alonso's addresses recounted earlier apply an equalizing effect to how consumers first engage with comic-originated characters ("spinner rack" or "movie theater"), in other messages emanating from Marvel, comics seem to be being reduced. The film division began in earnest in 1996, truly bearing fruit in 2008 with the Marvel-controlled, Paramount Pictures–distributed *Iron Man* (directed by Jon Favreau). As it matures, twenty cinematic entries and countless hours of television later, Marvel Studios' status has changed; much as Marvel Comics found itself switching industry leader positions with DC for the first time in 1971, MS—by most measures, current clear leader in popular film franchising—inhabits the identity of a winner, not that of an underdog.[34] With maturation, identity assumes complicated baggage; moreover, Marvel's reputation in the MCU era is all about deftly handled interlinked stories and chronologies. The PR story that MS can circulate has been that of an almost relentless rise; to incorporate this into its identity narrative should be less challenging than what faces DC today, another comic-based transmedia enterprise but one experiencing intermittent failure around big-budget film takes on its characters.[35] Nevertheless, where it might seem axiomatic that comics serve as "foundational texts," as per Matt Yockey, Marvel Studios' messages do not always support that story. MS saw fit to replace the rifling-pages comic motif that had served as company ident through thirteen features with the late 2016 release of *Doctor Strange* (directed by Scott Derrickson). The fanfare sequence now privileges comic pages for mere instants. They are replaced by an implied progression of forms: the pages morph into colorful Marvel Studios live-action figures; script notation and dialogue is subsequently overlaid on this image. Next, this hybrid screenplay/action representation starts to flicker with gentle movement (Captain America propels his shield towards the camera). After the barely moving Cap becomes fully animated, the final reveal (with camera pulling back) is that MCU excerpts, which appear as if projected on screens (connoting the final evolutionary stage), actually make up the underside of the Marvel logo.

The well-known fanfare sequence is promotional discourse and identity statement at once. Other statements show Marvel choosing when to accentuate comics "legacies" as something bearing on the present, and—equally—when not to. Thus, in a special feature included on the UK *Homecoming* 2-DVD set, the offscreen phrase "Spider-Man is the greatest superhero ever" (uttered by a producer) is accompanied not by MCU images, but by a montage of actual comic panels featuring the hero, as drawn by associated artists such as John Romita, Don Heck, and Joe Quesada. This seems more like selective flexibility than slippage.

Anxious symptoms like biennial relaunches and mothballing of once-flagship titles (*Fantastic Four*) demand to be read in a certain way. Are comics still at the heart of the business, for Marvel, under Disney? Derek Johnson maintains that the publishing division "remains a crucial site of legacy and identity" for all of Marvel—though Johnson's own piece frames one key concern as "how a comic book publisher works to stay a comic book publisher" amongst the sprawling activities of a transmedia mega-studio.[36]

Marvel was not the pioneer of the notion, but the publisher embraced nearly line-wide continuity in an interrelated superhero milieu as its prime mission. The tendency toward an increasingly complex, *planned* universe was well in play by the 1965 marriage of Reed and Susan Richards (the joyful event's seams bursting with Marvel superheroes).[37] The realization of a publisher employing its entire catalogue, interrelatedly, across the line was what Marvel did: a founding myth. It is known from the work of Sean Howe and others that the MU was stamped with a house identity through Jack Kirby being instructed to impose a style on newly joining artists.[38] The "Marvel Method" combined artist and writer in letting storytelling rest more on dynamic art layouts than the careful construction of scripts. This way of artificially inculcating consistency certainly cost the likes of Kirby, Steve Ditko, and often minimally credited artists much in the way of credit and pay, a most controversial reality of the Method when it came to Kirby. Marvel's line, however, flourished.

Elsewhere, Mike McKenny, Andy Livingstone, and I diagnosed the "personality" with which Marvel Studios broke out in Hollywood franchise filmmaking as crafted from elements strongly identified with the earlier orchestration of a Marvel comics "voice" and worldview.[39] For our purposes here, the question concerns whether the Marvel business of 2017, in a volatile comics market, could depend upon the same attitude to "legacy" as could Marvel Studios. The myths that were fostered by the perhaps unsurpassed creativity and fan-relatability of Marvel Comics' triumphant 1960s promulgated an unmistakable aura—embodied by Lee—that could efface unsightly behind-the-scenes moves (certainly, not all of which were the responsibility of Marvel creative and editorial staff). Marvel Studios has moments like this, even in a far shorter history. A well-known example concerns the termination of successful filmmakers' association with the studio, either through visions diverging (Edgar Wright, Joss Whedon), or their attraction of controversy (James Gunn).

For all the goodwill that is generally directed toward Marvel Studios, both divisions are parts of Disney. Some commentators explicitly drive a wedge between the parent and the publisher, but a commonly held view sees the Warner Brothers (DC) and Disney (Marvel) media conglomerates' approach to both publishers as "largely intellectual-property farms."[40] Others question what incentivizes Disney to support Marvel Comics in strengthening its market position "when they're making millions on the latest Marvel film."[41] Thus, the obvious tension in any MS reproduction of Marvel's heritage—the carnivalesque "Bullpen" culture—involves the agenda of its owner since 2009. With my coauthors, I have looked at such issues, but Disney—while synergistically moving theme-park rides and television-show content (like ABC-TV's *Castle*, 2009–16) through comic publications—has genuinely granted MS a degree of autonomy. We know, because Marvel/Disney went on record to ensure that we knew.[42] Disney is an expert in content and consumer product fields well beyond cinema yet finds it advantageous to let its brand lean on a relatively autonomous heritage imprimatur of Marvel Comics. The comics division still experiences problems, however. Next, we shall consider how Marvel Studios has used self-narrating and wise control of identity to make a clear passage around some of those same problems.

THE FIRST FAMILY

Alongside the retooled notions of legacy and homecoming clustering around the business in 2017, other constructions of Marvel's meanings persist. One echo of tradition conflates the Marvel Bullpen myth with a romanticization of studio president Kevin Feige and fellow executives. Marvel Studios projects a creative "family" structure, which carries both an authenticity and a multifaceted nature that assists when it is asserted even in the face of current—and *past*—threats to creative and industrial harmony.

Referring to the efforts to manage MS's public identity, Marc Graser subscribes to a heritage view, attributing success to "the consistency of [. . .] a core team of executives." Victoria Alonso, a top-ranking MS executive VP, describes the arrangement as "like having a family":[43] an image evolving from the aura of rude health and familiarity cultivated by Stan Lee's paratexts (such as his monthly "Soapbox" column). The image assures that the business chaos that afflicted Marvel Entertainment in the 1990s will not return (and maybe that a Feige culture will always stand up to Disney interference).[44] The "House of Ideas" needed benevolent stability well before Marvel Studios or Disney came along. The long-term nurturing of awkward projects is offered as evidence of stability. In the *Homecoming* DVD supplements, star Downey Jr. is interviewed and, being very on-message, credits the communication skills of Marvel leaders with the harmony underpinning success: "Just the fact that two massive studios can get along and share IP is to me really exciting. [. . .] I've known Amy [Pascal, lead Sony producer] forever and seeing her and Kevin [Feige] figure this out together is kind of great."[45]

"Homecoming" implies having been away in the first place. Different senses coalesce in how the movie uses homecoming, so a brief look at how it is constructed is warranted. In the diegesis, homecoming is a marker of the student year and celebration of the high school social system itself; but Marvel's industrial narrative adds more layers. Spider-Man returns to Marvel Studios, after a period where his creative fate was controlled by Sony; now restitution can be made for the wilderness era, before Sony's deal, when rights entanglements prevented any coherent live-action iteration.[46] Business challenges—implicitly including those due to earlier Marvel's lack of vision and financial stability—are surmounted, and the homecoming can proceed; but historic Marvel's incompetency is a relatively bland layer of meaning here. The materials around the DVD release hype the character's return as huge news, while a distant allusion to frosty former relations between Disney/Marvel and Sony is nevertheless made. Also permitted is a fleeting reference attaching failure to Sony, which alone, could not successfully develop a film universe around Spider-Man.[47] The Marvel and Sony representatives interviewed for the *Tangled Web* featurette spread the same message of collaboration, and the family characterization of Marvel governance recurs—even extending to interstudio relations. There is talk of the "need" for Sony to "have" Spider-Man, while by the same token, Spider-Man "needs" Marvel—quite an admission coming from Sony top brass (Pascal was once studio chairperson). This statement belongs with other positive readings of Marvel's core as stable, with the challenges of living with market conditions still imprinted by the loss of film licenses in the 1990s quietly fading away.[48]

Spider-Man emerges from this as an essential, historical asset for Marvel, allowing it to resurge even in comparison with the far more experienced film operation of Sony/Columbia (which nevertheless also benefits). Although the highly experienced Walt Disney Pictures identity is held out of direct view (as it often is in Marvel Studios promotions), Marvel can thus be presented as, once again, guarding the essences of comic narratives. To seal the point, early 1960s Ditko illustration adorns a sequence where Feige discusses what the MCU Spidey owes to the character's early comic status as "an alternative" to established heroes.[49]

When MS attempts to narrativize itself, it generally recalls a variant of the aura once kindled by showman Lee (Stan Lee, of course, continues to appear in each movie and many Marvel television shows). The "consistency" that Marvel Studios wants to enshrine in its image conjures up a version of legendary Bullpen days: a core family of comic pros, empowered to act responsibly with characters but firm enough to defend the company's "soul" from corporate upheaval.[50] A paternal lead creative makes this possible, and, like Lee, Feige is this brand of figurehead: good at publicity patter, firm in handling money-men, a wise channeler of creativity. Graser attributes the stability of MS's creative "flow" to Feige, identifying him—unusually for a Hollywood producer—with creative forces.[51] Even as early as 2008—year of the MCU debut *Iron Man*—press characterized Feige as the man holding Marvel's "film fibers" together, invoking the sense of a bustling universe controlled by a committed, superstrong individual. Devin Leonard attributes to Feige "a special understanding of [. . .] fans, superheroes, and narrative," noting how fans recognize him and chant supportively at an L.A. premiere.[52] MSs family style can, then, be seen as contiguous with the most acceptable parts of Marvel Comics' public identity, affirming the "cinematic destiny" narrative (confirming Johnson's view).[53] Such accounts of Feige's importance chime with other themes in Marvel Studios–related trade press: the organization appears creatively and financially sound, with positive aspects of its corporate story bound up into a man with a master plan (with shades of Stan Lee).

One of the threats to this positivity lies with the comics division. In 2017 its relations with fandom became embattled; the indifferently received *Secret Empire* spurred this, but inconsistent and divisive PR messages compounded it. Comics executive David Gabriel made public remarks about failed diversity initiatives, such as special arcs and replacements in major superhero identities.[54] Greeted with controversy, this sounded rather like Marvel defining such initiatives' acceptance as a matter for fan loyalty, and not a creative responsibility incumbent upon itself. The Gabriel affair jarred in juxtaposition to the values of race and gender tolerance for which Marvel deservedly attracted acclaim earlier in its history.[55] In October 2017 Marvel's YouTube channel published a video in the form of a to-camera piece with Stan Lee. By moving "Chairman Emeritus" Lee to the front line, a few months after the Gabriel story, Marvel was using its most iconic living creative to reinforce its traditions of inclusivity in narrative. A number of familiar themes, from family to legacy, were present in his language. Starting by asserting that Marvel's way is to reflect the world outside viewers' windows, he continues: "That world may change and evolve, but the one thing that will never change is the way we tell our stories of heroism. Those stories have room for everyone, regardless of their race, gender, religion or color of their skin. [. . .] We're all part of one big family [. . . and] you're part of that family; you're part of the Marvel Universe." Storytelling tradition fuses with liberal social mission. The video had close to 350,000 views by mid-December 2017, although Marvel discouraged further debate, perhaps understandably, by disabling comments underneath it.[56]

In the context of Gabriel's unpopular comments, ushering Spider-Man into the crowded MCU probably seemed a simple, organic next step in Marvel's overall project.[57] Even this, though, presented tests of coherence. The character is both "all new" to the MCU and challengingly old. The Sony-owned film character first manifested in the MCU via a brief cameo in *Captain America: Civil War* (Anthony and Joe Russo, 2016): a low-key introduction, this made Peter Parker's story but one thread of his mentor Tony Stark's narrative. Spider-Man would break out in *Homecoming*, released in July 2017. The film's commercial reception grew from initially average to strong.[58] *Homecoming* makes a point of Spider-Man/Peter's youth (and naivety), its script employing many familiar albeit minor faces from the Ditko-Lee Spider-Man world. However, the Spider-Man posited by the film, and Tom Holland's performance, marks an attempt to mix up and ultimately, perhaps, neutralize the distance between this incarnation of Spidey/Pete and earlier versions redolent of some idealized eternal adolescence (even though Marvel comics started to move away from this in the late 1960s, with Pete entering university followed by graduate school). This diverges from the characterological approach of Sony's film cycles, wherein Pete found work (in journalism or scientific research) and broadened his horizons in nonsuperhero company, while mourning his Uncle Ben (Martin Sheen, in two films).[59] A comic given away with the DVD set of *Homecoming* (and thus, it can be assumed, created with nonpurist readers in mind) reflected the same collection of tropes—a high school Peter, bearing little history, pursuing a classic villain, and a romantic subplot.[60]

LEGACY COMICS?

Marvel's publishing branch must necessarily confront the challenges of the future: the aging market for comic book readers, the lack of young readers waiting in the wings, and the frustrations of seeing other divisions within Marvel thrive in appeals to a new generation.[61]

The film division's progression may have seemed destined, but fans and other observers may wonder how the rest of the organization will catch up. This is particularly so since, to achieve MS's dominant market position, films once followed comics, in narrative and character terms; but, as the MCU body expands, that logic seems to have been abandoned.[62] In this context Axel Alonso's editorial encouragement for Marvel loyalists to understand and respect new readers brought in by the MCU makes sense.

One of the factors Marvel faces in fully synchronizing a stance on its own history is the diffuse state of the overall organization's identity, owing to its multi-sphere production commitments.[63] Instructive is Marvel's handling of Miles Morales, an alternate Spider-Man who, in his own universe, was perfectly authentic. Marvel engineered a comics event to bring a trickle of characters from the (once) purely counterfactual Ultimate Universe (a sort of sandbox for using alternative characters to revivify canonical storylines) across a narrative bridge into the mainstream MU.[64] This eventually brought the Afro-Latin American Morales into the new-old identity of Ultimate Spider-Man, via *The Death of Spider-Man*, a multi-*Ultimate* title crossover published between April and October 2011. Not impinging on Peter Parker's fortunes in the "mainstream," Morales's establishment was largely uncontroversial with fans (nevertheless antagonizing conservative media).[65] Marvel has consistently supported Morales's legitimacy, underscoring it with animated and—it seems—MCU iterations, along with his pivotal role in *Civil War II*, which was on sale while *Captain America: Civil War*—the major MS investment of 2016—was in theaters.[66] However, while such recastings are understood by many superhero-comic fans to be temporary and necessary, they create anxiety for others: when this happens to famous legacy characters, when code names are handed to new or minor characters, any sales increase is not always obviously causal. Worse, fan disquiet can result. Legacy itself, to a degree, is a Marvel proposal to counter such tensions.

Bart Beaty has explained today's shrinking comics market. Taking DC's *Superman* title as chief example, Beaty describes a nearly "vertical line downward" from postwar sales peaks, to 2010.[67] Although Marvel has frequently outsold DC and in fact still, as of early 2018, led in market share (almost 40 percent of the market in both dollars and units sold), the same sales plunge has hit both publishers. McMillan offers an update on the same phenomenon, slanting towards DC's recent ascendancy and gesturing toward the failure of successful Marvel-derived movies to boost comic sales.[68] For the reasons outlined by Johnson's assertion of a lack of symmetry to how Marvel "thrives" across different divisions, allied to the conditions Beaty analyzes, the publisher cannot afford to simply write off purists for whom Captain America must always be Steve Rogers (underlining the authoritative Mark Waid's usefulness to Legacy). This is since the younger group of adherents to characters like Jane Foster (erstwhile Thor) or Kamala Khan (as a Pakistani-American Muslim Ms. Marvel)—though sizable—is an inadequate replacement in dollar terms. The industry in general does not elaborate on digital sales, but Cocca reports that within a few issues of her 2013 introduction, Khan's title *Ms. Marvel* (vol. 3) had become "Marvel's top digital [. . . and] international seller."[69] Cocca further notes that sales for those newer characters also concentrate in cheaper digital issue and trade collection forms, thus counting less in dollar share. This logic explains why *Marvel Legacy* #1 restores "classic" Captain America and Wolverine (Logan) identities, shows the return of X-Man Jean Grey, and teases the FF. That said, the Hispanic American Robbie Reyes, another relatively fresh incumbent to a legacy character, sports the Ghost Rider mantle in *Legacy* #1, harmonizing with season 4 of television's *Marvel's Agents of S.H.I.E.L.D.* (2013–).

Media iteration promotes experimenting with versions of characters but must respect fan thinking regarding legitimacy and, additionally, licensor satisfaction. Licensors require "pure" versions of what characters offer; more iterations chip away at characters' stability. Cocca points out that the rotation of legacy hero mantles, where often the ratio of straight, white male characters in prime roles is reset, comfortably predates the change that followed in the wake of Miles Morales; and many fans can accept such developments.[70] As far back as the 1980s, Marvel creative-editorial figures like Mark Gruenwald were openly acknowledging this as an effective strategy.[71] In 1982, as Jason Shayer reports, writer Roger Stern had cocreated Monica Rambeau, inheritor of the moniker of a beloved male hero, the deceased Captain Marvel. Stern's storylines steered Rambeau to becoming the first Black female to lead the Avengers. Dismayed at a Marvel edict to relieve her of the role, Stern preferred to leave one of Marvel's highest-profile titles.[72]

Despite the broad public exposure for Marvel characters since 2000 (particularly after 2008–9's events: MCU initiation and Disney purchase), there are suggestions that comic book publishing is itself now a legacy market. Back in 2014, Marvel's plans to downplay the Fantastic Four and X-Men, while now rendered irrelevant by the Fox-Disney deal, stirred fans and aroused suspicion that "few compelling reasons existed for Marvel to continue producing legacy comics that fed external [. . .] film and television projects."[73] All associated titles paraded characters who were not, at the time, accessible to MS's plans, since owned by Fox, with the Fantastic Four's comic pulled outright (a temporary suspension, as *Legacy* #1 confirms). Now, Twentieth-Century Fox assets will pass to Disney, making MCU homecomings for the FF and popular mutant Deadpool virtually inevitable. Meanwhile, Sony has renewed the idea to exploit Spider-Man "universe" characters in films outside of MS control (beginning with Ruben Fleischer's *Venom* in 2018).

If discourses from within Marvel render comics' status as ambivalent, some see Marvel Studios' expansion as resting on the *same tactics* that killed off superhero publishing as mass entertainment. Bart Beaty's contention is that the techniques used by Marvel Studios in its extraordinary rise are "the exact same ones that rendered Marvel Comics a marginal publishing presence in the same era."[74] Noting key elements as the presence of a hardcore fan-pleasing approach through spiraling continuity and canon building in a "shared universe," Beaty offers that the MCU "trains" general audiences in this "'proper' method of engaging with [. . . its] texts" in the image of earlier modes of comic fandom.[75] For Beaty, MS's indulgence of crossovers, frequent Easter eggs, and "footnotes" that simulate Stan Lee–style editorial messages shapes the MCU as a media rebuilding of a world initially cast in comics. Pop culture press and the fan community supportively play continuity detectives to help out novices.[76] If Beaty's assessment is correct, the same commitment to narrative connectivity that has engaged MCU audiences has pushed casual readers out of comics, facilitating its dramatic decline.[77] As the fortunes of one division/sector rise, we may not expect the other to show either a significant rise or fall; and drawing a causal relationship between successful media ventures and comic sales is an inexact process. Still, industry commentators note that a full Hollywood agenda (in 2017 three popular MCU films, two new Netflix launches, and a Fox-Marvel movie) records no lasting salutary impact on Marvel sales in the period, whatever strategy is implemented.[78] Is the destiny of Marvel comics to feed projects in film, television, games, and toys? Where does an overdetermined comics event like Legacy fit with this? How comics can support the expansion toward cinematic realization, while maintaining their own luster, is an unanswered question that will supply more intrigue as Disney/Marvel marches on, particularly in the light of deals (such as with Fox) that, at least in publicly disclosed aspects, seem to hinge on Hollywood-facing policies.

CONCLUSION

The effects of Legacy proved, unsurprisingly, to be transient. Graham McMillan rated the relaunch "stalled," since it did not improve Marvel's annual performance relative to a resurgent DC, despite initial signs of a sales impact[79] *Amazing Spider-Man*—a couple of months after *Homecoming*'s release—doubled its previous (*Secret Empire*-connected) issue sales; they then, however, reverted to their previous standard, suggesting few permanent new fans had been won. *Legacy* #1 itself saw high sales along with the restarted main *Thor* series. Waid/Samnee's *Captain America* debut also piled on new buyers compared to the title's last regular issue dated October 2017 but within four issues was hovering at around 40 percent of its Legacy launch figure.[80]

A transitory sales pickup is not shocking, comparative to any company-wide relaunch; but Marvel's next rebrand/relaunch announcement—as Alonso-led initiatives made way for the new broom of Cebulski—almost mocked the Legacy premise with its rapidity. *Marvel Legacy* #1 hit shops in late September 2017; the announcement of "Fresh Start" rang out in February 2018, with just five months intervening. Led by a new creative team, *Avengers* #1 (by Jason Aaron and Ed McGuinness) saw even the higher, original Legacy numbering disappear (a small slice of text marking "LGY#691" underneath the prominent restarted number is present). Other companies have experimented with dual numbering over the years, but this is the first time that Marvel resorted to the tactic immediately following a campaign that professed to privilege history (acknowledged by the ambivalent retention yet reduction of the word "Legacy" as "LGY").

What seems certain is that Marvel has equally struggled with "newness" for a while. Cool receptions have greeted a number of past resets with various twists, but "Fresh Start"—instrumental to which is an FF revival, and other "originals" restored to their code names or classic situations—is certainly ironically named, for in some ways, of course, it continues Legacy's mission. Legacy provided no permanent solution for Marvel Comics; but understanding the need for it does bring focus to a larger puzzle with which the entire Marvel organization must deal if it wishes to institute a more diverse leading-character range (something it has demonstrably attempted) and thus continue to sincerely bill itself as a welcoming universe in the sense of Stan Lee's video, while preserving key heritage (and continuity) elements. Experts on brand and organization confirm the wisdom that "current needs or desired future image fuels the reinvention of the past."[81] Thus, Marvel strives to form a position where present needs both respect and are served by organizational heritage.

Examining how Marvel faces this challenge leads back to that critical moment of identity reshaping in the 1990s. In postbankruptcy reconstruction, the costly drift from core principles was corrected by Marvel remembering its own vast experience in storytelling. Executive Avi Arad—instrumental in the ultimate establishment of Marvel's film division—then advocated shouting to the world about the easy communicative properties of Marvel characters.[82] Arad's view, aligned with that of publisher Bill Jemas, strategically led Marvel's operational recovery in the postbankruptcy years. Interestingly, recent Marvel administrations can be seen to admire the same precept that Beaty argues when he brackets "arcane backstories" as discouraging lore for general audiences:[83] an Arad/Jemas-driven purification to star character essences brought renewal, and revenues to prop Marvel Entertainment up at this critical time (including the striking of X-Men and Spider-Man film deals; this, effectively, the leave-taking that Spider-Man had to endure so that a later homecoming could be possible).[84] In comics the Ultimate line reflected this, and a policy to enhance the credited status of its roster of writers and artists was welcomed as providing creative stability—and a dose of Bullpen legacy.[85]

The form this took strongly resembles the projection that Marvel Studios—as responsibly stewarded by Feige, Alonso, D'Esposito, and a small circle of trusted filmmakers—now maintains. That this was a defining moment of Marvel selectively appealing to its own history is obvious; it patterned how the identity of the company and its products has derived values from Marvel heritage ever since.

If a form of textuality springing directly from comics was too hard to reach, then the next best thing was a recognized, responsible guardianship of beloved characters. Marvel Studios has negotiated all of this rather well, although its official profession that comics still underlie everything has to be doubted, given examples we have considered of how that policy has faded.[86] It now comes to a problem, with its connected productions reaching some kind of apex following 2018's *Avengers Infinity War*, and a related film in 2019, after which reboot or renewal—in some form—is generally expected on a number of grounds (not least, well-known contractual arrangements with lead actors). This looks unlikely to apply to Holland's Spider-Man, however, with that character's next installment (*Spider-Man: Far from Home*, Jon Watts, 2019) set for a release after the Avengers film. The actor himself is in his early twenties.[87]

DC's well-received *Rebirth* in 2016 had illustrated that a "back to basics" relaunch can provide a period of success. What Marvel Comics seems to find problematic in living with the brand's history, Marvel Studios apparently takes in its stride, reconciling "old" and "new" (and an embarrassing rights problem from the past) with ease in *Homecoming*. Marvel Studios makes such moves to an accrual of credit, whereas failing to resolve old and new—in terms of managing continuity, or understanding fans' expectations for it—has (as Beaty argues) hastened decline for Marvel Comics. Marvel Studios' identity as "publisher" of the MCU texts interestingly draws on another important heritage element that is unconnected to the business of comics—plain, as MS is, in its admiration of methods of studio system era Hollywood. Once aspirational, this phase of filmmaking shapes practice even since MS became a citadel within Disney. Jerome Christensen's statement of this position—"The Hollywood studio [. . .] does its business right there on the screen"—maintains that both classical and (post) modern forms of American studio expression can be read as partly allegorical: films are stories about the business. This seems a very Marvel description, with Bullpen "characters" regularly spilling onto comic pages in the 1960s and 1970s, and Stan Lee and Jack Kirby established as part of the diegetic comics universe at an early stage. Legacy—in aspects like Valeria Richards's voiceover narration—partakes in Connor's notion, mentioned earlier, of "allegorical studio stories" carved into film fictions. He argues that a neoclassicism, melding classical and new, helped Hollywood studios adapt to an unfamiliarly "provisional production environment" after the 1970s.[88] This lesson was taken on board by Marvel Studios but proves more difficult to apply in Marvel Comics' sector.

The popular expansion of the MCU shows that, once settling its business and proving its stability, the company has found ways to more effectively involve returning and new consumers in its extensive shared universe. What is more, the consequent platform has been used to continue forging an identity narrative of renewal that also respects publishing tradition. Cooperation with

Sony over Spider-Man and the boosting of key executive images all make ample connection with the identity that served the publishing business well during the 1960s: a marker of authenticity, a perception of home or family, is put down. An initiative like Legacy—and the speedy retreat from it—demonstrates how the comics division cannot unproblematically pull off similar maneuvers; comics and publishing policy radiate uncertainty of how to affirm the company's complex hinterland of stories, identities, and histories.

NOTES

1. Derek Johnson, "Cinematic Destiny: Marvel Studios and the Trade Stories of Industrial Convergence," *Cinema Journal* 52, no. 1 (Fall 2012): 1–24.

2. Bart Beaty outlines these conditions in "Superhero Fan Service: Audience Strategies in the Contemporary Interlinked Hollywood Blockbuster," *Information Society* 32, no. 5 (2016): 319. Most of Marvel's current shows are delivered via its Netflix partnership; with Netflix reluctant to release figures, commercial take-up is difficult to gauge. That *Jessica Jones* season 2, 2017, has just become the eighth straight Marvel season with more in production would suggest that the franchise on Netflix is healthy; yet the *Iron Fist* show (season 1, 2017) was the franchise's first critical failure, as aggregator sites like Metacritic show. On network television, ABC-TV's *Marvel's Agents of S.H.I.E.L.D.* has had a tough time with ratings but survives; the initial season (2018) of *Runaways* has prospered on Hulu (and SyFy channel in the UK), while canceled shows include miniseries *Agent Carter* (two seasons, 2015–16) and *Inhumans* (2017).

3. M. Yockey, "This Island Manhattan: New York City and the Space Race in *The Fantastic Four*," *Iowa Journal of Cultural Studies*, no. 6 (Spring 2005): 30.

4. Axel Alonso, "Foreword," *All-New, All-Different Marvel Previews*, no. 1 (September 2015): 4.

5. Axel Alonso, "Legacy Lowdown: Axel Sez," *Marvel Legacy* 1, no. 1 (November 2017): 62.

6. Shannon Liao, "Marvel's Editor in Chief Apologizes for Pretending to Be a Japanese Man," *The Verge*, December 18, 2017, https://www.theverge.com/2017/12/18/16792070/marvel-editor-in-chief-akira-yoshida-cebulski-cultural-appropriation; Asher Elbein, "The Secret Identity of Marvel Comics' Editor," *The Atlantic*, December 17, 2017, https://www.theatlantic.com/entertainment/archive/2017/12/the-secret-identity-of-marvel-comics-editor/547829/.

7. William Proctor, "Schrödinger's Cape: The Quantum Seriality of the Marvel Universe," in *Make Ours Marvel: Media Convergence and a Comics Universe*, ed. Matt Yockey (Austin: University of Texas Press, 2017), 333.

8. A relevant example of this capturing Marvel's state of indecision between "the past" and "the future" was a badly received 2017 decision to stop printing a free code (voucher) for a digital comic, inside that issue's paid-for physical copy. With what fans had seen as a method of growing a "free" digital library seemingly replaced by issues of "classic" titles of lesser value, the move caused an outcry, leading Marvel to backtrack a few months later.

9. Coverage in Britain's *The Guardian*; for instance, see Sam Thielman, "Is Diversity to Blame for Marvel's Sales Slump—or Just a Lack of Imagination?" *The Guardian*, April 4, 2017, https://www.theguardian.com/books/2017/apr/04/marvel-comics-diversity-sales.

10. Derek Johnson, "'Share Your Universe': Generation, Gender and the Future of Marvel Publishing," in *Make Ours Marvel: Media Convergence and a Comics Universe*, ed. Matt Yockey (Austin: University of Texas Press, 2017), 148.

11. Johnson, "Share Your Universe," 157.

12. Cover dates will be given, although in the current era, the lag between the actual release of the single comic and the date on the cover has settled at around two months.

13. This shows in #789's narrative (October 2017). The basis of Spider-Man's Legacy storyline is the downfall of Peter Parker's tech company. Plot events connected to *Secret Empire* are tied off, with no change to the writer (Dan Slott had been on the title for a decade and was in situ into the Legacy era but left in 2018), and a subtly reorganized status quo around the hero set into place.

14. George Marston, "STEVE or 'STEVIL'? Tom Brevoort on SECRET EMPIRE, Fulfilling Promises & Who the Real CAP Is," *Newsarama*, September 14, 2017, https://www.newsarama.com/36401-tom-brevoort-secret-empire-interview.html.

15. A soul-searching Cap tangled up with a "Secret Empire" is bound, and partly intended, to bring to mind another story: the Watergate-echoing "Secret Empire" arc of the first half of 1974, chiefly written and drawn by Steve Englehart and Sal Buscema.

16. The return of Mark Waid, who first wrote the character in 1995, and his pairing with Chris Samnee, a popular artist with a purified "retro" style, was itself a signal of coming to terms with history. Reporting sites colluded with Marvel's desired message on this, privileging the narrative of a "classic" version of a character being restored (see the story: Newsarama Staff, "Classic CAP Is Back in CAPTAIN AMERICA 695 Preview," *Newsarama*, October 26, 2017, https://www.newsarama.com/37110-marvel-preview-1-captain-america-695.html).

17. As of this writing, the highest number of issues released in a Legacy-branded title was eight, for the bimonthly *Amazing Spider-Man* (issue #797 saw the branding quietly disappear).

18. Interestingly, in the autumn following *Spider-Man: Homecoming*, the elements included in *Amazing Spider-Man*'s primer segment relate strongly to the continuity underpinning Dan Slott's long term as writer, rather than particularly aiming to gel with the version presented by the movie. As discussed later, paratexts issued with *Spider-Man: Homecoming* replaced that role.

19. *Thor Ragnarok* (Taika Waititi, 2017) set a new level for the success of solo Thor movies, moving him onto a par with such as Iron Man; but the success of *Black Panther* (Ryan Coogler, 2018) was stupendous, and unexpected. As of May 2018, it was Marvel's leading American grosser, and had taken in $1.3 billion worldwide, elevating it to levels enjoyed by franchises like *Star Wars*. See BoxOfficeMojo, "Black Panther (2018)," http://www.boxofficemojo.com/movies/?page=main&id=marvel2017b.htm.

20. *Marvel Legacy* #1, 6–7.

21. See the discussion of Captain America's early 1970s experiences, particularly, in Michael Goodrum, *Superheroes and American Self-Image: From War to Watergate* (Abingdon: Routledge, 2016), 201–3.

22. Yockey, "This Island Manhattan."

23. Val opines, "Part of our legacy is that we're always getting lost" (38). On the Fantastic Four's treatment, see Johnson, "Share Your Universe," 138–39.

24. Martin Flanagan, Andy Livingstone, and Mike McKenny, *The Marvel Studios Phenomenon: Inside a Transmedia Universe* (London: Bloomsbury, 2016). On self-awareness in Marvel Studios' public identity, see 42–44, 197–98.

25. J. D. Connor, *The Studios after the Studios: Neoclassical Hollywood (1970–2010)* (Stanford, CA: Stanford University Press, 2015), 13 and passim.

26. *Marvel Legacy* #1, 33 and 58.

27. See, for one example, "Captain America's Empire: Reflections on Identity, Popular Culture and Post-9/11 Geopolitics," *Annals of the Association of American Geographers* 95, no. 3 (2005): 626–43.

28. Alex Widen, "*Captain America* #695 Review: Marvel Apologizes for the Last Two Years," Bam! Smack! Pow!, December 4, 2017, https://bamsmackpow.com/2017/11/10/captain-america-695-review/.

29. As might be expected of such a long-running fictional body of work, the time transpiring in the MU does not closely track the time of its readers' world. There have been efforts to calibrate the temporal flow of events in its texts to an external historical scale. The company has referred to something known as "Marvel Time"; its formula is discussed by Troy D. Smith, cited in Chris Tolworthy, "Marvel's Sliding Time Scale," *The Fantastic Four (1961–89) Was the Great American Novel*, June 20, 2014, http://zak-site.com/Great-American-Novel/marvel_time.html.

30. This trope has been explored in various ways in Cap's MCU coverage; see Flanagan, Livingstone, and McKenny, *Marvel Studios Phenomenon*, 98–107.

31. Jesse Schedeen, "*Captain America* #695 Review," IGN, November 1, 2017, http://uk.ign.com/articles/2017/11/01/captain-america-695-review; Widen, "*Captain America* #695 Review."

32. Marcus Sirois, "Issues with Comics,"' Facebook page, accessed December 9, 2017, https://www.facebook.com/groups/1691862497761406/.

33. Johnson, "Share Your Universe," 158.

34. See Flanagan, Livingstone, and McKenny, *Marvel Studios Phenomenon*, 13. For figures painting a comparative picture of Marvel Studios' success, see BoxOfficeMojo, "Franchise Index," http://www.boxofficemojo.com/franchises/.

35. Pertinently, two texts analyze fans' perceptions of DC's treatment of the logo that supports its comics trade dress and adorns movie idents, and the frequency with which DC displays its own branding/logo editorially as compared to Marvel. See Jim Edwards, "Why Everyone Hates DC Comics' Weird New Corporate Logo," *Business Insider*, January 17, 2012, www.businessinsider.com/why-everyone-hates-dc-comics-weird-new-corporate-logo-2012-1?op=1&IR=T#74-2; Marinus J. J. Van den Anker and Piet Verhoeven, "Corporate Communication: Analysing Marvel and DC," *Studies in Comics* 5, no. 1 (2010): 123.

36. Johnson, "Share Your Universe," 139, 141.

37. *Fantastic Four Annual* #3, 1965.

38. Sean Howe, *Marvel Comics: The Untold Story*, paperback ed. (New York: Harper Perennial, 2013), 50–51, 65.

39. Flanagan, Livingstone, and McKenny, *Marvel Studios Phenomenon*, 6–19; 46–50; 75–77.

40. Thom Pratt, "Marvel Comics Implosion: Are Politics, Readers or Combative Editorial to Blame?," *Kingdom Insider*, September 17, 2017, http://thekingdominsider.com/marvel-comics-implosion-politics/.

41. Asher Elbein, "The Real Reasons for Marvel Comics' Woes," *The Atlantic*, May 24, 2017, https://www.theatlantic.com/entertainment/archive/2017/05/the-real-reasons-for-marvel-comics-woes/527127/.

42. Flanagan, Livingstone, and McKenny, *Marvel Studios Phenomenon*, 161.

43. See Marc Graser, "How Marvel Guards Its Properties but Isn't Afraid to Take Chances with Its 'Galaxy,'" *Variety*, July 23, 2014, http://variety.com/2014/film/news/marvel-studios-guardians-of-the-galaxy-risk-1201266165/.

44. This is so since the relation between Disney's stewardship and control at Feigear level, as well as the intermediary role of the now-dissolved "Marvel Creative Committee," attracted much commentary. On the stability point, and how this relates to wider Disney structures, see Flanagan, Livingstone, and McKenny, *Marvel Studios Phenomenon*, 37–38, 72). The 'MCC'—a body that drew from comic talent—is discussed at 198–204.

45. "A Tangled Web," *Spider-Man: Homecoming*, directed by Jon Watts (Culver City, CA: Sony Pictures Home Entertainment, 2017), DVD.

46. See Liam Burke, *The Comic Book Film Adaptation: Exploring Modern Hollywood's Leading Genre* (Jackson: University Press of Mississippi, 2015), 16–17.

47. On Sony's efforts in this direction, see Matt Singer, "The *Amazing Spider-Man* Series: What Went Wrong?" *Screen Crush*, March 21, 2016, http://screencrush.com/the-amazing-spider-man-series-what-went-wrong/.

48. See Howe, *Marvel Comics*, 426–27; Derek Johnson, *Media Franchising: Creative License and Collaboration in the Culture Industries* (New York: New York University Press, 2013), 95–96. The Fox-Disney deal announcement (see below) means that the challenges really have receded, with only certain rights lying with Universal or any traditionally major Hollywood studios.

49. "Journey into Mystery," one of the featurettes on the *Thor Ragnarok* UK Blu-ray release (2018), takes precisely the same tack, albeit with a slant toward the artistry of Jack Kirby.

50. On this theme, see Dan Raviv, *Comic Wars: Marvel's Battle for Survival* (Sea Cliff, NY: Heroes Books, 2004), 35.

51. Graser, "How Marvel Guards."

52. Borys Kit, "Marvel's Universal Approach Makes It a World Apart from DC," *Hollywood Reporter*, May 12, 2008, https://www.hollywoodreporter.com/news/marvels-universal-approach-makes-a-111516; Devin Leonard, "The Pow! Bang! Bam! Plan to Save Marvel, Starring B-List Heroes," *Bloomberg*, April 4, 2014, http://www.bloomberg.com/bw/articles/2014-04-03/kevin-feige-marvels-superhero-at-running-movie-franchises.

53. Johnson, "Cinematic Destiny."

54. In Milton Griepp, "Marvel's David Gabriel on the 2016 Market Shift," *ICV2*, March 31, 2017, https://icv2.com/articles/news/view/37152/marvels-david-gabriel-2016-market-shift.

55. Lee and Kirby received much credit for the narrative of the X-Men. Its antibigotry message, frequently seen as allusively exploring the mid-sixties civil rights struggle, was regularly mapped from persecuted mutants onto the struggle of Black American society. Later the team's diverse roster reflected more communities of race and sexuality. Lee also worked on *Amazing Spider-Man* issues that pleaded for understanding for young drug addicts, and certain stories and characters were "firsts" for mainstream superhero narratives (Black Panther, for instance, was both the first Black and the first African headline superhero in American comics, in 1966). Marvel was credited with representing popular feminism in 1970s titles such as *She-Hulk* and *Ms. Marvel* (see Carolyn Cocca, *Superwomen: Gender, Power and Representation*, [New York and London: Bloomsbury: 2016], 184–91).

56. Marvel Entertainment, "A Message from Stan Lee," YouTube video, 1:18, posted by Marvel Entertainment, October 5, 2017, https://www.youtube.com/watch?v=sjobevGAYHQ.

57. See Billy Henehan, "NYCC '17: Retailer Outrage at the Marvel Retailer Panel!" *Comics Beat*, June 10, 2017, http://www.comicsbeat.com/nycc-17-retailer-outrage-at-the-marvel-retailer-panel/.

58. The film's US opening was below the level of other Spider-Man franchise debuts (from the Sony-only era), but the film went on to amass $334 million in North America and an additional $550

million internationally, placing it as one of the year's top worldwide earners. See BoxOfficeMojo, "Spider-Man: Homecoming (2017)," http://www.boxofficemojo.com/movies/?id=spiderman2017.htm.

59. The Uncle Ben character is significantly downplayed in *Homecoming*. Sheen appeared in Marc Webb's *The Amazing Spider-Man* and *The Amazing Spider-Man 2* (2012 and 2014). The previous, and unrelated, Sony cycle ran for three films (2002–7), was hugely successful, and starred Cliff Robertson in the Ben role.

60. B. Smith and J. L. Giles, *Spider-Man Homecoming: Marvel Custom Edition* #1, 2017.

61. Johnson, "Share Your Universe," 148.

62. Flanagan, Livingstone, and McKenny, *Marvel Studios Phenomenon*, 35–36, 201–2.

63. Johnson, "Share Your Universe," 147.

64. An extended example of Marvel's use of counterfactuality within the wider multiverse, this "sandbox" universe began with *Ultimate Spider-Man* #1 in 2000 and allowed experimentation with ideas and situations that could not be executed in—and would not affect—the established "Earth-616" MU, with its rich history and restrictions on permanent change. The UU was the epitome of major publisher reappropriation, as its headline characters had their origins resituated in the contemporary world, wiping away decades of narrative baggage that had been identified as off-putting to new readers but wishing to remain linked to core values. Importantly and deliberately, these were those readers discovering Marvel heroes at theaters in a new, globally effective era of superhero cinema from the late 1990s.

65. Johnson, "Share Your Universe," 158–59.

66. *Civil War II*, #1–8. Brian Michael Bendis and David Marquez et al. A relevant deleted scene in *Homecoming* featuring the actor Donald Glover seemed to hint at a family connection to Miles Morales. Phillip L. Cunningham looks at the context to why Glover has been much associated with debates around diversity and the Spider-Man character in general—see his "Donald Glover for Spider-Man," in *Web-Swinging Heroics: Critical Essays on the History and Meaning of Spider-Man*, ed. Robert Moses Peaslee and Robert G. Weiner (Jefferson, NC: McFarland, 2012), 22–8.

67. Beaty, "Superhero Fan Service," 320.

68. Graham McMillan, "DC Takes Over a Declining Market: Which Comics Sold Best in 2017," *Hollywood Reporter*, December 28, 2017, https://www.hollywoodreporter.com/heat-vision/best-selling-comics-2017-1070490.

69. Cocca, *Superwomen*, 210.

70. Cocca, *Superwomen*, 209.

71. Dwight J. Zimmerman, "Mark Gruenwald," *Comics Interview* 54 (1988): 5–23.

72. Jason Shayer, "Flashback: Roger Stern's *Avengers*," *Back Issue* 56 (April 2012): 8–34.

73. Johnson, "Share Your Universe," 147, 138.

74. Beaty, "Superhero Fan Service," 319.

75. Beaty, "Superhero Fan Service," 324.

76. Beaty, "Superhero Fan Service," 325.

77. In drawing his distinction between "casual" and "hardcore" audiences, Beaty does note the different scale of a line of comics, involving thousands of texts per decade, where a decade of MS production represents under twenty features and—currently—around 250 one-hour episodes of TV.

78. McMillan, "DC Takes Over."

79. McMillan, "DC Takes Over."

80. All figures reported throughout this piece reflect totals shipped to comic shops, as is industry practice. John Jackson Miller, "October 2017 Comic Book Sales Figures," *ComicChron*,

November 2017, http://www.comichron.com/monthlycomicssales/2017/2017-10.html. For *Captain America* figures, see John Jackson Miller, "November 2017 Comic Book Sales Figures," *ComicChron*, December 2017, http://www.comichron.com/monthlycomicssales/2017/2017-11.html.

81. Dennis A. Gioia, Majken Schultz, and Kevin G. Corley, "Organizational Identity, Image, and Adaptive Instability," in *Organizational Identity: A Reader*, ed. Mary Jo Hatch and Majken Schultz (Oxford: Oxford University Press, 2004), 361.

82. Not every Legacy title subscribed to the "reset of status quo" principle used by *Amazing Spider-Man*, or the restatement of character essence employed in Waid's *Captain America* story; some of the ways in which creative teams interpreted "legacy" to stress a different direction did in fact recover relatively arcane plot points and characters from popular periods as far back as the 1980s. This was noted in some X-Men titles, and it could also be seen in the resurrection of certain titles such as *Marvel Two-in-One Featuring The Thing*.

83. Beaty, "Superhero Fan Service," 318; Deron Overpeck, "Breaking Brand: From NuMarvel to MarvelNOW! Marvel Comics in the Age of Media Convergence," in *Make Ours Marvel: Media Convergence and a Comics Universe*, ed. Matt Yockey (Austin: University of Texas Press, 2017), 164, 181.

84. Howe, *Marvel Comics*, 392–417.

85. Flanagan, Livingstone, and McKenny, *Marvel Studios Phenomenon*, 65.

86. For example, Johnson ("Share Your Universe," 149) cites the head of Marvel Television, Jeph Loeb, interviewed in 2013: "We want everyone to realize that it all starts [. . .] with comic books."

87. As played by Holland, the character is given an amusing trait around the preservation of pop-cultural knowledge, which he occasionally translates into effective battle action (referencing films from *Star Wars* and *Alien* sagas, as well as in-joke film *Footloose*, beloved of the leader of the Guardians of the Galaxy). To the amazement of more seasoned colleagues like Stark, Parker/Spidey calls these texts "really old movies."

88. Jerome Christensen, *America's Corporate Art: The Studio Authorship of Hollywood Motion Pictures* (Stanford, CA: Stanford University Press, 2012), 3; Connor, *Studios after the Studios*, 13.

WORKS CITED

Aaron, Jason, Esad Ribic, et al. "Marvel Legacy." *Marvel Legacy*, #1. New York: Marvel Comics, 2017.

Alonso, Axel. "Foreword." *All-New, All-Different Marvel Previews* 1, #1. New York: Marvel Comics, September 2015.

Alonso, Axel. "Legacy Lowdown: Axel Sez." *Marvel Legacy*, #1. New York: Marvel Comics, 2017.

Beaty, Bart. "Superhero Fan Service: Audience Strategies in the Contemporary Interlinked Hollywood Blockbuster." *Information Society* 32, no. 5 (2016): 318–25.

Box Office Mojo. "Franchise Index." December 15, 2017. http://www.boxofficemojo.com/franchises/?view=Franchise&sort=sumgross&order=DESC%20. Accessed September 9, 2018.

Burke, Liam. *The Comic Book Film Adaptation: Exploring Modern Hollywood's Leading Genre*. Jackson: University Press of Mississippi, 2015.

Christensen, Jerome. *America's Corporate Art: The Studio Authorship of Hollywood Motion Pictures*. Stanford, CA: Stanford University Press, 2012.

Cocca, Carolyn. *Superwomen: Gender, Power and Representation*. New York: Bloomsbury, 2016.

Connor, J. D. *The Studios after the Studios: Neoclassical Hollywood (1970–2010)*. Stanford, CA: Stanford University Press, 2015.

Cunningham, Phillip L. "Donald Glover for Spider-Man." In *Web-Swinging Heroics: Critical Essays on the History and Meaning of Spider-Man*, edited by Robert Moses Peaslee and Robert G. Weiner, 22–28. New York: McFarland Press, 2012.

Dittmer, Jason. "Captain America's Empire: Reflections on Identity, Popular Culture and Post-9/11 Geopolitics." *Annals of the Association of American Geographers* 95, no.3 (2005): 626–43.

Edwards, Jim. "Why Everyone Hates DC Comics' Weird New Corporate Logo." *Business Insider*, January 17, 2012. www.businessinsider.com/why-everyone-hates-dc-comics-weird-new-corporate-logo-2012-1?op=1&IR=T#74-2. Accessed September 9, 2018.

Elbein, Asher. "The Real Reasons for Marvel Comics' Woes." *The Atlantic*, May 24, 2017. https://www.theatlantic.com/entertainment/archive/2017/05/the-real-reasons-for-marvel-comics-woes/527127/. Accessed September 9, 2018.

Gioia, Dennis A., Majken Schultz, and Kevin G. Corley. "Organizational Identity, Image, and Adaptive Instability." In *Organizational Identity: A Reader*, edited by Mary Jo Hatch and Majken Schultz, 349–76. Oxford: Oxford University Press, 2004.

Goodrum, Michael. *Superheroes and American Self-Image: From War to Watergate*. Abingdon: Routledge, 2016.

Graser, Marc. "How Marvel Guards Its Properties but Isn't Afraid to Take Chances with Its 'Galaxy.'" *Variety*, July 23, 2014. http://variety.com/2014/film/news/marvel-studios-guardians-of-the-galaxy-risk-1201266165/. Accessed September 9, 2018.

Henehan, Billy. "NYCC '17: Retailer Outrage at the Marvel Retailer Panel!" Comics Beat (blog), June 10, 2017. http://www.comicsbeat.com/nycc-17-retailer-outrage-at-the-marvel-retailer-panel/. Accessed September 9, 2018.

Howe, Sean. *Marvel Comics: The Untold Story*. New York: Harper Perennial, 2013.

Johnson, Derek. "Cinematic Destiny: Marvel Studios and the Trade Stories of Industrial Convergence." *Cinema Journal* 52, no. 1 (Fall 2012): 1–24.

Johnson, Derek. *Media Franchising: Creative License and Collaboration in the Culture Industries*. New York: New York University Press, 2013.

Johnson, Derek. "'Share Your Universe': Generation, Gender and the Future of Marvel Publishing." In *Make Ours Marvel: Media Convergence and a Comics Universe*, edited by Matt Yockey, 138–63. Austin: University of Texas Press, 2017.

Kit, Borys. "Marvel's Universal Approach Makes It a World Apart from DC." *Hollywood Reporter*, May 12, 2008. https://www.hollywoodreporter.com/news/marvels-universal-approach-makes-a-111516. Accessed on September 9, 2018.

Lee, Stan. *Origins of Marvel Comics*. New York: Marvel Enterprises, 1997.

Leonard, Devin. "The Pow! Bang! Bam! Plan to Save Marvel, Starring B-List Heroes." *Bloomberg*, April 4, 2014. http://www.bloomberg.com/bw/articles/2014-04-03/kevin-feige-marvels-superhero-at-running-movie-franchises. Accessed on September 9, 2018.

Liao, Shannon. "Marvel's Editor in Chief Apologizes for Pretending to be a Japanese Man." *The Verge*, December 18, 2017. https://www.theverge.com/2017/12/18/16792070/marvel-editor-in-chief-akira-yoshida-cebulski-cultural-appropriation. Accessed September 9, 2018.

McMillan, Graham. "DC Takes Over a Declining Market: Which Comics Sold Best in 2017." *Hollywood Reporter*, December 28, 2017. https://www.hollywoodreporter.com/heat-vision/best-selling-comics-2017-1070490. Accessed September 9, 2018.

Marston, George. "STEVE or 'STEVIL'? Tom Brevoort on SECRET EMPIRE, Fulfilling Promises & Who the Real CAP Is." *Newsarama*, September 14, 2017. https://www.newsarama.com/36401-tom-brevoort-secret-empire-interview.html. Accessed September 9, 2018.

Marvel Entertainment. "A Message from Stan Lee." YouTube video, 1:17. October 5, 2017. https://www.youtube.com/watch?v=sjobevGAYHQ. Accessed September 9, 2018.

Miller, J. J. "November 2017 Comic Book Sales Figures." *ComicChron*, December 2017. http://www.comichron.com/monthlycomicssales/2017/2017-11.html. Accessed September 9, 2018.

Miller, J. J. "October 2017 Comic Book Sales Figures." *ComicChron*, November 2017. http://www.comichron.com/monthlycomicssales/2017/2017-10.html. Accessed September 9, 2018.

Newsarama Staff. "Classic CAP Is Back in *CAPTAIN AMERICA* 695 Preview." *Newsarama*, October 26, 2017. https://www.newsarama.com/37110-marvel-preview-1-captain-america-695.html. Accessed September 9, 2018.

Overpeck, Deron. "Breaking Brand: From NuMarvel to MarvelNOW! Marvel Comics in the Age of Media Convergence." In *Make Ours Marvel: Media Convergence and a Comics Universe*, edited by Matt Yockey, 164–86. Austin: University of Texas Press, 2017.

Pratt, Thom. "Marvel Comics Implosion: Are Politics, Readers or Combative Editorial to Blame?" The Kingdom Insider. September 17, 2017. http://thekingdominsider.com/marvel-comics-implosion-politics/. Accessed September 9, 2018.

Proctor, William. "Schrödinger's Cape: The Quantum Seriality of the Marvel Universe." In *Make Ours Marvel: Media Convergence and a Comics Universe*, edited by Matt Yockey, 319–46. Austin: University of Texas Press, 2017.

Raviv, Dan. *Comic Wars: Marvel's Battle for Survival*. Sea Cliff, NY: Heroes Books, 2004.

Rodriguez, Ashley. "Marvel May Soon Lose Its Avengers." *Quartz*, November 28, 2017. https://qz.com/1139562/marvel-may-soon-lose-its-avengers-as-the-actors-contracts-expire. Accessed September 9, 2018.

Schedeen, Jesse. "*Captain America* #695 Review. *IGN*, November 1, 2017. http://uk.ign.com/articles/2017/11/01/captain-america-695-review. Accessed on September 9, 2018.

Shayer, Jason. "Flashback: Roger Stern's *Avengers*." *Back Issue* 56 (April 2012): 8–34.

Smith, Brian, J. L. Giles, et al. "School of Shock." *Spider-Man Homecoming [Marvel Custom Edition]*, #1. New York: Marvel Comics, 2017.

Thielman, Sam. "Is Diversity to Blame for Marvel's Sales Slump—or Just a Lack of Imagination?" *The Guardian*, April 4, 2017. https://www.theguardian.com/books/2017/apr/04/marvel-comics-diversity-sales. Accessed on September 9, 2018.

Tolworthy, Chris. "Marvel's Sliding Time Scale." *The Fantastic Four (1961–89) Was the Great American Novel*, June 20, 2014, http://zak-site.com/Great-American-Novel/marvel_time.html. Accessed on September 9 2018.

Van den Anker, Marinus J. J., and Piet Verhoeven. "Corporate Communication: Analysing Marvel and DC." *Studies in Comics* 5, no. 1 (2010): 117–29.

Waid, Mark, Chris Samnee, et al. "Home of the Brave Part 1." *Captain America* 8, #695. New York: Marvel Comics, 2017.

Widen, Alex. "*Captain America* #695 Review: Marvel Apologizes for the Last Two Years." *Bam!Smack!Pow!*, December 4, 2017, https://bamsmackpow.com/2017/11/10/captain-america-695-review/. Accessed on September 9, 2018.

Wright, Bradford W. *Comic Book Nation: The Transformation of Youth Culture in America*. Paperback ed. Baltimore: Johns Hopkins University Press, 2003.

Yockey, Matt. "This Island Manhattan: New York City and the Space Race in *The Fantastic Four*." *Iowa Journal of Cultural Studies*, no. 6 (Spring 2005): 58–79.
Zimmerman, Dwight J. "Mark Gruenwald." *Comics Interview* 54 (1988): 5–23.

CHAPTER TWO

DIANA IN NO MAN'S LAND

Wonder Woman and the History of the World War

BRIDGET KEOWN AND MARYANNE RHETT

In 1941 William Moulton Marston, Elizabeth Holloway Marston, and Harry George Peter gave the world Wonder Woman, a character who joined the ranks of Superman and Captain America to fight the forces of fascism and tyranny. She was, according to Marston, intended as a symbol of female empowerment and an inspirational icon for women. She was also a product of her time and place: a world of supervillainy needing superheroes. And she was the result of several decades of liberalization that resulted in expanded notions of women's identity, psychology, and suffrage, all of which allowed Wonder Woman and her alter-ego Diana Prince the space to revolutionize the world of comics. In 2017, in the wake of a tumultuous year and presidential campaign season marked by discussions and debates over sexism, feminism, and the historic significance of women in the public sphere, the release of Patty Jenkins's 2017 film *Wonder Woman* was hailed as a feminist triumph. As the first in over a decade to feature a female superhero, and the first superhero movie to be directed by a woman, Wonder Woman herself was described by Rosyln Sucas as "a hero for our time," and a triumph for the DC Comics film franchise, bringing in nearly $822 million in worldwide box office earnings.[1] While *Wonder Woman* spoke specifically to the issues of the world in which it was released, *Wonder Woman* was also a historical film, placing its titular heroine in the trenches of the western front in late 1918.[2]

Despite the fictional basis of the film, by introducing Diana Prince into a real-world, historical setting, the filmmakers created a reality on screen that made a number of statements about the nature of warfare and women in 1918 that are both anachronistic and theoretically problematic. This chapter looks at the false reality constructed by the film *Wonder Woman*, particularly around the treatment of German soldiers as prototype Nazis and the gendered nature of heroism depicted in the film's many war scenes. It also pushes back against the notion that scholars see Wonder Woman as a significant character only for either aesthetic or historical reasons. In this latter case, we argue that Wonder Woman *is* history, a product of a specific time and place and that altering her placement *in* history alters history. A similar but less drastic parallel to this revision of history can be seen in the 1970s television Wonder Woman. As Tim Hanley points out, "By turning World War II into a fight just between America and the Nazis, the war became a battle between the forces of ultimate good and the forces of ultimate evil."[3] Such a lack of ambiguity obscures the complexities of Wonder Woman as a character, as well as the historical context in which she was created.

To understand the ways in which the 2017 film manipulated the character, it is important to understand the history of Wonder Woman's creation and early evolution. In 1941 William Moulton Marston, inspired by his wife Elizabeth Holloway Marston, as well as illustrator H. G. Peter, cocreated the character of Wonder Woman with them. She joined the ranks of such illustrious DC heroes as Superman and Batman to fight the forces of fascism and tyranny. She was intended, from the very first, to be a feminist icon, representative of the highly sexualized and idealistic brand of feminism espoused by Marston, Holloway, and their eclectic social network. Inspired by thinkers such as Margaret Sanger coupled to his own notions of future matriarchal societies, Marston declared that women would one day rule the world, fulfilling both their own sexual desires and those of the men they subjugated.[4] Hanley notes, "Wonder Woman was a superior superhero, and intentionally so. . . . His [Marston's] worldview was unique, remarkably progressive, and all of his theories were channeled into his creation."[5] Wonder Woman, and her alter-ego Diana Prince, was a product of her time and place: a world of supervillainy needing superheroes and, more importantly to Marston, *superheroines*. To understand why Diana/Wonder Woman was needed at that particular moment demands an understanding of the women and stories that came before her, of the decades of liberalization that resulted in expanded notions of women's identity, psychology, and suffrage, and how this allowed Wonder Woman the space to revolutionize the world of comics.

When Marston first pitched the Wonder Woman idea to comic book publisher Max Gaines, he had to convince Gaines that a female-centric storyline would sell, particularly, as Gaines contended, because "every female pulp and comic-book heroine . . . had been a failure."[6] Marston countered that "the comics' worst offense was their bloodcurdling masculinity."[7] For Marston, who spent years working on psychological questions of power and love, what the comics industry and readers of comics needed was a hero (heroine) who could break the "exclusively masculine rules [and] be tender, loving, affectionate, and alluring."[8] Marston wished to reinvigorate a woman's place, making an image of her as a powerful leader, and subsequently realigning what power meant. His efforts were aided by the reality that "women [had] been making comics since their inception, and there was even something resembling gender parity in readership prior to the implementation of the Comics Code in 1954."[9] What is more, Marston was talking about "exclusively masculine rules" not only within the confines of the comics' covers but in the very statesmanship of global politics as well. Wonder Woman was intended to be a foil to the rising tide of fascism and all the (toxic) masculine markers that came alongside.

None of Marston's intentions necessarily dissuaded anticomics activists from denouncing Wonder Woman as a tool of fascism. In 1945 Jesuit and anticomics crusader Walter J. Ong decried Superman as a Nazi and Wonder Woman as a practitioner of "Hitlerite paganism," who "is only a female Superman, preaching 'the cult of force, spiked, by means of her pretentiously scanty 'working' attire, with a little commercial sex. . . .' When not in her outré 'working' clothes she habitually wears a suitcoat and tie among the jeweled guests at luncheon parties and at formal evening affairs."[10] Ong's frustration with Wonder Woman's rejection of traditional forms of maternal femininity reflects both the social tension of the time over gender expression and performance among working women, and the emergence of a new kind of femininity that could be capable, strong (indeed, overpowering), and yet effortlessly beautiful and feminine—an image embodied in Gal Gadot's Wonder Woman, who makes use of an evening gown to conceal her sword in the 2017 film. Still, despite the sentiment of anticomics crusaders, Wonder Woman was not a fascist heroine. She was, just like Captain America, "created expressly to fight the Nazi threat."[11] As Lepore has noted, Wonder Woman "left Paradise to fight fascism with feminism, in 'America, the last citadel of democracy, and of equal rights for women!'"[12] What is more, Kailyn Kent observes, "The *Wonder Woman* comics were an intentional manifesto, meant to instill radical concepts of femininity, masculinity, sexuality and heroism into children."[13] For Marston, his work was intended to aid in "the growth in the power of women," and to curb the rising tide of militant masculinity by encouraging men to yield—indeed, to submit—to the power of strong and compassionate women.[14]

Over the course of the late 1800s through to the 1920s, comics in newspapers and magazines showed, with great regularity, images of women bound, gagged, tied up, and otherwise restrained by their political and/or medical repression. In Margaret Sanger's 1923 *Birth Control Review*, one woman was held down by the ball and chain of "unwanted babies," while Lou Rogers's "Tearing off the Bonds" from *Judge* depicted another woman undoing the bonds of political oppression. Rogers's work may even have been the ultimate influence on how Wonder Woman was drawn. The original artist for Wonder Woman, Harry George Peter, worked alongside Rogers at *Judge*, and while it is not clear that Peter was directly influenced by Rogers's style, the similarities are striking. What is more, Peter, like Marston, was closely aligned with the suffrage movement.[15] Interestingly, while the bondage of pre–Wonder Woman women signaled needed societal changes, in the Wonder Woman series it was perceived in vastly different ways, perhaps in part due to the fact that by the time Wonder Woman came to be, the bondage of antisuffrage had long been broken.

The bondage ubiquitous in early Wonder Woman issues became problematic for Max Gaines, as an increasing number of readers expressed concern at the sexual fetishism brought into the mainstream by the title. Marston, who was by no means a sexual prude, waved off Gaines's concerns with two interrelated arguments. First, the sexual fantasies and fetishes that arose from Wonder Woman were, to his mind, healthy and necessary.[16] Second, for Marston, Wonder Woman was representative of "love bonds" as juxtaposed with "male bonds of cruelty and destruction; between submitting to a loving superior or deity and submitting to people like the Nazis, Japs, etc."[17] Wars, Marston said, "will only cease when humans *enjoy being bound*."[18] This tenuous argument held enough water for Gaines that Wonder Woman continued in her pursuit of justice, occasionally fettered, whipped, manacled, tied up, and enslaved. It was clear that Wonder Woman was progeny of suffrage and Progressive era feminism, and the antithesis of the fascist regimes of Europe and Asia.

The protofeminist and feminist narrative of *Wonder Woman* has ebbed and flowed with the comic's history just as much as it has in other media. If we accept a traditional academic notion of "waves" of feminism, it becomes apparent that if the first wave "molded Wonder Woman, second-wave feminists helped break her out of comic book hell," and the current state of feminism continues to both shape the character and be shaped by the character.[19] *Ms.* magazine's choice to use Wonder Woman on the inaugural cover, Hunt asserts, "course-corrected [the comic] in the early 1970s back to her World War II persona."[20] In *Wonder Woman: Spirit of Truth*, by Paul Dini, art by Alex Ross, white, middle-class, and largely Anglo-American feminism came head to head with global identity constructions and other regional notions of feminism. Forced to understand that her "traditional attire" was anything but in the Middle East, Wonder Woman donned an *abaya* in her effort to stop evildoers.[21] The response to this depiction of Wonder Woman "passing" as Middle Eastern sparked a great deal of debate about her identity as a global icon for feminism. In the wake of September 11, 2001, a depiction of a traditional American heroine in this way was not surprising, but it did reinforce the growing sentiment that Wonder Woman may not be a hero for all. In subsequent years Islamic superheroines have come into being as a corrective to this issue. G. Willow Wilson's *Ms. Marvel*, reimagined as a teenage Pakistani American from Jersey City, New Jersey, is most notable in this set. Conscious of her Islamic faith and her American cultural identity, Kamala Khan (Wilson's *Ms. Marvel*) straddles the costume divide in converting a "burkini" (Islamic-style swimsuit) into a superhero's costume.

The "West v. the Rest" mentality that underlay *Spirit of Truth* has not vanished, even in the wake of more diverse and globally conscious superheroes.

Commentary in the wake of the release of *Wonder Woman* the movie, in particular the casting of Gal Gadot, an Israeli who had served in the Israeli Defense Forces, reignited a great deal of this debate. The tensions about the nature of feminism and what it looks like were well developed by Nida Sheriff in a blog post for *Medium*. Sheriff, taking the stance that "Gal Gadot is not Wonder Woman," spoke to the tension her casting created: "Are you a feminist that is overjoyed by Wonder Woman and is willing to ignore oppression for it? Or are you a feminist that is willing to ignore one of the most seminal events in women's cinema for the oppression of Palestine?"[22] While lauded for giving audiences a "hero for our times," the film reinforced the Western-centric notions of feminism that pervaded the comics' "wave" history.

WONDER WOMAN IN THE TRENCHES

Patty Jenkins and the production team of *Wonder Woman* reimagined Diana's place in history, both as a feminist icon in a postmodern world and as a hero for the World War I era. Because of Wonder Woman's independent, unhindered personality and her ultimate goal of securing lasting world peace needed to fit within the historical context and gendered confines of World War I, filmmakers needed to change the historical reality in which she appeared. First, and perhaps most obviously, they needed to create stark, unmistakable villains in a historical situation that featured very few such characters, in order to clearly show Diana/Wonder Woman as a hero(ine). At the opening of the film, German soldiers are described in language reflective of Anglo-American "Hun" propaganda, caricatures of heartless, animalistic marauders, rather than men. To ensure Wonder Woman remained a foil for fascism and toxic masculinity, this imagery and villainy of her opponents needed to be driven home. Recognizable "fascists" had to be present in World War I; thus, *Wonder Woman* employs narrative and visual clues to transform soldiers of the German Imperial Army into soldiers of the Third Reich. For example, General Ludendorff sports a three-prong collar tab on his uniform, a component not adopted until 1941. Moreover, although the *Stahlhelm* helmets worn by many German soldiers in the film were first introduced in 1916 before the campaign at Verdun, the style of helmet shown in the film is far more reminiscent of the later, refurbished *Vulkanfiber* models developed in the 1930s for senior staff officers.[23]

While these clues visually link the German soldiers in the film to the Nazi legacy, further historic connections to the Nazi era are made in the films' narrative. Dr. Maru's "vials of energizer," broken and inhaled by Ludendorff, recall the widespread development of and heavy reliance on methamphetamines during the Nazi regime. As Nathan Ohler has shown, doctors were revered in Nazi military settings for their ability "to maintain the performance of the individual and where possible to increase it."[24] Dr. Maru's work, and its effect on Ludendorff, is highly reminiscent of the widespread reliance of those within the Third Reich on new and increasingly powerful drugs. Finally, the vicious assassination of the German High Command in the film carries far more resonance to the Night of Long Knives in 1934, during which the Nazi paramilitary *Sturmabteilung* were assassinated to consolidate Hitler's power, than it does to any event of World War I. As Chris DeRosa observes, the presence of Ludendorff, who became a Nazi in later life, lends an artificial continuity between World War I and World War II, and makes the blurring and telescoping of historical events seem not only easy but justifiable.[25] Nevertheless, it is critical to remember that the Ludendorff of 1918 did not mastermind a gas attack on civilians or assassinate members of the German high command.[26] To portray him as such a man not only is historically inaccurate but critically overlooks the ways in which power and violence can corrupt and blight over time.

These changes radically affect how the history and reality of World War I is portrayed throughout the film, imposing a binary of "good" and "evil" on the combatants. Despite attempts to discuss the ambiguities of war and of the people who fight it, *Wonder Woman*'s portrayal of World War I does not stray far from the explanation that Steve Trevor provides to Diana after landing in Themyscira: "I'm one of the good guys, and those are the bad guys."[27] By portraying himself as an individual, Steve Trevor immediately singles himself out as the protagonist, as a man of action, while relegating all the Germans who followed him into the land of the Amazons to a single, stereotypical evil. From this first moment, then, German soldiers assume the faceless aspect of the kind of archvillains who must be defeated at all costs. This interpretation continues when Diana first encounters German soldiers in action on her brief tour of the Belgian trenches, before her defining walk across No Man's Land. There, Trevor tells her, "This is No Man's Land, Diana. It means no man can cross it, alright? This battalion has been here for nearly a year and they barely gained an inch. Alright? Because on the other side, there are a bunch of Germans pointing machine guns at every square inch of this place."[28] The German soldiers are positioned opposite—the implication is that they, too, are immobile behind their machine guns—remaining largely unseen, and wholly anonymous.

Such an interpretation is not an accurate portrayal, for two important reasons. The first is rooted specifically in historical accuracy; the war being fought in late 1918, particularly in the Flanders area, was no static war. With the collapse of the German Spring Offensive (or *Kaiserschlacht*) in July, it was clear to all that the end of the war was eminent. Renewed Allied offensives were quickly organized to avoid another long winter of waiting, resulting in huge gains for the Allied forces, fortified by the newly arrived US Army. The war continued, but it became a war of movement, marked by savage, intimate violence and all-out destruction; the German army desperately attempted to stall the Allied offensive, and the Allies attempted to push the German army past the brink of exhaustion. The second reason has more to do with issues of audience compassion. By placing the Germans in the trenches opposite Steve Trevor and his band of rugged individuals, the filmmakers are absolved from showing actual German soldiers as they would have appeared at this time—largely young, dirty, and desperate. Instead, Steve Trevor continues to impose upon them the kind of violent, amoral characteristics that so often characterize Nazis in films of World War II—and of numerous other comic book storylines.

The potentially misleading representation of history in *Wonder Woman* extends to, and is enacted through, its central protagonist. Here, too, the filmmaker's attempts to both create a postmodern heroine and simultaneously shoehorn Diana Prince/Wonder Woman into an earlier time period results in several significant complications. Overall, the narrative used by Jenkins was not dramatically different from some of the first issues of the comic: in the film, Diana meets Steve Trevor in much the same way she meets him in the book, and the concern her fellow Amazons express for her leaving Paradise Island follows a similar script. However, unlike the comic series, Trevor in the movie knows Diana and Wonder Woman as one, not as two distinctly different women. This notable change points more toward the modern context in which the film was produced—Diana/Wonder Woman can now be a whole person, accepted for all that she is by the man who works with her. Indeed, where Chris Pine's Steve Trevor attempts to limit Diana, he does so out of concern for the social stigmas to which she will be subjected. He serves to protect and anchor her in a time period to which she does not belong: helping her find the proper clothes, how to speak to authorities, and how to perform femininity in 1918. In essence, Trevor's role is to teach Diana to go undercover, just as he has done, in the society she has infiltrated. However, the fact that both Diana and Steve operate in a manner more akin to the postmodern world of the film than in their historical context emphasizes how out of place they are and, specifically, how out of place is Diana. Marston's Diana/Wonder Woman was the outcome of what Olive Byrne noted as the "one outstanding benefit to humanity from the first World War. . . . Women . . . emerged from a false haremlike protection and began taking over men's work."[29] Wonder Woman was begotten of this awakening, not developed alongside it. In attempting to inhabit both the past and the cinematic present, Diana seems to settle in neither place.

Though Diana's interactions with Steve Trevor emphasize their comparative feminist enlightenment, the narrative arc of the film refuses to challenge conventional stereotypes regarding the gendered nature of subjectivity or heroism. The audience hears Diana's interpretation of the world around her, but their tour of it is provided by Trevor and his men. This insistence on defining the world through the male gaze has some interesting implications for the portrayal of women in history and in the film. Though her presence is accepted by the men around her, in part because of her physical appeal, there is never a time when Diana is offered the chance to remake the patriarchy in the way that Marston intended. That Wonder Woman is a feminist is implied in her ability to fight "like a man," her bemused disdain for women's fashions of the 1910s, and the passing suggestion of the suffragette movement more clearly indicated by the character Etta Candy. In the opening of the second issue of *Wonder Woman*, the narrator asks, "Why does she fight for America . . . [to] battle for freedom, democracy, and womankind thru-out the world!"[30] In Jenkins's film the plight of mortal women, specifically, is only secondary, if not tertiary, to the antiwar storyline that unfolds, and Diana's realization of her powers as a superhero(ine). As a result, the real contributions of actual women in World War I and the suffrage movement, which helped to make the notion of a female superhero a socially acceptable one, go generally overlooked.[31]

This is especially problematic in a work set in World War I, because of the historiographical legacy that has yet to fully incorporate women's active role in the conflict. The strict social, cultural, and political emphasis on "traditional gender roles," both during and after the war, meant that those gender roles and expectations largely survived intact, obscuring how women's identities, behavior, and work changed during the war, as well as the long-term effects of their war work on future generations.[32] By performing alongside men, and eschewing all female relationships, the 2017 *Wonder Woman* film contributes to the sidelining of women, rather than celebrating their achievements. In this evaluation we focus specifically on British society, into which Diana strides after leaving Themyscira.

A (WONDER) WOMAN'S PLACE IS . . .

As a result of male enlistment and later conscription, British women took jobs in a large number of new fields and industries. According to a report from the War Cabinet Committee on Women in Industry, by July 1918 approximately 7,310,500 women were doing some form of paid labor in industry, commerce, agriculture, transport, and national and local government, an increase of 23 percent over the total estimated four years earlier.[33] Moreover, women from more-privileged backgrounds performed volunteer work at home and abroad in organizations like the Red Cross or the Voluntary Aid Detachment, or through private endeavors such as funding their own hospitals and ambulances. It has been estimated that as many as sixty thousand women served in armed forces in some capacity (including the Women's Land Army), and that some twenty-five thousand were stationed along the western front.[34] Such work was physically demanding, emotionally taxing, and, in some cases, psychologically traumatizing. It was also the focus of intense scrutiny, as women gained increasing social independence through their work outside the home and their earning of independent wages. Despite attempts in postwar Britain to return women to imagined prewar gender norms, their war work not only helped them forge alliances with other women but opened new job opportunities for future generations to seek education and employment outside the home. Marston himself noted how the work taken up by women in World War I allowed women in World War II

> to now fly heavy planes successfully; they help build planes, do mechanics' work. In England they've taken over a large share of all manual labor in fields and factories; they've taken over police and home defense duties. In China a corps of 200,000 women under the supreme command of Madame Chiang Kai-shek perform the dangerous function of saving lives and repairing damage after Japanese air raids. This huge female strong-arm squad is officered efficiently by 3,000 women. Here in this country we've started a Women's Auxiliary Army and Navy Corps that will do everything men soldiers and sailors do except the actual fighting. Prior to the First World War nobody believed that women could perform these feats of physical strength. But they're performing them now and thinking nothing of it.[35]

However, as *Wonder Woman* emphasized, the historical experiences of women are still portrayed as secondary in significance. In its interpretation of the western front, and the war as a whole, the 2017 *Wonder Woman* reinforces this view. The only other woman who appears and speaks in the "real world" (that is, World War I) is Etta Candy, who remains fixed in an office throughout the action of the film. This is particularly striking when one remembers that, in Marston's comics, Etta is a member of the Holliday Girls, a sorority who worked with Wonder Woman to round up a ring of Nazi spies, including Doctor Poison. Their telepathic communication allowed them to work in concert despite the difference between them. In Jenkins's film, Etta's only communication is with Steve Trevor.

Instead, the narrative focuses on the experiences and suffering of the male characters. Steve Trevor, despite the remarkable mobility afforded to him as a spy, emphasizes his and his fellow soldiers' helplessness when he tells Diana in the trench of their tale: "This battalion has been here for nearly a year and they barely gained an inch."[36] His comrade, Charlie, a Scottish sniper (played by Ewan Bremmer), suffers from psychological trauma, recognized as "shell shock" in this historical context, and is unable to fire his rifle. The women that we do see are Belgian civilians and are nearly silent and effectively helpless. Although her actions are performed out of a sense of altruism, Diana's walk across No Man's Land is shown as restoring the Allied soldiers to the role of active combatant and triumphant warrior, with soldiers following her and carrying out an assault on the German trench.

Perhaps no scene was more widely celebrated in this regard than the one in which Diana, determined to liberate a small Belgian village, climbs out of the Allied trench and crosses No Man's Land, accomplishing that which no man, and no army, ever could. Though not initially intended to be a cinematic act of feminism—indeed, Diana's slow-motion walk in her revealing costume might very well be read by some as a trademark example of the "male gaze"—this scene, more than the film as a whole, has been highlighted as a critically important moment for women and for feminism in cinema.[37] Diana's walk across No Man's Land brought some audience members to tears and was lauded by reviewers as a landmark moment in filmmaking. "Witnessing a woman hold the field, and the camera, for that long blew open an arguably monotonous genre," noted the *Los Angeles Times*, in an article that included numerous tweets from women who wept while watching Diana brave her way across the hellscape of battle.[38] For thousands of audience members, many of whom were women, Diana's march across a desolate landscape, wrecked and rendered uninhabitable by men, represented a metaphorical stance against the aggressively, even violently, patriarchal political moment in which the film was released. As Alicia Lutes observed in a post on Nerdist, "We all had to grow up and shed our naïveté about what was happening around us. We had to stand up and accept the responsibility to change the world was on us. I saw that Diana saw this, and felt empowered by her confidence to know that, in spite of what the men around her said, she *was* strong enough to do what they could not."[39] One article featured by the *Huffington Post* even reasoned that "had the film been released a year earlier, a woman would be in the White House today."[40]

As powerful and memorable as this scene is, from a historical perspective it encapsulates the central contradiction of this "woman-centered" (and potentially feminist) film, about a female, feminist character. Repeatedly, *Wonder Woman* emphasizes that, in order to be a hero, indeed in order to claim any subjectivity, a character needs to act like a man (and also to be physically appealing to a man). Rather than emphasizing the significant contributions of women within the historical context of World War I, Diana's heroism comes from performing like a male combatant, in a sexualizing costume that makes her a visual feast for the men who swarm around her. The relationship between male and female adventure comics is an important distinction here, in underscoring the difference between the intention of the Wonder Woman film and how it was perceived. As Lillian Robinson observes, "whereas male adventure comics borrow chiefly the names and salient attributes of mythological figures, thus appropriating the status of authentic epic . . . the tales of female superheroes embellish and extend the myths or turn them inside out."[41] Instead of creating her own moment in history, Diana's walk is instead the repetition of the same walk that millions of men had performed before her, and her heroism rests on her ability to fulfill their mission by enduring the withering machine-gun fire on their behalf. Diana's superior strength is put to use, not as the peacemaking force that Marston envisioned but as a champion of the kind of "blood-curdling masculinity" that he specifically opposed. Though there is dancing when the village is liberated, it is the celebration of a moment before war resumes—war in which Diana takes part as a combatant, and not as a peacekeeper.

This scene is emblematic of the lack of focus paid to Marston's intentions for his heroine. In 1943 Marston published an article in the *American Scholar* explaining why his *Wonder Woman* was so necessary among the enormous number of comic books available to young readers. In it he argued that the intense, "blood-curdling masculinity" was one of the industry's most glaring faults.[42] Further, Marston notes, the spirit of altruism, and the ideals that support such a spirit, had been consistently disparaged, specifically because they were qualities typically associated with women: "It's smart to be strong. It's big to be generous. But it's sissified, according to exclusively masculine rules, to be tender, loving affectionate, and alluring. 'Aw, that's girl's stuff!' snorts our young comics reader. 'Who wants to be a *girl*?' And that's the point; not even girls want to be girls so long as our feminine archetype lacks force, strength, power."[43] Marston's insistence in creating *Wonder Woman* was that heroism was not to be found only on battlefields, or through cataclysmic showdowns, but through empathy, compassion, and allyship. For all that Diana's march across No Man's Land is a feat of remarkable courage, selfless determination, and cinematic triumph, it, and indeed the entire film, obscures both Marston's stated form of heroism and the unique ways in which women served during World War I. As a result, commentary on this portion of the film consistently disregards the fact that Diana's iconic march is performed out of a spirit of altruism, to rescue imperiled civilians, and not out of martial spirit. That the civilians she rescues are gendered as female further completes this metaphor of active male combatants and silent, incapable women.

This emphasis on male subjectivity can also be seen in the physical identity of Dr. Poison, also known in this iteration as Isabelle Maru. Maru, another creation of Marston's, first appeared as a Nazi scientist, clad in a gender-obscuring bodysuit and a mask that obscured her eyes and nose, in *Sensation Comics* #2 (1942). Arguably, the disfigurement of Dr. Maru in the film, from which she does not suffer in the comics, may align her with the historical narrative of the "Hiroshima Maidens": women disfigured by the atomic bombing of Hiroshima and brought to the US to receive reconstructive surgery.[44] Ironically, Dr. Poison in the comics was the disguise of a Japanese woman, Princess Maru. In the 2017 film, Dr. Maru's bodysuit is exchanged for a more feminine dress, and a slim porcelain mask that obscures much of actress Elena Anaya's face. Moreover, for the purposes of Jenkins's work, Dr. Maru had to be relocated to the Ottoman Empire, as Japan fought on the side of the Entente Powers. The use of a scarred female villain, whose face is rendered unnatural, inspired well-deserved conversation on the long and uncomfortable history of associating female "ugliness" or disfigurement with moral evil. However, from a historical standpoint, it is crucial to understand how, taken out of specific historical context and without further exploration of her character, Dr. Maru's mask places her within a male-centered story of injury and rehabilitation.

Though the percentage of men who survived injury during World War I was higher than in any previous conflicts, the result was millions of veterans who returned from war with life-changing scars, missing appendages, and severely injured faces. Approximately 280,000 men from Great Britain, Germany, and France returned from service with maxillofacial injury, defined as injury to the jawbone and to the soft tissues of the face.[45] Such wounds were a direct result of trench warfare, where shrapnel and snipers often hit the face as it emerged "over the top." These men and, more specifically, their injuries were widely used in the immediate postwar world by those eager to make a statement about the real costs of war.[46] A delegation of facially wounded French soldiers (known as *les gueules cassées*: literally, the broken faces) was present at the signing of the Treaty of Versailles, a living reminder to the German delegation of their War Guilt, as well as a statement against the violence of the war as a whole. Medically, attempts to return these men to some equivalent of their prewar appearance and functionality led to remarkable developments in plastic surgery and facial prosthetics, not the least of which were slim porcelain masks intended to be worn over the injured part of the face and blend seamlessly with the adjoining skin. Though hot, cumbersome, and, for many, extremely unsettling in their static verisimilitude, these masks were—and are still—a visual symbol not only of war's damage to male combatants but also of the potential for healing.[47]

The revelation of Dr. Poison without her mask, which comes during the climactic showdown between Wonder Woman and Ares, reveals the extent of Isabelle Maru's injuries. In a historical context, her facial injuries relate Dr. Maru within a history of female labor and suffering that denotes an abstract feminism akin to Diana's walk across No Man's Land. One such example is of the female employees in matchstick factories who suffered from "phossy jaw," formally known as exposed bone osteonecrosis of the jaw. This condition, resulting from the mixing of yellow phosphorus and the carbon dioxide in human breath, began with jaw pain and swelling, progressed to the exposure of the bones of the jaw, and often led to brain damage and organ failure.[48] The London matchgirls' strike of 1888 by the women and teenage girls employed at the Bryant and May Factory in protest at the working conditions that facilitated the onset of this condition played a crucial role in the British labor movement. Closer to the period in which the *Wonder Woman* film is set, Maru's injuries also recall the plight of the "Radium Girls," women employed in painting "glow-in-the-dark" watch faces with radium, who suffered agonizing tumors, lethal internal damage, and necrosis of the jaw to such an extent that dentists were able to remove a patient's jawbone "merely by putting his fingers in her mouth and lifting it out."[49] Women at a factory in New Jersey sued the US Radium Corp. for poisoning and won.[50] Their legal action became a landmark case in the history of workplace safety and regulations. Here again is another example of women's labor being overlooked in a story of male-oriented "heroism." However, even though Dr. Maru's injuries visually related her to this legacy of women disfigured by their workplace, who reclaimed their agency and subjectivity through protest, this legacy is never discussed, nor is Dr. Maru provided with a backstory that might explain what happened to her. As with the German soldiers, the less known about enemies, the less risk of audience sympathy for their plight. Instead, the film shows only her mask, a mask that intimately recalls the prosthetics developed for facially injured male First World War veterans. Just as Diana's walk across No Man's Land insisted on a historically masculine performance of subjectivity, Isabelle Maru's face recalls a male narrative of injury and potential recovery. Both women remained bound and obscured by historically male narratives, rather than emphasizing the female, feminist history that the film purports, or is purported by audiences, to present.

For all that superhero movies are sources of "escapist entertainment" and flights of imaginative fancy, the fact remains that film creates reality. This is true within the context of the viewing, as the audience gathers to witness a coherent, cohesive storyline, but also within the broader context whereby historical films help us visualize, interpret, and understand the past. Though the 2017 *Wonder Woman* film was indubitably a fictional story, it utilized a well-documented historic moment to tell its tale, manipulating historical facts and interpretations to fit the needs of the fictional plot. Additionally, the film manipulated the history of Marston's Wonder Woman character in order to make her more accessible to a twenty-first-century audience. These changes have significant ramifications for the portrayal of history, on the micro- and macro-levels. This chapter has provided several examples of the problematic nature of using a real-world historical setting as a backdrop, as well as adapting a character to a different time period. In so doing, we hope to enrich the historical backdrop of the *Wonder Woman* film into a complex, three-dimensional world that more accurately reflects the historical realities of World War I, and the portrayal of Wonder Woman and the female characters around her.

NOTES

1. This "a hero for our time" notion is fairly cliché at this point, but Roslyn Sucas centered her article on the concept, situating the movie in the larger geopolitical realities of the spring and summer of 2017. Roslyn Sucas, "Can Gal Gadot Make Wonder Woman a Hero for Our Time?" *New York Times*, May 4, 2017, accessed November 26, 2017, https://nyti.ms/2paNGNQ.

2. Sucas, "Can Gal Gadot Make Wonder Woman a Hero for Our Time?"

3. Tim Hanley, *Wonder Woman Unbound: The Curious History of the World's Most Famous Heroine* (Chicago: Chicago Review Press, 2014), 221.

4. Jake Coyle, "In Year of Wonder Woman, the Remarkable Tale of Her Creation," *Seattle Times*, October 19, 2017, accessed May 22, 2018, https://www.seattletimes.com/nation-world/in-year-of-wonder-woman-the-remarkable-tale-of-her-creation/; Hanley, *Wonder Woman Unbound*, 17.

5. Hanley, *Wonder Woman Unbound*, 43.

6. Jill Lepore, *The Secret History of Wonder Woman* (New York: Vintage Books, 2015), 187.

7. Lepore, *Secret History of Wonder Woman*, 187.

8. Lepore, *Secret History of Wonder Woman*, 187.

9. Betsy Gomez, ed., *She Changed Comics: The Untold Story of Women Who Changed Free Expression in Comics!*, ed. Comic Book Legal Defense Fund (Berkeley, CA: Image Comics, 2016), i.

10. "Are Comics Fascist?" *Time*, October 22, 1945, 69.

11. Glen Weldon, "Superheroes and the F-Word: Grappling with the Ugly Truth under the Capes," NPR, November 16, 2016, accessed May 22, 2018, https://www.npr.org/sections/monkeysee/2016/11/16/502161587/superheroes-and-the-f-word-grappling-with-the-ugly-truth-under-the-capes.

12. Jill Lepore, "The Surprising Origin of Wonder Woman," *Smithsonian Magazine*, October 2014, accessed May 22, 2018, https://www.smithsonianmag.com/arts-culture/origin-story-wonder-woman-180952710/#2vgYSEWupZrRdlK8.99.

13. Kailyn Kent, "Resuscitating Wonder Woman," The Hooded Utilitarian, January 15, 2015, accessed May 22, 2018, http://www.hoodedutilitarian.com/2015/01/resuscitating-wonder-woman/.

14. Kelli E. Stanley, "Suffering Sappho! Wonder Woman and the (Re)Invention of the Feminine Ideal," *Helios* 32, no. 2 (2005): 149.

15. "She Changed Comics: Lou Rogers, Advocate for Women's Rights," Comic Book Legal Defense Fund, March 17, 2017, accessed November 30, 2017, http://cbldf.org/2017/03/she-changed-comics-lou-rogers-advocate-for-womens-rights; also see Gomez, *She Changed Comics*, 21–22.

16. Marston's background in psychological research goes a long way in helping us understand why he saw *Wonder Woman* as an educational outlet for reorienting society vis-à-vis sexuality and emotion. Noah Berlatsky's *Wonder Woman: Bondage and Feminism in the Marston/Peter Comics, 1941–1948* is an excellent starting point for unraveling these issues. In a blog post discussing the book's arguments, Kailyn Kent notes: "Marston theorized that the world would be a better place if people learned to accept and practice both dominance and submission, as opposed to harshly overpowering others. Neither dominance nor submission was considered the superior state, and Marston links both in a pleasurable, loving cycle that ultimately leads to world peace." The Hooded Utilitarian, January 15, 2015, accessed August 21, 2018, http://www.hoodedutilitarian.com/2015/01/resuscitating-wonder-woman/.

17. Lepore, *Secret History of Wonder Woman*, 243; also see Noah Berlatsky, *Wonder Woman: Bondage and Feminism in the Marston/Peter Comics, 1941–1948* (New Brunswick, NJ: Rutgers University Press, 2015).

18. Lepore, *Secret History of Wonder Woman*, 238.

19. Kristin Hunt, "Wonder Woman Was Created by a Male Feminist Who Loved Bondage and Matriarchy," Vice, June 2, 2017, accessed July 31, 2018, https://broadly.vice.com/en_us/article/kzqaj9/wonder-woman-was-created-by-a-male-feminist-who-loved-bondage-and-matriarchy.

20. Hunt, "Wonder Woman Was Created."

21. Paul Dini and Alex Ross, *Wonder Woman: Spirit of Truth* (DC Comics, 2001), 23.

22. Nida Sheriff, "Feminism of Oppressors (or 'Why I Won't See Wonder Woman' or 'Why Some Feminists Will Be Pissed')," Medium, June 7, 2017, accessed August 10, 2018, https://medium.com/@nidasheriff/feminism-of-oppressors-or-why-i-wont-see-wonder-woman-or-why-some-feminists-will-be-pissed-723b8fd914f8.

23. Brian C. Bells and Kevin Lyles, *Wehrmacht Combat Helmets 1933–45* (New York: Osprey, 2004), 12.

24. Quoted in Nathan Ohler, *Blitzed: Drugs in the Third Reich*, trans. Shaun Whiteside (Boston: Houghton Mifflin Harcourt, 2017), 36.

25. Carol Pinchefsky, "What Wonder Woman Got Right and Wrong about World War I," *SyFy Wire*, June 20, 2017, accessed August 21, 2018, http://www.syfy.com/syfywire/what-wonder-woman-got-right-and-wrong-about-world-war-i.

26. Pinchefsky, "What Wonder Woman Got Right and Wrong."

27. Patty Jenkins, dir., *Wonder Woman* (Burbank, CA: Warner Brothers Studios, 2017).

28. Jenkins, *Wonder Woman.*

29. Olive Richard, "Our Women Are Our Future," *Family Circle*, August 14, 1944. Articles for *Family Circle* by Olive Richard, the pseudonym of Olive Byrne, should be read in the context of her role as Marston's live-in second wife/lover.

30. Charles Moulton, "Wonder Woman," *Sensation Comics* #2 (DC Comics, 1942).

31. Lillian S. Robinson, *Wonder Women: Feminisms and Superheroes* (New York: Psychology Press, 2004), 7.

32. See Susan R. Grayzel, *Women's Identities at War: Gender, Motherhood, and Politics in Britain and France during the First World War* (Chapel Hill: University of North Carolina Press, 1999).

33. Cited in Gill Thomas, *Life on All Fronts: Women in the First World War* (Cambridge: Cambridge University Press, 1989), 9. Although research indicates that women who were not in wage-earning work before the war did not enter the workforce during the war in large numbers, it is true that the type of work that wage-earning women did during the war did diversify considerably.

34. Laura Doan, "Topsy-Turvydom: Gender Inversion, Sapphism, and the Great War," *GLQ: A Journal of Lesbian and Gay Studies* 12, no. 4 (2006): 517.

35. Richard, "Our Women Are Our Future."

36. Jenkins, *Wonder Woman.*

37. See James Mottram, "Wonder Woman 'Not a Feminist Hero,' Says Groundbreaking Movie's Female Director," *South China Morning Post*, May 22, 2017, accessed September 15, 2017, http://www.scmp.com/culture/film-tv/article/2094961/wonder-woman-not-feminist-hero-says-groundbreaking-movies-female.

38. Meredith Woerner, "Commentary: Why I Cried through the Fight Scenes in 'Wonder Woman,'" *Los Angeles Times*, June 5, 2017, accessed September 15, 2017, http://www.latimes.com/entertainment/herocomplex/la-et-hc-wonder-woman-crying-20170605-htmlstory.html.

39. Alicia Lutes, "How Wonder Woman's No Man's Land Tells a Radical Story about Trust," *Nerdist*, June 3, 2017, accessed September 15, 2017, http://nerdist.com/wonder-woman-no-mans-land-scene/.

40. G. Roger Denson, "The Wonder Woman 'No Man's Land' Scene Is Rooted in History, Myth and Art," *Huffington Post*, August 5, 2017, accessed September 16, 2017, http://www.huffingtonpost.com/entry/the-wonder-woman-no-mans-land-scene-is-rooted-in_us_59498fcae4b0710bea889a18.

41. Robinson, *Wonder Women*, 7.

42. William Moulton Marston, "Why 100,000,000 Americans Read Comics," *American Scholar* 13, no. 1 (1943–44): 42.

43. Marston, "Why 100,000,000 Americans Read Comics," 42.

44. For further information, see Hilary E. L. Elmendorf, "Enduring the Unendurable: The Hiroshima Maidens in Postwar Japan and Cold War America," thesis, American Studies, Washington State University, 2004.

45. Fiona Reid, "Losing Face: Trauma and Maxillofacial Injury in the First World War," in *Psychological Trauma and the Legacies of the First World War*, ed. Jason Crouthamel and Peter Leese (London: Palgrave Macmillan, 2017), 26.

46. See, for example, the artwork of Otto Dix and George Beckmann, as well as Ernst Friedrich's *War against War*, published in Germany in 1924. In France, *les gueules cassées* formed a fraternal association that provided support for facially injured veterans but also lobbied for greater acceptance and assistance from society and the government for their service and sacrifice.

47. See Reid, in *Psychological Trauma and the Legacies of the First World War*, 41. The presence of a masked character in other contemporary media, such as *Boardwalk Empire*, speaks to the power of these masks to this day.

48. For more information, see Robert E. Marx, "Uncovering the Cause of 'Phossy Jaw' circa 1850 to 1906: Oral and Maxillofacial Surgery Closed Case Files—Case Closed," *Journal of Oral and Maxillofacial Surgery* 66, no. 11 (2008): 2356–63.

49. Quoted in Kate Moore, *The Radium Girls* (London: Random House, 2016), 40.

50. See Moore, *Radium Girls*.

WORKS CITED

"Are Comics Fascist?" *Time*, October 22, 1945, p. 69.

"She Changed Comics: Lou Rogers, Advocate for Women's Rights." Comic Book Legal Defense Fund, March 17, 2017. http://cbldf.org/2017/03/she-changed-comics-lou-rogers-advocate-for-womens-rights/. Accessed November 30, 2017, 2017.

Bells, Brian C., and Kevin Lyles. *Wehrmacht Combat Helmets 1933–45*. New York: Osprey, 2004.

Berlatsky, Noah. *Wonder Woman: Bondage and Feminism in the Marston/Peter Comics, 1941–1948*. New Brunswick, NJ: Rutgers University Press, 2015.

Brevet, Brad. "Disappointing August 2017 Closed Out the Worst Summer Movie Season in over 10 Years." Box Office Mojo, September 20, 2017. http://www.boxofficemojo.com/news/?id=4326&p=.htm. Accessed November 26, 2017.

Conley, Bridget. "Theories of Violence from Superhero Blockbusters." Reinventing Peace, June 22, 2017. https://sites.tufts.edu/reinventingpeace/2017/06/22/theories-of-violence-from-superhero-blockbusters/. Accessed August 9, 2018.

Coyle, Jake. "In Year of Wonder Woman, the Remarkable Tale of Her Creation." *Seattle Times*, October 19, 2017. https://www.seattletimes.com/nation-world/in-year-of-wonder-woman-the-remarkable-tale-of-her-creation/. Accessed May 22, 2018.

Dini, Paul, and Alex Ross. *Wonder Woman: Spirit of Truth*. DC Comics, 2001.

Denson, G. Roger. "The Wonder Woman 'No Man's Land' Scene Is Rooted in History, Myth and Art." *Huffington Post*, August 5, 2017. http://www.huffingtonpost.com/entry/the-wonder-woman-no-mans-land-scene-is-rooted-in_us_59498fcae4b0710bea889a18. Accessed September 16, 2017.

Doan, Laura. "Topsy-Turvydom: Gender Inversion, Sapphism, and the Great War." *GLQ: A Journal of Lesbian and Gay Studies* 12, no. 4 (2006): 517–42.

Elmendorf, Hilary E. L. "Enduring the Unendurable: The Hiroshima Maidens in Postwar Japan and Cold War America." Thesis, American Studies, Washington State University, 2004.

Gomez, Betsy, ed. *She Changed Comics: The Untold Story of Women Who Changed Free Expression in Comics!* Edited by Comic Book Legal Defense Fund. Berkeley, CA: Image Comics, 2016.

Grayzel, Susan R. *Women's Identities at War: Gender, Motherhood, and Politics in Britain and France during the First World War*. Chapel Hill: University of North Carolina Press, 1999.

Hanley, Tim. *Wonder Woman Unbound: The Curious History of the World's Most Famous Heroine*. Chicago: Chicago Review Press, 2014.

Hunt, Kristin. "Wonder Woman Was Created by a Male Feminist Who Loved Bondage and Matriarchy." Vice. June 2, 2017. https://broadly.vice.com/en_us/article/kzqaj9/wonder-woman-was-created-by-a-male-feminist-who-loved-bondage-and-matriarchy. Accessed July 31, 2018.

Jenkins, Patty, dir. *Wonder Woman*. 2017.

Kaplan, Laurie. "When the War Was Over: The Return of the War Nurse." In *Writings of Persuasion and Dissonance in the Great War, That Better May Follow Worse*, edited by David Owen and Cristina Pividori, 65–80. Leiden: Brill Rodopi, 2016.

Kent, Kailyn. "Resuscitating Wonder Woman." The Hooded Utilitarian. January 15, 2015. http://www.hoodedutilitarian.com/2015/01/resuscitating-wonder-woman/. Accessed on May 22, 2018.

Lepore, Jill. *The Secret History of Wonder Woman*. New York: Vintage Books, 2015.

Lepore, Jill. "The Surprising Origin of Wonder Woman." *Smithsonian Magazine*, October 2014. https://www.smithsonianmag.com/arts-culture/origin-story-wonder-woman-180952710/#2vgYSEWupZrRdlK8.99. Accessed on May 22, 2018.

Lutes, Alicia. "How Wonder Woman's No Man's Land Tells a Radical Story about Trust." Nerdist. June 3, 2017. http://nerdist.com/wonder-woman-no-mans-land-scene/. Accessed September 15, 2017.

Marston, William Moulton. "Why 100,000,000 Americans Read Comics." *American Scholar* 13, no. 1 (1943–44): 35–44.

Marx, Robert E. "Uncovering the Cause of 'Phossy Jaw' circa 1850 to 1906: Oral and Maxillofacial Surgery Closed Case Files—Case Closed." *Journal of Oral and Maxillofacial Surgery* 66, no. 11 (2008): 2356–63.

Moore, Kate. *The Radium Girls*. London: Random House, 2016.

Mottram, James. "Wonder Woman 'Not a Feminist Hero,' Says Groundbreaking Movie's Female Director." *South China Morning Post*, May 22, 2017. http://www.scmp.com/culture/film-tv/article/2094961/wonder-woman-not-feminist-hero-says-groundbreaking-movies-female. Accessed September 15, 2017.

Moulton, Charles. "Wonder Woman." *Sensation Comics*, January 1942.

Ohler, Norman. *Blitzed in Nazi Germany*. New York: Houghton Mifflin Harcourt, 2017.

Pinchefsky, Carol. "What Wonder Woman Got Right and Wrong about World War I." June 20, 2017. *SYFY Wire*. http://www.syfy.com/syfywire/what-wonder-woman-got-right-and-wrong-about-world-war-i. Accessed July 30, 2017.

Reid, Fiona. "Losing Face: Trauma and Maxillofacial Injury in the First World War." In *Psychological Trauma and the Legacies of the First World War*, edited by Jason Crouthamel and Peter Leese, 25–48. London: Palgrave Macmillan, 2017.

Richard, Olive. "Our Women Are Our Future." *Family Circle*, August 14, 1944.

Robinson, Lillian S. *Wonder Women: Feminisms and Superheroes*. New York: Psychology Press, 2004.

Sheriff, Nida. "Feminism of Oppressors (or 'Why I Won't See Wonder Woman' or 'Why Some Feminists Will Be Pissed')." Medium. June 7, 2017. https://medium.com/@nidasheriff/feminism-of-oppressors-or-why-i-wont-see-wonder-woman-or-why-some-feminists-will-be-pissed-723b8fd914f8. Accessed August 9, 2018.

Stanley, Kelli E. "Suffering Sappho!" Wonder Woman and the (Re)Invention of the Feminine Ideal." *Helios* 32, no. 2 (2005): 143–71.

Sucas, Roslyn. "Can Gal Gadot Make Wonder Woman a Hero for Our Time?" *New York Times*, May 4, 2017. https://nyti.ms/2paNGNQ. Accessed November 26, 2017.

Thomas, Gill. *Life on All Fronts: Women in the First World War*. Cambridge: Cambridge University Press, 1989.

Watson, Janet S. K. *Fighting Different Wars: Experience, Memory, and the First World War in Britain*. Cambridge: Cambridge University Press, 2004.

Weldon, Glen. "Superheroes and the F-Word: Grappling With the Ugly Truth under the Capes." National Public Radio. November 16, 2016. https://www.npr.org/sections/monkeysee/2016/11/16/502161587/superheroes-and-the-f-word-grappling-with-the-ugly-truth-under-the-capes. Accessed May 22, 2018.

Woerner, Meredith. "Commentary: Why I Cried through the Fight Scenes in 'Wonder Woman.'" *Los Angeles Times*, June 5, 2017. http://www.latimes.com/entertainment/herocomplex/la-et-hc-wonder-woman-crying-20170605-htmlstory.html. Accessed on September 15, 2017.

CHAPTER THREE

FLAGS OF OUR FATHERS

Imperial Decline, National Identity, and Allohistory in Marvel Comics

LAWRENCE ABRAMS AND KALEB KNOBLAUCH

From 1945 to 1975, the last of the nineteenth-century European empires disappeared from the map. A wave of national independence movements, starting with India and moving quickly across the African continent and Southeast Asia, swept them away. At the crest of the wave, during the 1960s, Marvel began to examine the role of European empires in their fictional world, questioning the value of imperialism and critiquing the many destructive elements of imperial rule. Furthermore, Marvel stories began to imagine historical and political alternatives to imperial conquest while real efforts at decolonization began to achieve independence for states under British and French control. This interest in themes of empire and decolonization was not an organized or concerted effort on the part of Marvel writers and editors but part of the publisher's ongoing engagement with contemporary political and social issues in the pages of its superhero comics. As we will show, many Silver and Bronze Age superhero comics take descriptive and speculative approaches to this theme, as a kind of allohistory about imperialism and decolonization during the mid-twentieth century.

During the Silver Age of superhero comics, a new generation of writers, artists, and readers introduced significant innovations to the superhero genre.[1] Many of these comics introduced new character types that humanized the superhero. Most fans credit Marvel writer Stan Lee and artist Jack Kirby—fixtures of Marvel Comics and its predecessor since 1940—for ushering in this new era of superhero stories. Characters created by Lee and Kirby had realistic problems that accompanied their fantastic new abilities.

The Silver Age superhero's powers changed as well. Genetic mutation and manipulation, exposure to radiation, and scientific experimentation provided the new generation of heroes with their abilities—not always for the better. Bruce Banner's exposure to gamma radiation gave him superpowers that transformed him into a hero but also a dangerous monster. The Fantastic Four were hit by cosmic radiation that transformed and deformed their bodies. Mutants in the Marvel universe present a range of abilities and appearances, and in many cases their mutations result in great personal anguish and social ostracism.[2] The ability of superhero comics to reflect fears of technological modernity captured the imagination of readers. Scientific origins for powers were nothing new: lab accidents created superpowered people in the Golden Age of comics as well—Jay Garrick, the original Flash, gained his powers after exposure to a hard water gas—but during the Silver Age the specter of atomic power loomed large in comics. Following the Silver Age, superheroes would be less paragonic but even more relatable.[3]

Contemporary social conflict featured prominently in Silver Age superhero comics.[4] Famously, Lee and Kirby's *X-Men* borrowed liberally from the civil rights movement; mutant leaders Charles Xavier and Magneto clashed over mutant responses to bigotry and violence, mediating, if crudely, the positions of Martin Luther King Jr. and Malcolm X. Early *X-Men* stories included racialized insults about mutants and addressed issues of passing, racial violence, and systemic oppression.[5] Looking back on the history of the X-Men, writer Chris Claremont declared, "The X-Men are hated, feared, and despised collectively by humanity for no other reason than they are mutants. What we have here, intended or not, is a book that is about racism, bigotry and prejudice."[6] The series addresses these themes in a more generalized way. Richard Reynolds calls it a "parable of the alienation of any minority" rather than as a direct mediation of the civil rights movement.[7] As is evident from subsequent readings of the series, a range of marginalized groups can read themselves into the X-Men.[8]

While the X-Men are the most widely known example of Silver Age social commentary, they are far from unique, and the civil rights movement was not the only historical inspiration for superhero comics.[9] Black Panther's adventures in the American South and his frequent residence as a public school teacher in Harlem both reveal America's systemic racial inequalities.[10] And, more recently, Captain Britain stories explicitly pit the hero against the conservative policies of Thatcherite Britain.[11] The sense of social insecurity in these midcentury comics reflects a larger concern with global affairs in a Cold War context.

By 1974 a new wave of heroes began to emerge. Notable among these for its responsiveness to global issues, nationalism, and the legacy of imperial violence was the Punisher. Frank Castle is a disillusioned Vietnam veteran who lost his family to the mob. He operates as a murderous vigilante outside the law. On the surface the Punisher bears little resemblance to the archetype of the righteous star-spangled heroes of the Gold or Silver Ages. Garbed in black with a white skull emblazoned on his chest in place of a flag, the Punisher nonetheless fits within a recognizable trend during the decade. He enforces his own views of the law and morality of the state, frequently against or among ethnic minorities, and more than any other hero, is directly born out of the frustration and chaos of the Vietnam War.[12] The Punisher is likewise the inspiration for entire follow-on generations of antiheroes and villains cast in his mold.[13] And as we will show, many other Marvel stories began to reimagine the geopolitical struggles of the Cold War.

Matthew Costello argues that "the changes in the material reality of America—particularly the assumption of a global role and a political economy that had become nationally integrated—required a reformed vision of the American self."[14] Recent studies of Silver Age superhero comics have shown how Marvel also incorporated Cold War politics and contemporary cultural tensions. Bradford Wright argues that superheroes represented "the epitome of the modern adolescent fantasy," and therefore the fantastical narratives both are inherently appealing and address feelings of powerlessness in the reader.[15] These factors also account for the substantial drop in reader interest by the end of the Second World War and its subsequent rebound during the 1960s, which Michael Goodrum charts, arguing that superhero comics helped to define the boundaries of American identity, acceptable values, and how the rest of the world should perceive American culture.[16] Charles Henebry traced the transformation of Tony Stark, who embodied the nation's capitalist spirit, and as Iron Man embodied its technological and productive potential, from a Cold Warrior to an internationalist progressive in the wake of the Vietnam War.[17] Matthew Yockey situates the *Fantastic Four*, uniquely among superhero comics of the time, directly in the context of the space race. Threats from outer space, or terrestrial threats that came from outer space, engaged with growing American anxieties over Soviet successes, starting with Sputnik, the Soviet satellite put into orbit in 1957.[18] Ramzi Fawaz has argued that the *Fantastic Four* "dramatized a fantasy of bodily vulnerability to the forces of science and to the social norms of national citizenship in the era of anticommunism."[19] The bodies of Reed Richards and his team contradicted their self-image by embodying countercultural figures of the 1960s: the left-wing intellectual, the liberal feminist, the youth activist, and the "maladjusted queer."[20] This is all to say that many scholars have turned their attention to the capacity of Marvel Comics to incorporate contemporary political and cultural debates, and thus help shape how the histories of those debates are remembered and reproduced in popular culture.

This chapter examines Marvel superhero comics in the context of decolonization, the collapse of European imperialism, and the rise of American hegemony. First, we argue that Marvel's *Black Panther* reimagines the history of Western colonial rule just as the wave of national independence movements hit its zenith. Though Black Panther has been the subject of many recent critical analyses, from fan blogs to acclaimed scholarly studies like Adilifu Nama's *Super Black*, most of these studies address the character through an explicitly American lens.[21] Our focus is on anglophone empire, broadening the range of analytical possibility for these artifacts of popular culture. In the second part of this chapter, we argue that, through its British superheroes, particularly Captain Britain and Union Jack, Marvel writers and artists reexamined British national identity and explored the fault lines of British society following the loss of the empire. Marvel heroes also contributed to a reevaluation of American national identity, not just as Cold Warrior but as the head of a new kind of empire. We use these topics to argue that superhero comics were not limited to tracking or renegotiating American values and identity but became part of a more global process of identity making in the twentieth century.

ALLOHISTORY AND THE BLACK PANTHER

Allohistory (alternatively called conjecture history, what-if history, and alternate history) speculates on different versions of history: what if, for example, the United States lost World War II, the Confederacy won the Civil War, or the American Revolution never took place?[22] Other allohistorical stories take real historical events (such as Frank Miller's *300*) or settings (such as steampunk) and intentionally fictionalize hem.[23] To give one example of allohistory in the superhero genre, in February 1940 Jerry Siegel and Joe Shuster were commissioned to write a short comic for *Look* magazine called "How Superman Would End the War," in which the Man of Steel kidnaps Hitler and Stalin and drags them before an international court at the League of Nations, where they are convicted of "modern history's greatest crime—unprovoked aggression against defenseless countries."[24] This comic may be the first allohistorical superhero comic, but it was not the last. Ever since Captain America landed his famous haymaker on Hitler, superhero comics have frequently engaged in allohistorical narratives.[25] Gavriel Rosenfeld argues that allohistories largely come in two forms: fantasy and nightmare scenarios.[26] Rosenfeld writes:

> Fantasy scenarios envision the past as superior to the present and thereby express a sense of dissatisfaction with the way things are today. Nightmare scenarios, by contrast, depict the past as inferior to the present and thereby express a sense of contentment with the status quo. Fantasy and nightmare scenarios, moreover, have different political implications. Fantasy scenarios tend to be liberal, for by envisioning a better past, they see the present as wanting and thus implicitly support changing it. Nightmare scenarios, by contrast, tend to be conservative, for by viewing the past in negative terms, they ratify the present and thereby reject the need for change.[27]

Allohistories are also inherently presentist; they do not investigate the past on its own terms, as historians strive to do, but instrumentalize the past in order to comment on the present. As allohistories, Marvel characters such as the Black Panther, Captain Britain and Union Jack, and the X-Men allow the reader to project the possibilities of Third World independence from great power hegemony, critique America's history of racial violence and internal colonialism, examine Britain's imperial past and changing social relations, and criticize the damaging legacy of English and American imperialism.

In 1966, its fifth year in publication, Stan Lee and Jack Kirby's *Fantastic Four* was one of Marvel's most successful titles. The series featured many of Marvel's Silver Age heroes. In issue #52, the Fantastic Four were gifted a highly advanced flying car from "an African chieftain, called . . . the Black Panther!"[28] Ben Grimm, the Thing, quips, "Never heard of 'im! But how does some refugee from a Tarzan movie lay his hands on this kinda gizmo?"[29] Condescension quickly turned to awe as the team traveled to Wakanda to meet their mysterious benefactor. Wakanda, in the Marvel universe, is a small African nation over which the Panther rules. The Fantastic Four land in a biomechanical forest and are tested by the Panther in a staged attack. This "attack" was more a test of character, and once the Panther was satisfied—having demonstrated his superiority over the white visitors—he invited the team to his court.[30] In issue #53, Reed Richards (Mr. Fantastic, the leader of the Fantastic Four) marveled at the ceremony T'Challa had organized to greet the heroes: "Though the Wakanda tribe lives in the tradition of their forefathers, they possess modern, super-scientific wonders we can only marvel at!"[31]

From this exciting introduction, the Black Panther began a half century of adventures that crossed continents and grappled with some of the most difficult social and political issues in both American and international contexts. In 2016 Marvel celebrated the fiftieth anniversary of the character, including debuting a new series under the direction of acclaimed author Ta-Nehisi Coates, and introduced the Panther to the Marvel Cinematic Universe in *Captain America: Civil War*. Throughout a fifty-year history, the adventures of the Black Panther—the longest-running Black superhero character—have addressed diverse geopolitical issues, reimagined African sovereignty outside of colonial influences, and confronted American racial politics and neocolonialism.[32]

T'Challa is both the king and superpowered defender of the nation of Wakanda, which Marvel currently locates on the western shore of Lake Victoria.[33] Unlike other superhero aliases, Black Panther is not an invented nom de guerre but is an office of the leader of the Panther Clan, the largest tribe in Wakanda.[34] The Black Panther is charged with protecting the tribe, and kingdom, against outside threats. T'Challa assumed the mantle after his father was killed by the mercenary Ulysses Klaw. Aside from protecting the people of Wakanda, the Black Panther is also charged with securing the country's deposits of "vibranium," a fictional metal that has allowed Wakanda to achieve a level of technological prowess unmatched by any other country in the Marvel universe. Vibranium provides the majority of Wakandan wealth and is also a key material in the armor, weapons, and tools of many of the Marvel heroes. Famously, it is also the key material component of Captain America's shield. The Black Panther's outfit, a ceremonial habit, is laced with the metal, protecting the wearer from all manner of attacks. Attempts to plunder Wakanda of its most valuable resource are often the origin of conflicts with supervillains and foreign governments, and, increasingly, from within.

These early Black Panther stories raise one of the most significant themes of the Black Panther comics: exploitation and plunder of African resources. In Black Panther's second-ever appearance, he explains to Reed Richards that vibranium, at the time a sound-absorbing metal, existed only within the borders of Wakanda; in fact, stealing this metal was the reason Ulysses Klaw came to Wakanda in the first place.[35] Four years later, in *Astonishing Tales* #6 and #7, Dr. Doom stages his own invasion of the country in search of the metal, after torturing Wakandans and tunneling through the country to find the location of the deposits.[36] The parallels to historical incidents of torture and environmental destruction in colonies like Belgian Congo for rubber, South Africa for diamonds, or Morocco for phosphorous are obvious. In fact, conflicts between Spain and Morocco, and then between Morocco and Western Sahara, over phosphorous mining rights were contemporary with the publication of these comics.

Like the fictional Wakanda, Morocco maintains a strategically significant source of mineral wealth; Morocco possesses the world's largest phosphate reserves. In 1958 Spanish geologists discovered the reserves—1.7 billion tons—outside the city of Smara. Over the next two decades, Spanish and other Western investors developed the phosphate mines to extract and export the resource. In 1975 one *New York Times* article declared, "Suddenly, Spanish Sahara Matters," and Western Sahara attracted intense international attention for its newfound wealth.[37] Almost from the outset, understanding resource extraction in the Western Sahara has been central to understanding the conflict that erupted over control of the mines.[38] Ownership of the mines even delayed Spain's efforts at decolonization, as the World Bank recognized Western Sahara as the most resource-rich state in Northern Africa.[39] Morocco, too, sought to gain control over Western Sahara, following the 1975 Treaty of Madrid, which handed Western Sahara over to Morocco. Morocco even petitioned the International Court of Justice to recognize its historical claims to the region. Ongoing conflict over the mines and Western Sahara has remained one of the central reasons for the stalemate between Morocco and Western Sahara and has resulted in the displacement and violence against the Sahrawi who have lived and worked in the mines but have never reaped the benefits of their own natural wealth. Contemporary and later

Black Panther stories use this historical dynamic in an allohistorical imagining of an African society that could retain the means of production of their own natural resources. But despite this utopian vision, the comic retains the troubling potentials of violence and internecine conflict.

Throughout the various runs of *Black Panther* comics, conflicts over vibranium serve as a reminder of whom and what the Panther is protecting, and this great responsibility exceeds those of most comic book heroes. Later runs also began to reconsider the utopianism of Wakanda. Illegal mining operations take center stage in *Jungle Action* #7 in 1973, and again in *Captain America* #414 and #415 in 1993. In the latter case, the competition in illegal mining came from the "Savage Land," a utopia in the Antarctic, and the competition from this other "savage" land nearly tanked the Wakandan economy.[40] In 1990's *Marvel Superheroes* #1, Black Panther even faces a rogue member of the royal cabinet, Mubaru, who tried to steal the ore and stage a coup.[41] And in *Black Panther: Panther's Prey*, a miniseries published the same year, Wakandan native Solomon Prey attempts to blow up the entire deposit, and the conflict reveals a major drug smuggling and crack cocaine epidemic in the country.[42] Written at the height of the so-called crack epidemic of the late 1980s and 1990s, this short story serves as a troubled reflection of contemporary social and political fears.

In early issues of Jack Kirby's *Black Panther* (1977–1979) fights over vibranium take on new meanings and draw on one of the painful truths of real-life histories of resource extraction. In issues #8 through #10, T'Challa faces a coup from Jakarra, his top general, who, after being exposed to raw vibranium ore, developed mutated powers that far exceeded the Black Panther's. It takes the efforts of the entire Wakandan royal family to put an end to the coup.[43] Subsumed by the power of this strange metal, the general believes that he can master both it and rule of the Wakandan nation. However, the literal melding of military man and the metal only leads to further division and violence within the kingdom. The symbolism here is particularly rich and underscores the complex and often destructive relationships between colonial mineral wealth and political violence. The bloody history of diamond mining in western Africa provides a real-world parallel. Across numerous countries—Sierra Leone, Liberia, and the Democratic Republic of Congo are only some of the most famous examples—diamonds intensified civil wars and financed repressive military regimes and rebel militias. Whereas in earlier comics, vibranium provides a clear material and social good, *Black Panther* #8–10 shows mineral wealth exacerbating social divisions and nearly toppling the kingdom. Furthermore, despite T'Challa's ultimate success, Kirby's *Black Panther* also traffics in contemporary racist notions of inherent African instability and the lack of effective self-governance.

NEOCOLONIAL ALLOHISTORY

One intriguing offshoot of this theme of resource extraction involves interactions between the Black Panther and Captain America. In *Tales of Suspense* #97, T'Challa asks Captain America to come to his aid against the Nazi scientist Baron Zemo and his orbiting solar gun.[44] This is one of the few times T'Challa ever asks for American aid. More often, American presence in Wakanda was at best a nuisance, or at worst a threat to Wakandan security. Cap is so often used as a representative of the United States, and the implications of interactions between the two characters is worth exploring as a theme of American involvement in the so-called Third World.

In *Captain America* #414 and #415, the arrival of Captain America to Wakanda inadvertently allowed an invasion of the country. Several comics set during the Second World War also feature invasions, in these instances, by Nazis looking to exploit the resources of Wakanda to help win the war.[45] Through this series of Western invaders, these Black Panther stories echo the criticism of Aimé Césaire that before Europeans were the victims of the Nazis, "they were its accomplices . . . before it was inflicted on them . . . they have absolved it . . . because, until then, it had been applied only to non-European peoples."[46] In *Black Panther* #30, Christopher Priest, the Marvel writer who shifted the focus of the Panther comics to address more explicitly geopolitical issues, Captain America meets the Black Panther—this time the Black Panther is T'Chaka, the father of T'Challa—in a brief confrontation that turns on its head most conventions (stereotypes) of the colonial encounter. T'Chaka clearly has an intellectual, as well as a tactical, advantage over the Americans and even plays on stereotypes of the ignorant savage in need of Western assistance. This is the original trope of Black Panther and Wakanda in *Fantastic Four* #52, now turned on its head. T'Chaka has an understanding of the geopolitical and geostrategic picture of the war that is completely above the American hero's. Eventually the two heroes come to a mutual respect that helps to draw Wakanda closer to the international community, but it was the Wakandans who determined the pace of change. In a reversal of real-world American foreign relations, the natives rejected, because they did not need or want it, America's help.[47] This comic poses a scenario in which the rest of the world/the Third World does not need the United States. It poses significant questions: how important is technological superiority in a colonial or neocolonial encounter, and what happens if or when that advantage disappears? This is a myth of African liberation of sorts, or liberation of the so-called Third World from Western hegemony, rooted in the era of decolonization.

In the miniseries *Captain America/Black Panther: Flags of our Fathers*, by Reginald Hudlin and illustrated by Denys Cowan, these dynamics are explored in greater depth. In this series Hitler sends Baron von Strucker—a mainstay

Captain America villain—to Wakanda to capture the vibranium supplies for the German war machine. This comic parallels the German scramble for the Baku oilfields during the Second World War. In the comic, as in the Second World War, the German need for mineral resources was a matter of national survival and success in the war effort.[48] When Captain America and his allies Nick Fury and the Howling Commandos arrive in Wakanda, they encounter German soldiers' heads mounted on spikes as uncharacteristically gruesome evidence of the Black Panther's claim that Wakanda can take care of itself.[49] In the second issue, Captain America learns that Black Panther—this time the king Azzuri, the grandfather of T'Challa (a minor retcon from Priest's *Black Panther* #30)—is already aware of his secret identity, thanks to a massive global spy network, inverting the real-life network of Western intelligence agents inserting themselves into the governments of the Third World.[50] The third issue introduces another historical dynamic: proxy wars. The Nazis ally with a neighboring tribe, the White Gorilla clan, to aid in the war with Wakanda; this new relationship also sparks a debate among the Nazi leaders on the role of racial politics, who see their White Gorilla allies as racially inferior.[51]

The conclusion of this series has the Black Panther and Captain America driving out the Nazis, with a threat from the Panther that, should the Nazis ever return, he would invade Germany himself. Once again we see Captain America receiving a vibranium shield as a sign of gratitude, and throughout this series the Panther is clearly dominant, dictating the terms under which the Americans leave Wakanda and refusing to get involved in the war outside Wakandan borders.[52] This conclusion raises one more allusion. Following the Second World War, leaders of the Third World, for example, in French Indochina, concluded that the West was not necessary as a protector; in the case of the French, they abandoned the territory to the Japanese. This was a critical moment in the decline in colonial control, and much of the characterization of Black Panther in this miniseries echoes the defiance of Cold War leaders like Ho Chi Minh, and Guevara's address to the Tricontinental. The "Flags of Our Fathers" miniseries evokes significant historical themes from the Second World War, the Cold War, and most importantly the geopolitical effects of decolonization, often blurring the conflicts in ways that suggest American self-confidence after the "End of History," but inverts the relationship between the United States and the developing world, reflecting a newfound insecurity during the war on terror.

ALLEGORIES OF THE NATION

The Black Panther comics, reexamined through the lens of anticolonial allohistory, demonstrate the often-deep engagement of superhero comics and historical themes. And the choice of Black Panther for this essay rides a new wave of popular and scholarly interest in the character, following the release of Ryan Coogler's *Black Panther* (2018). Other, less well-known heroes in the Marvel stable also engage in allohistorical narratives. Through Marvel's British superheroes—specifically Captain Britain and Union Jack, both prominent in the UK but virtually unknown elsewhere—we can see how Marvel Comics illustrated contemporary debates over national identity, and indeed a sense of national crisis, as the British Empire declined in the twentieth century.

Since the earliest days of political consolidation and developing nationalism, it has been common practice to portray the nation-state in an embodied human form.[53] In the anglophone Western world it is possible to reel off their names like a who's who of historical symbolism: Columbia, Britannia, Hibernia, Scotia, Uncle Sam, John Bull, Ms. Canada, and Sawney Scot just to name a few. Historians have subjected these personifications to their due scrutiny, but in addressing comic book symbols of the nation in the anglophone sphere, our focus has been overly narrow. In basic terms our focus has been too American.

The flag-draped superhero was there from the very beginning of the Golden Age. There are few images in comics more iconic than the cover of *Captain America Comics* #1 as Cap gives Hitler the haymaker he so richly deserved in December 1940, a whole year before America entered World War II. But by the early Silver Age of comics, the nationalist heroes were in decline. Declining sales, backlash to the hypernationalism of McCarthyism, censorship over fears of homosocial relationships between older male heroes and their young boy wards, and growth of other pulp comic media like mystery and romance comics led to the shelving of numerous superhero titles until their resurgence in the mid-1970s.

Prior to 1975 non-American nationalist flag superheroes with their own titles or long-running stories as parts of a team were very rare. This is because the superhero as a genre despite its transnational immigrant roots is fundamentally American in origin and economic base and took time to develop into a more international genre.[54] *The Invaders* (1976) was the first serious attempt to bridge the Atlantic anglophone market in a kind of "special relationship" approach to publishing. *The Invaders* was written by an American creative team as a deliberately anachronistic set of stories set during World War II and featured a team-up of Captain America, Namor, and the Human Torch. This was a revival of the extremely patriotic teams, like the All-Winners Squad, which were originally published during the war. However, joining *The Invaders* in issue #8 was an all-new British superhero, an unpowered special commando named Union Jack. Retconned into the timeline of the Marvel comic book universe as part of a multinational team from World War I, previously unseen by readers and known as Freedom's Five, Union Jack at the time of *The Invaders* in World War II is now a retired old soldier and lord named James Montgomery Falsworth.

In Lord Falsworth's Union Jack we see a particularly American take on British identity and geopolitics. He is a member of the nobility, an unpowered operative from an older generation's more gentlemanly war. His principal villain from his heyday is the nefarious lieutenant of Dracula, a vampire named Baron Blood. Union Jack enthusiastically comes out of retirement in World War II to help Captain America and the Invaders to face off a new vampiric threat to his children from Baron Blood. But it is clear that he is no longer in his prime. Meanwhile, it is revealed that Baron Blood is actually his Nazi-sympathizing brother John Falsworth. Union Jack becomes disabled in the fight to bring down his brother, but his daughter Jacqueline is granted powers and goes on to fight in numerous adventures with the Invaders and others as the speedster heroine Spitfire, while his son, Brian, will eventually take up the mantle of Union Jack. Both Spitfire and Union Jack feature in *The Invaders* until its conclusion in 1979, and in other titles from then on.

The powers gained by Spitfire are also revelatory. She is faster than the speed of sound, resilient, and capable of regeneration. Her power set is also deeply rooted in the odd circumstances of her origin story. In later years she is revealed to be a latent mutant but originally gains her powers from the combination of a vampire bite by her uncle Baron Blood and a blood transfusion from the original Human Torch, an android.[55] By gaining powers Spitfire far surpasses her unpowered father and brother and is thus an easy-to-digest allegory of feminism and generational change for British and American readers. Her superhero moniker is derived from the famous RAF fighter plane that defended Britain's skies during WWII, and despite her noble background she serves in the Women's Volunteer Service Corps even before gaining powers. This continues the familiar practice in *The Invaders* of rooting a 1970s comic in a narrative of WWII triumphs but giving the characters a more progressive modern slant. This is apparent when Spitfire joins the Invaders team as a full member, even outright declaring, "Now I can take my father's place—as an Invader!"[56] This was an action that would have been unusual in the actual WWII comics *The Invaders* sets out to mimic but one that is commonplace in 1977 in the wake of the feminist and women's liberation movements in the US and UK in the 1960s and 1970s.[57]

There is a lot to unpack here in only a few dozen pages of pulp over four issues. The privilege of class and noblesse oblige in comics is an interesting spin on the power and responsibility trope endemic to the genre. Baron Blood also provides a mirror for the dark side of the class privilege of nobility which was rapidly becoming a relic of an older imperial past by the comic's publication in the 1970s. The passing of the mantle of Union Jack from Lord Falsworth to his son is likewise a ready example of popular culture reacting to broader generational shifts in British society. The decline of the old empire and Union Jack's lack of powers compared to his American teammates is also interesting, as it is firmly reminiscent of the final passages of Tennyson's "Ulysses," which has been frequently used in popular culture as an allegory for the decline of the British Empire.[58] However, the view of empire and identity in *The Invaders* is colored here by the fact it was never actually written by a British creative team. As such, it is helpful, then, to compare *The Invaders* with Marvel's other notable attempt to capture the British Empire, and by extension the British market, in comics.

For a British character written by Britons for Britons we must turn back to 1975 and Marvel UK's second strategy to boost British comics sales. This second strategy, which should be dubbed the "Jerusalem" approach, was very simple. Its purpose was to create a British flag hero as a direct counterpart and opposite number for Captain America. The result was the powerful if unimaginatively named Captain Britain. This direct parallel is particularly valuable in establishing what became common differences between American and British superheroic norms. Notable among these is that Captain Britain sets the tone for the predominance of magic or the supernatural as the basis for many of the new British superheroes, compared with Americans and their technology. Like Union Jack, Captain Britain is of the nobility, Lord Brian Braddock. But he is by contrast a young and fashionable university student of physics. He originally gains his powers from an amulet granted to him by Merlin in the Siege Perilous and frequently blends science and magic to achieve his goals.

Created by British expat Chris Claremont, *Captain Britain* unfortunately "floundered commercially," failing to live up to Marvel UK's hopes.[59] Chris Claremont's run as writer lasted only ten issues after being told to tone down the political allegory in his stories. "Claremont, who scripted the series in those early days, seems to have been a little constricted by corporate decisions concerning the character."[60] The title was frequently plagued by editorial clashes about politics, half-finished plotlines, a cost-cutting transition from full color to black-and-white, which incensed fans, and an incoherent direction for the character's arc. London's *Financial Times* described it as a "farrago of illiterate SF nonsense."[61] The solo title *Captain Britain Weekly* lasted only a year. However, the character developed a small but loyal fan following and has remained in print in partnerships or teams sporadically but consistently since 1976.

The paired continuity and constant disruption is important, because it allowed the creative staff to constantly reinvent the character. Most comics undergo four main phases of their development: impassioned creation, replacement of creative staff with a new vision, radical reinvention and deconstruction, and finally synthesis along lines of fan expectations.[62] The frequent difficulties of *Captain Britain*'s publication history demonstrate this in an accelerated fashion. Classic decisions faced by most Bronze and Modern Age heroes such as whether or not to use lethal force, whether to submit to state authority, and whether to simply hang up the super suit are forced into the narrative with incredible rapidity in Captain Britain's storylines. Nowhere is this more apparent than in the reinvention and literal rebirth of the character in his second solo title volume in 1985 under the writing of Alan Moore.

This revival of the character on the cusp of the Modern Age of Comics under the pen of the godfather of the Modern Age provides some of the best gems in *Captain Britain* for analysis. Despite being told to tone down the politics, Moore (and even more so his artist Alan Davis) ramped it up.[63] Captain Britain receives new and altered powers; his uniform was altered from the classic heraldry to a more modern flag outfit complete with technology to supplement his magical powers and based loosely on the Horse Guards uniform. He faces off with the government over registration and protests the treatment of the poor under a faux-Thatcherite regime, his sister became psychic and decidedly less feminist than her original incarnation in the 1970s before eventually joining the X-men herself as the mutant Psylocke, and his ancestral family manor is destroyed. This kind of chaos and upheaval was typical of Alan Moore's writing and characteristic of the birth of the Modern Age.

Captain Britain's story, like Union Jack's, does not end in the 1980s but continues to develop throughout the Modern Age of comics. While his second solo run was also short-lived, Captain Britain survives as a frequent team leader or member on teams. Notable among these are Excalibur (the UK's Avengers), the Knights of Pendragon (alongside Union Jack), and MI-13 (UK's answer to S.H.I.E.L.D. but for magic). Most recently his powers have taken on a new twist as well. In current comics Captain Britain is literally powered by his own confidence in the righteousness of his cause and his country and is the headmaster of the Braddock Academy, where he trains the next generation of British superheroes.

The largest change Moore made to the character was the introduction of the Captain Britain Corps, a police force for the multiverse,[64] each universe represented by its own version of Captain Britain shaped by different historical divergences that shape their respective realities. This introduces a self-reflective nationalism to the comic that is only reinforced by the names of the story arcs of the 1980s run. These titles include classic phrases from the hymnal *Jerusalem* like "Dark Satanic Mills" and the crossover story in *Captain America* #305–6 "Walk upon England." "Walk upon England" is especially notable for this, as it is only the second encounter between Captains Britain and America. In this plotline, they work together to take down a magical foe, but Captain America is forced to bow to Captain Britain's superior knowledge of magic, experience, and territoriality and let Merlin extradite the foe to another dimension. In the final scene, they are both clear allegories for national identity and hegemony, going so far as to omit Captain from each other's names, and expressing belief in the righteousness of their cause. This scene is also particularly amusing as it is a far cry from their first meeting and team-up in the 1970s, which begins when Captain Britain punches Captain America for interfering in a fight between Captain Britain and a Welsh police inspector who was attempting to unmask Captain Britain.

CONCLUSION: AFTER EMPIRE

The ongoing focus on the nation and the global role of the superhero that develops during the Bronze and early Modern Ages matures into two recognizable trends in the latter half of the Modern Age. The first is a more critical look at the nation-state and the domestic legacies of imperial violence and oppression, and the second is a parallel critique of the role of the superpowered (state or hero) in a global interventionist role. For this chapter we have chosen two brief examples that demonstrate these trends especially well in the post-9/11 Modern Age comics environment. While comics fans generally lack a term for a new age after the Modern Age, the allohistorical and presentist nature of comics and comics media do reflect some significant developments in the years following the 9/11 terror attacks in the United States and escalation of conflict in the years to follow.[65]

The first example is the return of Union Jack in a special miniseries. Published in 2006 as a response to the 7/7 London terror bombings of the previous year, the special volume *Union Jack: London Falling* is a distinctly Modern Age update to the character, with valuable insight to be drawn from the changes. As we have already discussed, the great utility of comics is their adaptability and rapid responsiveness to changes in the social, cultural, and political environment. This new Union Jack is a perfect example. His name is Joseph Chapman, he is the son of a shipbuilder from Manchester, and a far cry from his aristocratic predecessors. Chapman is a champion of the people, helping them evacuate when his superiors at MI-5 had tried to hush up the seriousness of the threat while secretly evacuating senior officials and wealthy friends. Union Jack takes help where he can get it from work crews and ordinary Londoners, because all the real heroes like Captain Britain are "off on one of their secret infinity wars or whatever," and Union Jack and the temporary and tenuous support of his allies Sabra and Arabian Knight are all Britain has.[66] This is a darker, grimmer, more fallible look at the national flag superhero that has become typical of the post-9/11 Modern Age comic.

The *London Falling* special culminates in the triumph of Union Jack and his reluctant and cantankerous allies defeating the threat, but not without help from ordinary Londoners, and not without casualties. The final battle ends with the Union flag literally frozen in mid-wave in the wreckage of Trafalgar Square.[67] What we see here is not the triumphalist national narratives of earlier ages of comics but recognition of the decline of the power of the West and the imperial nation-state. This trend is especially reinforced only a few years later in the 2010 *Xenogenesis* run of *Astonishing X-Men.*

Xenogenesis is reflective of the second major trend we highlight for later, Modern Age comics. It is fitting that a comic run that investigates the role of international intervention be a run of the X-Men. Following a prior cancellation, the X-men were revived as a superhero team in 1975 and—reflective of the expanding international focus of the Bronze Age—were one of the first truly international teams. The new team was made up of Professor X (British), Sunfire (Japanese), Banshee (Irish), Wolverine (Canadian), Nightcrawler (German), Colossus (Russian), Thunderbird (Native American), and Storm (nominally a mix of Black American, Kenyan, and Egyptian, though really a catch-all racial stand-in for all of Africa).

By 2010 the composition of the X-Men had changed radically, but its international tenor remains. Of special importance to this story, though, is Storm. At this point in the Marvel comics continuity, Storm is actually married to King T'Challa of Wakanda, the Black Panther. In this run King T'Challa, and by extension Wakanda, is one of the principal funders of Mutantes Sans Frontières (Mutants without Borders). The MSF in this case is a stand-in for any number of international aid organizations, though its Wakandan funding inverts the normal postimperial, Western-dominated international aid relationships.[68] This is just the first of several obviously allohistorical reflections present in this run.

After the Black Panther calls on the X-Men and MSF to investigate a crisis in his neighboring fictional state of Mbangawi in East Africa, the subsequent pages of the entire first issue of the run amount to a primer on the history of conflict in modern Africa. Cyclops plays the role of the well-meaning, optimistic, but patronizing American aid organization. Storm fills the role of native African guide and supposed expert on all things "African." And finally, Wolverine steps in as the voice of the jaded representative of the old empires laying out a series of depressing facts for an ignorant teammate and declaring "never known a trip to this part o' the world that didn't go bad the second my feet touched the dirt."[69]

What ties "Xenogenesis" so perfectly together, though, is not simply the framing of an African problem with an American or international aid solution but what caused the problem in the first place. In the second issue, the X-Men encounter a British-educated African warlord named Dr. Joshua N'Dingi. But the postimperial legacy actually runs far deeper. In the third issue, Ndingi reveals that he is a former MI-13 agent who returned to his home country to assume control after his father's death and rails at the X-Men for their self-interested meddling in African affairs. The parallels and contrasts to Black Panther are readily evident. Furthermore, the X-Men learn that the cause of the problem they are there to combat is a direct result of an event known as a "Jasper's Warp."[70] The Warp and the cybernetic Furies that accompany it are in fact originally Captain Britain villains from the 1980s.[71] What we see here is a direct parallel in the comics for the postimperial crises often left behind by decolonization that linger well into the present day.

Social change and conflict has remained a significant feature of Marvel's stories from the Silver Age of comics onward. The use of allohistorical narratives provides an underexamined lens for comics scholars to evaluate comics' potential for historical engagement. As we have shown, Marvel's focus on political issues outside the United States began early in the Silver Age, particularly with the Black Panther stories—and rapidly expanded and became sharply self-critical in the wake of the Vietnam War—to become a frequent element of their superhero comics, even with its less popular characters. In Marvel's foreign-market imprints, also, this engagement with postcolonial national identity achieved particular prominence. While we examined these trends in only Marvel's extensive stable, there remains a vast untapped potential among other publishers and comics genres.

NOTES

1. We use the following descriptive chronology for American superhero comics: The Golden Age comprises superhero comics published from the late 1930s to circa 1950, the Silver Age from 1956 to 1970, the Bronze Age from 1970 to 1985, and the Modern Age from 1985 to the present. This periodization, particularly regarding the Bronze and Modern Ages, is frequently contested. We have little to contribute to those arguments, which are often used far too rigidly. But insofar as they provide chronological signposts, we continue to use this shorthand.

2. Examples here are numerous: Rogue cannot touch other people without possibly crippling or killing them, Legion's powers manifest as dissociative identity disorder, and Jean Grey's inability to control her telekinesis leads to her death and rebirth as the destructive Phoenix. The point is that, for mutants, powers come at a great personal cost.

3. Gardner Fox and Harry Lampert, "The Origin of the Flash," *The Flash* #1 (All-American Publications, 1940).

4. This is not exclusive to Silver Age Comics; Golden Age comics also featured contemporary social conflict but with some differences. Whereas a Golden Age Superman comic might feature a corrupt senator (*Action Comics* #1) or address workers' safety in a coal mine (*Action Comics* #3), Silver Age comics and beyond were more willing to address broad social ills and systematic oppression.

5. A clear example of these themes can be found in Stan Lee and Jack Kirby, "The Uncanny Threat of . . . Unus, the Untouchable," *X-Men* #8 (Marvel Comics, 1964).

6. Mikhail Lyubansky, "Prejudice Lessons from the Xavier Institute," in *The Psychology of Superheroes: An Unauthorized Exploration*, ed. Robin S. Rosenberg (Dallas: Benbella Books, 2008), 76.

7. Richard Reynolds, *Superheroes: A Modern Mythology* (Jackson: University Press of Mississippi, 1992), 79.

8. See, for instance, Michael Loadenthal, "Professor Xavier Is a Gay Traitor! An Antiassimilationist Framework for Interpreting Ideology, Power, and Statecraft," *Journal of Feminist Scholarship* 6 (2014); and Lawrence Baron, "*X-Men* as J-Men: The Jewish Subtext of a Comic Book Movie," *Shofar* 22, no. 1 (2003): 44–52.

9. The Fantastic Four's ill-fated flight took place in the context of the space race. In their first comic, Reed Richards wants to get to deep space to beat the Russians. Tony Stark, after a significant delay, involves himself in the war in Vietnam. And, at the cusp of the Silver and Bronze Age divide, in a famous and controversial issue of *The Amazing Spider-Man* (#96, 1971), Peter Parker intervenes when Harry Osborne develops a drug addiction. This issue was, in fact, created at the request of the Nixon administration, which saw comics as a potential messaging tool in its "war on drugs."

10. Working under the pseudonym of "Luke Charles," Black Panther taught at the absurdly inappropriately named Andrew Jackson High School.

11. Thatcher has even been lampooned as the crime lord Vixen. She also appeared as Captain Britain from an alternate universe. See Chris Claremont and Ron Wagner, "Someone Will Die for This!" *Excalibur* #32 (Marvel Comics, 1990), and Chris Claremont and Ron Wagner, "Cat on a Hot Tin Roof," *Excalibur* #33 (Marvel Comics, 1991).

12. Cord Scott, "The Alpha and the Omega: Captain America and the Punisher," in *Captain America and the Struggle of the Superhero*, ed. Robert G. Weiner (London: McFarland, 2009), 125–27.

13. Notorious among these is the 1980 British comic *Judge Dredd*, a satire of the Punisher (and by extension American violence). The titular character's morality in service to national law is so warped that he is morally superior only to a genocidal maniac like his nemesis Judge Death. Similarly descended from the Punisher is the Modern Age Marvel character Nuke (1986), also a Vietnam War veteran named Frank, and a steroidal, cybernetically enhanced murderer who paints the American flag on his face.

14. Matthew J. Costello, *Secret Identity Crisis: Comic Books & the Unmasking of Cold War America* (New York: Continuum, 2009), 31.

15. Bradford Wright, *Comic Book Nation: The Transformation of Youth Culture in America* (Baltimore: Johns Hopkins University Press, 2003), 1.

16. Michael Goodrum, *Superheroes and American Self Image from War to Watergate* (London: Routledge, 2016), 11.

17. Charles Henebry, "Socking It to Shell-Head: How Fan Mail Saved a Hero from the Military-Industrial Complex," in *The Ages of Iron Man: Essays on the Armored Avenger in Changing Times*, ed. Joseph J. Darowski (Jefferson, NC: McFarland, 2015), 95–97.

18. Matthew Yockey, "The Island Manhattan: New York City and the Space Race in *The Fantastic Four*," *Iowa Journal of Cultural Studies* 6 (Spring 2005): 59, accessed May 26, 2018, http://dx.doi.org/10.17077/2168-569X.1125.

19. Ramzi Fawaz, *The New Mutants: Superheroes and the Radical Imagination of American Comics* (New York: New York University Press, 2016), 66.

20. Fawaz, *New Mutants*, 69–70.

21. See chapter 2 in Adilifu Nama, *Super Black: American Pop Culture and Black Superheroes* (Austin: University of Texas Press, 2011).

22. Gavriel Rosenfeld, "Why Do We Ask 'What If?' Reflections on the Function of Alternate History," *History and Theory* 41, no. 4 (December 2002): 90–103.

23. Maryanne A. Rhett, "Leagues, Evildoers and Tales of Survival: Graphic Novels and the World History Classroom," in *Graphic Novels and Comics in the Classroom: Essays on the Educational*

Power of Sequential Art, ed. Carrye Kay Syma and Robert G. Weiner (Jefferson, NC: McFarland, 2013), 116–7.

24. Jerry Siegel and Joe Shuster, "How Superman Would End the War . . ." *Look*, February 27, 1940, accessed May 26, 2018, https://archive.org/stream/HowSupermanWouldEndTheWar/look#page/n1/mode/2up.

25. Joe Simon and Jack Kirby, "Meet Captain America," *Captain America* #1 (Marvel Comics, 1941).

26. Many scholars make this point. See, for example, Christoph Rodiek, *Erfundene Vergangenheit: Kontrafaktische Geschichtsdarstellung (Uchronie) in der Literatur* (Frankfurt: V. Klostermann, 1997), 30.

27. Rosenfeld, "Why Do We Ask," 93.

28. Stan Lee and Jack Kirby, "The Black Panther," *Fantastic Four* #52, Marvel Comics, 1966, 2.

29. Lee and Kirby, "Black Panther," 2.

30. See Goodrum, 122–27, where he discusses the racial and national tensions that play out over these two *Fantastic Four* issues.

31. Stan Lee and Jack Kirby, "The Way It Began!," *Fantastic Four* #53 (Marvel Comics, 1966), 1.

32. Bob Almond, afterword to *Black Panther: The Complete Collection, Vol. 2*, by Christopher Priest (Marvel Comics, 2015).

33. See Ta-Nehisi Coates, *Black Panther: A Nation under Our Feet*, bk. 1 (Marvel Comics, 2016).

34. The origin of the character's name is complicated. There is an obvious similarity to the Black Panther Party for Self-Defense, founded by Huey P. Newton and Bobby Seale in October of 1966 in Oakland, California. Newton and Seale took the image of a black panther from the Lowndes County Freedom Organization, founded in 1965. This potential connection was reinforced in Ryan Coogler's film *Black Panther* (2018) by retconning the villain, Erik Killmonger, as a Wakandan boy who grew up in 1990s Oakland. For his part, Stan Lee maintains that any similarity between the two names is merely coincidence. In an interview with *Alter Ego* (#104, 2011) Lee said that he was inspired by characters from early pulp novels and regrets the association. Jack Kirby's concept art labels him as the Coal Tiger, and the character's name was changed for a time to the Black Leopard to distance the comic from the Black Panther Party. The controversy is addressed directly in the comics as well. In *Fantastic Four* #119 (1972), T'Challa tells Ben Grimm, the Thing, "I contemplate a return to your country, Ben Grimm, where [Black Panther] has—*political* connotations. I neither condemn nor condone those who have taken up the name, but *T'Challa* is a law unto *himself*. Hence the new name—a *minor* point, at best, since the panther is a leopard." The name was changed back nine months later in *Avengers* #105 (1972), in which he says, "I did not want my *personal* goals and tribal *heritage* confused with *political* plans made by *others*," but "I am not a *stereotype*. I am *myself*. And I am—the *Black Panther*."

35. Lee and Kirby, *Fantastic Four* #53.

36. Gerry Conway and Barry Smith, "The Tentacles of the Tyrant," *Astonishing Tales* #6 (Marvel Comics, 1971); Roy Thomas and Herb Trimpe, "And If I Be Called a Traitor," *Astonishing Tales* #7 (Marvel Comics, 1971).

37. Paul Ellman, "Ownership Is Crucial," *New York Times*, August 3, 1975.

38. On the topic of resource extraction and conflict in Western Sahara, see Paul Collier and Anke Hoeffler," On the Economic Causes of Civil War," *Oxford Economic Papers* 50 (1998): 563–73; Paul Collier and Anke Hoeffler, "Greed and Grievance in Civil War," *Oxford Economic Papers* 56,

no. 4 (2004): 563–95; and Mats Berdal and David M. Malone, *Greed and Grievance: Economic Agendas in Civil Wars* (Boulder, CO: Lynne Rienner, 2000).

39. World Bank (1974), cited in Pedro Pinto Leite, "International Legality versus Realpolitik: The Cases of Western Sahara and East Timor," in Pedro Pinto Leite and Claes Olsson, *The Western Sahara Conflict* (Uppsala: Nordiska Afrikainstitutet, 2006), 16.

40. Mark Gruenwald, Rik Levins, and M. C. Wyman, "Escape from AIM Isle," *Captain America* #414 (Marvel Comics, 1993); Mark Gruenwald and Rik Levins, "Savage Landings," *Captain America* #415 (Marvel Comics, 1993). The Antarctic setting evokes fin de siècle "Hollow Earth" fiction, typified by Edgar Rice Burroughs's *At the Earth's Core* and Jules Verne's *Journey to the Center of the Earth.* What began in the eighteenth century as a literary trope of the pole as an exotic wasteland—à la Coleridge's "Rime of the Ancient Mariner" or Mary Shelley's *Frankenstein*—became by the end of the century a credible scientific theory: that either at the poles or beneath them there existed a tropical lost world. Incidentally, in later Marvel continuity, the Savage Land is recognized by the United Nations as an international wildlife preserve and is therefore protected from any commercial exploitation, furthering the relevance of resource extraction to these comics.

41. Robert Ingersoll and Mike Gustovich, "Conflagration," *Marvel Superheroes* #1 (Marvel Comics, 1990).

42. Don McGregor and Dwayne Turner, *Black Panther: Panther's Prey*, pt. 1 (Marvel Comics, 1991).

43. See Jack Kirby, *Black Panther* #8–10 (Marvel Comics, 1978).

44. Stan Lee and Gene Colan, "And So It Begins—!," *Tales of Suspense* #97 (Marvel Comics, 1968).

45. The use of Nazis in these stories complicates the message for readers, serving as a substitute for communist expansionism as well as projecting American imperialism onto a third party. Matthew Costello also addresses the slippage between Nazis and communists in superhero comics. See Costello, *Secret Identity Crisis*, 61.

46. Aimé Césaire, *Discourse on Colonialism* (New York: Monthly Review Press, 1972), 3.

47. Christopher Priest and Norm Breyfogle, "The Story Thus Far," *Black Panther* #30 (Marvel Comics, 2001).

48. Emily Meierding, "Do Countries Fight over Oil?" in *The Palgrave Handbook of the International Political Economy of Energy*, ed. T. Van der Graaf, B. Sovacool, A. Ghosh, F. Kern, and M. Klare, 441–60 (London: Palgrave Macmillan, 2016). Meierding argues that Germany's attacks against the Russian Caucasus (1941–42), along with Iraq's invasion of Kuwait (1990) and Japan's invasion of the Dutch East Indies (1941–42), are the only major military campaigns ever launched solely for control of oil. They did this because if they failed to gain control over the oil, their governments would have collapsed.

49. Reginald Hudlin and Denys Cowan, "Part 1," *Captain America/Black Panther: Flags of Our Fathers* #1 (Marvel Comics, 2010).

50. Reginald Hudlin and Denys Cowan, "Part 2," *Captain America/Black Panther: Flags of Our Fathers* #1 (Marvel Comics, 2010).

51. Reginald Hudlin and Denys Cowan, "Part 3," *Captain America/Black Panther: Flags of our Fathers* #1 (Marvel Comics, 2010).

52. Reginald Hudlin and Denys Cowan, "Part 4," *Captain America/Black Panther: Flags of our Fathers* #1 (Marvel Comics, 2010).

53. Linda Colley, *Britons: Forging the Nation; 1707–1837* (New Haven: Yale University Press, 2014), 133.

54. Fan letter on the subject from David Gordon-MacDonald quoted in J. M. DeMatteis and M. Zeck, "Mean Streets," *Captain America* #272 (Marvel Comics, 1982).

55. Roy Thomas and Frank Robbins, "An Invader No More," *The Invaders #11*, Marvel Comics, 1976; Dan Slott and Rita Fagiani, "Young Blood," *Marvel Comics Presents #89*, Marvel Comics, 1991. The corruption of old-fashioned British nobility cured by the technological innovation of new American ways.

56. Roy Thomas and Frank Robbins, *Invaders* #11.

57. Roy Thomas and Frank Robbins, "To the Warsaw Ghetto," *The Invaders* #12 (Marvel Comics, 1977). Notable exceptions like Wonder Woman notwithstanding, female lead title characters or equal partners on teams remained relatively scarce until the late 1960s.

58. While the poem is rife with British imperial allegory, the relevant lines are as follows: "We are not now that strength which in old days; Moved earth and heaven, that which we are, we are; One equal temper of heroic hearts, Made weak by time and fate, but strong in will; To strive, to seek, to find, and not to yield."

59. Alan Davis et al., *Captain Britain Omnibus* (New York: Marvel Books, 2009), 659.

60. Davis et al., *Captain Britain Omnibus*, 614. Exact details of these publisher constraints are scarce, but they play a significant role in the history of the title.

61. Davis et al., *Captain Britain Omnibus*, 658.

62. Marc DiPaolo, *War, Politics and Superheroes: Ethics and Propaganda in Comics and Film* (London: McFarland, 2011), 31.

63. Davis et al., *Captain Britain Omnibus Vol.* 2, vii.

64. Alan Moore and Alan Davis, "Rough Justice," *The Daredevils* #7 (Marvel Comics, 1983). This issue is especially noteworthy, as it the first-ever mention of the now-famous Marvel Universe-616 numbering, the prime universe of all Marvel stories in their internal chronology. It is unclear from where exactly Moore drew inspiration for the multiversal Captain Britain Corps. Universal or multiversal police forces are a common trope in comics (Green Lanterns, Nova Corps, various short stories in British comic magazines like *Eagle* or *2000AD*) and science fiction since Michael Moorcock coined the now-common use of the multiverse terminology in 1970. However, the multiverse concept first entered popular knowledge in 1952, a year before Moore was born, when it was proposed by quantum physicist Erwin Schrödinger at a lecture in Dublin, Ireland, and has been a staple of genre fiction ever since. For more on this, see John Gribbin's *Erwin Schrödinger and the Quantum Revolution* (London: Bantam Press, 2012).

65. DiPaolo, 18–19. At the 2018 Comics Studies Society Conference, Adrienne Resha proposed the term "Blue Age" for comics written after the 2007 launch of ComiXology.

66. Christos N. Gage and Mike Perkins, "Enemies of the Crown/London Falling (Part 1)," *Union Jack* #1 (Marvel Comics, 2006).

67. Christos N. Gage and Mike Perkins, "London Falling (Part 4)," *Union Jack* #4 (Marvel Comics, 2007).

68. Warren Ellis and Kaare Andrews, *Astonishing X-Men: Xenogenesis* #1 (Marvel Comics, 2010).

69. Ibid. Wolverine enumerates many common tropes about Africa: corruption, genocide, AIDS, child soldiers, etc. This plays directly into the myths of a "Broken Africa" that are common in modern histories of the continent. Some of these myths remain so common in popular conception that introductory history texts for teaching the history of the continent still require a section dedicated to debunking them. Erik Gilbert and Jonathan T. Reynolds, *Africa in World History: From Prehistory to the Present* (Upper Saddle River, NJ: Prentice Hall, 2012), xxiii.

70. Warren Ellis and Kaare Andrews, *Astonishing X-Men: Xenogenesis* #3 (Marvel Comics, 2010).

71. Warren Ellis and Kaare Andrews, *Astonishing X-Men: Xenogenesis* #4 (Marvel Comics, 2010); Alan Moore and Alan Davis, "A Crooked World," *Marvel Super-Heroes (UK)* #387 (Marvel UK, 1982).

WORKS CITED

Almond, Bob. Afterword to *Black Panther: The Complete Collection Vol. 2*. By Christopher Priest. New York: Marvel 2015.

Baron, Lawrence. "X-Men as J Men: The Jewish Subtext of a Comic Book Movie." *Shofar: An Interdisciplinary Journal of Jewish Studies* 22, no. 1 (2003): 44–52. https://muse.jhu.edu/ (accessed July 4, 2018).

Berdal, Mats, and David M. Malone. *Greed and Grievance: Economic Agendas in Civil Wars*. Boulder, CO: Lynne Rienner, 2000.

Césaire, Aimé. *Discourse on Colonialism*. New York: Monthly Review Press, 1972.

Coates, Ta-Nehisi. *Black Panther: A Nation under Our Feet*. Bk. 1. New York: Marvel Comics, 2016.

Colley, Linda. *Britons: Forging the Nation; 1707–1837*. New Haven: Yale University Press, 2014.

Collier, Paul, and Anke Hoeffler. "On the Economic Causes of Civil War." *Oxford Economic Papers* 50 (1998): 563–73.

Collier, Paul, and Anke Hoeffler. "Greed and Grievance in Civil War." *Oxford Economic Papers* 56, no. 4 (2004): 563–95.

Conway, Gerry, and Barry Smith. "The Tentacles of the Tyrant." *Astonishing Tales* #6. New York: Marvel Comics, 1971.

Costello, Matthew J. *Secret Identity Crisis: Comic Books & the Unmasking of Cold War America*. New York: Continuum, 2009.

Davis, Alan, Alan Moore, Jamie Delano, and Chris Claremont. *Captain Britain Omnibus*. New York: Marvel Books, 2009.

DeMatteis, J. M., and M. Zeck. "Mean Streets." *Captain America* #272. New York: Marvel Comics, 1982.

DiPaolo, Marc. *War, Politics and Superheroes: Ethics and Propaganda in Comics and Film*. London: McFarland, 2011.

Ellis, Warren, and Kaare Andrews. *Astonishing X-Men: Xenogenesis* #1. New York: Marvel Comics, 2010.

Ellis, Warren, and Kaare Andrews. *Astonishing X-Men: Xenogenesis* #3. New York: Marvel Comics, 2010.

Ellis, Warren, and Kaare Andrews. *Astonishing X-Men: Xenogenesis* #4. New York: Marvel Comics, 2010.

Ellman, Paul. "Ownership Is Crucial." *New York Times* (1923–Current file); August 3, 1975; ProQuest Historical Newspapers: The New York Times, pg. 145. Accessed May 26, 2018.

Fawaz, Ramzi. *The New Mutants: Superheroes and the Radical Imagination of American Comics*. New York: New York University Press, 2016.

Gage, Christos N., and Mike Perkins. "Enemies of the Crown/London Falling (Part 1)." *Union Jack* #1. New York: Marvel Comics, 2006.

Gage, Christos N., and Mike Perkins. "London Falling (Part 4)." *Union Jack* #1. New York: Marvel Comics, 2007.

Gilbert, Erik, and Jonathan T. Reynolds. *Africa in World History: From Prehistory to the Present.* Upper Saddle River, NJ: Prentice Hall, 2012.

Goodrum, Michael. *Superheroes and American Self Image from War to Watergate.* London: Routledge, 2016.

Gribbin, John. *Erwin Schrödinger and the Quantum Revolution.* London: Bantam Press, 2012.

Gruenwald, Mark, Rik Levins, and M. C. Wyman. "Escape from AIM Isle." *Captain America* #414. New York: Marvel Comics, 1993.

Gruenwald, Mark, and Rik Levins. "Savage Landings." *Captain America* #415. New York: Marvel Comics, 1993.

Henebry, Charles. "Socking It to Shell-Head: How Fan Mail Saved a Hero from the Military-Industrial Complex." In *The Ages of Iron Man: Essays on the Armored Avenger in Changing Times.* Edited by Joseph J. Darowski. Jefferson, NC: McFarland, 2015.

Hudlin, Reginald, and Denys Cowan. *Captain America/Black Panther: Flags of Our Fathers.* New York: Marvel Comics, 2010.

Ingersoll, Robert, and Mike Gustovich. "Conflagration." *Marvel Superheroes* #1. New York: Marvel Comics, 1990.

Kirby, Jack. *Black Panther.* Vol. 2. New York: Marvel Comics, 2006.

Lee, Stan, and Gene Colan. "And So It Begins—!" *Tales of Suspense* #97. New York: Marvel Comics, 1968.

Lee, Stan, and Jack Kirby. "The Black Panther." *Fantastic Four* # 52. New York: Marvel Comics, 1966.

Lee, Stan, and Jack Kirby. "The Way It Began!" *Fantastic Four* #53. New York: Marvel Comics, 1966.

Leite, Pedro Pinto, and Claes Olsson. *The Western Sahara Conflict: The Role of Natural Resources in Decolonization.* Uppsala: Nordiska Afrikainstitutet, 2006.

Loadenthal, Michael. "Professor Xavier Is a Gay Traitor! An Antiassimilationist Framework for Interpreting Ideology, Power, and Statecraft." *Journal of Feminist Scholarship* 6 (2014): 13–46.

Lyubansky, Mikhail. "Prejudice Lessons from the Xavier Institute." In *The Psychology of Superheroes: An Unauthorized Exploration,* edited by Robin S. Rosenberg. Dallas: Benbella Books, 2008.

McGregor, Don, and Dwayne Turner. *Black Panther: Panther's Prey.* Pt. 1. New York: Marvel Comics, 1991.

Meierding, Emily. "Do Countries Fight over Oil?" In *The Palgrave Handbook of the International Political Economy of Energy,* edited by T. Van der Graaf, B. Sovacool, A. Ghosh, F. Kern, and M. Klare, 441–60. London: Palgrave Macmillan, 2016.

Moore, Alan, and Alan Davis. "A Crooked World." *Marvel Super-Heroes (UK)* #387. London: Marvel UK, 1982.

Moore, Alan, and Alan Davis. "Rough Justice." *The Daredevils* #7. New York: Marvel Comics, 1983.

Priest, Christopher, and Norm Breyfogle. "The Story Thus Far." *Black Panther* #30. New York: Marvel Comics, 2001.

Reynolds, Richard. *Superheroes: A Modern Mythology.* Jackson: University Press of Mississippi, 1992.

Rhett, Maryanne A. "Leagues, Evildoers and Tales of Survival: Graphic Novels and the World History Classroom." In *Graphic Novels and Comics in the Classroom: Essays on the Educational Power of Sequential Art,* edited by Carrye Kay Syma and Robert G. Weiner, 111–19. Jefferson, NC: McFarland, 2013.

Rodiek, Christoph. *Erfundene Vergangenheit: Kontrafaktische Geschichtsdarstellung (Uchronie) in der Literatur.* Frankfurt: V. Klostermann, 1997.

Rosenfeld, Gavriel. "Why Do We Ask 'What If?' Reflections on the Function of Alternate History." *History and Theory* 41, no. 4 (December 2002): 90–103.

Scott, Cord. "The Alpha and the Omega: Captain America and the Punisher." In *Captain America and the Struggle of the Superhero*, edited by Robert G. Weiner, 125–34. London: McFarland, 2009.

Siegel, Jerry, and Joe Shuster. "How Superman Would End the War . . ." *Look*, February 27, 1940. https://archive.org/stream/HowSupermanWouldEndTheWar/look#page/n1/mode/2up (accessed May 26, 2018).

Simon, Joe, and Jack Kirby. "Meet Captain America." *Captain America* #1. New York: Marvel Comics, 1941.

Slott, Dan, and Rita Fagiani. "Young Blood." *Marvel Comics Presents* #89. New York: Marvel Comics, 1991.

Thomas, Roy, and Frank Robbins. "An Invader No More." *The Invaders* #11. New York: Marvel Comics, 1976.

Thomas, Roy, and Frank Robbins. "To the Warsaw Ghetto." *The Invaders* #12. New York: Marvel Comics, 1977.

Thomas, Roy, and Herb Trimpe. "And If I Be Called a Traitor." *Astonishing Tales* #7. New York: Marvel Comics, 1971.

Wright, Bradford. *Comic Book Nation: The Transformation of Youth Culture in America*. Baltimore: Johns Hopkins University Press, 2003.

Yockey, Matthew. "The Island Manhattan: New York City and the Space Race in *The Fantastic Four*." *Iowa Journal of Cultural Studies* 6 (Spring 2005): 58–79. http://dx.doi.org/10.17077/2168-569X.1125. Accessed May 26, 2018.

CHAPTER FOUR

THE BUCKAROO OF THE BADLANDS

Carl Barks, Don Rosa, and (Re)Envisioning the West

PETER CULLEN BRYAN

Often overlooked in the annals of comics scholarship, Disney comics provide a unique perspective on American history. They are a step removed from the larger media empire, the advantage of Walt's disinterest in many of the aspects of his empire, and provide an interesting counterpoint to many depictions of American history in that era. During their heyday in the late 1950s and early 1960s, Disney's comics (particularly *Uncle $crooge*) offered an alternative to the various adult-oriented western and horror comics, as well as the superheroes that would eventually come to dominate the industry. These comics portrayed an Old West more grounded in lived reality than the two-fisted tales of cowboy heroics, or even Walt Disney's *Davy Crockett* trilogy from the early 1950s that portrayed life as more of a happy-go-lucky adventure. The comics of Carl Barks, freed from editorial oversight, created more grounded stories and would contribute to further revisionist efforts with Barks's successor, Don Rosa.

CARL BARKS THE REALIST

Carl Barks's work set in an Old West reflects a sort of revisionist history, but one more keenly aware of the rough reality, with swindling bankers and inclement weather a greater threat than bank robbers or Cherokee raiders (indeed, Barks's work possessed a more sympathetic view of Native Americans than many other publications at the time). The relation between history and authenticity in Don Rosa's work is key to understanding his creative process, and the manner in which it was received by a new generation of readers. Also key is the presentation of an alternative version of the American West to wide and diverse audiences, as posited by myth-symbol with Barks and Rosa playing with the notions of what the West was.[1] Both creators stood in opposition to prevailing notions of the homogenized West of the midcentury, though they interrogated the myths in different fashions, utilizing images within their comic books to make arguments about the realities within the West.[2] Carl Barks and Don Rosa both played upon national myths while nevertheless subverting their weight and meaning, attempting to re-create a true version of the Old West, or at least one truer than contemporary pop culture versions.

The western as a genre dominated postwar American culture, though comics were more diffuse. The superheroes that had been so significant in the invention of the comic book had been displaced by other genres. Bradford Wright explains that "the majority of comic books published in the early 1950s were devoted to funny animals, romance, and innocuous adventure stories, but an increasing minority indulged tastes for controversial and provocative subject matter."[3] Western comics were never quite as dominant as the western was in other media but still featured in the comic books of the day. These comics were not immune to the larger issues of postwar culture; Tom Engelhardt explains that "the western, which in the 1950s achieved a dominant position on the small screen at home as well [as the movie theater] remained a particularly white genre (even though one-quarter or more of nineteenth-century cowboys had been black)."[4] The Old West featured in the comics was often drawn from the cowboys in other media; William Savage locates half a dozen long-running cowboy comics featuring the likes of Tom Mix and Gene Autry, most running from the mid-1940s until the late 1950s, in keeping with the larger cowboy fad of the period.[5] These figures had an additional function, however. Savage goes on to explain that

> comic-book cowboys could address contemporary social problems because of the anachronistic nature of their existence. They went on horseback and camped out at night and had to do with rather primitive Indians, but there was no historical context. They rode the mid-twentieth-century West, among cars and trucks and planes and speedboats and all manner of technological wonders, suggesting that the mainstream meandered freely through the outback and that western social issues were merely American social issues writ rural.[6]

The operative point is that these figures were unstuck from their alleged point of origin, instead dealing with the more salient issues of the day (particularly drug dealing). This is the context in which Carl Barks is writing, offering a different view of the West.

Carl Barks's version of the American West is harder-edged than contemporary comics and western films (his career in comics ran from the early 1940s to the mid-1960s, coinciding with the dominance of the western in popular culture).

His stories were couched in a sense of reality, which Don Rosa expands into a realistic tale of the difficulties inherent in making a fortune on the frontier. Both writers seem to draw heavily from historical sources; Scrooge's story is more akin to something like William Breckenridge's *Helldorado* than John Ford's *Stagecoach* and mediates elements of the revision westerns that became common in the interregnum between Barks and Rosa.[7] Both authors placed a heavy emphasis on authenticity. Barks drew upon *National Geographic* to represent a verdant and surprisingly realistic representation of the real world, just with ducks and dogs in place of humans, tying the history of Scrooge into real historic events when possible. Andrew Lendacky writes, "[Barks] actually did research, utilizing a file of old *National Geographic* magazines to ensure an authentic look for the physical environment he recreated as the backdrop to the Duck's adventures."[8] While the physical environments possessed some authenticity, the problems of *National Geographic*, particularly its portrayal of nonwhites as Other, were present in the Barks comics.[9]. Lendacky continues that "Barks, although a native of the Northwest, apparently had an affinity for the Southwest, if one can judge by the number of stories he has written that have the Southwest or South of the Border physical settings."[10] Barks was born in 1901, little more than a generation removed from the reality, and his youth spent on a cattle ranch (with the attendant encounters with actual cowboys) likely influenced the creation of a more grounded vision of the West. Lacking the life experience of his predecessor, Rosa took it a step further, building upon the body of work that Barks had crafted, expanding more deeply into the real world through diligent research and expert opinions.

Fredrick Jackson Turner famously intoned the "closing of a great historic moment" during the World's Columbian Exposition in 1893.[11] Drawing from census data, Turner contended that the spirit of settlement and progress would no longer spread wide, raising concerns about the future development of American identity. Lynn Harter contends that "the mythic image that anchors the frontier thesis is that of the frontiersman, a heroic character who ventured forth into uncharted territory, supposedly independent of others' symbolic and material resources, to win a decisive victory against all odds."[12] The loss was more of possibility than of any physical space; 1893 was the same year that introduced the world to the Ferris wheel, spray paint, alternating current, and brownies, and would hardly mark the end of the frontier in popular imagination. Butch Cassidy and the Sundance Kid still roamed, the Klondike gold rush was still a few years away, the Nome and Fairbanks gold rushes in the following years, and the Indian Wars still saw skirmishes into the new century. The romanticization of the West had begun well before this moment, evidenced by William "Buffalo Bill" Cody's Wild West show, the first of which was performed in 1883, and Mark Twain's *Huckleberry Finn*, wherein the title character promises "to light out for the territory" at the novel's conclusion, as well as dime novels more generally.[13]

Even Walt Disney played a role in this, both in producing the *Davey Crockett* television films and the larger Disneyland project, which John Wills explains as "[turning] history into interactive entertainment . . . the studio breathed life into lost, dead, and departed historical objects. Disney tapped nostalgia for historic America and reminded visitors of 'the good old ways.'"[14] Still, Turner's thesis informs how the frontier would come to be understood, the Old West that was, and was a crucial element of the development of the modern American empire in the twentieth century.[15]

The frontier is an amorphous thing, as much a state of being as a physical space. The borders were at best temporary and arbitrary, pushed ever outward by successive generations of traders, miners, farmers, and ranchers that inexorably transformed the landscape and destroyed or drove out the native inhabitants. These migrations occurred at various points in history, and from various directions, whether of mountain men traveling south along the Rocky Mountains from Canada, prospectors taking the long boat ride from New York to San Francisco, or various waves of immigration from nearly every continent. Turner's conception of the frontier posits it as a space that has a way of removing the European-ness of its settlers, engendering a unique American character informed by the wide-open spaces, lack of history (at least in the traditional, European sense), harshness of survival, and interactions with Native Americans. Turner posits that this space allowed for the flowering of both capitalism and democracy: "the frontier is productive of individualism . . . it produces antipathy of control, and particularly to any direct control. The tax-gatherer is viewed as representative of oppression."[16] While the worth of an individual and the entitlement to the fruits of one's own labors did not spring forth from the American character (after all, there are over two dozen mentions of tax collectors in the New Testament alone), it was adopted as an intrinsic aspect of the western settler.

The nature of the dispersed territorial governments and limited federal oversight reconstituted the myths of the creation of America, that the country's very origin was inexorably linked to the oppressions of Old Europe alone, and that westward expansion constituted an extension of America's founding character. It is a space where men are men, challenging the forces of nature; Harter argues that "the masculine subjectivity embodied by the frontiersman is one characterized primarily by isolation and independence. The frontier narrative functions as a textual guide that directs the formation of not only individual identities (e.g., the farmer as the lone hero) but also organizational form (e.g., the proclivity for structures that privilege individualism)."[17] This myth was refined and simplified over time, bent to a dozen different political causes, whitewashed over the course of generations. Turner's scholarship is a relic, a crucial foundation of the study of American culture but one that reflects the prevailing cultural notions of what the frontier was. Richard Slotkin contends:

> Turner's approach is essentially "nostalgic." By dwelling on the naive perfection of the pre-modern frontier past, Turner implies a critique of the corruption of the present. The Frontier of the past appears as a place in which, once upon a time, the political and social life of a European people was transformed, morally regenerated, and given a distinctively democratic direction.[18]

Thus, Turner's approach understands the West as an end result, as though a switch is flipped with the close of the frontier, and the hierarchy of power that results is almost predestined. Slotkin recognizes the faults of Turner, which would come into play within the character of Uncle Scrooge, albeit for a very different audience. Similarly, David Nye argues, "Ask most Americans how the first settlers lived and they will talk about log cabins. It was not so, but later generations superimposed this vision on all of the American past."[19] These versions of the past have little relation to the reality of life is historical settings but nevertheless inform perceptions of the country's history and contemporary interactions with that same history. Turner's conception of the West was simplistic, but no more so than the westerns and other popular culture texts that followed.

DONALD DUCK AND THE SHERIFF

Carl Barks was born in 1901, a few months before his eventual employer Walt Disney. Like Disney, Barks spent his youth on what remained of the frontier. Disney's youth in small-town Missouri was echoed in Barks's childhood on an Oregon homestead, though the transformation of the American landscape had already reached parts of the Midwest. Whereas Disney had access to basic amenities (electricity, running water), Barks lived a rural life, including riding to school in a wagon for several years, and he did not even attend high school.[20] Moreover, the young Barks encountered remnants of the West that was; he recalls that "real cowboys would come in those outfits . . . my brother and I, we just worshipped those fellows. And oh, what vulgar-talking men they were!"[21] Barks contends that they shared few stories of their work, though some anecdotes slip through in interviews. He came of age in this space, and it was a significant influence on his work; he noted, "I have a love for the Old West, the wide-open spaces. I can remember when I myself was a young boy with plenty of room to roam around in, with a gun to shoot and horses to ride. It was part of the formation of my character, I guess."[22] Even his home of Merrill, Oregon, had a brush with history; Barks remarked that "the last of the Indian wars was fought there in the 1880s, something like that, which was close to where I'd lived."[23] Despite his lack of formal education, Barks was nevertheless intrigued by history, and elements of the American West filtered into his work in the decades to come.

Barks pursued drawing, drifting from Oregon to San Francisco to Minneapolis, before winding up at Walt Disney Studios in Los Angeles, finding work as an animator in 1934. His talents seemed better suited to writing, particularly in Donald Duck cartoons, and he transferred to the story department in 1937. Barks remained there until 1942, when he quit for health reasons, taking up work as a chicken farmer, though he was soon hired to produce work for the burgeoning Disney comics on a freelance basis on the recommendation of one of his old writing partners and was given considerable freedom in the stories he wrote.[24] While his initial output was relatively slow, he would soon become the most prodigious writer of Donald Duck comics. By the time he retired in 1966, he had produced some seven hundred stories across his career, including the stories that introduced Uncle Scrooge McDuck.

The West and the frontier always loomed in the Carl Barks canon. His work is the re-creation of the frontier of his imagination, a space that still existed within living memory, one that had changed little in spite of Turner's proclamation, one that he had lived.[25] Electrification would not occur in the rural areas of the Pacific Northwest until after World War I, and life had continued in much the same fashion as it had for several generations. Barks's experience would not have been far removed from someone like Laura Ingalls Wilder, and his vision of the West was couched in that hardscrabble reality.[26] This upbringing engendered in Barks a certain distrust of the modern world and technology, as Thomas Andrae explains: "Barks's conservatism and critical stands toward modernity inform many of the cartoons on which he worked . . . anxieties about a loss of masculine authority and control, a dread of the feminine, and fears of technological progress."[27] Barks's work naturally harked back to frontier mentalities, the same concepts that Turner had posited, though it remained out of step with many of the prevailing notions appearing in western narratives of the era. Andrae continues that "at the same time, Barks was a staunch individualist, and the cartoons also express an antiauthoritarian ethic exemplified in the nephews' struggle for freedom against Donald, and Barks's satire of war propaganda and military discipline."[28] Barks's playful sensibilities belied certain deeply held values that undergirded the comics, though he did not fit clearly into a single category. While his work embodied certain frontier ideals, it was more complicated than simple politics. He created dichotomies between the pastoral ideals of rural life and the rush of urban life but often underlined the faults of both.[29] His conclusions more often indicated that people were alike all over, that small-town folks and primitive tribes could be just as greedy as big-city capitalists, though with a marked preference for the simple life.[30] The excursions in Barks's stories often visited premodern spaces, be they lost South American tribes or old ghost towns, but even these spaces were grounded in realism. Inhabitants of these spaces were no more noble or honest than the city dwellers, reflecting a certain idea of commonality in human experience.

"The Sheriff of Bullet Valley" (*Four Color* #199) finds Donald Duck taking up the job of sheriff's deputy in a rural town, playing upon the tropes of the western. Donald's adventures in the story are entirely informed by his awareness of the rules and narratives of western films, which naturally drives much of the story's plot. It is self-aware of the tropes of the western genre, and that those tropes no longer exist within modernity. Barks opens with "gone now are the outlaws, the stage robbers, the cow thieves! Gone, too, the grim-lipped sheriffs that hunted them down! All that remains of the Old Wild West is its legends!"[31] Barks takes the opportunity to poke fun at the silliness of many of the pop-cultural expectations of frontier life, but it is infused with some sense of loss. Much of the plot is driven by Donald's assumption that the western films of which he is fond are true to life. Donald's genre savviness is dangerous, as in an early scene when he is tricked out of his horse by the local cattle rustlers (who burn their brand into the animal while he is distracted), and he assumes that the sheriff is the actual villain, thinking, "Maybe he wanted me to get killed! I begin to smell a plot! There was a mix-up like this in the picture 'Fagin's Fangs'! Horace Mustang jailed hundreds of innocent men before he discovered the leader of the rustlers was his kindly old grandmother!"[32] Donald views the events of the story through the lens of genre, assuming that the West resembles his steady diet of cowboy movies. In a later instance, he arrests an innocent rancher after he surmises (incorrectly) a dastardly plot. Donald explains, "Old Diamond has 300 thin steers in the pasture! He hides 'em in a canyon then steals 300 fat steers from the Double X to put in their place . . . clever old guy! But I saw the same trick in the picture 'Shuddering Saddles'!"[33] His popular-culture knowledge overrides common sense, which is coupled with his overwhelming stubbornness, creating most of the conflict in the story. Even during the final confrontation with the villainous Blacksnake, Donald laments "all I have to do is put my guns on him and take him in! This is so easy it's not even fun!"[34] This leads directly to a moment when Donald drops his guard, when Blacksnake claims, "Nobody but a coward would do a trick like that! Put your guns back in their holsters and draw even—like a brave man should!"[35] Once more, Donald's awareness of genre conventions is nearly the death of him, as he responds, "I'm no coward! Rimfire Remington always does this in his pictures!"[36] Donald is of course immediately shot several times by the villain.

Barks's West is a dangerous space, and one that does not play by the rules of the western as a genre. Donald's inability to see Bullet Valley as anything other than a western causes no end of difficulty to the innocents in the story and draws out the conflict much longer than it likely would have taken. Thomas Andrae argues, "Barks's story is not just an elegiac tale about the passing of the West but a moral fable that concerns the redemption of frontier values in the modern era . . . the way in which Western films inculcate a confusion between myth and reality becomes a central premise of the story."[37] Donald's ultimate triumph in the story is the result of his stubbornness and dumb luck, while the functionality of the tropes of the western are questioned in the modern setting.

Donald's success occurs when he finally breaks from the western cinema that informs much of his behavior in the story; as Donald states, finally capturing Blacksnake, that "it's not the way Rimfire Remington would do it, but it's way more fun!"[38] Donald Duck becomes a tool to interrogate the myths of the West; after all, Barks had known real cowboys, had grown up on the frontier, and recognized too well the gulf between the shining history and the muddy reality. Geoffrey Blum states that "something of a frontiersman himself, Barks was concerned with the fate of old-timers who had helped build [frontier towns]."[39] Donald's many failed efforts to capture the criminal underscore the limits of the frontier ideal that had taken hold in the postwar era but echo also the loss of the true frontier in favor of a facsimile that little resembles the rough and dangerous life lived on the fringes of civilization. Donald Duck in "Bullet Valley" is presented as a tourist, a day-tripper without any reckoning of the reality of frontier life, to the degree that he disrupts the investigation into the cattle rustlers. He is not equipped to survive in that space and would likely have died on multiple occasions were it not for his oversized sheriff's badge and the intervention of his nephews (who prove slightly more genre savvy, perhaps better able to recognize the inaccuracies portrayed in western cinema). Donald is perhaps indicative of others who pine for a West that never truly was; Barks knew the dangers and difficulties of frontier life and was keenly aware that the people who wished for a return to frontier values likely had no idea of what life on the frontier fully entailed.

SCROOGE McDUCK THE FRONTIERSMAN

Scrooge McDuck might be Barks's most vibrant and well-realized creation. An unrepentant capitalist, he embodies more than just unrestrained greed, reflecting the spirit of American competitiveness in all endeavors. An unrepentant capitalist in the mold of the nineteenth-century robber barons, to the degree that fellow Scotsman Andrew Carnegie likely served as an inspiration (it is no accident that one of Scrooge's rivals is named John Rockerduck, certainly a reference to Carnegie's rival John Rockefeller), though with slightly more humanity than other depictions of the archetype. Scrooge is the very embodiment of the traits that Turner outlined decades earlier: "coarseness and strength combined with acuteness and inquisitiveness . . . that masterful grasp of material things, lacking in the artistic but powerful to effect great ends; that restless, nervous energy; that dominant individualism . . . these are the traits of the frontier."[40] Scrooge further encompasses the bootstraps myth, infused with the image of the lone hero on the frontier, and the immigrant who arrives in America only to travel ever westward, though the chronology is a bit skewed; Barks was never concerned with keeping details straight from story to story and scattered details of Scrooge's backstory across dozens of different issues, usually as a setup for the narrative. Details emerged over time: Scrooge as a prospector, as a rancher, as an explorer; Barks's only full-length story set in Scrooge's youth (detailing his time as a riverboat captain on the Mississippi) was featured in a special digest "Uncle Scrooge Goes to Disneyland" in 1957.

These moments were restricted to snatches of dialogue or the occasional splash panel, but a common thread was his role as a frontiersman. The younger Scrooge never tarried in a city for long, instead seeking out wide-open spaces that promised untold riches to the brave and hardy. The stories allowed for Barks to wax poetic about the lost frontier as well. Barks remarked of his story "Back to the Yukon": "Nostalgia about the gold rush country and the old dance-hall girls had a lot to do with my thinking on that story. There were still some dance-hall girls alive and around and they'd get a write-up in the paper once in a while. I had tried to make Goldie a believable person because I thought that people were interested in what became of these girls."[41] Barks recalled the West-that-was and sought to bring life to that reality, honoring those who had lived it. Goldie in "Back to the Yukon" is long past her glory days, living out of a battered shack in the wilderness, carrying on the best she can. While the story sees her better off thanks to the uncommonly generous actions of Scrooge, the story nevertheless reckons with the remnants of the Old West: broken dreams and broken bodies, the promise of the frontier long closed.

While Scrooge's fortune has several origin stories, the most resilient is the acquisition of the wealth during the Alaskan gold rush. Scrooge's success is the result of supreme effort, achieved only by himself, wealth physically produced from the land itself by hard labor. He seeks out a claim deep in the hinterlands, braving hostile weather and menacing loan sharks, producing a fortune from Klondike gold. Scrooge's success reflects a certain frontier ideal of individualism, allowing Scrooge to remain clean of the more negative aspects of nineteenth-century wealth acquisition (he is no robber baron, after all). It avoids the sticky problems of the exploitation of labor (though that accusation would be lobbied against him for his treatment of family members, notably in Dorfman and Mattelart's *How to Read Donald Duck*), as well as any deeper interrogation of the capitalist system.[42] Andrae argues that "[Barks] narrates his stories as if they are real events yet simultaneously deconstructs the premises on which they are based . . . the contradictions made apparent by these stories invite us to critically examine rather than passively consume the popular formulas, myths, and stereotypes he portrays."[43] Scrooge had achieved his wealth by being "tougher than the toughies and smarter than the smarties," offering a simplistic worldview that replicated the same myths of the American West that had been propagated for decades, albeit with a little more grit and mud. Blum elaborates that "the combination of rugged heroism, ragged lawlessness, and instant riches appeals to our national imagination . . . for those who came after, it became the portrait of a nation: noble at times, ugly at others, but undoubtedly America."[44] Scrooge becomes emblematic of the transformation of America's frontier into something else, a process that would be more fully explored in the stories of Don Rosa.

The work of Carl Barks was largely bereft of any continuity, though that was hardly uncommon for other comic books of the era. The status quo remained inviolable: even though Donald ended "The Sheriff of Bullet Valley" as the town's new sheriff, it was never remarked upon or referenced again, and Scrooge's incredible wealth always found its way back to his money bin even if it had been sunk to the bottom of a lake. The characters and their personalities were generally consistent (Scrooge softened a bit as the years wore on, a bit less world-weary with age), but there were no attempts to tell larger stories by the time of Barks's retirement in 1966. The series went into decline, overshadowed by Silver Age superheroes that began to increasingly deal with real-world issues as the Bronze Age dawned, and while sparse reprints continued, it was not until the 1980s that new content began to be created once more.[45] The most enduring of the new generation of artists was a middle-aged engineer, Don Rosa, who had grown up as a fan of the Barks stories and found a niche as the successor to Barks's legacy.

DON ROSA THE REVISIONIST

Don Rosa differs from Barks in experience and background. Rosa was born into a relatively wealthy family of builders and educated at the University of Kentucky; his drawing was nevertheless self-taught, as with Barks, whom he had idolized in his youth. The majority of Rosa's writing constituted sequels to or reimaginings of Barks's stories, involving return trips to exotic locales and efforts to solidify the world that Barks had created. In particular, Scrooge's time on the frontier is a major focus of Rosa's work, be it the Old West or the Klondike. Rosa explains his methodology: "I constructed a list of every 'fact' about Scrooge's youth that was ever revealed in a Barks tale, no matter how minute or obscurely buried the morsel of history may have been. Next, I assembled these 'facts' into a timeline, mixing in actual historical events and people to give it an authentic feel."[46] Rosa's West, as an extension of Barks's, is not a wild space of high-noon showdowns and bank robberies, but rather the birthplace of modern capitalism. It is no accident that Scrooge, an idealized symbol of the promise of twentieth-century capitalism, makes his fortune there and finds his identity. Rosa's reinterpretation of the character's history serves to reconstruct the West that was: Scrooge is present at a great many major historical moments, though nevertheless on the fringe, never entering the grand stage of history. These stories mixed so-called Barksian Facts with real historical research to create a fuller picture of the life Scrooge had lived. Rosa takes the moments laid out by Barks to their logical conclusion, while emphasizing the gritty realities of frontier life. These stories deconstructed the mythology of the West, locating the real-life individuals and portraying the events as they would have happened (albeit with a comical touch).

"The King of the Klondike" includes encounters with several historical figures but more distinctly features mud. Rosa's West (in this case, Skagway, Alaska; and Dawson City, Yukon Territory) is covered in mud, with the first two pages including Scrooge's efforts to navigate half a mile of mudflats to reach the shore.[47] In this moment Scrooge encounters dime-novel hero Wyatt Earp, who introduces himself threateningly with "Don't you recognize my famous buntline special?"[48] Earp proves to be a violent, egotistical brute, engaging in a barroom brawl, challenging a would-be gunslinger: "It's me you want! The Wyatt Earp! Brave, courageous, and bold—the whole bit . . . I demand you shoot me!"[49] Rosa makes fun of the idea of the western hero, casting Earp as a petty, violent brute, offering a tarnishing image of the white-hat cowboy. Later in the story, the villainous Dawson City crimelord Soapy Slick is introduced as a stand in for the real-life Skagway politician/criminal Jefferson Randolph "Soapy" Smith, engaging in the same underhanded behavior of which Smith was often accused; here, Soapy is a loan shark and gambling kingpin who engages in claim jumping, similar to the historical Soapy.[50] Soapy is the primary antagonist of Scrooge, though the difficulty of the environment (the mud and the cold) proves more of a hindrance to Scrooge's efforts. In Rosa's reckoning of the West, there are few "good" individuals, with nearly every character in the story proving either outright malicious or simply ineffectual (as with the Mounties that appear near the conclusion of the story).[51] Rosa laments, "I had to include Skagway in this tale; after all, another disappointing truth is that it was the American Skagway that was actually the lawless, crime-ridden murder capital of North America, not the peaceful Canadian town of Dawson City where the Northwest Mounted Police kept law and order. But that's America for you."[52] The reality of Klondike gets in the way of the storytelling to some extent, but the message of Rosa echoes that of Barks: that the frontier is dangerous, unfriendly, and consistently covered in mud.

Rosa's stories in general try to stick as close as they can to the facts and real-life figures that inhabited the wilderness: many historical figures, both well-known and obscure, turn up throughout his adventures there, ranging from Teddy Roosevelt and Wild Bill Hickok to Murdo MacKenzie and Sam Steele. The American frontier keeps drawing Scrooge back: though he initially adventures as a riverboat captain, circumstances cause him to take up a job as a cowboy, and soon after as a prospector. Rosa uses these experiences to weave his story; at the start of "Raider of the Copper Hill" (*U$* 288), Scrooge laments, "Bad timing is my life story! I bought a riverboat right before the railroads put 'em out of business! Then I got into cattle, but there's no future there, either!"[53] This West is not a land of endless opportunity but one of broken dreams. Success is achieved more through luck and timing than grit and determination. Rosa explains the story: "I have woven my tale around the founding of the famous (real-life) Anaconda Copper Mine . . . this was a beautiful situation in which to place the young and callow Scrooge, and then teach him he won't be able to retain success until he wins it wholly of his own hard work!"[54] Scrooge achieves success more through legal chicanery and the assistance of a wealthy benefactor than through hard work, and his success is short-lived. Rosa uses the story to question the myth of the self-made man, though Scrooge will eventually embody that particular trope.

Scrooge's excursions take him across the world in search of gold, participating in several major gold rushes yet invariably returning to the United States, first to Arizona, and later to the Klondike. Rosa further grounds the stories within historical reality by weaving the Barks stories into actual history, introducing historic figures to enhance the connections to the past. Rosa's work, particularly the epic *Life and Times of Scrooge McDuck*, was couched in authenticity, just as Barks's was, while also remaining true to the classic canon. Rosa remarked, "The sense of authentic history that is one of the most salient aspects of Barks' great adventure sagas—perhaps that's the one thing that makes me, like many others, find Scrooge to be a more fascinating character than Donald, who seems to live only in the present."[55] Rosa builds upon this history in his stories, expands upon the themes and tone of Barks by delving deeper into Scrooge's time on the frontier. The period is portrayed in loving detail, deeply researched, and Rosa took pains to portray life on the frontier accurately. Scrooge works menial jobs, barely scraping by (and even then, occasionally relying on assistance from allies and loan sharks), his fated fortune seemingly forever out of reach. He becomes a hardened frontier spirit over time, his youthful optimism sharpening into a distrust of the world. This transformation embodies the landscape, the loss of the independence allowed by the frontier playing out within the character of Scrooge.

The frontier seems to be ever fading into the distance through *The Life and Times of Scrooge McDuck*. Scrooge is always lighting out for the territories in the fashion of Huckleberry Finn, one step ahead of the sprawl of civilization. He departs the Mississippi River for the Dakotas and Montana, from there stopping in Arizona. The story in Arizona, "The Vigilante of Pizen Bluff," reads the closest to a traditional western, with Scrooge facing off against the Dalton gang, with the assistance of Buffalo Bill and elements of his Wild West Show. The story subverts the myths of the Wild West, when at one point Buffalo Bill explains, "But if we don't have an exciting climax to this chase, P.T.'s publicity scheme will be worthless!"[56] Buffalo Bill and Scrooge's uncle Pothole proceed to imagine half a page's worth of pulp heroics, including Bill claiming, "I pin two more to the wall with Bowie Knives," while Pothole "busts a table across a row of Daltons."[57] These statements directly parody the silliness of many classic western tropes, but there is an underlying sense of seriousness to the story as a whole. Buffalo Bill's concluding monologue intones, "Our glory days are quickly coming to an end! The great Indian tribes are all on reservations and we frontiersman are in silly Wild West shows! This year's census shows that the frontier has now disappeared . . . we're officially relics of a bygone age!"[58] This is Rosa at his most metatextual, echoing bluntly Turner's frontier thesis.[59]

Rosa's stories are more direct in their portrayal of life in the Old West. The brief snippets of Barks were woven into full-length stories, borrowing elements of reality to create a more complete portrait of the historical moment; Rosa notes, "As always, I've mixed much accuracy into this biography to give it a feel of authenticity."[60] Every major character that is not a Barks creation is a historical figure. Barks himself made use of a few real-world figures in his stories; for instance, "Soapy" Slick appears as an antagonist in a single Barks story but is featured as a major villain in Rosa's work. Comics scholar Geoffrey Blum explains that "where Barks dabbled and borrowed, Rosa researches his stories in painstaking detail, drawing maps . . . when Barks deftly but cavalierly combined features of two cities, Rosa goes out of his way to apologize for the inaccuracy . . . [Rosa] has sought to flesh out Scrooge's myth and tidy inconsistencies in the timeline."[61] Barks's world-building reflected his own experiences and interactions, which Rosa in turn enhanced, bringing it closer to the reality, explaining, "The setting and events are as authentic as possible. I also tried to tell a bit more than some readers may know (or want to know) about Klondike gold prospecting."[62] In Rosa's version, the West was dustier, muddier, and lonelier. The wide-open spaces were even more vibrant, yet also more lonesome. Rosa's Scrooge suffers loneliness in his efforts to pull wealth from the land; in Barks's version, he is always joined by his nephews or other relations, but in *The Life and Times*, he is most often on his own or interacting with some stranger who will depart on some other path at the end of the story. While this plays upon certain larger myths of the Old West ("riding off into the sunset" may be the best-known trope produced by a western), it captures a certain truth. The glory achieved by Scrooge is through blood, sweat, and tears; when he returns to Dawson City after striking gold, he is exhausted, dirtied, and virtually unrecognizable, echoing many of the lonesome images of cowboys in Goetzmann's *West of the Imagination*.[63] There is little glee in his triumph. Neither does life become particularly easier as the stories progress;

the frontier is not a space that can be tamed, as such efforts simply result in its disappearance.

The portrayal of the Old West in the Scrooge McDuck comics of Carl Barks and Don Rosa stands apart from contemporary images of that space. The western craze that consumed film, television, and comics was avoided on the pages of Barks, with Rosa further deconstructing the idealized West that persisted in the American imagination. Here, frontier life is almost entirely bereft of glamour, the streets are paved with mud and wooden planks, hard work rarely pays off (and when it does, Scrooge is too exhausted to really enjoy it). The sense of loss is palpable, that the frontier is very quickly closing, and even Alaska is falling to the forces of civilization by the end of Scrooge's time there. Barks knew the frontier from his youth and worked it into the history of Scrooge, capturing small moments and details of the reality, subtly echoing his own experiences. Rosa seeks the historical truth, locating historic figures present at major crossroads (or at least that could have been plausibly present) and using them to signify the changes that were occurring, occasionally quite directly commenting on the close of the frontier. The motivations of the two writers are similar; both endeavor to capture a sense of reality and correct the myths of the West while still playing in that space. Barks writes an elegy for the frontier he missed by accident of birth, while Rosa constructs a masterwork of scholarship and fandom that serves as a towering monument to the work of Barks. The frontier is idealized within these stories, just as it is in the American mind, but both authors locate the pieces of truth buried deep within those myths and illustrate the way things were.

NOTES

1. Bruce Kuklick's "Myth and Symbol in American Studies" expands on the work of Henry Nash Smith and Leo Marx, arguing that the scholar should endeavor to understand how certain concepts were viewed in order to better contextualize their place within American history, with an eye toward the individual and beyond the view of the intellectual. William Goetzmann's *West of the Imagination* focuses on the imagery of the Old West, particularly the traditional paintings that helped to solidify the American "understanding" of what the West was. Both emphasize the use of images in the creation of cultural memories about history, relevant here in interpreting the versions put forward by Barks and Rosa.

2. Richard Slotkin states that "for most Americans—to the perpetual dismay of westerners—the West became a landscape known through, and completely identified with, the fictions created about it. Indeed, once that mythic space was well established in the various genres of mass culture, the fictive or mythic West became the scene in which new acts of mythogenesis could occur—in effect displacing both the real contemporary region and historical Frontier as factors in shaping the on-going discourse of cultural history." Richard Slotkin, *Gunfighter Nation* (Norman: University of Oklahoma Press, 1998), 61–62.

3. Bradford Wright, *Comic Book Nation* (Baltimore: Johns Hopkins University Press, 2001), 155.

4. Tom Engelhardt, *The End of Victory Culture* (Amherst: University of Massachusetts Press, 2007), 34.

5. William Savage, *Commies, Cowboys, and Jungle Queens: Comic Books and America, 1945–1954* (Hanover, NH: Wesleyan University Press, 1990), 67.

6. Savage, *Commies, Cowboys*, 69.

7. William M. Breakenridge, *Helldorado: Bringing Law to the Mesquite* (Lincoln: University of Nebraska Press, 1992); John Ford, dir., *Stagecoach* (1939; Beverly Hills: United Artists, 2010).

8. Andrew Lendacky, "The Carl Barks Stories and Racial and Cultural Stereotyping," *Barks Collector*, no. 16 [1980], 8.

9. Chris York, discussing the role of Native Americans in western comics, notes that "it has been long established that the reduction of cultures into one-dimensional caricatures makes their dismissal both ideologically and physically a much easier task for the dominant culture." Chris York, "Beyond the Frontier: *Turok, Son of Stone* and the Native American in Cold War America," in *Comic Books and the Cold War, 1946–1962: Essays on Graphic Treatment of Communism, the Code, and Social Concerns* ed. Chris and Rafiel York (Jefferson, NC: McFarland, 2014), 179.

10. Lendacky, "Carl Barks Stories," 9–10.

11. Frederick Jackson Turner, *The Frontier in American History* (Malabar, FL: Robert E. Kreiger, 1985), 1.

12. Lynn Harter, "Masculinity(s), the Agrarian Frontier Myth, and Cooperative Ways of Organizing," *Journal of Applied Communication Research* 32 (2004): 91.

13. Mark Twain, *The Adventures of Huckleberry Finn* (New York: Dover, 1994), 222.

14. John Wills, *Disney Culture* (New Brunswick, NJ: Rutgers University Press, 2017), 63.

15. Other authors, notably Ariel Dorfman and Armand Mattelart, would more closely link Donald Duck and American imperialism, specifically in a South American context. Their work emphasizes the translation and propagandistic aspects of the Disney output, though it lies outside the scope of this chapter. Ariel Dorfman and Armand Mattelart, *How to Read Donald Duck: Imperialist Ideology in the Disney Comic Book* (New York: International General, 1991).

16. Turner, *Frontier in American History*, 30.

17. Harter, "Masculinity(s), the Agrarian Frontier Myth," 93.

18. Slotkin, *Gunfighter Nation*, 34–35.

19. David Nye, *America as Second Creation* (Cambridge: MIT Press, 2003), 46.

20. Malcolm Willits, Don Thompson, and Maggie Thompson, "The Duck Man," *Duckburg Times*, no. 10/11 (March 27, 1981): 3–4.

21. Donald Ault, *Carl Barks: Conversations* (Jackson: University Press of Mississippi, 2003), 55.

22. Ault, *Carl Barks*, 104.

23. Ault, *Carl Barks*, 56.

24. Willits et al., "Duck Man," 12.

25. Barks's parents were both born a few years before the outbreak of the Civil War in Missouri, with his father heading to California on the back of a freight train in the 1880s, before arriving in Oregon to take advantage of the Homestead Act.

26. Amy Singer's examination of the portrayal of economic inequality in *Little House on the Prairie* echoes the discussions of Barks here and perhaps finds common ground with the two texts. Amy Singer, "Little Girls on the Prairie and the Possibility of Subversive Reading," *Girlhood Studies* 8, no. 2 (Summer 2015): 4–20.

27. Thomas Andrae, *Carl Barks and the Disney Comic Book* (Jackson: University Press of Mississippi, 2006), 31.

28. Andrae, *Carl Barks and the Disney Comic Book*, 31–32.

29. John Wills explains the rise of Disney's emphasis on the natural world: "The rise of Disnature is important as it corresponds to the fall of real nature in our lives. Tied to the demographic shift away from farms and toward the metropolis, the demise of daily interaction with the 'great outdoors' left an experiential void in the twentieth century." Wills, *Disney Culture*, 114. This process plays out in Barks's work as well as in more mainstream Disney fare, though it tends to reflect the philosophy of Carl Barks more than that of Walt Disney.

30. This was a common theme among Barks stories; Peter Schilling Jr. remarks of the Donald Duck story "Lost in the Andes" that "Donald represents that heroic dream—that some happy accident will come along when we least expect it, and send us on a journey. Donald has no illusions that he's [. . .] going to make any money . . . he presses forward for the thrill of adventure." Peter Schilling Jr., *Carl Barks' Duck: Average American* (Minneapolis: Uncivilized Books, 2014).

31. Barks, "The Sheriff of Bullet Valley," *Four Color* #199, 3.

32. Barks, "Sheriff of Bullet Valley," 8.

33. Barks, "Sheriff of Bullet Valley," 13.

34. Barks, "Sheriff of Bullet Valley," 29.

35. Barks, "Sheriff of Bullet Valley," 29.

36. Barks, "Sheriff of Bullet Valley," 29.

37. Andrae, *Carl Barks and the Disney Comic Book*, 80–81.

38. Barks, "Sheriff of Bullet Valley," 33.

39. Geoffrey Blum, "Dawson: Imagination's Doorway," *Walt Disney Giant* #1 (September 1995), 29.

40. Turner, *Frontier in American History*, 37.

41. Carl Barks, *Uncle Scrooge McDuck* (Berkeley, CA: Celestial Arts, 1987), 64.

42. Dorfman and Mattelart, *How to Read Donald Duck*, 70–71.

43. Andrae, *Carl Barks and the Disney Comic Book*, 78.

44. Blum, "Dawson," 26.

45. According to figures available through ComicChron, in 1960, the Duck comics published by Dell had sales figures averaging just over two million copies a month across two titles (*Uncle $crooge* and *Walt Disney Comics and Stories*). By 1969, it had declined to 272,000 per month for *Walt Disney Comics and Stories* (data for *Uncle $crooge* are unavailable for that year). "Comic Sales Figures for 1960," *ComicChron*, accessed August 25, 2018, http://comichron.com/yearlycomicssales/postaldata/1960.html.

46. Rosa, *Life and Times*, 70.

47. Don Rosa, "The King of the Klondike," *Uncle $crooge* #292, 1–2.

48. Rosa, "King of the Klondike," 2.

49. Rosa, "King of the Klondike," 3.

50. Rosa, "King of the Klondike," 4–5.

51. Rosa, "King of the Klondike," 22.

52. Rosa, "King of the Klondike," 25.

53. Rosa, *Life and Times*, 68.

54. Rosa, *Life and Times*, 81.

55. Rosa, *Life and Times*, 155.

56. Don Rosa, "The Vigilante of Pizen Bluff," *U$* #306, 15.

57. Rosa, "Vigilante of Pizen Bluff," 16.

58. Rosa, "Vigilante of Pizen Bluff," 21.

59. This echoes Slotkin as well, who writes "in Cody's farewell tours, that nostalgia for the 'Old West' that had been the basis for his first success gave way to a new form of sentiment: a nostalgia not for the reality but for the myth—not of the frontier itself, but for the lost glamour of Buffalo Bill's Wild West." Slotkin, 87.

60. Rosa, *Life and Times*, 70.

61. Blum, "Dawson," 28.

62. Rosa, *Life and Times*, 132.

63. William Goetzmann, *West of the Imagination* (W. W. Norton, 1986).

WORKS CITED

Andrae, Thomas. *Carl Barks and the Disney Comic Book: Unmasking the Myth of Modernity*. Jackson: University Press of Mississippi, 2006.

Ault, Donald, ed. *Carl Barks: Conversations*. Jackson: University Press of Mississippi, 2003.

Barks, Carl. "The Sheriff of Bullet Valley." *Donald Duck* #199, October 1948.

Barks, Carl. *Uncle Scrooge McDuck: His Life and Times*. Celestial Arts, 1987.

Blum, Geoffrey. "Dawson: Imagination's Doorway." In *Walt Disney Giant No. 1*, September 1995, 26–29.

Dorfman, Ariel, and Armand Mattelart. *How to Read Donald Duck: Imperialist Ideology in the Disney Comic Book*. New York: International General, 1991.

Engelhardt, Tom. *The End of Victory Culture: Cold War America and the Disillusioning of a Generation*. Amherst: University of Massachusetts Press, 2007.

Goetzmann, William. *West of the Imagination*. New York: W. W. Norton, 1986.

Harter, Lynn. "Masculinity(s), the Agrarian Frontier Myth, and Cooperative Ways of Organizing: Contradictions and Tensions in the Experience and the Enactment of Democracy." *Journal of Applied Communication Research* 32, no. 2 (2004): 31–53.

Horn, Maurice. *Comics of the American West*. Winchester, VA: Winchester Press, 1977.

Lendacky, Andrew. "The Carl Barks Stories and Racial and Cultural Stereotyping." *Barks Collector* no. 16 [1980], 6–22.

Kuklick, Bruce. "Myth and Symbol in American Studies." *American Quarterly* 24, no. 4 (1972): 435–50.

Nye, David. *America as Second Creation: Technology Narratives and New Beginnings*. Cambridge: MIT Press, 2003.

Rosa, Don. "The King of the Klondike." Uncle $crooge #292, June 1995.

Rosa, Don. *The Life and Times of Scrooge McDuck*. Timonium, MD: Gemstone, 2005.

Rosa, Don. "The Vigilante of Pizen Bluff." *Uncle Scrooge* #306, October 1996.

Savage, William. *Commies, Cowboys, and Jungle Queens: Comic Books and America, 1945–1954*. Hanover, NH: Wesleyan University Press, 1990.

Schilling, Peter, Jr. *Carl Barks' Duck: Average American*. Minneapolis: Uncivilized Books, 2014.

Singer, Amy. "Little Girls on the Prairie and the Possibility of Subversive Reading." *Girlhood Studies* 8, no. 2 (Summer 2015): 4–20.

Slotkin, Richard. *Gunfighter Nation: The Myth of the Frontier in Twentieth-Century America.* Norman: University of Oklahoma Press, 1998.

Turner, Fredrick Jackson. *The Frontier in American History.* Malabar, FL: Robert E. Kreiger, 1985.

Twain, Mark. *The Adventures of Huckleberry Finn.* New York: Dover, 1994.

Willits, Malcolm, Don Thompson, and Maggie Thompson. "The Duck Man." *Duckburg Times,* no. 10/11, March 27, 1981.

Wills, John. *Disney Culture.* New Brunswick, NJ: Rutgers University Press, 2017.

Wright, Bradford. *Comic Book Nation: The Transformation of Youth Culture in America.* Baltimore: Johns Hopkins University Press, 2001.

York, Chris. "Beyond the Frontier: *Turok, Son of Stone* and the Native American in Cold War America." In *Comic Books and the Cold War,* ed. Chris York and Rafiel York, 179–90. Jefferson, NC: McFarland, 2014.

HISTORICAL TRAUMA

CHAPTER FIVE

VICTOR CHARLES AND MARVIN THE ARVN

Vietnamese as Enemy and Ally in American War Comic Books

STEPHEN CONNOR

Wading waist-deep through a Vietnamese swamp, desperately fending off yet another ambush and unable to distinguish enemy from ally, a frustrated and battle-fatigued Lt. James Kramer lamented, "Why couldn't I fight in a nice, simple war?"[1] Lieutenant Kramer, of course, never fought in the jungles of Vietnam but rather across the pages of Charlton Comics' *Army War Heroes*. His story, "This Crummy War," published in October 1968, serves as a useful starting point to consider the intersection of the Vietnam War, comic books, popular culture, and history. To that end, this chapter considers the telling and retelling of American intervention in the pages of war comic books and asks: In what ways did war comics construct the Vietnamese as enemy and as ally?[2]

Despite the distinction as America's longest war in the twentieth century, the American intervention in Vietnam received comparatively little attention in war comic books.[3] Even less consideration was given to the war's central actors, the Vietnamese themselves. Much like the vast historiography of the war in Southeast Asia, until very recently war comics presented the conflict without the Vietnamese.[4] Those who did appear were overwhelmingly bit-part extras. Almost universally their depiction and significance had little to do with the overall narrative. This is not entirely surprising; the protagonists of war comics, like the readership, were American. Rather, the Vietnamese served other needs, initially as confirmation of Washington's official telling of the war and, after 1975, as part of a wider sense-making and retelling.[5] To locate the Vietnamese in American war comics, this chapter focuses on depictions of two of these constituencies: enemy and ally in the intervention and postwar eras. We begin, however, with a consideration of what "Vietnamese" meant in the pages of war comic books.

TELLING THE WAR: WARTIME REPRESENTATIONS OF THE VIETNAMESE

As others have noted, war comic books set in the Second World War and particularly in the Pacific theater presented an enemy based on familiar, long-held racialized tropes.[6] Indeed, for historian John Dower, such representations of the bestial Asiatic "Other" not only dehumanized the enemy but also contributed to the overwhelming racial violence in the Pacific. These visions, he contended, fit snugly into long-standing American fears and representations of the "Orient" and the "Yellow Peril."[7] However, even as such enduring images remained usable and, as we shall see, central to depictions into the 1960s, the complicated and contradictory realities of American intervention in Vietnam, in effect a civil war, presented comic book creators with a fundamental problem. In short, war comics needed to present differing versions of the Vietnamese, who, it was understood, shared identical "racial" features yet fundamentally different ideologies and possibilities.[8] The challenge of representing friend/foe, both of whom occupied the same landscape, was further compounded by creators' and audiences' profound and enduring unfamiliarity with the historical, cultural, and even geographic realties of Vietnam. Particularly in the early 1960s, few Americans clearly understood who exactly the enemy was, what they wanted, or what they even looked like.[9] Indeed, the answer to two of the three questions was the same: the "bad guys" were Vietnamese, and they looked Vietnamese, as did the "good guys."

Of course, the need to distinguish antagonist from protagonist within a perceived homogeneous ethnicity was not particularly new to war comics. In previous cases, however, conventional war shaped the setting of the story and contributed tidy divisions to clearly differentiate ally from enemy. The unconventional nature of the war in Vietnam, however, makes such neat separations far less applicable. Consequently, while creators could rely to a certain extent on traditional, dehumanizing representations to signify the enemy, the "friendly" status of both South Vietnamese allies and the general population required altering and sometimes downplaying traditional characterizations, an effort that often proved incomplete and unsatisfactory. Representing the conflict in intervention era war comics presented creators with a profound problem. How, in a medium long reliant on racialized prompts to present the "Oriental" as Other, and even more recently as subhuman, could some Vietnamese be established as enemy and others as ally?

"A SCORPION IN A HAYSTACK": THE VIETNAMESE AS ENEMY

In war comics published during and immediately after the American war in Vietnam, stories largely featured familiar imagery, stereotypes, and scenarios that focused on the importance of the intervention rather than the unique nature of the war.[10] Initially creators faced the challenge of addressing and representing the war's "setting," what historians have called the village war, and the nature of the conflict as a counterinsurgency. In short, unlike World War II and Korea, Vietnam was a war without fronts, a conflict not just against an enemy but for a population. For writers and artists comfortable and familiar with characterizations of the "Oriental" Other, the creative toolbox to render this proved limited. Even more challenging was the reality that creators could not rely solely on tried and tested rhetorical, narrative, and visual techniques that had shaped depictions of the enemy during the most recent conflicts, World War II and the Korean War. In the intervention era, enemy status could not be conferred by simply "re-skinning" the racialized, "Oriental" adversary prominent in earlier war comics.[11] Quite simply, neither the Japanese nor the Chinese enemy could readily be recast as Vietnamese. On the one hand, both during the war and after, many Americans lamented the impossibility of distinguishing "good" Vietnamese from "bad."[12] Yet, on the other hand, all Vietnamese were certainly not alike. Indeed, unlike representations of the Japanese or Chinese, in Vietnam stories how the enemy looked was insufficient to establish enemy status, as images alone left little to distinguish friend from foe.[13] To resolve this identity crisis and confer adversarial status on some Vietnamese, representations moved beyond solely physical caricature to engage and portray the alien nature of communism as the foundation of enemy identity. To do so creators depicted enemies whose word and deeds were as diabolical as their ideology. By presenting a range of specific visual and dialogue cues, creators established enemy "otherness," why some Vietnamese were the enemy and others allies within a perceived homogeneous ethnicity.

Until the publication of Marvel's *The Nam* in the late 1980s, Charlton's *Fightin' Marines* produced the longest run of Vietnam stories in American war comics and is perhaps most representative of the challenges creators faced in depicting the Vietnamese enemy during the Silver Age.[14] While one-off stories did occasionally feature in the anthology book, the serial exploits of cigar-chomping Sgt. "Shotgun" Harker and his cowardly, effeminate sidekick, Private "Chicken" Smith, provide the best examples.[15] In "Village of Fear," set in the imagined "safe" village of Dinh Nat, Shotgun and Chicken hunt for souvenirs "for the tourist trade in Saigon."[16] Over the course of their search, Viet Cong insurgents emerge from the shadows to ambush them twice, capturing Chicken Smith. Ultimately, several shootouts and fistfights later, the Marines not only defeat the skulking insurgents but also befriend the terrorized village headman, Ki Lingh, liberate his village, and, as he put it "relieved [his] people of a terrible threat." Two issues later, in "The Deadly Shadows," Shotgun and Chicken patrol yet another village, this time in the Mekong Delta. Unsurprisingly, given the nature of the enemy, and reinforced by the feature's title, the area is far from safe, despite the assurances of the Vietnamese Army and local population that "only loyal to Saigon villagers left."[17] The villagers are, in fact disguised insurgents, plotting to murder the marines in their sleep. Predictably, after a series of firefights and fisticuffs, the Americans triumph and once again liberate the villagers.

In these two stories of Shotgun Harker and Chicken Smith, and indeed the majority of intervention era comic books, depictions of the Vietnamese enemy largely lacked the anthropomorphized and outsized features common in the World War II era.[18] While some caricature lingered, such depictions were usually reserved for villainous leaders rather than anonymous Viet Cong foot soldiers.[19] Indeed, as physical representation alone was insufficient to distinguish friend from foe, creators relied on dialogue and behavior to demonstrate what the enemy thought—indeed, why they were the enemy. The result was a "Red Enemy in Vietnam," cruel and cunning, a hybrid of two stereotypes: Oriental and Communist.[20]

While "elusive as a smoke wisp" and "dangerous as a scorpion in a haystack," behavior established the bulk of the Vietnamese enemy as automatons without agency, and capable of following only the simplest directions.[21] Dubbed at best "V.C." and "Charlie" and, at worst, "slope-head," most Vietnamese enemies served only as props to be punched, kicked, stabbed, choked, and shot.[22] American interaction was largely reduced to combat, often hand-to-hand, against a nebulous collection of yellow faces clad in black pajamas who sprang from the shadows in a jungle or village, menacing combatant and civilian alike. Communist behavior centered on a predictable range of violent actions with the ambush and wave assault the most popular.[23] Whether targeting civilians or American forces, attack came from the shadows, usually en masse, with the enemy pressing the assault until determined American intervention broke their fighting spirit and thwarted their sinister plans.[24] Often too the "dirty tricks" and traps of the enemy resulted in a capture, interrogation, escape sequence during which the plans of a single Vietnamese leader were revealed and foiled, usually after a multipanel "donnybrook." In these scenarios the enemy leadership conformed to a set of recognizable tropes with an inscrutable, yet physically weak and cowardly, "mastermind" undone by the brains, but more commonly the brawn, of the American hero.[25] In depicting Vietnamese insurgents, acting communist presented a treacherous, zealous, barbarous enemy who, akin to the schoolyard bully, turned spineless and weak when "socked in the nose," a popular and recognizable if not particularly sophisticated metaphor for Cold War confrontation and containment.

The sequential nature of the comic book allowed such predictable action to be paired with dialogue to not only tell the story but establish and confirm enemy status. Unsurprisingly, in intervention era comics, Vietnamese communists expressed themselves, however stiltedly, in English. Further, the Vietnamese enemy's dialogue was most often narrow in scope, limited to three forms: exclamations, lies, and rants.[26] As mentioned, insurgents, who are clearly mindful of the martial prowess of American forces, attack by ambushing their foes.[27] While not a wholly unwarranted characterization given the nature of guerilla warfare, representations were more indicative of an inept Pearl Harbor–esque sneak attack than a coordinated insurgent strategy. As part of the strike, enemies routinely shouted catch-phrases such as "Die! Die, Joe!" and most commonly simply "Kill!" Such exclamations ensured that readers understood quickly and unequivocally that communists intend only violence. When met by American firepower and, very often, pugilism, however, their defeat inevitably followed.

As Cold War Americans were well aware, Communism, treacherous and conspiratorial by nature, lurked in the shadows, relying as often on subterfuge as surprise in the effort to destroy freedom and liberty. Conveniently, traditional and familiar renderings of the "Oriental" as inscrutable and insidious meshed well with characterizations of the Communist, striking without warning but lacking the "guts" for a fair fight. As both "Oriental" and Communist, the Vietnamese enemy was presented as liar and imposter. In "The Deadly Shadows," for example, a Viet Cong fighter masquerading as a civilian declares the village safe, assuring Shotgun and Chicken: "No Viet Cong here . . . all *good* Vietnamese," while two menacing insurgents skulk along the side of a splash page just out of sight of the marines. A few panels later, unconvinced and harboring "this weird feeling as though I'm in danger," the suspicious Private Smith confronts another disguised insurgent creeping up behind him. Clearly attempting to hide a knife inside his shirt, the diminutive insurgent explains, "Me not Charlie . . . me *good* villager." Routinely, such subterfuge proved far more successful than the sneak attack/frontal assault, as Americans, trust-worthy and fair-minded by nature, often fell for the ruse and were captured.[28] Indeed, throughout the Harker and Smith stories, the duo was taken prisoner no less than twelve times, providing an opportunity for the enemy to "speak communist" and ultimately reveal their plans and receive their comeuppance. Most often this meant a rant that ranged from name-calling with "Yankee liar!" and "American gangsters," popular insults, to the multipanel soliloquy in which the enemy leader threatened, tortured, and insulted, all the while extoling the virtues of communism and condemning the evils of capitalism.[29]

In World War II comics, the Japanese were the enemy because they were Japanese. In the intervention era, the nature of the conflict required the construction of an ideological rather than a purely racial foe. Speaking and acting communist meant being a communist, establishing some Vietnamese as enemy while simultaneously reinforcing to the readership a larger message: the moral obligation of the United States to oppose Communism, even if that meant intervention in a "crummy war" in Southeast Asia. After all, other Vietnamese were in need of American assistance.

"PLUCKY LITTLE BANTAMS": THE ALLY IS THE VIETNAMESE

Nearly three years before significant military commitment in Vietnam, war comic books had already begun to depict and contextualize American intervention.[30] From the outset, almost all creators and publishers reflected the Kennedy and Johnson administrations' view that the insurgency represented a mounting existential threat to South Vietnam.[31] Without American aid it was only a matter of time before another Asian domino tumbled.[32] The central challenge for creators was not to demonstrate why the Vietnamese should resist the communist menace. After all, American audiences required little explanation of *why* Communism should be contained. Rather the task was to demonstrate *how* it could be confronted. For American planners and comic book creators alike, the answer was the same: create allies from the Vietnamese who had shaken off native apathy and passivity to begin a process of enlightenment and political maturity. Saving Vietnam from "communist guerillas . . . ever more active and ruthless," required that the United States aggressively "supply, and instruct [the Vietnamese] in ways of halting the Red . . . terror."[33] To effectively do that necessitated an American "helping hand" to construct reliable allies from the most unreliable of materials: the Vietnamese themselves.[34] In intervention era comics this meant the Army of the Republic of Vietnam (ARVN).

Unsurprisingly, depictions of allied Vietnamese decreased as direct American intervention escalated. In effect, as the US sent more troops to Vietnam, the ARVN faded further into the background, increasingly irrelevant. In the first few years of American intervention, however, war comics routinely depicted the ARVN in stories focused on the advisory and training role played by small, elite groups of American Special Forces.[35] Specifically, Dell Comics, *Jungle War Stories* and *Tales of the Green Beret*, running thirteen and five issues respectively, provided the most comprehensive depictions.[36] In these books creators explained the necessity, logic, and nature of intervention, while casting Vietnamese allies as an important, if secondary, constituency.[37]

"Second Chance," published in September 1967 in *Tales of the Green Beret*, succinctly presented both the peril and potential of Vietnamese as ally. In the story an ARVN unit led by Captain Drang and aided by US advisers Major Barker and Sergeant "Champ" Benton were betrayed by a Viet Cong infiltrator and drawn into an ambush.[38] Facing a battle-hardened enemy, the Vietnamese panicked, and only the level-headed intervention of the Green Berets staved off massacre. In the aftermath Captain Drang appealed to the Americans to "give them a second chance," admitting that while his men did panic, they were at heart "brave men" who only required "more training." Predictably, the sympathetic American soldiers agreed, setting up an "Ambush School" to develop both the necessary skills and, more importantly, the grit and courage needed to defeat the

NLF. Unbeknownst to the newly trained ARVN, however, wily Viet Cong General Kyo had learned of their preparation and set a clever trap. In short order, the Vietnamese and their advisors were drawn into an ambush, but, unlike in their earlier encounter, "the Vietnamese [held] on doggedly." Facing overwhelming odds, Captain Drang, the "plucky little bantam . . . [requested] an airstrike right near his own position," gallantly insisting that "if the Vietnamese [ARVN] . . . must die . . . let us take many Cong butchers with us!" Mortally wounded, the Vietnamese commander ordered his men to charge the enemy, saying, "This time it is the Cong who panic and brake [*sic*]." The story concluded with Captain Drang's burial and Major Barker's eulogy, during which he reminded the ARVN that "one Vietnamese Captain had faith in them. . . . All he wanted was a second chance to prove that his men could fight," "a second chance to fight for your country's freedom . . . and you justified his trust in your courage!"[39]

"Second Chance" demonstrated that the ARVN, akin to the wider population, required American leadership and training to "hold them together" and unlock their natural virtue while suppressing their latent vice.[40] Without such hands-on support, the ARVN "were unpredictable . . . they'd cracked under pressure before and they might do it again."[41] While capable of developing and learning, neither bravery nor martial prowess came easily for the Vietnamese, inherently physically weak, timid, fickle, and often pacific by nature.[42] In the end, only American know-how and can-do spirit could empower their Vietnamese allies to "push onward with determination" and contribute to the salvation of their nation.[43]

Constructing a Vietnamese ally that readers could recognize and accept challenged creators to represent their friendly status while still relying on visually recognizable stereotypes of the Oriental that were equally applicable to the enemy.[44] Again only behavior could square the circle. However, while the enemy, the antagonist, did play an important role in the narrative, creators and readers alike understood that Vietnamese allies were never the main feature. Unsurprisingly and universally, white Americans occupied center stage, reinforcing the notion that winning the war would largely be the result of US determination. Indeed, whatever the effort and contribution of the ARVN, Vietnamese and American were never equals but rather were cast in a paternalistic relationship founded on the demonstrative ideological and cultural supremacy of the United States. Further, whereas establishing the Vietnamese enemy required a wide range of cues beyond simply assumed ethnic qualities, representing allies leaned heavily on precisely that. The tension for creators was to portray Oriental otherness without dehumanizing the Vietnamese in toto. For the ARVN, this meant that actions followed a formulaic trajectory from passivity to reticence to activity, establishing them as Oriental enough to be other but also worthy enough to be liberated, protected and nurtured.[45] To that end their behavior needed to reinforce the notion that most Vietnamese could be converted and that they harbored, however submerged, an inherent longing for liberal democratic values, even if unable to clearly articulate them.

Both historically and in intervention era war comic books, assisting the ARVN served as an important explanation for intervention. As the war progressed and it became increasingly obvious that training and advising alone were insufficient to secure victory, the United States increasingly assumed a more direct role in the war effort. In the pages of American war comics, this meant that when considered at all as anything more than props and landscape, the ARVN suffered from a reductionism that presented it as an apolitical, amorphous raw material to be molded. Intervention era comic books portrayed the ARVN as work in progress yet worthy of the gift of freedom, thanks of course to the benevolence of the United States. For American readers, intervention appeared as twin moral imperatives: a duty to protect the Vietnamese based on their intrinsic humanness, however conventionally rendered, and the need to champion the universalism of liberal democracy. In the aftermath of the war, however, such optimistic depictions were irrevocably shattered and the ARVN transformed from "how we can win" to "why we lost."

RETELLING THE WAR: POSTWAR REPRESENTATIONS OF ENEMY AND ALLY

The fall of Saigon in April 1975 confirmed that the United States lost the war in Vietnam. Yet in the pages of American war comics, the end of the conflict hardly registered at all. Indeed, the few remaining war comics continued as they had since the early 1970s, simply ignoring the war altogether.[46] Only in the 1980s, concurrent with the growing "Vietnam boom" in popular culture, did the war return to the pages of war comic books.[47] Beginning in 1986 with the publication of Marvel Comics' *The 'Nam* and quickly followed by Apple Comics *Vietnam Journal* in 1987, creators claimed that their works were an effort to give the war meaning and relevance, at least for Americans.[48]

In the first issue of *The 'Nam*, Doug Murray, himself a Vietnam veteran, offered readers "the real thing—or at least as close to the real thing as we can get in a newsstand comic bearing the Comics Code seal."[49] The series, intended initially to be published in real time, promised both historical accuracy and to present "what the war was really like for those who fought in it."[50] For Murray, Marvel provided the opportunity to reach a postwar uninformed generation with a war comic "designed as a way to present a representative history," a retelling of "what happened to people in that war," or at least the grunt's-eye view of it.[51]

Akin to Murray, Don Lomax, veteran and author of the long-running *Vietnam Journal*, remained focused on the common American soldier. Yet rather than writing history, he considered his series an ongoing act of remembrance and sense-making.[52] Lomax bluntly stated: "I'm not doing a history book. I take it from the grunt's eye view and they didn't have any goddam idea why they were there. I don't think people in my story should have any idea why they are there. Nobody knew why they were there . . . nobody knew what they were doing."[53]

These post-1975 Vietnam War comic books intended to provide a specific retelling of the war that offered contemporary significance to the American reader.[54] Consequently, the Vietnamese were constructed largely devoid of historical or political context.[55] Indeed, in both *Vietnam Journal* and *The 'Nam*, creators rarely focused at all on the Vietnamese enemy. When they did appear, they were largely confined to two roles: attacker and target. Often artists signified an enemy presence only with shadowy figures and a sound effect of incoming fire, while in other cases they silently emerged from the jungle in a well-coordinated charge, only to be cut down in a myriad of gruesome, if not wholly inaccurate, ways. In some sense, little changed from the previous generation of war comics, as the enemy continued as part of the landscape across which stories of the American experience were retold.[56] Yet similarities to intervention era comics notwithstanding, the reality of defeat required that creators fundamentally recast some Vietnamese as tough and worthy enough to have prevailed.

"VICTOR CHARLES": THE FORMIDABLE ENEMY

As part of a wider sense-making process, images and idioms were reconstructed, sometimes jarringly, to present Vietnamese enemies as formidable adversaries. In important ways a more historically accurate representation emerged as insurgents and North Vietnamese (PAVN) soldiers no longer rush wildly toward American forces to fight hand-to-hand or simply cower or run in the face of adversity.[57] In other words, "Charlie definitely [had] his shit together!"[58]

Establishing a formidable enemy meant that the Vietnamese routinely succeeded in killing, wounding, and maiming American forces, often in significant numbers.[59] Indeed, unencumbered by the Comics Code, *Vietnam Journal*'s portrayal of combat was noted by popular, comic industry, educational and academic commentators as not just graphic but also "like the real thing": "realistic," "gritty," and "brutally honest."[60] For example, Lomax focused considerable attention on the 1968 Tet Offensive, with an emphasis on the horrific street fighting in Hue and the siege at Khe Sanh.[61] While the Vietnamese enemy proved ultimately unsuccessful in besting the Americans, it was not for lack of effort or ability, characterizations that are largely historically accurate.[62] In another story set during the bloody 1969 operation in the A Shau Valley, Lomax depicted combat as reminiscent of the merciless battles of the Pacific War.[63] Throughout the issue American paratroopers fought and eventually annihilated "hardcore regulars . . .

prepared to fight to the last man." While the Vietnamese were not belittled but rather afforded parity with American soldiers in a comradeship of arms, their motivation to refuse surrender was incomprehensible. In the aftermath of the battle, one soldier pointedly asked: "What the hell are these people made of?! Damn fine soldiers!" Indeed, while Lomax reconsidered how the enemy fought and presented the enemy as a formidable and worthy foe, the enigmatic "Asian" remained as inexplicable as ever.[64]

In *The 'Nam* combat was similarly depicted, if more sanitized, and the enemy also recast as experienced, illusive, and determined.[65] Further, in line with his desire for historical accuracy, Murray regularly considered the village war, and in a ground-breaking issue, Saigon itself.[66] Early in the series, protagonist Private Ed Marks headed to the capital for rest and relaxation. While there he and his comrades survived two terrorist bombings carried out by shadowy Viet Cong insurgents.[67] Such representations, while highlighting the enemy's calculating ruthlessness, also established them as innovative, elusive, and resourceful, features denied them in wartime depictions. In both *Vietnam Journal* and *The 'Nam*, Viet Cong insurgents and PAVN soldiers were dedicated, effective, and capable, if brutal and often fool-hardy.[68] Gone was the incompetent and buffoonish enemy, reimagined and retold as aggressive, motivated, and skillful, drawing on lessons learned fighting not just the American military but the French and Japanese before them. Perhaps even more importantly, postwar creators engaged, however marginally, a key consideration largely absent from earlier war comics, namely, why the enemy fought.

Postwar comics made significant efforts to represent an enemy perspective, largely related to *how* the Vietnamese enemy fought and died. More haltingly creators also considered enemy motivation, *why* they fought, in both a personal and collective sense. The most comprehensive effort to represent the enemy motivation came in the final issue of *The 'Nam*. Written by Lomax, "The Letter" traced the journey of a young girl's drawing from her village in the North to her father, an NLF commander, hiding near Saigon. After the 1968 Tet Offensive, five-year-old Yen Luong understood that her father's three-year absence would end only "when the American colonists [were] driven from their land and Vietnam [could] reunite with the south and again be one," an interpretation of the war learned at the knee of her mother.[69] With faint hope that it would find its way to her father, Yen's drawing headed south, first with her departing cousin Tuan, a young PAVN conscript. Along the route Lomax introduced a series of characters as the letter passed from hand to hand, ultimately delivered to her father moments before his death in an American airstrike. As they carried the drawing, each character demonstrated a primary motivator: why they fought and, more importantly, why they would die.

In "The Letter," while more nuanced than intervention era representations, the Vietnamese enemy expressed only one motivation limited to ideological programing, nascent nationalism, or revenge. Rarely did creators consider ideological solidarity as a significant motivator, generally continuing the wartime tradition of presenting Communism as little more than manipulation, soon exposed by the enemy's brutality or the careless waste of life at the hands of a cynical leadership. In an extension of the speaking communist tradition of earlier war comics, idealism as motivation was presented as lie or naiveté, expressed as catch-phrases juxtaposed with atrocity or military blunder.[70] In "The Letter," for example, Lomax presented an extended conversation in which Tuan and his PAVN cell discussed the necessity of defeating the "Imperialist running dogs." While not a wholly inaccurate reflection of Communist Party, rhetoric and significant in articulating their nationalist aspirations, such dialogue cast their sentiment as naive, and the soldiers simply victims of "indoctrination . . . begun virtually at birth," their lives casually thrown away by their "leader's policy of reunification."[71] Indeed, as part of his underlying effort to reconstruct the war as little more than senseless wastage and carnage, Lomax inserted Wilfred Owen's famous line "*Dulce et decorum est pro patria mori*." While a dubious statement from the mouth of a young, rural PAVN volunteer, the reference reflected a popular post-1975 view that Vietnam had been a "grim exercise in futility," a notion familiar to American readers, if not the North Vietnamese.[72]

Whatever the limitations of engaging enemy ideology on its own terms, postwar narratives did reflect important realities about the PAVN's (and North Vietnam's) public interpretation of the war as an anticolonial struggle. Indeed, on three occasions in *The 'Nam*, nascent nationalism and the Vietnamese historical tradition of resistance to foreign intervention served as "the cause" in the construction of a determined, tenacious, and ultimately victorious enemy.[73] Overwhelmingly, however, the enemy proved decidedly apolitical, motivated by personal experience akin to what David Kilcullen termed "accidental guerillas syndrome."[74] While this characterization too put little stock in genuine ideological solidarity as a motivator, equally it also marked an important departure from depictions of the enemy as communist lackey and considered the nature of the war in Vietnam. In an insurgency, Murray understood, the way the war was prosecuted had the potential to not only destroy but also to create and replenish the enemy. Retelling Vietnam required creators to represent what was in effect two wars: one to search and destroy the enemy, and the other to win the hearts and minds of the population. While postwar comic books overwhelming depicted conventional combat rather than the "Other War" of pacification, the violence, missteps, and atrocities that alienated civilians whose loyalty was to be won did not go unmentioned. When considering enemy motivation, creators suggested that intervention on behalf of a failed, unresponsive South Vietnamese regime engendered "accidental guerrillas."[75] Many enemy fought as a response to extraneous violence as atrocities committed (or tolerated) by South Vietnamese forces or their American allies pushed otherwise passive Vietnamese into the arms of the insurgents, providing a way to fight back or at least exact some measure of personal revenge.[76] The true enemy was Communism and its hardcore agents who manipulated and exploited legitimate grievances, subverted nationalist aspirations, and placed American servicemen in an impossible predicament, namely, facing popular resistance on behalf of a corrupt ally who was, in effect, the lesser of two evils. Free of ideological taint, the "average" Vietnamese enemy became a foe whose motivations creators and readers alike could at least empathize with and understand, if not agree with.

Perhaps even more importantly in the context of the late Cold War, such representations allowed victory to go to the enemy Vietnamese rather than their official ideology. With little thoughtful representation, let alone discussion, appreciation, or understanding of political and ideological motivations, the primary depiction as a largely apolitical "common" soldier provided a means through which the victorious enemy was both a formidable and, at least on the battlefield, worthy foe.[77] But it is also true that even as postwar creators attributed agency of a kind, in large measure the Vietnamese enemy remained "as faceless and impersonal as the body-count reports used by the Americans to judge the war's progress," a trait that continues to linger in both the academic and popular treatments of the war.[78] In effect, the Vietnam enigma continued.[79]

Even as postwar creators challenged some representations common in intervention era comics, the enemy's brutality, targeting combatants and civilians alike, remained prominent and recurring.[80] In *Vietnam Journal*, Lomax depicted atrocity on a grand scale, such as the massacre of civilians in Hue in 1968.[81] Other stories focused on the mistreatment of captured Americans, in which the explicit torture and murder amounted to little more than wanton brutality rather than "enhanced" interrogation.[82] In such cases GI.s resisted maltreatment and bravely faced their fate stoically. The most graphic representations of enemy atrocity, however, focus on Vietnamese villagers. In "The Ballad of Luther Wolfe," insurgents hunt for a lost American soldier hiding in a nameless hamlet. In the course of their search, the enemy interrogates and murders a young mother before bayoneting her infant child. Even mainstream publisher Marvel, while adhering to the Comics Code, presented depictions of atrocity. In "Humpin' the Boonies," US soldiers patrolling a pacified village discover the decomposing remains of slaughtered civilians, prompting Private Marks to query, "How could anybody human do this?"[83] Images of atrocity and brutality, while certainly more comprehensive and graphic than wartime depictions, served much the same purpose, namely to deny enemy claims of legitimacy and popular support. In a retelling of the war, the Vietnamese enemy may have been a formidable, perhaps even at times a worthy, adversary, yet they were far from "liberators."[84]

The postwar Vietnamese enemy reflected key characteristics denied or inverted in intervention era comics chiefly: discipline, courage, tenacity, and however roughly defined, motivation. Further, to a certain extent, postwar narratives did challenge the "long tradition of belittlement" in war comics, as creators recast the enemy Vietnamese and American soldiers as "brothers in arms," tied together through the shared experience of combat in a brutal war.[85] Of course such depictions also absolved American forces of defeat at the hands of "lesser men." Yet even as creators attempted to render the enemy "realistically," these Vietnamese rarely departed from bit-part players, a largely faceless and impersonal, even elemental, foe.[86] Also in evidence were representations of savage brutality that, however historically accurate, were detached from careful consideration of perpetrator motivation. In the end, a complex depiction of the Vietnamese insurgent remained elusive, and the enemy continued as an opaque, if humanized, "Other."

"MARVIN THE ARVN": THE UNWORTHY ALLY

In postwar comic books, however limited the attention paid to the enemy, even less consideration was given to Vietnamese allies. Unwilling to answer the question "Why did we lose in Vietnam?" with the rather obvious answer—because of the Vietnamese enemy creators proved largely in step with a popular interpretation that claimed Vietnamese allies, not Americans, had lost the war. In this explanation the United States found itself fighting on behalf of a corrupt regime and alongside an unmotivated, incompetent Army of the Republic of Vietnam.[87] Juxtaposed with the formidable, if ruthless, "Victor Charles" was "Marvin the ARVN," the cowardly, craven South Vietnamese soldier too focused on rape and robbery to defend his country or appreciate the aid of the United States.[88] Highlighting characteristics formerly attributed in intervention era narratives to the enemy, in the postwar retelling of the war it was Vietnamese allies who refused to fight for their freedom and thus were ultimately responsible for surrendering it. In this way creators engaged a particular paradox also reflected in some of the historiography: the Vietnamese ally had lost the war, while the Vietnamese enemy had not won it, at least from the United States. In effect, postwar comics provided a narrative that again exonerated the American GI, if not the intervention, and reinforced the interpretation that war had been lost everywhere but on the battlefield.

Simply put, the ARVN soldier exhibited none of the martial prowess attributed to the enemy. Indeed, when facing each other, "Victor Charles" consistently bested and often routed "Marvin." When the South Vietnamese army featured at all, readers could expect catastrophe to follow as facing any opposition, ARVN units withered and immediately required the intervention of their American allies.[89] Military success, readers were reminded, required US aid and, inevitably, casualties.[90] In *Vietnam Journal* Lomax recounted the Vietnamese army's triumphant striking of the NLF flag and the raising of the republic's during the 1968 battle for Hue. In his telling, US Marines defeated a determined foe in brutal street fighting only to be "up-staged again" as "Marvin the ARVN" arrived to hoist their flag only after the shooting had stopped.[91]

What "Marvin" lacked in fighting spirit, he more than made up for in brutality. In virtually every extended depiction of the ARVN, the narrative centered on war crimes ranging from the torture and execution of prisoners to rape and murder of civilians.[92] In "Cordon and Search," for example, Lomax focused on their casual and routine cruelty. During a village search, civilians are abused and raped, while in another scene, an interrogator murders a suspected insurgent by shoving a grenade in his mouth and pushing him from a helicopter.[93] In *The 'Nam*, depictions of ARVN brutality were considerably less graphic when compared with *Vietnam Journal*. Different also were the nature and source of the violence. In both issues detailing allied atrocity, the incidents take place under American supervision with the ARVN acting as "enforcers."[94] Yet these depictions were not intended to understand their behavior but rather positioned them as accomplices to whom violence and atrocity came naturally and easily. In effect, as "willing executioners" and likely perpetrators, the narrative focused on American behavior, offering the critique that "our side" should have known and should have done better.

While, as we have seen, postwar creators did acknowledge anticolonial ethnonationalism as a motivator for enemy resistance, this was not, incipient or otherwise, extended to ARVN soldiers. In the absence of any solidarity with the Saigon regime, "ARVN turds" simply used the war to enrich themselves, regardless of the impact on the survival of the republic.[95] As an institution, the Vietnamese military was riddled with corruption, from the conscripted "farm boys" who looted enemy corpses to war-profiteering commanders and rear echelon army bureaucrats.[96] In "The Gratitude of His People," writer Chuck Dixon makes the point bluntly with Major Phouc, an ARVN officer focused more on gambling on an enemy sniper's next target than actively engaging insurgents. Having killed the Vietnamese enemy sniper, the story's American protagonist reflects: "One [enemy] guy with a rifle, keepin' all them Marvins home in their bunkers. One guy worth two hundred of them. Never thought about it till now. Little man's gonna win this war."[97] The Vietnamese major and his "toy soldiers" not only required Americans to do "their job" for them but inevitably would lose the war itself.

Almost universally, *Vietnam Journal* reinforced the Vietnamese army's "reputation for being lazy, inept soldiers who would throw their weapons down and run rather than fight."[98] As cowardly, disordered, and undisciplined, the ARVN closely resemble intervention era characterizations of the enemy. While, strictly speaking, postwar representations were certainly not as improbable as earlier depictions and were in some measure roughly based on historical incidents, the dominance of such portrayals proves reflective of a lingering collective memory of the ARVN.[99] Ultimately, the South Vietnamese allies were not allies at all, and consequently the war was unwinnable. Try as they might, no measure of American intervention could defend a state that refused to defend itself.[100] As Lomax put it:

> ARVN momma-san's boys who were supposed to defend the perimeter collapsed. Discipline went out the window. They were left sobbing like babies, begging for mercy with their little hands in the air. A lot of good it did them. Most were executed on the spot. Charlie don't like crybabies. I took command of the remaining ARVN with little protest from their indecisive officers and NCO's . . . and we beat them [the NVA] back proving that they could do it with . . . confidence in the individual leading them. It may seem . . . I'm painting all ARVN with a broad brush . . . I've seen individual bravery, just not in their chain of command.[101]

On several occasions both *Vietnam Journal* and *The 'Nam* did present alternate representations of the Vietnamese ally. Yet even these depictions more often reinforced rather than challenged traditional characterizations. Early in *The 'Nam*, Murray devoted an entire issue to engaging the Vietnamese perspective. In "The Good Ol Days," Private Marks chatted with Duong, a former Viet Cong insurgent who now served as a Kit Carson scout for the US Army.[102] However unlikely the conversation, it allowed Murray to provide both an overview of Vietnamese history and the journey from enemy to ally, from Viet Cong to *Chieu Hoi* (defector).

Initially just a "simple farmer," Duong is moved by the execution of his wife by French forces collaborating with the Japanese to join the Viet Minh as a nationalist. He is inspired not by ideology but "Uncle Ho's" familiar insistence that "men [were] created equal." Apolitical, he returns to the fields after liberation, rejoining the Viet Minh only in their later anticolonial fight against the French. The remainder of the narrative shows Duong trapped in the middle, between a South Vietnamese government "as bad as the French" and an increasingly unjust and violent insurgency intent on "oppressing the people." In the end, unable to reconcile American altruism with the NLF's senseless brutality, Duong defects through the Open Arms program and joins American forces, "where I have been accepted." Significantly, Murray presents the United States not as a successor to the Japanese and French, but rather as an ally and benefactor sharing Duong's vision of personal and national liberation denied by the NLF and their northern masters.

At one level "The Good Old Days" represents an effort to "put a face" on an ally in much the same way Murray had done with Private Marks, as representative of the American "everyman." But at another level, there is little everyman about Duong. Rather, as a former Viet Cong insurgent, effectively an allied "accidental guerilla," he maintains a personal and legitimate commitment to the war effort and possesses proven capabilities as a skilled and effective soldier.[103] In the notably few efforts to depict the Vietnamese as "good allies," postwar creators disproportionally focused on everyone *but* the regular ARVN grunt. Only the "cream of the ARVN," often elite units or former enemies, matched up to American forces, earning their respect and confidence with their dedication and fighting prowess.[104] In effect, the Vietnamese ally needed to demonstrate that they were as good as an average American.[105]

While the ARVN collectively remained suspect, so too could singular Vietnamese prove themselves capable allies through individual acts of bravery, self-sacrifice and loyalty in service of their American comrades. Quite simply, valuable Vietnamese acted as "sidekicks," fighting against the enemy and for their allies rather than in the service of their state. Their significance to the retelling of the war therefore lay in their kinship with the American soldier.[106] Selfless, motivated and stoic, this ally parallels the fate of the US GI, who was, in the end, betrayed by those who had asked them to serve.

Both wartime and postwar creators echoed Gen. William Westmoreland's view in June 1965 that South Vietnam could not "survive without the active commitment of US ground combat forces" able to "accomplish what the Army of the Republic of Vietnam could not."[107] Clearly, only American leadership provided and enforced the necessary discipline, bravery, and ingenuity that allowed ARVN soldiers to overcome their natural propensity for disorder, cowardice, and inscrutability.[108] In the initial twenty-five years after the fall of Saigon, postwar comic book characterizations of the ARVN proved largely in step with popular interpretations of the war. To date, however while historians have begun to challenge the dominant "Marvin" representation and consider a range of factors that ultimately led to the final collapse of the Vietnamese military, war comics have not.[109] Indeed, quite the opposite occurred. While comic book creators have expressed a renewed interest in retelling the Vietnam war in recent years, the ARVN have suffered a fate worse than caricature, namely, insignificance.

PUTTING THE VIETNAMESE BACK IN THE WAR

War comic books remain on the periphery of the medium. While superheroes dominate, whether in comic book stores or movie theaters, creators, publishers, and readers alike have shown little interest in reviving the genre. Even in 1990, as interest and readership in *The 'Nam* waned, Murray noted that "the general perception of the comics industry *throughout* [was] superheroes. There's no place in the market for detective stories, westerns or war stories and that books like *The 'Nam* and *Vietnam Journal* [were] novelties."[110] For Murray, whatever his initial hopes and creative direction, there was, at least at Marvel Comics "no room for precise, historical truth."[111]

Of course, war comics were never intended to present a historically representative or comprehensive narrative of the conflict. To do so, as Murray rightly noted, required a "book devoted to the Vietnamese. And certainly there's not an American comic book company that would be that"—a sentiment largely as true in 2018 as 1990.[112] Yet, just as the Vietnam war as a subject of academic inquiry continues to flourish, invigorated no doubt by the series of post-9/11 American military interventions, so too have a few comic creators begun to draw a past that includes the Vietnamese. Yet such works are not, in the strictest sense, war comics but rather employ Vietnam as a setting and metaphor. One example is Jason Aaron's *The Other Side*, a five-issue miniseries published by DC Comics, and a spiritual successor to Archie Goodwin's stories in *Blazing Combat*. On the one hand, Aaron's focus on Vo Binh Dai, a PAVN soldier, presented a retelling of the war that considered history, motivation, and war experiences from a Vietnamese perspective. On the other hand, such important depictions and subversions notwithstanding, *The Other Side* "defies genre definition" and proves less a war comic and more "a psychological horror story."[113] More significant, however, are recent graphic novels such as *Vietnamerica: A Family's Journey* and *The Best We Could Do*.[114] Such works represent a long-absent voice and record the experiences of the Vietnamese diaspora after 1975. Finally, Marcelino Truong's *Such a Lovely Little War: Saigon 1961–63*, set in the early days of the American intervention, masterfully intertwines historical, political, and familial narratives long overlooked in mainstream war comic books. In doing so, Truong refocuses the "grunt's eye view," an essential corrective that reminds readers that any "representative history," any retelling of the conflict, necessitates deeper consideration of both enemy and ally.[115]

As we have seen, the Vietnamese remained as landscape and supporting cast in the telling and retelling of an American tale. Yet it is also true that representing the conflict in war comic books did force creators to confront its complexity and uniqueness and develop representations to reflect this reality, requiring innovation and reconceptualization in order to provide relevance and meaning. In the end, however, perhaps the most the striking feature of Vietnam war comics is just how little the Vietnamese mattered at all. It is therefore imperative for storytellers and historians alike to investigate how, when, and why they do matter, for as Viet Thanh Nguyen reminds, "the war has not ended" and cannot possibly end until the Vietnamese are placed at its very heart.

NOTES

1. "This Crummy War," *Army War Heroes* #27 (Charlton Comics, 1968).

2. For a fuller discussion of the state and decline of war comics, see Bradford Wright, *Comic Book Nation: The Transformation of Youth Culture in America* (Baltimore: Johns Hopkins University Press, 2001); and Leonard Rifas, "War Comics," in *The Routledge Companion to Comics*, ed. Frank Bramlett, Roy Cook, and Aaron Meskin (New York: Routledge, 2017), 183–91. For discussions of Vietnam era comic books more generally, see Wright, *Comic Book Nation*, 189–99; Cord Scott, *Comics and Conflict: Patriotism and Propaganda from WWII through Operation Iraqi Freedom* (Annapolis: Naval Institute Press, 2014), 17–77; David Huxley, "'The Real Thing': New Images of the Vietnam War in American Comic Books," in *Vietnam Images War and Representation*, ed. James Aulich and Jeffrey Walsh, 160–70 (Basingstoke: Palgrave Macmillan, 1989); Robert Kodosky, "Holy Tet Westy! Graphic Novels and the Vietnam War," *Journal of Modern Culture* 44, no. 5 (2011): 1047–66; Richard Young, "'The Real Victims' of the Vietnam War: Soldier versus State in American Comic Books," *Journal of Modern Culture* 50, no. 3 (2017): 561–84; Bryan Vizzini, "When (Comic) Art Imitates Life: American Exceptionalism and the Comic Book Industry in the Vietnam War Era," in *The Vietnam War in Popular Culture: The Influence of America's Most Controversial War on Everyday Life Vol. 1*, ed. Ron Milam (Santa Barbara, CA: Praeger, 2016), 359–78; Cathy Schlund-Vials, "Comics Captured America's Opinions about the Vietnam War," https://theconversation.com/comics-captured-americas-growing-ambivalence-about-the-vietnam-war-83756; Peter Rollins, "Using Popular Culture to Study the Vietnam War: Perils and Possibilities," in *Why We Fought: America's Wars in Film and History*, ed. Peter Collins and John O'Connor (Lexington: University Press of Kentucky, 2008), 367–89; Lori Maguire, "The Avengers Always Stand Ready to Do Their Part": The Avengers and the Vietnam War," in *The Ages of the Avengers: Essays on the Earth's Mightiest Heroes in Changing Times*, ed. Joseph Darowski, 12–24 (Jefferson, NC: McFarland, 2014).

3. Particularly helpful in contextualizing Vietnam era comics are: Scott, *Comics and Conflict*; Chris Murray, "*Popaganda*: Superhero Comics and Propaganda in World War Two," in *Comics & Culture: Analytical and Theoretical Approaches to Comics*, ed. Anne Magnussen and Hans-Christian Christiansen, 141–55 (Copenhagen: Museum Tusculanum Press, 2000); Lisa Mundey, *American Militarism and Anti-Militarism in Popular Media, 1945–1970* (Jefferson, NC: McFarland, 2012), 159–208.

4. See George Herring, "Peoples Quite Apart: Americans, South Vietnamese, and the War in Vietnam," *Diplomatic History* 14, no. 1 (Winter 1990): 1–23; Michael Klein, "Cultural Narrative and the Process of Re-collection: Film, History and the Vietnam Era," in *The Vietnam Era: Media and Popular Culture in the US and Vietnam*, ed. Michael Klein (London: Pluto Press, 1990), 9–10; Carl Boggs and Tom Pollard, *The Hollywood War Machine: U.S. Militarism and Popular Culture* (Boulder, CO: Paradigm, 2007), 90–91, 95; Walter Hoelbling, "US Fiction about Vietnam: The Discourse of Contradiction," in Klein, *Vietnam Era*, 130.

5. According to Wright, Charlton "expounded an unqualified endorsement of U.S. intervention." Wright, *Comic Book Nation*, 189–90.

6. John Dower, *War without Mercy: Race and Power in the Pacific War* (New York: Pantheon Books, 1986), 10, 77–181; also see Wright, *Comic Book Nation*, 30–55, 110–21; Christopher Field, "'He Was a Living Breathing Human Being': Harvey Kurtzman's War Comics and the 'Yellow Peril' in 1950s Containment Culture," in *Comic Books and the Cold War, 1946–1962: Essays on Graphic Treatment of Communism, the Code and Social Concerns*, ed. Chris York and Rafiel York, 30–44 (Jefferson: McFarland, 2012); Scott, *Comics and Conflict*, 41–47, 49–52.

7. Dower, *War without Mercy*, 77–78; also see Nathan Madison, *Anti-Foreign Imagery in American Pulps and Comic Books* (Jefferson, NC: McFarland, 2013); Sheng-Mei Ma, *The Deadly Embrace: Orientalism and Asian American Identity* (Minneapolis: University of Minnesota Press, 2000); Charles Hardy and Gail F. Stern, eds., *Ethnic Images in the Comics* (Philadelphia: Balch Institute for Ethnic Studies Museum, 1986); Jeff Yang and Daniel Kim, "Marvels & Monsters: Unmasking Asian Images in U.S. Comics, 1942–1986," http://www.janm.org/exhibits/marvels-monsters/ and http://www.npr.org/2011/08/11/139536088/marvels-and-monsters-unveils-asians-in-comics.

8. Johannes Fabian, *Time and the Other: How Anthropology Makes Its Object* (New York: Columbia University Press, 2002), 164.

9. See Frank Longevall, "'There Ain't No Daylight": Lyndon Johnson and the Politics of Escalation," in *Making Sense of the Vietnam Wars: Local, National and Transnational Perspectives*, ed. Mark Philip Bradley and Marilyn Young (Oxford: Oxford University Press, 20008), 108; and William Hammond, *Reporting Vietnam: Media & Military at War* (Lawrence: University Press of Kansas, 1998), 1–18.

10. James Sandy, "A Paneled Perspective: The United States and the Vietnam War Examined through Comic Books," in *The Vietnam War in Popular Culture: The Influence of America's Most Controversial War on Everyday Life Vol. 2*, ed. Ron Milam, 245–49 (Santa Barbara: Praeger, 2016); and Scott, *Comics and Conflict*, 58–69. For a profound and short-lived intervention era war comic counternarrative to this prowar perspective, see Archie Goodwin, *Blazing Combat!* (Seattle: Fantagraphic Books, 2009).

11. Dower, *War without Mercy*, 77–181; Madison, *Anti-Foreign Imagery*, 121–33; also see Vizzini, "When (Comic) Art Imitates Life," 373; David Huxley, "Naked Aggression: American Comic Books and the Vietnam War," *Comics Journal*, no. 136 (July 1990): 110–11.

12. In a 1963 issue of *Jungle War Stories*, published almost two years prior to significant American intervention, readers were informed: "Viet Cong soldiers are frequently hard to distinguish from the rest of the Vietnamese population because of the black calico peasant pajamas which they wear on all occasions . . . even when going into battle!" See "The Face of the Vietcong," *Jungle War Stories* #4 (Dell Comics, 1963).

13. This is not to say that familiar stereotypes did not exist. For example, "The Enemy in Vietnam," *Jungle War Stories* #4 (Dell Comics, 1963), presented a blond, shirtless American standing with his arm extended out from his shoulder. Standing under this arm is a diminutive Vietnamese man. While the Vietnamese figure is drawn free of traditional, racialized features, the text reads: "The typical Viet Cong Guerrilla is a scrawny, unkept [*sic*] 100-pounder who barely comes up to the average GI's shoulders." See Dower, *War without Mercy*, 35; Brian Woodman, "A Hollywood War of Wills: Cinematic Representation of Vietnamese Super-Soldiers and America's Defeat in the War," *Journal of Film and Video* 55, no. 2/3 (Summer/Fall 2003): 44–58; Madison, *Anti-Foreign Imagery*, 121–33.

14. Vizzini, "When (Comic) Art Imitates Life," 371–74.

15. Significantly, the Harker and Smith stories in *Fightin' Marines* #94 and #96 were published in November 1970 and March 1971 respectively, just as US commitment to the war wound down. See Scott, *Comics and Conflict*, 55; Vizzini, "When (Comic) Art Imitates Life," 371–74.

16. Joe Gill, "Village of Fear," *Fightin' Marines* #94 (Charlton Comics, 1970). The fictional village, located "forty miles west of Hanoi," placed it about three hundred miles on the "wrong side" (north) of the Demilitarized Zone.

17. Joe Gill, "The Deadly Shadows," *Fightin' Marines* #94 (Charlton Comics, 1971).

18. Dower, *War without Mercy*, 77–181.

19. For an example, see Joe Gill, "Buckshot & Ballots," *Fightin' Marines* #79 (Charlton Comics, 1968); Joe Gill, "Hanoi Ambush," *Fightin' Marines* #82 (Charlton Comics, 1968); "The Brainwashers," *Fightin' Marines* #93 (Charlton Comics, 1970); "Charley Trap," *Fightin' Marines* #103 (Charlton Comics, 1972); "The Voice of the Enemy," *Fightin' Marines* #105 (Charlton Comics, 1972). Alternatively, in "Hanoi Hacker," *Fightin' Marines* #98 (Charlton Comics, 1971), the villain is represented as an Oriental bald behemoth, shirtless, muscular, tall but whose hubris leads to his demise.

20. "Enemy in Vietnam"; also see Vizzini, "When (Comic) Art Imitates Life," 368–71; Matthew Costello, *Secret Identity Crisis: Comic Books and the Unmasking of Cold War America* (New York: Continuum 2009), 62.

21. "Enemy in Vietnam."

22. For a representative example, see Joe Gill, "The Hidden Guns in the DMZ," *Fightin' Marines* #83 (Charlton Comics, 1969). Dialogue examples are found in Joe Gill, "The Viet Cong and the Peaceniks," *Fightin' Marines* #92 (Charlton Comics, 1970), and "The Name of the Game," *Fightin' Marines* #97 (Charlton Comics, 1971). Hand-to-hand combat proved popular in other war era comics as well. An excellent example is found in the exploits of former Green Beret captain Phil Hunter. With the aid of young Vietnamese woman, Hunter scoured the jungle in search of his twin brother, a captured pilot. In *Our Fighting Forces* #99–106 (DC Comics, 1966–1967), virtually every story forces Hunter to rely on his martial arts skills to defeat insurgents. For a brief report on the series, see "Pop Goes the War," *Newsweek*, September 12, 1966. Further examples are found in "Operation Red Eye," *Tales of the Green Beret* #1 (Dell Comics, 1967).

23. For similar representations in other intervention era war comics, see Charlton Comics' *Army War Heroes* #23 and #27, and *Fightin' Army* #74, #144, and #158, as well as Dell's *Tales of the Green Beret* #1–5. In several issues of *Jungle War Stories*, a one-page illustrated essay provided a more comprehensive discussion of the insurgency. While perhaps more nuanced, they remained in step with contemporary depictions of the enemy as brutal, insidious, subversive, and conspiratorial.

24. For a representative example, see "The Deadly Shadows," "Operation: Ten Little Indians," *Tales of the Green Beret* #2 (Dell Comics, 1967). For an example of a counternarrative, see "Special Forces!," in Goodwin, *Blazing Combat!*, 91–98.

25. See "Second Chance," *Tales of the Green Beret* #4 (Dell Comics, 1967).

26. See "Operation: Ten Little Indians."

27. Also see Joe Gill, "A Tough War," "Operation: Ten Little Indians," "Jungle Justice," *Tales of the Green Beret* #2 (Dell Comics, 1967), and Robert Kanigher, "No Mercy in Vietnam," *Our Fighting Forces* #99 (DC Comics, 1966). In Kanigher's story the insurgents deployed a unique if improbable device, an exploding Kewpie doll.

28. Gill, "The Deadly Shadows"; also see "Silence at Station Seven," *Jungle War Stories* #2 (Dell Comics, 1963).

29. Also see "Hanoi Ambush," "The Brainwashers," "The Voice of the Enemy," "Viet Cong Victim," *Fightin' Marines* #104 (Charlton Comics, 1972). Capture scenes also appear in other war stories, such as Howard Liss, "Trial by Fury," *Our Fighting Forces* #106 (DC Comics, 1967); and "Find . . . Fix . . . Fight . . . Finish," *Tales of the Green Beret* #2 (Dell Comics, 1967).

30. See "The Powder Keg," "Crash Landing," and Kurtzman, "Dien Bien Phu"; also see Konrad Jarausch, Christian Ostermann, and Andreas Etges, "Rethinking Representing, and Remembering the Cold War: Some Cultural Perspectives," in *The Cold War: Historiography, Memory, Representation*, Konrad Jarausch, ed. Christian Ostermann and Andreas Etges (Berlin: de Gruyter GmbH), 7–11.

31. *Jungle War Stories* #1 (Dell Comics, 1962) explained the conflict straightforwardly: "In 1954, in Geneva, it [Indochina] was partitioned into North and South Vietnam. Since then, the southern country has been constantly plagued by invasion of Communist guerillas from the north, called Viet Cong." The Vietnamese enemy was established as "communist guerillas" who had "become ever more active and ruthless." As noted previously, Warren Publishing's *Blazing Combat!* provided a contemporaneous counternarrative. Also see Sandy, "Paneled Perspective," 248–49.

32. *Jungle War Stories* cautioned readers: "While the territory currently considered in the possession of South Vietnam is placed at more than one-half Vietnam's total area of 125,000 square miles . . . this figure is true only for the daylight hours. At night—when its guerrillas roam the land at will—it is estimated that North Vietnam actually controls more than 70 per cent of the Nation!" Also see "A Figure That Matters," *Jungle War Stories* #7 (Dell Comics, 1964).

33. *Jungle War Stories* #1 and "Vietnam Battle Facts," *Jungle War Stories* #2 (Dell Comics, 1963).

34. "The Helping Hand," *Jungle War Stories* #5 (Dell Comics, 1963); also see Fabian, *Time and the Other*, 144–47; and Costello, *Secret Identity Crisis*, 81.

35. "Americans as swaggering heroes" is also evidenced in earlier comic books. See Zou Yizheng, "Flying Tigers and Chinese Sidekicks in World War II American Comic Books," in *The 10 Cent War: Comic Books, Propaganda and World War II*, ed. Trischa Goodnow and James Kimble (Jackson: University Press of Mississippi, 2016), 52–55.

36. Wright, *Comic Book Nation*, 189–99; Scott, *Comics and Conflict*, 59; Kodosky, "Holy Tet Westy!," 1053–54; *Tales of the Green Berets*, published by Dell in 1967, was based on Robin Moore's 1965 bestseller of the same name.

37. For an early example, see "Vengeance in Vietnam," *Jungle War Stories* #1 (Dell Comics, 1962).

38. The notion of traitor posing as ally remained prominent and fit snugly with preexisting notions of the "Asian" as inscrutable traitor. For further examples, see "Introducing 'Shotgun' Harker and The Chicken," *Fightin' Marines* #78 (Charlton Comics, 1968); "Hey Charlie, Surprise!" *Fightin' Marines* #80 (Charlton Comics, 1968); Gill, "Deadly Shadows"; Liss, "Trial by Fury"; "Blood Loyalty," *Our Fighting Forces* #105 (DC Comics, 1967); "The Traitor," *Tales of the Green Beret* #1 (Dell Comics, 1967); "Violence in the Air," *Jungle War Stories* #4 (Dell Comics, 1963); "Die by Water or Fire" and "Frontal Assault," *Guerilla War* #12 (Dell Comics, 1965). For the untrustworthy, if not traitorous, ARVN, see "The Switcheroo" and "Ring of Fire," *Jungle War Stories* #5 (Dell Comics, 1963).

39. "Second Chance."

40. See "Second Chance," "Mission: Strangle," *Jungle War Stories* #4 (Dell Comics, 1963), and "Save or Be Saved," *Jungle War Stories* #7 (Dell Comics, 1964). Only in *Blazing Combat* were

the ARVN depicted as brutal, willing to torture and commit atrocities against the enemy and civilians alike.

41. "Second Chance." On occasion individual Vietnamese, mainly officers, were capable of bravery and possessed fine leadership qualities. Along with Captain Drang, see ARVN Major Ksor in "Find . . . Fix . . . Fight . . . Finish," *Tales of the Green Beret* #2 (Dell Comics, 1967).

42. A range of other stories also presented limitations inherent in the Vietnamese. For cowardice in combat, see "Requiem for a Red," *Jungle War Stories* #1 (Dell Comics, 1962). For fear of the environment and inability to navigate jungle terrain, see "M-U-D Spells Disaster," *Jungle War Stories* #4 (Dell Comics, 1963). For physical weakness, see "Deadly Masquerade," *Jungle War Stories* #7 (Dell Comics, 1964). Also see Yizheng, "Flying Tigers and Chinese Sidekicks," 57–61.

43. Also see "Deadly Masquerade," in which US leadership and training empowered the ARVN to "fight like savages!" a sentiment echoed in "Fear in the Delta," *Jungle War Stories* #6 (Dell Comics, 1964), and "Saving Face," *Army Attack* #1 (Charlton Comics, 1964).

44. Edward Said, *Orientalism* (New York: Vintage Books, 2003), 21.

45. See "The Deadly Shadows," "The Name of the Game," and "Verdict: Guilty as Charged!" *Fightin' Marines* #99 (Charlton Comics, 1971).

46. See George Herring, *America's Longest War: The United States and Vietnam* (New York: McGraw-Hill, 1986), 273; Andrew Dagilis, "Uncle Sugar vs. Uncle Charlie: An Interview with *The 'Nam*'s Creator, Doug Murray," *Comics Journal*, no. 136 (July 1990): 64–65; Huxley, "Naked Aggression," 112; Doug Murray, "Interview with Brian Jacks," *Slush Factory*, May 2001, http://www.slushfactory.com/features/articles/052502-murray.php; Doug Murray, "Interview with Charlie Rose," *CBS News Washington*, June 4, 1987, https://www.youtube.com/watch?v=qwfB9bCs4kw; Paula Span, "Vietnam: The Comic Book War: Marvel Brings Out a Dark, Gritty and Popular Series," *Washington Post*, September 10, 1986; Sandy, "Paneled Perspective," 249.

47. While the two most significant comic books in the genre were *The 'Nam* and *Vietnam Journal*, other publications included: Ronald Ledwell, *In Country Nam* (Survival Art Press, 1986); *Semper Fi': Tales of the Marine Corps* #1, #2, and #6 (Marvel Comics, 1988–1989); Doug Murray, *Hearts & Minds: A Vietnam Love Story* (Marvel Comics, 1991); Will Eisner, *Last Day in Vietnam* (Dark Horse Comics, 2000); Jason Aaron, *The Other Side* (Vertigo, 2007); Joe Kubert, *Dong Xoai, Vietnam 1965* (Vertigo, 2011).

48. Sandy, "Paneled Perspective," 249–54; Richard Young, "There Is Nothing Grittier than a 'Grunt's Eye View': American War Comic Books and the Popular Memory of the Vietnam War," *Australasian Journal of American Studies* 34, no. 2 (2015): 75–93; Arnold Isaacs, *Vietnam Shadows: The War, Its Ghosts, and Its Legacies* (Baltimore: Johns Hopkins University Press, 1997), 1–8; Paula Span, "Vietnam."

49. Murray purported that "every action, every fire fight . . . [was] based on fact." Doug Murray, Editorial "Incoming," *The 'Nam* (Marvel Comics, 1986).

50. Murray, Editorial "Incoming"; also see Dagilis, "Uncle Sugar vs. Uncle Charlie," 72.

51. Dagilis, "Uncle Sugar vs. Uncle Charlie," 63, 71.

52. Leonard Rifas, "Interview with Don Lomax," *Comics Journal*, no. 136 (July 1990): 88, 102.

53. Rifas, "Interview with Don Lomax," 102. Almost universally in war comics, apart from short phrases and exclamations, text was presented in English, usually accompanied by an editorial comment noting the translation from the specific language. In line with *Vietnam Journal*'s specific goal of retelling the war as largely incomprehensible to the average GI, Lomax broke from traditional comic conventions by presenting Vietnamese dialogue untranslated.

54. Michael Klein, "Cultural Narrative and the Process of Re-collection: Film, History and the Vietnam Era," in *The Vietnam Era: Media and Popular Culture in the US and Vietnam*, ed. Michael Klein (London: Pluto Press, 1990), 10–11, 13; Cathy Schlund-Vials, "Re-seeing Cambodia and Recollecting *The 'Nam*," in *Looking Back on the Vietnam War: Twenty-First-Century Perspectives*, ed. Brenda Boyle and Jeehyun Lim (New Brunswick, NJ: Rutgers University Press, 2016), 156–57.

55. Marvel's *The 'Nam* focused almost exclusively on the American perspective. Only in two issues was the narrative presented from their perspective. See Doug Murray, "Good Old Days," *The 'Nam* #7 (Marvel Comics, 1987); and Don Lomax, "The Letter," *The 'Nam* #84 (Marvel Comics, 1993).

56. For a representative example, see Don Lomax, "Hamburger Hill," *Vietnam Journal: Book Seven: Valley of Death* (Caliber Comics, 2011), and "63 Charlie," *Vietnam Journal: Book Eight: Brain Dead Horror* (Transfuzion, 2011). Also see Amy Kiste, "Re-creating Vietnam: A Semiotic Analysis of *The 'Nam*, a Comic Book Representation of the War," paper presented at the 7th Annual International Conference on Culture and Communication, Philadelphia, PA, October 5–7, 1989, 15–16.

57. Don Lomax, "Inch by Inch," *Vietnam Journal: Book Five: Tet '68* (Caliber Comics, 2010), and Don Lomax, "Sanctuary," *Vietnam Journal: Book Seven: Valley of Death* (Caliber Comics, 2011); also see Kiste, "Re-creating Vietnam," 15–16.

58. Lomax, "Hamburger Hill."

59. See "63 Charlie." In intervention era war comics as well as Marvel's *The 'Nam*, American casualties and deaths were represented but rarely prominently depicted. In general, death was quick and sanitized, as depicted in Doug Murray, "Pride Goeth," *The 'Nam* #9 (Marvel Comics, 1987).

60. Lomax based *Vietnam Journal* on his experiences in his tour of duty in Vietnam in the mid-1960s. Graphic violence abounds throughout the series. For representative examples, see Don Lomax, "American Involvement Vietnam," *Vietnam Journal: Book One: Indian Country* (Transfuzion, 2009), and "Blood Stripe," *Vietnam Journal: Book Seven: Valley of Death* (Caliber Comics, 2011). Lomax considered the graphic nature of his depictions in Rifas, "Interview with Don Lomax," 88. Also see Sandy, "Paneled Perspective," 252–53; and Kiste, "Re-creating Vietnam," 1.

61. Don Lomax, *Vietnam Journal: Book Five: Tet '68* (Caliber Comics, 2010). For depictions of the Tet Offensive in *The 'Nam*, see Doug Murray, "Hue: City of Death," *The 'Nam* #25 (Marvel Comics, 1988); and Don Lomax, "Streets of Blood," *The 'Nam* #81 (Marvel Comics, 1993).

62. Don Lomax, *Vietnam Journal: Book Five: Tet '68*; also see Lomax, "Sanctuary." Additionally, Hue was featured in Michael Palladino, "Reunion," *Semper Fi': Tales of the Marine Corps* #1 (Marvel Comics, 1988).

63. Don Lomax, "Re-group," *Vietnam Journal: Book Seven: Valley of Death* (Caliber Comics, 2011).

64. For further representative examples of combat, see Lomax, *Vietnam Journal: Book Five: Tet '68*; and Don Lomax, "77 Days in Hell," *Vietnam Journal: Book Six: Bloodbath at Khe Sanh* (Caliber Comics, 2011).

65. An excellent example can be found in Chuck Dixon, "C-Note," *The 'Nam* #48 (Marvel Comics, 1990).

66. See Doug Murray, "Three Day Pass," *The 'Nam* #3 (Marvel Comics, 1987); also see Doug Murray, "'Humpin' the Boonies," *The 'Nam* #5 (Marvel Comics, 1987); Chuck Dixon, "The Ville," *The 'Nam* #61 (Marvel Comics, October 1991); Michael Palladino, "Village War," *Semper Fi': Tales of the Marine Corps* #2 (Marvel Comics, 1989); Bernard Grenier, *War without Fronts: The USA*

in Vietnam (New Haven: Yale University Press, 2010); Richard Hunt, *Pacification: The American Struggle for Vietnam's Hearts and Minds* (Boulder, CO: Westview Press, 1995).

67. "Three Day Pass."

68. For representative examples, see Don Lomax, "Hill 875," *Vietnam Journal: Book Three: From the Delta to Dak To* (Caliber Comics, 2010); Don Lomax, "The Last Patrol," *Vietnam Journal: Book Six: Bloodbath at Khe Sanh* (Caliber Comics, 2011). Lomax noted that the Vietnamese enemy "had to be good . . . they were fighting this humongous war machine with just rocks and spear guns." Rifas, "Interview with Don Lomax," 90. Presumably, Lomax's contention relies on exaggeration to make his point.

69. "The Letter."

70. See "Streets of Blood" and "The Letter" as representative examples.

71. "The Letter." The universality of such sentiment has long been challenged in historiography. For an excellent study of the particular nature, structure, and process of the Vietnamese "revolutionary conflict," see Jeffrey Race, *War Comes to Long An: Revolutionary Conflict in a Vietnamese Province* (Berkeley: University of California Press, 2010), 173–93; Merle L. Pribbenow, trans., *Victory in Vietnam: The Official History of the People's Army of Vietnam, 1954–1975*, Military History Institute of Vietnam (Lawrence: University Press of Kansas, 2002); Douglas Pike, *PAVN: People's Army of Vietnam* (New York: Da Capo Press, 1991), 216; William Duiker, *Vietnam: Nation in Revolution* (Boulder, CO: Westview Press, 1983); Francis FitzGerald, *Fire in the Lake: The Vietnamese and the Americans in Vietnam* (New York: Vintage Books, 1972).

72. Mark Atwood Lawrence, *The Vietnam War: A Concise International History* (New York: Oxford University Press, 2008), 177; David Elliot, "Official History, Revisionist History and Wild History," in *Making Sense*, e Bradley and Young, 277–304; Brenda Boyle, "Naturalizing War: The Stories We Tell about the Vietnam War," in *Looking Back on the Vietnam War: Twenty-First-Century Perspectives,* ed. Brenda Boyle and Jeehyun Lim (New Brunswick, NJ: Rutgers University Press, 2016), 187–90; Boggs and Pollard, *Hollywood War Machine*, 99–101.

73. See Doug Murray, "The Good Ol' Days, *The 'Nam* #4 (Marvel Comics, 1988); Doug Murray, "Family Affair;" *The 'Nam* #39 (Marvel Comics, 1989); and "The Letter"; also see Dagilis, "Uncle Sugar vs. Uncle Charlie," 69.

74. David Kilcullen, *The Accidental Guerrilla: Fighting Small Wars in the Midst of a Big One* (Oxford: Oxford University Press, 2009), 1–38.

75. See "Family Affair," and Don Lomax, "Old Ghosts," *The 'Nam* #75 (Marvel Comics, 1992).

76. See "The Good Ol' Days." Also see Murray, *Hearts and Minds*. Only on two occasions did *Vietnam Journal* consider enemy motivation. However, in both cases the enemy was not ethnic Vietnamese but Montagnard. See "The Enemy," and Don Lomax, "The Diary," *Vietnam Journal: Series Two, Volume One: Incursion* (Caliber Comics, 2017). Focus on the Montagnard can also be found in Kubert, *Dong Xoai*.

77. See Doug Murray, "Thanks for Thanksgiving," *The 'Nam* #22 (Marvel Comics, 1988).

78. Michael Lee Lanning and Dan Clegg, *Inside the VC and the NVA: The Real Story of North Vietnam's Armed Forces* (New York: Ballantine Books, 1992), 3. Also see Kiste, "Re-creating Vietnam," 11–12, 16.

79. Lanning and Clegg, *Inside the VC and the NVA*, 16.

80. Dower, *War without Mercy*, 110.

81. For representations in *Vietnam Journal*, see Don Lomax, "Hue: The Imperial City," and "Inch by Inch," *Vietnam Journal: Book Five: Tet '68* (Caliber Comics, 2010). For representations

in *The 'Nam*, see "Hue: City of Death" and "Streets of Blood." Also useful are James Willbanks, *The Tet Offensive: A Concise History* (New York: Columbia University Press, 2006), and Edwin Moïse, *The Myths of Tet: The Most Misunderstood Event of the Vietnam War* (Lawrence: University of Kansas Press, 2017).

82. Don Lomax, "Coastal Pink and Almond Eyes," and "MIA," *Vietnam Journal: Book Four: M.I.A.* (Caliber Comics, 2010). Also see Doug Murray, "Auld Acquaintance," *The 'Nam* #26 (Marvel Comics, 1989).

83. "Humpin' the Boonies." Also see Dagilis, "Uncle Sugar vs. Uncle Charlie," 74. For depictions of atrocity during the Tet Offensive in Marvel Comics, see "Hue: City of Death," while mistreatment of American prisoners of war can be found in "Auld Acquaintance," and Chuck Dixon., "Every Kind of People," *The 'Nam* #60 (Marvel Comics, 1991); "The Ville;" and "Village War."

84. See Don Lomax, "House to House," *The 'Nam* #80 (Marvel Comics, 1993). In "Auld Acquaintance," Murray described atrocity: "It was a mass grave. People who wouldn't go along with the V.C. Hundreds of them. I don't know what kind of . . . I just don't know." Also see Kiste, "Re-creating Vietnam," 11–12, 16; and Boggs and Pollard, *Hollywood War Machine*, 95.

85. Dower, *War without Mercy*, 110; "The Ville"; Chuck Dixon, "The Gratitude of His People," *The 'Nam* #65 (Marvel Comics, 1992).

86. Rifas, "Interview with Don Lomax," 89–90.

87. Dagilis, "Uncle Sugar vs. Uncle Charlie," 67.

88. Rifas, "Interview with Don Lomax," 90; Dagilis, "Uncle Sugar vs. Uncle Charlie," 68.

89. Rifas, "Interview with Don Lomax," 89–90.

90. In "Inch by Inch," the Marines turn their guns on the ARVN in a tense standoff. Also see Don Lomax, "Didi," *The 'Nam* #72 (Marvel Comics, 1992).

91. Don Lomax, "The Citadel," *Vietnam Journal: Book Five: Tet '68* (Caliber Comics, 2010). A challenge to Lomax's view that the "Vietnamese never learned to fight" is found in George Smith, *Siege at Hue* (Boulder, CO: Lynne Rienner, 1999), 165–78.

92. On the cover of "Beginning of the End," *The 'Nam* #24 (Marvel Comics, 1988), artist Andy Kubert interpreted one of the war's most infamous images: Eddie Adams's photograph of General Nguyễn Ngọc Loan's execution of Nguyễn Văn Lém in 1968. Importantly, Murray contextualized the incident historically by referencing Lém's (alleged) participation in the assassination of several of Loan's men and their families. A panel featured in the execution is also featured in Lomax's run on the series in "House to House." Both *Vietnam Journal* and *The 'Nam* also featured American atrocities alongside allied and enemy ones. The war brutalized all combatants without distinguishing nationality, ideology, or justness of cause. In short, a bad war turned men bad. Representative examples are found in "From Cedar Fall, with Love;" Doug Murray, "The Bombs Bursting," *The 'Nam* #18 (Marvel Comics, 1988); Doug Murray, "Phoenix," *The 'Nam* #34 (Marvel Comics, 1989); Don Lomax, "Old Ghosts," *The 'Nam* #75 (Marvel Comics, 1992). Doug Murray, "Sounds of Silence," *The 'Nam* #35 (Marvel Comics, 1989) included a discussion of the My Lai massacre from the perspective of a returned American veteran. *The 'Nam* #75 addressed atrocity and My Lai 4 throughout the entire issue. Of particular significance in the issue is an essay entitled "What Is an Atrocity?" written by veteran Lee R. Russell. American atrocities are also represented in Don Lomax, "Dust-Off," and "Hawks of the Dark Horse," *Vietnam Journal: Book Two: Iron Triangle* (Caliber Comics, 2009). Also see: Huxley, "Naked Aggression," 111; Boggs and Pollard, *Hollywood War Machine*, 99–100; and Kendrick Oliver, *The My Lai Massacre in American History and Memory* (Manchester: Manchester University Press, 2006). For a recent and controversial

historical treatment of US atrocity, see Nick Turse, *Kill Anything That Moves: The Real American War in Vietnam* (New York: Henry Holt, 2013).

93. See Don Lomax, "Cordon and Search," *Vietnam Journal: Book Four: M.I.A.* (Caliber Comics, 2010. Also see Gina Weaver, *Ideologies of Forgetting: Rape in the Vietnam War* (Albany: State University Press of New York, 2010).

94. "From Cedar Fall, with Love" and "Phoenix."

95. Academic study of motivation and the ARVN remains highly underdeveloped. See Robert Brigham, *ARVN: Life and Death in the South Vietnamese Army* (Lawrence: University Press of Kansas, 2006) for a representative example. For an assessable survey, see Spencer Tucker, *Vietnam* (Lexington: University Press of Kentucky, 1999).

96. "Beginning of the End;" Chuck Dixon, "Duty Elsewhere," *The 'Nam* #64 (Marvel Comics, 1992).

97. "The Gratitude of His People."

98. Don Lomax, "The Plain of Reeds," *Vietnam Journal: Book Three: From the Delta to Dak To* (Caliber Comics, 2010).

99. Don Lomax, "Yankee Station, Part One," *The 'Nam* #77 (Marvel Comics, 1993); also see Lomax, "Sanctuary"; and James Willbanks, *The Battle of An Loc* (Bloomington: Indiana University Press, 2005).

100. \ Lomax made the point particularly bluntly in "Yankee Station, Part Two," *The 'Nam* #78 (Marvel Comics, 1993).

101. Lomax, "Sanctuary."

102. "The Good Old Days."

103. "The Good Old Days" offered a "composite of . . . three different VC" to provide "a clear picture of the roots of the war—the reason Charlie fought as long and as hard as he did." In effect, Murray reinforced the notion that only a former enemy could and would fight as hard as the enemy. Also see "Streets of Blood." For representative examples in *Vietnam Journal,* see Don Lomax, *Vietnam Journal: Book One: Indian Country* (Transfuzion, 2009); "Coastal Pink and Almond Eyes"; and Don Lomax, "The Sniper," *Vietnam Journal: Series Two, Volume One: Incursion* (Caliber Comics, 2017). Also see Tal Tovy, "From Foe to Friend: The Kit Carson Scout Program in the Vietnam War," *Armed Forces & Society* 33, no. 1 (2006): 78–93; and Brigham, *ARVN.* In *Vietnam Journal,* virtually all "good allies" were in fact specifically identified as Montagnard, a persecuted minority.

104. "Plain of Reeds."

105. Specific elite units consisted of a range of formations such as a Civilian Irregular Defense Group (CIDG), ARVN Rangers, Kit Carson Scouts, a Provincial Reconnaissance Unit (PRU), "Tunnel Rats," a particularly capable Regional Forces detachment ("Ruff Puffs"), and, in one case, a "CIA Intel Agent." Examples are found in *The 'Nam* #62, #63, #74, #80, and #81. In *Vietnam Journal,* Lomax also praised elite units such as the Kit Carson Scouts and *Biet Dong Quan* (ARVN Rangers). See "Plain of Reeds" and Don Lomax, "The Lost Platoon," *Vietnam Journal: Book Eight: Brain Dead Horror* (Transfuzion, 2011).

106. See Lomax, "Streets of Blood." Captain Lu, a faithful ARVN officer, explained his motivation for fighting: "I was sick of the jokes putting down the ARVN soldiers. 'Wanna buy an ARVN rifle? It's never been fired and only been dropped once.' To some extend it might be true but ARVN died well over two to one compared with the Americans. And their blood was just as red and their families missed them and grieved for them just as long as for any other."

107. Moïse, *Myths of Tet*, 11.

108. See Chuck Dixon, "The Weight," *The 'Nam* #43 (Marvel Comics, 1990); Don Lomax, "Operation: Chicken Lips," *The 'Nam* #70 (Marvel Comics, 1992); Don Lomax, "Return to Brass Hat," *The 'Nam* #71 (Marvel Comics, 1992); "Didi." Also see Kiste, "Re-creating Vietnam," 14. Vietnamization and the later period of the war, including the infamous battle for An Loc during the 1972 Easter Offensive, were specifically detailed in *The 'Nam* #70–72.

109. Lam Quang Thi, "A View from the Other Side of the Story: Reflections of a South Vietnamese Soldier," in *Rolling Thunder in a Gentle Land: The Vietnam War Revisited*, ed. Andrew Wiest, 105–22 (Oxford: Osprey, 2006); Andrew Wiest, *Vietnam's Forgotten Army: Heroism and Betrayal in the ARVN* (New York: New York University Press, 2008); Brigham, *ARVN;* George Veith, *Black April: The Fall of South Vietnam, 1973–75* (New York: Encounter Books, 2013).

110. Dagilis, "Uncle Sugar vs. Uncle Charlie," 82.

111. Dagilis, "Uncle Sugar vs. Uncle Charlie," 65, 82.

112. Dagilis, "Uncle Sugar vs. Uncle Charlie," 71.

113. Kodosky, "Holy Tet Westy!," 1050–52; also see Aaron, *Other Side.*

114. GB Tran, *Vietnamerica: A Family's Journey* (New York: Villard Books, 2010); Thi Bui, *The Best We Could Do: An Illustrated Memoir* (New York: Abrams Comicart, 2016).

115. Marcelino Truong, *Such a Lovely Little War: Saigon 1961–63* (Vancouver, BC: Arsenal Pulp Press, 2016).

WORKS CITED

Aaron, Jason. *The Other Side*. Vertigo, 2007.

"A Figure That Matters." *Jungle War Stories* #7. Dell Comics, 1964.

"Blood Loyalty." *Our Fighting Forces* #105. DC Comics, 1967.

Boggs, Carl, and Tom Pollard. *The Hollywood War Machine: U.S. Militarism and Popular Culture*. Boulder, CO: Paradigm, 2007.

Boyle, Brenda. "Naturalizing War: The Stories We Tell about the Vietnam War." In *Looking Back on the Vietnam War: Twenty-First-Century Perspective*, edited by Brenda Boyle and Jeehyun Lim, 187–90. New Brunswick, NJ: Rutgers University Press, 2016.

"The Brainwashers." *Fightin' Marines* #104. Charlton Comics, 1972.

Brigham, Robert. *ARVN: Life and Death in the South Vietnamese Army*. Lawrence: University Press of Kansas, 2006.

Costello, Matthew. *Secret Identity Crisis: Comic Books and the Unmasking of Cold War America*. New York: Continuum, 2009.

Dagilis, Andrew. "Uncle Sugar vs. Uncle Charlie: An Interview with *The 'Nam*'s Creator, Doug Murray," *Comics Journal*, no. 136 (July 1990): 64–65.

"Deadly Masquerade." *Jungle War Stories* #7. Dell Comics, 1964.

"Die by Water or Fire." *Guerilla War* #12. Dell Comics, 1965.

Dixon, Chuck. "C-Note." *The 'Nam* #48. Marvel Comics, 1990.

Dixon, Chuck. "Duty Elsewhere." *The 'Nam* #64. Marvel Comics, 1992.

Dixon, Chuck. "Every Kind of People." *The 'Nam* #60. Marvel Comics, 1991.

Dixon, Chuck. "The Gratitude of His People." *The 'Nam* #65. Marvel Comics, 1992.

Dixon, Chuck. "The Ville." *The 'Nam* #61. Marvel Comics, October 1991.

Dixon, Chuck. "The Weight." *The 'Nam* #43. Marvel Comics, 1990.
Dower, John. *War without Mercy: Race and Power in the Pacific War.* New York: Pantheon Books, 1986.
Duiker, William. *Vietnam: Nation in Revolution.* Boulder, CO: Westview Press, 1983.
Eisner, Will. *Last Day in Vietnam.* Dark Horse Comics, 2000.
"The Enemy in Vietnam." *Jungle War Stories* #4. Dell Comics, 1963.
Fabian, Johannes. *Time and the Other: How Anthropology Makes Its Object.* New York: Columbia University Press, 2002.
"The Face of the Vietcong." *Jungle War Stories* #4. Dell Comics, 1963.
"Fear in the Delta." *Jungle War Stories* #6. Dell Comics, 1964.
Field, Christopher. "'He was a Living Breathing Human Being': Harvey Kurtzman's War Comics and the 'Yellow Peril' in 1950s Containment Culture." In *Comic Books and the Cold War, 1946–1962: Essays on Graphic Treatment of Communism, the Code and Social Concerns*, edited by Chris York and Rafiel York, 30–44. Jefferson, NC: McFarland, 2012.
"Find . . . Fix . . . Fight . . . Finish." *Tales of the Green Beret* #2. Dell Comics, 1967.
FitzGerald, Francis. *Fire in the Lake: The Vietnamese and the Americans in Vietnam.* New York: Vintage Books, 1972.
"Frontal Assault." *Guerilla War* #12. Dell Comics, 1965.
Gill, Joe. "The Brainwashers." *Fightin' Marines* #93. Charlton Comics, 1970.
Gill, Joe. "Buckshot & Ballots." *Fightin' Marines* #79. Charlton Comics, 1968.
Gill, Joe. "Charley Trap." *Fightin' Marines* #103. Charlton Comics, 1972
Gill, Joe. "Hanoi Ambush." *Fightin' Marines* #82. Charlton Comics, 1968.
Gill, Joe. "Hanoi Hacker." *Fightin' Marines* #98. Charlton Comics, 1971.
Gill, Joe. "The Hidden Guns in the DMZ." *Fightin' Marines* #83. Charlton Comics, 1969.
Gill, Joe. "The Name of the Game." *Fightin' Marines* #97. Charlton Comics, 1971.
Gill, Joe. "A Tough War," "Operation: Ten Little Indians," and "Jungle Justice." *Tales of the Green Beret* #2. Dell Comics, 1967.
Gill, Joe. "The Viet Cong and the Peaceniks." *Fightin' Marines* #92. Charlton Comics, 1970.
Gill, Joe. "Village of Fear" and "The Deadly Shadows." *Fightin' Marines* #94. Charlton Comics, 1970.
Gill, Joe. "The Voice of the Enemy." *Fightin' Marines* #105. Charlton Comics, 1972.
Goodwin, Archie. *Blazing Combat!* Seattle: Fantagraphic Books, 2009.
Grenier, Bernard. *War without Fronts: The USA in Vietnam.* New Haven: Yale University Press, 2010.
Hammond, William. *Reporting Vietnam: Media & Military at War.* Lawrence: University Press of Kansas, 1998.
"Hanoi Ambush." *Fightin' Marines* #104. Charlton Comics, 1972.
Hardy, Charles, and Gail F. Stern, eds. *Ethnic Images in the Comics.* Philadelphia: Balch Institute for Ethnic Studies Museum, 1986.
"The Helping Hand." *Jungle War Stories* #5. Dell Comics, 1963.
Herring, George. *America's Longest War: The United States and Vietnam.* New York: McGraw-Hill, 1986.
Herring, George. "Peoples Quite Apart: Americans, South Vietnamese, and the War in Vietnam." *Diplomatic History* 14, no. 1 (Winter 1990): 1–23.
"Hey Charlie, Surprise!" *Fightin' Marines* #80. Charlton Comics, 1968.
Hoelbling, Walter. "US Fiction about Vietnam: The Discourse of Contradiction." In *The Vietnam Era: Media and Popular Culture in the US and Vietnam*, edited by Michael Klein, 9–10. London: Pluto Press, 1990.

Hunt, Richard. *Pacification: The American Struggle for Vietnam's Hearts and Minds*. Boulder, CO: Westview Press, 1995.

Huxley, David. "Naked Aggression: American Comic Books and the Vietnam War." *Comics Journal*, no. 136 (July 1990): 110–11.

Huxley, David. "'The Real Thing': New Images of the Vietnam War in American Comic Books," in *Vietnam Images War and Representation*, edited by James Aulich and Jeffrey Walsh, 160–70. Basingstoke: Palgrave Macmillan, 1989.

"Introducing 'Shotgun' Harker and The Chicken." *Fightin' Marines* #78. Charlton Comics, 1968.

Isaacs, Arnold. *Vietnam Shadows: The War, Its Ghosts, and Its Legacies*. Baltimore: Johns Hopkins University Press, 1997.

Jarausch, Konrad, Christian Ostermann, and Andreas Etges. "Rethinking, Representing, and Remembering the Cold War: Some Cultural Perspectives." In *The Cold War: Historiography, Memory, Representation*, edited by Konrad Jarausch, Christian Ostermann, and Andreas Etges, 1–18. Berlin: de Gruyter GmbH, 2017.

Jungle War Stories #1. Dell Comics, 1962.

Kanigher, Robert. "No Mercy in Vietnam." *Our Fighting Forces* #99. DC Comics, 1966.

Kilcullen, David. *The Accidental Guerrilla: Fighting Small Wars in the Midst of a Big One*. Oxford: Oxford University Press, 2009.

Kiste, Amy. "Re-creating Vietnam: A Semiotic Analysis of *The 'Nam*, a Comic Book Representation of the War," paper presented at the 7th Annual International Conference on Culture and Communication, Philadelphia, PA, October 5–7, 1989, 15–16.

Klein, Michael. "Cultural Narrative and the Process of Re-collection: Film, History and the Vietnam Era." In *The Vietnam Era: Media and Popular Culture in the US and Vietnam*, edited by Michael Klein, 10–11. London: Pluto Press, 1990.

Kodosky, Robert. "Holy Tet Westy! Graphic Novels and the Vietnam War." *Journal of Modern Culture* 44, no. 5 (2011): 1047–66.

Kubert, Joe. *Dong Xoai, Vietnam 1965*. New York: Vertigo, 2011.

Lanning, Michael Lee, and Dan Clegg. *Inside the VC and the NVA: The Real Story of North Vietnam's Armed Forces*. New York: Ballantine Books, 1992.

Lawrence, Mark Atwood. *The Vietnam War: A Concise International History*. New York: Oxford University Press, 2008.

Ledwell, Ronald. *In Country Nam*. Weymouth, MA: Survival Art Press, 1986.

Liss, Howard. "Trial by Fury." *Our Fighting Forces* #106. DC Comics, 1967.

Lomax, Don. "American Involvement Vietnam." *Vietnam Journal: Book One: Indian Country*. Transfuzion, 2009.

Lomax, Don. "Coastal Pink and Almond Eyes," and "MIA." *Vietnam Journal: Book Four: M.I.A.* Caliber Comics, 2010.

Lomax, Don. "Cordon and Search." *Vietnam Journal: Book Four: M.I.A.* Caliber Comics, 2010.

Lomax, Don. "The Diary." *Vietnam Journal: Series Two, Volume One: Incursion*. Caliber Comics, 2017.

Lomax, Don. "Didi." *The 'Nam #72*. Marvel Comics, 1992.

Lomax, Don. "Dust-off" and "Hawks of the Dark Horse." *Vietnam Journal: Book Two: Iron Triangle*. Caliber Comics, 2009.

Lomax, Don. "Hamburger Hill," "Sanctuary," "Re-group," and "Blood Stripe." *Vietnam Journal: Book Seven: Valley of Death*. Caliber Comics, 2011.

Lomax, Don. "Hill 875." *Vietnam Journal: Book Three: From the Delta to Dak To*. Caliber Comics, 2010.

Lomax, Don. "House to House." *The 'Nam* #80. Marvel Comics, 1993.

Lomax, Don. "Inch by Inch." *Vietnam Journal: Book Five: Tet '68*. Caliber Comics, 2010.

Lomax, Don. "The Letter." *The 'Nam* #84. Marvel Comics, 1993.

Lomax, Don. "The Lost Platoon." *Vietnam Journal: Book Eight: Brain Dead Horror*. Transfuzion, 2011.

Lomax, Don. "Old Ghosts." *The 'Nam* #75. Marvel Comics, 1992.

Lomax, Don. "Operation: Chicken Lips." *The 'Nam* #70. Marvel Comics, 1992.

Lomax, Don. "The Plain of Reeds." *Vietnam Journal: Book Three: From the Delta to Dak To*. Caliber Comics, 2010.

Lomax, Don. "Return to Brass Hat." *The 'Nam* #71. Marvel Comics, 1992.

Lomax, Don. "77 Days in Hell." *Vietnam Journal: Book Six: Bloodbath at Khe Sanh*. Caliber Comics, 2011.

Lomax, Don. "63 Charlie." *Vietnam Journal: Book Eight: Brain Dead Horror*. Transfuzion, 2011.

Lomax, Don. "The Sniper." *Vietnam Journal: Series Two, Volume One: Incursion*. Caliber Comics, 2017.

Lomax, Don. "Streets of Blood." *The 'Nam* #81. Marvel Comics, 1993.

Lomax, Don. *Vietnam Journal: Book One: Indian Country*. Transfuzion, 2009.

Lomax, Don. "Yankee Station, Part One." *The 'Nam* #77. Marvel Comics, 1993.

Lomax, Don. "Yankee Station, Part Two." *The 'Nam* #78. Marvel Comics, 1993.

Longevall, Frank. "'There Ain't No Daylight': Lyndon Johnson and the Politics of Escalation." In *Making Sense of the Vietnam Wars: Local, National and Transnational Perspectives*, edited by Mark Philip Bradley and Marilyn Young, 98–99. Oxford: Oxford University Press, 2008.

Ma, Sheng-Mei. *The Deadly Embrace: Orientalism and Asian American Identity*. Minneapolis: University of Minnesota Press, 2000.

Madison, Nathan. *Anti-Foreign Imagery in American Pulps and Comic Books*. Jefferson: McFarland, 2013.

Maguire, Lori. "The Avengers Always Stand Ready to Do Their Part": The Avengers and the Vietnam War." In *The Ages of the Avengers: Essays on the Earth's Mightiest Heroes in Changing Times*, edited by Joseph Darowski, 12–24. Jefferson: McFarland, 2014.

The Military History Institute of Vietnam. *Victory in Vietnam: The Official History of the People's Army of Vietnam, 1954–1975*. Translated by Merle L. Pribbenow. Lawrence: University Press of Kansas, 2002.

"Mission: Strangle." *Jungle War Stories* #4. Dell Comics, 1963.

Moïse, Edwin. *The Myths of Tet: The Most Misunderstood Event of the Vietnam War*. Lawrence: University Press of Kansas, 2017.

"M-U-D Spells Disaster." *Jungle War Stories* #4. Dell Comics, 1963.

Mundey, Lisa. *American Militarism and Anti-Militarism in Popular Media, 1945–1970*. Jefferson: McFarland, 2012.

Murray, Chris. "*Pop*aganda: Superhero Comics and Propaganda in World War Two." In *Comics & Culture: Analytical and Theoretical Approaches to Comics*, edited by Anne Magnussen and Hans-Christian Christiansen, 141–55. Copenhagen: Museum Tusculanum Press, 2000.

Murray, Doug. "Auld Acquaintance." *The 'Nam* #26. Marvel Comics, 1989.

Murray, Doug. Editorial. "Incoming." *The 'Nam*. Marvel Comics, 1986.

Murray, Doug. "Family Affair." *The 'Nam* #39. Marvel Comics, 1989.

Murray, Doug. "The Good Ol' Days." *The 'Nam* #4. Marvel Comics, 1988.
Murray, Doug. "Good Old Days." *The 'Nam* #7. Marvel Comics, 1987.
Murray, Doug. *Hearts & Minds: A Vietnam Love Story*. Marvel Comics, 1991.
Murray, Doug. "Hue: City of Death." *The 'Nam* #25. Marvel Comics, 1988.
Murray, Doug. "Interview with Brian Jacks." *Slush Factory*, May 2001, http://www.slushfactory.com/features/articles/052502-murray.php. Accessed on 25 September 2018.
Murray, Doug. "Interview with Charlie Rose." *CBS News Washington*, June 4, 1987, https://www.youtube.com/watch?v=qwfB9bCs4kw. Accessed on 25 September 2018.
Murray, Doug. "Phoenix," *The 'Nam* #34. Marvel Comics, 1989.
Murray, Doug. "Pride Goeth," *The 'Nam* #9. Marvel Comics, 1987.
Murray, Doug. "Sounds of Silence," *The 'Nam* #35. Marvel Comics, 1989.
Murray, Doug. "Thanks for Thanksgiving," *The 'Nam* #22. Marvel Comics, 1988.
Murray, Doug. "Three Day Pass," *The 'Nam* #3. Marvel Comics, 1987.
"The Name of the Game." *Fightin' Marines* #99, Charlton Comics, 1971.
Oliver, Kendrick. *The My Lai Massacre in American History and Memory*. Manchester: Manchester University Press, 2006.
"Operation: Chicken Lips." *The 'Nam* #70. Marvel Comics, 1992.
"Operation Red Eye." *Tales of the Green Beret* #1. Dell Comics, 1967.
Palladino, Michael. "Reunion." *Semper Fi': Tales of the Marine Corps* #1. Marvel Comics, 1988.
Palladino, Michael. "Village War." *Semper Fi': Tales of the Marine Corps* #2. Marvel Comics, 1989.
Pike, Douglas. *PAVN: People's Army of Vietnam*. New York: Da Capo Press, 1991.
"Pop Goes the War." *Newsweek*, September 12, 1966.
Race, Jeffrey. *War Comes to Long An: Revolutionary Conflict in a Vietnamese Province*. Berkeley: University of California Press, 2010.
"Requiem for a Red." *Jungle War Stories* #1. Dell Comics, 1962.
Rifas, Leonard. "Interview with Don Lomax." *Comics Journal*, no. 136 (July 1990): 88, 102.
Rifas, Leonard. "War Comics." In *The Routledge Companion to Comics*, edited by Frank Bramlett, Roy Cook, and Aaron Meskin, 183–91. New York: Routledge, 2017.
"Ring of Fire." *Jungle War Stories* #5. Dell Comics, 1963.
Rollins, Peter. "Using Popular Culture to Study the Vietnam War: Perils and Possibilities." In *Why We Fought: America's Wars in Film and History*, edited by Peter Collins and John O'Connor, 367–89. Lexington: University Press of Kentucky, 2008.
Said, Edward. *Orientalism*. New York: Vintage Books, 2003.
Sandy, James. "A Paneled Perspective: The United States and the Vietnam War Examined through Comic Books." In *The Vietnam War in Popular Culture: The Influence of America's Most Controversial War on Everyday Life, Vol.* 2, edited by Ron Milam, 245–49. Santa Barbara, CA: Praeger, 2016.
"Save or Be Saved." *Jungle War Stories* #7. Dell Comics, 1964.
"Saving Face." *Army Attack* #1. Charlton Comics, 1964.
Schlund-Vials, Cathy. "Comics Captured America's Opinions about the Vietnam War." https://theconversation.com/comics-captured-americas-growing-ambivalence-about-the-vietnam-war-83756. Accessed September 9, 2018.
Schlund-Vials, Cathy. "Re-seeing Cambodia and Recollecting *The 'Nam*." In *Looking Back on the Vietnam War: Twenty-First-Century Perspectives*, ed. Brenda Boyle and Jeehyun Lim, 156–74. New Brunswick, NJ: Rutgers University Press, 2016.

Scott, Cord. *Comics and Conflict: Patriotism and Propaganda from WWII through Operation Iraqi Freedom*. Annapolis: Naval Institute Press, 2014.

"Second Chance." *Jungle War Stories* #4. Dell Comics, 1963.

"Second Chance." *Tales of the Green Beret* #4. Dell Comics, 1967.

Semper Fi': Tales of the Marine Corps #1, #2, and #6. Marvel Comics, 1988–1989.

"Silence at Station Seven." *Jungle War Stories* #2. Dell Comics, 1963.

Smith, George. *Siege at Hue*. Boulder, CO: Lynne Rienner, 1999.

Span, Paula. "Vietnam: The Comic Book War: Marvel Brings Out a Dark, Gritty and Popular Series." *Washington Post*, September 10, 1986.

"The Switcheroo." *Jungle War Stories* #5. Dell Comics, 1963.

Thi, Bui. *The Best We Could Do: An Illustrated Memoir*. New York: Abrams Comicart, 2016.

Thi, Lam Quang. "A View from the Other Side of the Story: Reflections of a South Vietnamese Soldier." In *Rolling Thunder in a Gentle Land: The Vietnam War Revisited*, edited by Andrew Wiest, 105–22. Oxford: Osprey, 2006.

"This Crummy War." *Army War Heroes* #27. Charlton Comics, 1968.

Tovy, Tal. "From Foe to Friend: The Kit Carson Scout Program in the Vietnam War." *Armed Forces & Society* 33, no. 1 (2006): 78–93.

"The Traitor." *Tales of the Green Beret* #1. Dell Comics, 1967.

Tran, G. B. *Vietnamerica: A Family's Journey*. New York: Villard Books, 2010.

Truong, Marcelino. *Such a Lovely Little War: Saigon 1961–63*. Vancouver, BC: Arsenal Pulp Press, 2016.

Tucker, Spencer. *Vietnam*. Lexington: University Press of Kentucky, 1999.

Turse, Nick. *Kill Anything That Moves: The Real American War in Vietnam*. New York: Henry Holt, 2013.

Veith, George. *Black April: The Fall of South Vietnam, 1973–75*. New York: Encounter Books, 2013.

"Verdict: Guilty as Charged!" *Fightin' Marines* #99. Charlton Comics, 1971.

"Viet Cong Victim." *Fightin' Marines* #104. Charlton Comics, 1972.

"Vietnam Battle Facts." *Jungle War Stories* #2. Dell Comics, 1963.

"Violence in the Air." *Jungle War Stories* #4. Dell Comics, 1963.

"The Voice of the Enemy." *Fightin' Marines* #104. Charlton Comics, 1972.

Vizzini, Bryan. "When (Comic) Art Imitates Life: American Exceptionalism and the Comic Book Industry in the Vietnam War Era." In *The Vietnam War in Popular Culture: The Influence of America's Most Controversial War on Everyday Life Vol. 1*, edited by Ron Milam, 359–78. Santa Barbara: Praeger, 2016.

Weaver, Gina. *Ideologies of Forgetting: Rape in the Vietnam War*. Albany: State University Press of New York, 2010.

Wiest, Andrew. *Vietnam's Forgotten Army: Heroism and Betrayal in the ARVN*. New York: New York University Press, 2008.

Willbanks, James. *The Battle of An Loc*. Bloomington: Indiana University Press, 2005.

Willbanks, James. *The Tet Offensive: A Concise History*. New York: Columbia University Press, 2006.

Woodman, Brian. "A Hollywood War of Wills: Cinematic Representation of Vietnamese Super-Soldiers and America's Defeat in the War." *Journal of Film and Video* 55, no. 2/3 (Summer/Fall 2003): 44–58.

Wright, Bradford. *Comic Book Nation: The Transformation of Youth Culture in America*. Baltimore: Johns Hopkins University Press, 2001.

Yang, Jeff, and Daniel Kim. "Marvels & Monsters: Unmasking Asian Images in U.S. Comics, 1942–1986." http://www.janm.org/exhibits/marvels-monsters/ and http://www.npr.org/2011/08/11/139536088/marvels-and-monsters-unveils-asians-in-comics. Accessed September 9, 2018.

Yizheng, Zou. "Flying Tigers and Chinese Sidekicks in World War II American Comic Books." In *The 10 Cent War: Comic Books, Propaganda and World War I*, edited by Trischa Goodnow and James Kimble, 52–55. Jackson: University Press of Mississippi, 2016.

Young, Richard. "The 'Real Victims' of the Vietnam War: Soldier versus State in American Comic Books." *Journal of Modern Culture* 50, no. 3 (2017): 561–84.

Young, Richard. "There Is Nothing Grittier than a 'Grunt's Eye View': American War Comic Books and the Popular Memory of the Vietnam War." *Australasian Journal of American Studies* 34, no. 2 (2015): 75–93.

CHAPTER SIX

MAGNETO THE SURVIVOR

Redemption, Cold War Fears, and the "Americanization of the Holocaust" in Chris Claremont's *Uncanny X-Men* (1975–1991)

MARTIN LUND

In the cinematic versions of the X-Men franchise, the character Magneto as played by both Ian McKellen and Michael Fassbender is unequivocally a Jewish Holocaust survivor.[1] This identity was established in the opening scene of *X-Men* (2000) and has been part of the character's silver screen presence ever since. The cinematic Magneto's Jewishness has since also been applied in several analyses of the comics franchise and character, to bolster the claim that the comics character is also Jewish and has been so for decades—a projection mapped by some comics scholars and critics onto comics published both after and *before* the film.

Director Bryan Singer has described the establishment of Magneto's Jewishness in his first *X-Men* film more as a matter of historical consistency than anything else: "In the comic book, he was in a concentration camp, but he was not necessarily Jewish [. . .] I made that decision that morning because that's the way it worked. Jews were transported primarily together, and if I was going to put yellow stars on these extras, I was going to be putting one on young Erik."[2] But, as Singer notes, in the comics' continuity Magneto was not definitively Jewish, and would not be so until 2008, in the miniseries *Magneto Testament*.[3] Certainly, by that time it had been established for decades and beyond the shadow of a doubt that Magneto was a survivor of Auschwitz, but associations of Jewishness were not always part of that identity; Magneto's identity was fluid, with his potential Jewish identity sometimes hinted at and sometimes dismissed.

This chapter focuses on Magneto as he appeared in Chris Claremont's 1975–1991 run as writer of *X-Men*, later *Uncanny X-Men*.[4] It is crucial to frame and delimit this material because Magneto is often treated as if he were an organic whole, with description freely mixing character developments that occurred over decades, without considering the fact that many different writers and artists have been involved in (re)creating the character. By projecting the work of earlier and later writers onto Claremont, commentators often identify Magneto as Jewish.[5] Without a clear articulation of which version of a character is the subject of any given study, such projection is always a possibility. No comic-book character is static, few characters in superhero comics are the product of a single creator, and continuity brings both depth and sprawl in characterization; the result of serialization is often a multiplicity of character iterations that are identical or similar in many respects but radically different in others.[6]

According to political scientist Matthew J. Costello, the retelling of comics characters' origin stories permits the incorporation of elements that had previously not been there, changes that signal new visions of the meaning of characters and shifts in the culture these characters reflect.[7] Generic Holocaust references appeared throughout Claremont's run, but nowhere did they figure more prominently than in his long, and ultimately abortive, rewriting of Magneto into a death camp survivor and occasional tragic antihero. This process has often resulted in overstated assumptions about Magneto's identity.

To understand how and why Magneto was made into a survivor requires a look into the history of how the Holocaust has been understood in the US and, particularly, how it was understood at the time when (and since) Claremont first introduced the idea that Magneto was a survivor, in 1981. Importantly, Claremont left Magneto's ethnicity as a gap in the metatext. In *Uncanny X-Men* #149 (September 1981), the issue preceding the introduction of Magneto's Auschwitz background, the X-Men's leader Xavier was even pointedly used to keep Magneto explicitly ambiguous: "Magneto! Origin, unknown. Although his features are Caucasian, probably Nordic—antecedents, unknown."[8] Why, then, did Magneto become a survivor? And how was this identity framed?

THE AMERICANIZATION OF THE HOLOCAUST

Historian Jonathan Sarna writes, "Today, most Americans know more about the Holocaust than about any single event in the entire history of the Jewish people."[9] That, however, does not necessarily mean that most Americans' knowledge of the Holocaust is particularly deep; neither does the near-universal agreement in the US that the Holocaust must be remembered mean that what is known about it is clear-cut.[10] As historian Peter Novick puts it, "Americans are exhorted that they must 'confront' and 'remember' the Holocaust, but what is it they are to confront and remember?"[11]

When Claremont introduced the Holocaust into Magneto's backstory, it was not an unknown quality in American comics: some images of the camps had appeared (mostly without Jewish victims) in WWII era comics; the postwar decades had introduced a few stories—including one in which Batman fought a survivor out for revenge (*Batman*, no. 237, December 1971); and Art Spiegelman had started serialization of his soon-to-be Pulitzer-winning *Maus*.[12] But the Holocaust was still rare in comics, as it was in other areas of US popular culture at the time. The Holocaust is one of the most contentious events in human history, and myriad meanings have been attributed to and abstracted from it over the years. Following the Second World War, what is now called the Holocaust remained in the cultural periphery; only slowly did it emerge into Jewish American, and later national American, historical consciousness.[13]

Further, Novick, historian Alvin H. Rosenfeld, and others have argued that in this slow emergence, the Holocaust has been "Americanized."[14] Testimonies from outside the US like Elie Wiesel's *Night* (US publication 1960) and Primo Levi's *Survival in Auschwitz* (1959) had been important in making the Holocaust known, but they had not had much success in the US; a heavily edited version of Anne Frank's diary was among the only sources for Holocaust remembrance that were widely known to Americans before 1978.[15] Rosenfeld writes that the cruelties and deprivations of the Nazi genocide of Jews are so alien to the American mind-set, accustomed to an (idealized) ethos of goodness, innocence, optimism, liberty, diversity, and equality, that they are virtually incomprehensible: "The Holocaust has had to enter American consciousness, therefore, in ways that Americans could readily understand on their own terms. These are terms that promote a tendency to individualize, heroize, moralize, idealize, and universalize."[16]

Such tendencies were evident already in various American 1950s versions of Anne Frank's diary, which stressed her optimism while softening her suffering, but the most significant development in Americanization occurred from the late 1970s through early 1990s. The TV miniseries *Holocaust* (1978) presented the Holocaust within a soap-operatic framework and was followed by further representations that "in the aggregate [. . .] served to firmly affix the Holocaust on the American cultural map."[17] In many ways Americanization culminated in 1993, with Stephen Spielberg's *Schindler's List* and the opening of the National Holocaust Memorial Museum on the National Mall.[18] Part of this Americanizing process was a new focus on survivors and their stories; also beginning around 1978, just years before Magneto took on the mantle, Holocaust survivors went from having been "isolated and avoided" to figures who were to many "heroic witnesses, tellers of tales, redeemers of the human spirit and of hope," in part as a response to a larger turn toward prizing survival in US culture.[19] It is in this context, and with these contours, that Magneto was turned into a survivor.

INSCRIBING THE HOLOCAUST

Magneto first appeared in *X-Men* #1, in September 1963. Over the years, he was many things to the X-Men but always a blustering and unselfconsciously evil villain and mutant supremacist terrorist. During Claremont's tenure Magneto drifted further and further away from this original framing, in what journalist Arie Kaplan describes as "a more personal and more openly Jewish journey than ever before, leaving all talk of metaphor behind."[20] Magneto's journey was indeed personal, as was that of many of Claremont's—and indeed Marvel's—characters in these years, but neither openly Jewish nor devoid of metaphor.[21] At first, while remaining bombastic and cocky, Magneto sought revenge for personal slights rather than power.[22] In *X-Men* #125 (September 1979), however, emotional depth emerged with the revelation that he had lost a wife, Magda, under tragic circumstances.[23] Then, in an argument with the X-Man Cyclops in *Uncanny X-Men* (*UXM*) #150 (October 1981), Magneto expressed sorrow over the recent death of another X-Man. Deepening the tragedy of his newfound past, Magneto here says: "I know . . . something of grief. Search through my homeland, you will find *none* who bear my name. Mine was a large family, and it was slaughtered—without mercy, without remorse."[24]

The statement's meaning, however, is not revealed until the issue's climax, when, believing that he has killed Kitty Pryde, a young and explicitly Jewish X-Man, in the heat of battle, he mentions the loss of his own daughter, Anya. After her murder, Magneto says, he resolved to "not rest 'til I had created a world where my kind—mutants—could live free and safe and unafraid. Where such as you, little one, could be happy. Instead, I have *slain* you." He adds: "I remember my own childhood—the gas chambers as [*sic*] *Auschwitz*, the guards joking as they herded my family to their death. As our lives were nothing to them, so *human* lives became nothing to me." Unable to maintain his blustering bravado, Magneto adds Cold War connotations when he concludes, melancholy and in subversive echo of John F. Kennedy's inaugural address: "I believed so much in my destiny, in my personal vision, that I was prepared to pay any price, make any sacrifice to achieve it. But I forgot the innocents who could suffer in the process. Can you not appreciate the irony, Ororo? In my zeal to remake the world, I have become much like those I have always hated and despised."[25]

What prompted the fight was Magneto's decision to hold the world hostage and threaten to "*end* life on earth as you know it," unless granted total political control. He delivers his ultimatum by projecting his image into the White House, the Kremlin, and other seats of world power. The persecution of mutants, underscored by its soon-to-be-introduced Holocaust corollary, motivates his extremism: "I and my fellow mutants have been hunted down and slain like wild animals. Those killings will stop. *All* killing will stop. The nuclear powers have the capability of expunging *all life* from this planet. Daily, the risk of such a holocaust increases, yet the leaders of those nations seem not to care." Some even regard nuclear war as desirable. "You are welcome to exterminate yourselves, if you wish," Magneto says, "but in the process, you might destroy my people as well. That I will not allow."[26]

Claremont's own sparse notes for the issue are suggestive: "Magneto's master plan [. . .] surrender or else—(anti nuke message?)/goal admirable—means wrong/scott leads x-men against him." At a time when nuclear holocaust loomed larger than ever since the Cuban Missile Crisis, when Auschwitz had become "an Image of the Modern Malaise" and the Holocaust was becoming a "convenient symbol for the prevailing sense of helplessness" of the day, it is perhaps unsurprising that the two would intersect in this way, even though it might seem off-putting to many.[27]

On the same notes page cited above, Claremont adds: "moral conflict" (connected with "anti-mutant paranoia"); "holocaust"; "link /w Kitty." There is also a diagram tracing character relations that connects Magneto and Xavier with each other, and each with both Kitty and the Holocaust. The most noteworthy element in this is the fact that Kitty's name has a Star of David next to it, while Magneto's does not.[28] This suggests that whether or not Magneto was Jewish did not matter for the purposes of introducing the Holocaust in relation to nuclear disarmament: Magneto's actions give the story its force; Kitty's Jewishness, its pathos.

The unimaginable destructive potential of Magneto's ultimatum and its attendant wrongness are presented in extreme terms in this story; a second, global, Holocaust looms, and those he "has always hated and despised" are framed not only as the Nazis but as their potential successors: Reagan, Thatcher, Brezhnev, and other leaders who were now playing with people's lives. This ties into a post-Watergate moral realignment that historian John Lewis Gaddis labels a "recovery of equity," after which public opinion increasingly questioned the Cold War and its long-held assumptions. Particularly disturbing were the doctrine of Mutual Assured Destruction (MAD), "hostage-taking on a massive scale [. . .] deliberately placing civilian populations at risk for nuclear annihilation," and the fact that in their conduct of the Cold War, American leaders seemed to be abandoning the very values they claimed to fight for.[29] In this context, and with its overt ties to it, *UXM* #150's introduction of the Holocaust then appears as a heavy-handed warning about the cost of moral compromise and the potential for global calamity in the pursuit of what is nonetheless perceived as a righteous goal.[30] Echoing the ideas underlying the recovery of equity as they sit together after Kitty's apparent death, the X-Man Storm tells Magneto: "The dream was good, *is* good. Only the dreamer has become corrupted."[31]

Claremont's inscription of the Holocaust into Magneto's story continued in a "flashback" in *UXM* #161 (September 1982), when Xavier is in a coma, fighting an alien infestation. The flashback places Magneto and Xavier's first meeting in Haifa just after the Korean War. Xavier, a psychologist, recalls being summoned to see if he could cure Gabrielle Haller, a "catatonic schizophrenic" former Dachau inmate. Telepathically entering her mind, Xavier forces his way through her mental defenses: "[I]f she *has* found peace within herself, have I the right to force her to confront her past, her present? *Yes*!" The ensuing confrontation briefly addresses suffering in the Holocaust, but through the trope of Xavier's superpowers and in literally inhuman terms, making its representation less immediate: the SS guards are fanged demons and ogres rather than conscious, political, human agents, and the crematoria become the gates of hell.[32]

A montage-panel on the next page shows how "over the weeks that follow—and with the aid of her constant companions Xavier and Magnus—Gaby bridges the gap between child- and adulthood, her old life in Holland and her new one in Israel, *with remarkable ease*."[33] She and Xavier even become romantically involved. Thus, the Holocaust's terrible reality is alleviated. The story then promptly turns to the kidnapping of Gabrielle by ex-Nazi terrorists in outlandish uniforms brandishing high-tech weaponry, and her subsequent action-packed rescue by Xavier and Magneto, all over lost Nazi gold.

When Xavier first arrives in Haifa, Magneto is already there. The location is, of course, suggestive of Jewishness, but not definitive. Xavier notices Magneto's tattoo, but his interlocutor replies before he can ask: "*Auschwitz*. I grew up there." "And your family," asks Xavier. "I have no family, Dr. Xavier. Anymore," says Magneto, adding to his litany of loss. The two grow close, but Xavier realizes that Magneto has been "deeply scarred" by his own experiences, and their ideological positions concerning mutant-human relations prove too different for their friendship to last. Magneto leaves after they defeat the terrorists, his parting words marked by mistrust and loss: "In time, you will learn what I have learned—that even those you love will turn from you in horror when they discover what you truly are. Mutants will not go meekly to the gas chambers. We will fight . . . and we will win!"[34]

Neither of the story's survivors forgets, but their approaches to the past differ. On the one hand, Magneto dwells in bitterness, hawkish anger, and wrong-headed paranoia, which is again explained in terms of personal loss and tragedy, making it individual and thus more relatable. It is also clearly framed as wrong, a verdict illustrated by Magneto taking the recovered Nazi gold with him and thus tainting his mission for mutant supremacy from the outset. On the other hand, the flashback's closure is optimistic, affirmative, and typically American in its sentimental affirmation of life and love. Gabrielle, who returned to a catatonic state during the rough-and-tumble rescue, wakes up despite being scared, despite risking being hurt, because she hears Xavier's voice and follows it out of her shell: "Oh, Charles," she says, "it's so wonderful to be alive!"[35] Even more clearly than Magneto, Gabrielle changes from being a survivor viewed as "archetypal victim[], guilty, ghostly, silent, and estranged" into a symbol of hope and the human spirit.[36]

REDEMPTIVE AFFIRMATION

Having established Magneto as a deeply scarred and wayward man, Claremont then began redeeming him. At one point, in the 1982 graphic novel *God Loves, Man Kills*, when Magneto confronts the X-Men and Cyclops asks if his vision of a mutant dictatorship is better than a world in which mutants are feared, the villain rebuffs him: "Do not take that tone with me, boy. I have lived under a dictatorship . . . and seen my family murdered by its servants. When I rule, it will be for the betterment of *all*." He will eliminate discontent, he says, and the freedoms lost will not be noticed even in the most "libertarian" of states.[37] Unable to convince his adversaries, he leaves, but the Magneto who sought to rule because he thought might makes right is gone, replaced by an idealist for whom the ends justify the means. Later, in *UXM* #196 (August 1985), he even stops another X-Man from killing a man who has assaulted Xavier, with the rationale that it would make her no better than those who hate and fear them.[38]

Then, in *UXM* #199 (November 1985), Magneto, Kitty Pryde, and the shape-shifting mutant Mystique (in disguise) attend a Holocaust "Remembrance Day" gathering. Much has been made of this in secondary literature. Kaplan describes it as showing Magneto and Kitty "bond[ing] over their shared Jewish heritage," and as being "one of the first sustained efforts to work openly Jewish characters into an established superhero book."[39] For literary scholar Cheryl Alexander Malcolm, Magneto "instructs" Kitty in the importance of Holocaust remembrance." He becomes "a Jewish mentor" who "urges" Kitty to address the gathering.[40] According to librarian Robert G. Weiner and historian Lynne Fallwell:

> Because Magneto was a survivor, the plot of the stories brought to light the problems of racism and fear of others to a wide audience. One of the most telling narratives appears in *X-Men 199–200* (1985), when Shadowcat (Kitty Pryde—a young Jewish character, whose extended family members perish in the camps) goes with Magneto to speak at the Holocaust Memorial Museum in Washington, DC. The ultimate message of her talk is "Never Again" can we allow something like the Holocaust to occur.[41]

The descriptions quoted above all inflate the scene's importance. Magneto had never displayed any Jewish heritage to bond over with Kitty. He never "instructs" Kitty in "the importance of Holocaust remembrance," nor does he become a "mentor" who "urges" her to do anything. When Kitty speaks, she does not deliver a talk; she asks, on behalf of her recently deceased grandfather, if anybody knows anything about her great-aunt.[42] All this happens in eight panels on one page, as part of a larger story with a different moral.

The setting and timing of this comic are noteworthy, however; cover dated November 1985, the comic was published just months after Ronald Reagan's controversial visit to German soldiers' graves (in May), which had been predated by an initial unwillingness to visit a concentration camp, and statements that seemed to suggest that he was equating the suffering of the Holocaust's victims with that of Germans who were victims of a single madman's whims.[43] As such, Claremont was writing this script in a context where the importance of remembrance was being discussed in the media, and it is likely that he was affected by this. More importantly, the sequence takes place at the "National Holocaust Memorial," which is likely a reference to the announced but still-unbuilt United States Holocaust Memorial Museum. (The cornerstone would not be laid for another three years, and it would not open until 1993.) The memorial has been a contentious symbol of Americanization since the 1980 decision to fund it, on the recommendation of a presidential commission charged with representing the American people with a mandate to balance Jewish specificity with a mission to combat hate and oppression, prevent genocide and crimes against humanity, and strengthen democracy.[44]

Placing Magneto and Kitty there favorably highlights a still nonexistent symbol of the Holocaust as something other than the murder of six million European Jews and persecution of countless others. In the story, remembrance and witness appear as means of prevention and ensuring that something like the Holocaust never happens again, but in a way that suggests a universalizing impulse: the survivors and Mystique speak in generalized or vague terms of "man's inhumanity to man" and the "systematic, institutionalized extermination of one people by another." Only once is the fact that Jews were especially targeted mentioned, and then in a comparative way, as part of Magneto's "nightmare" mutant future. When the Holocaust is explicitly connected to the open-ended sign of mutantcy in this way, the dire image of a potential future acquires the character of a lesson about diversity and tolerance and serves as a metaphorical warning about victimization in general.[45]

Furthermore, Magneto is here not only a survivor but also a rescuer, merging in his character two groups of people that were at the time becoming increasingly prominent as affirmative symbolic figures that could "balance" suffering with images of hope in American Holocaust memory.[46] A couple of survivors who recognize Magneto tell Kitty that they knew her relative in the Warsaw resistance, before she died at Auschwitz. "We would have died, too, if not for this scoundrel," they tell her about Magneto: "He'd been at that accursed place from the very start.

He saved many of us." Surprised, Kitty asks: "You were a hero?" Hardly, replies Magneto. Heroism meant holding on to one's humanity, and so, "If I am a hero, then so is every man and woman who survived."[47] Here, the Holocaust's victims and perpetrators, while not forgotten, are obscured by heroic types who were, by any measure, tragically far fewer.

Then, abruptly, the government-affiliated Freedom Force comes to arrest Magneto, and a classic superhero battle ensues. Magneto and Kitty triumph with the X-Men's aid, but Magneto nonetheless surrenders himself, citing the fear he inspires. This willingness to abide by the rule of law further emphasizes how he is turning into a more democratic, "American," character:

> You did not see the faces of my friends when they saw me reveal my powers. They were terrified—as my wife, Magda, was so many years ago. My powers saved our lives—yet she was more afraid of them, and me, than of the secret police butchers who murdered our daughter. Look at what we have done to this place. Think what I have done to the world. [. . .] Have I become the image of those I hated? [. . .] I am through running and hiding. For my own salvation—for the good of mutantkind—the time has come at last to take a stand . . . to face my accusers, and my *fate!*"[48]

In his impassioned defense at his trial (in *UXM* #200, December 1985), Magneto further muddles the meaning of the Holocaust in Claremont's X-Men comics when he sweeps from rationalizing the destruction of a Soviet submarine as self-defense to a critique of the Cold War powers he had earlier threatened: "By what right do those self-same great powers hold *me* hostage, with their nuclear arsenals?! I am a citizen of neither the United States nor the Soviet Union . . . yet they possess the capacity to slay me and mine. I live, I prosper, solely because two men on opposite sides of the globe choose to keep the peace." From there he moves to a Holocaust-referencing historical critique of human cruelty writ large:

> My dream, from the start, has been the protection and preservation of my own kind, mutants. To spare them the fate my family suffered in Auschwitz—and do not tell me such a thing cannot happen again, because that is a lie! You humans slaughter each other because of the color of your skin, or your faith or your politics—or for no reason at all—too many of you hate as easily as you draw breath. What's to prevent your adding us to that list?![49]

Magneto then goes on to take individual responsibility for his actions and makes a plea for mutant rights: "I am the reason mutants are unjustly feared. That is why I am here, why I will abide by the court's decision. My hope is to make the world understand the reasons for my being. But, most of all, to punish *me* for my crimes—and, no longer, my people."[50] Before anything can come of it, the revenge-seeking children of the ex-Nazi that Magneto and Xavier fought in the *UXM* #161 flashback attack the court. After their defeat, Xavier lies dying and passes his torch to Magneto, saying that his looking after the X-Men and teaching the New Mutants (another mutant team) will "stand as a far nobler monument—and better safeguard to mutantkind—than your martyrdom at this trial."[51]

The Cold War references in this story again point to international tensions, which were then in their last hot flash, and are once more phrased with a type of MAD-as-hostage-taking rhetoric underlying the Holocaust references.[52] Also noteworthy are the references to principle and rights. Gabrielle Haller, who serves as Magneto's counsel, references recent history, which is "full of accused, and admitted terrorists—thieves and murderers—whom the international community later accepted, even welcomed as statesmen," and asks if someone fighting for a just cause should be judged by the same standards as one who acts from greed.[53] This speech likely references Israeli Prime Minister Menachem Begin implicitly. This, combined with the prosecution's and gallery's willingness to condemn Magneto, might be a sideways swipe at the UN, which at the time still had not retracted its 1975 "Zionism = Racism" resolution and staged "annual ritual condemnations" of Israel. Thus, "The Trial of Magneto" possibly, but partially, reflects a widespread disaffection among Jewish supporters of Israel with a UN human rights system that had been on the increase since Israel's territorial expansion following the Six-Day War of 1967.[54] But the story is more palpably connected with the Cold War and as such is grounded in American democratic discourses.

CHANGING THE PAST

After the trial, with Magneto teaching the New Mutants as Xavier's successor, the Holocaust largely disappeared from the regular *UXM* series and Magneto's characterization until the end of Claremont's tenure.[55] Between the mid-1980s and early 1990s, however, Marvel issued the reprint series *Classic X-Men*, which Claremont used to further reshape Magneto, by rewriting parts of two previously published comics and filling in gaps in the metatext with a couple of short vignettes. *Classic* #12 (August 1987) reprinted *X-Men* #104 (April 1977) with an added page where a still-unredeemed Magneto monologically calls Xavier a fool for not realizing that Magneto is mutantkind's only hope for survival against the world's untrustworthy governments: "I have lived through one *Holocaust*. Never again. The world will be brought to my heel—our race guaranteed survival and prosperity for all time—and all who oppose me, especially traitors such as you and your brats . . . will receive the fate they so richly deserve."[56] *Classic* #19

(March 1988) added a scene to *X-Men* #113 (September 1978) in which Magneto reflects about his wife: "Foolish woman—it was such as she who made me what I am! If she—who loved me—was terrified of my mutant power, think how the rest of humanity will react!—Has reacted! I endured one death camp—in Auschwitz—I will not see another people fear what they do not understand and destroy what they fear."[57] These examples again use the Holocaust comparatively, reiterating antiprejudicial sentiment and mistrust of Cold War leadership in the day's hyperbolic terms, but in a much more immediate way, appearing as a type of generalized rhetoric of victimization.

The first Magneto vignette, "A Fire in the Night" (*Classic* #19), revisits Magneto while he was still a fugitive terrorist. In the form of a nightmare, it tells of his escape from Auschwitz, the happy life he made with his wife, Magda, and daughter, Anya, and its abrupt end in Anya's fiery death and Magda's subsequent departure in fear of Magneto's newly and violently manifested powers. Here, Magneto survived the Holocaust and found a joy with his family that healed his wounds; again, it is loss and heartache, not victimhood, which ultimately pushes him over the edge. He wakes up from his nightmare to see a fire across the way, a mother and daughter caught in the conflagration with no hope of survival: "A pity," he thinks, "but no concern of mine." Lying to himself, he claims to care only for his own kind. By the next page, however, he comes to the rescue and shows that he is not the monster he has been made out to be. When the father and husband of the rescued says that he can never repay him, Magneto replies that, actually, he can: "By telling the world how your family was saved by *Magneto*. Magneto the terrorist, Magneto the super-villain, Magneto the *mutant*. Remember me always, m'sieu. I could have let them perish—but I chose *life!*" Magneto may be all of those things and more, the man answers, but "first and foremost—you have proved yourself a *man!*"[58] Thus, Magneto's symbolic proto-redemptive step of rescuing surrogates for his lost loved ones is vindicated and the rightness of his willingness to come the rescue of those unlike him affirmed.

In "I, Magneto" (*Classic* #12), Magneto serves as a US asset hunting Nazi war criminals sometime after the Nuremburg trials; "I was only following orders," Magneto's target says, before asking if Magneto expects him to "receive a fair trial . . . from *Jews?*"[59] This "Magneto before Magneto" brings to mind real-world Nazi hunters like Simon Wiesenthal or the Mossad agents who brought Adolf Eichmann to his widely publicized 1961 trial. The story appeared at a time when the American Justice Department had an active program dedicated to tracking down, denaturalizing, and deporting immigrants accused of involvement in the Holocaust. "I, Magneto" was published soon after the trial of John Demjanjuk, known by testimony as "Ivan the Terrible" of Treblinka, and the subsequent revelations of the Justice Department's misconduct in his denaturalization.[60] But, again, Nazism and the Holocaust remain in the periphery rather than coming to the center: Magneto accuses the man of killing women and children "on the Russian front," and the tragedy is Magneto's loss of another close companion, his beloved physician Isabelle.[61] Isabelle becomes collateral damage when Magneto's handlers come to dispose of him for hunting the "wrong" Nazi, that is, one working with the US against the USSR.[62] This is likely Claremont taking early American Cold War policy to task, critiquing America's postwar rehabilitation of West Germany and the enlistment of former Nazis in the establishment of the CIA and in the space program, among other things. Thus, the Holocaust here mixes with the same familiar elements: the loss of family and loved ones, and the tethering of Magneto's extremism in Cold War moral compromise.

Magneto's redemption was ultimately unsuccessful; going against years of character development, others wrote him as a straight villain in the 1989–1990 crossover storyline "Acts of Vengeance," after which he gradually reverted back to his old self. A few months before Claremont's departure, in *UXM* #274–75 (March–April 1991), Magneto and his allies battle a villainess strongly reminiscent of his original heartless and megalomaniacal self. Here, perhaps because of the aborted redemption, Holocaust suffering is more directly addressed than ever before, and there is less hope: the encounter with the villainess primes Magneto's memory. He recalls his family being shot by Nazis, hears "the echo of der führer's voice in the radio of memory, smell[s] the awful stench of the sick and dying as the cattle cars brought the condemned to Auschwitz," and remembers "carting the bodies by the hundreds[,] by the thousands . . . from the death house to the crematorium." He wears red, he says, in honor of the dead.[63]

But, again, the Holocaust is quickly combined with other tragedies: Magneto also recalls his daughter's and Isabelle's deaths, and he fears that he is about to lose Rogue, another loved one. It is interesting in this connection to note the conflict between Magneto and his ostensible ally Colonel Semyanov, the father of a sailor who had been on a Soviet submarine sunk by Magneto in *UXM* #150. "I am sorry for your loss," Magneto tells the colonel. "Which is more than I ever heard . . . for the slaughter of those I loved." Semyanov's reply is surprising and telling: "Your . . . daughter, you mean?"[64] The conflict between Magneto and Semyanov again roots distrust and hatred in the Cold War and personal loss, rather than in Holocaust and collective victimization. This conflict plays an important role in catalyzing Magneto's questioning of his attempt to carry on after Xavier and, by the end of the story, to abandon redemption. The next time he and the X-Men meet, in *X-Men* (volume 2) #1 (October 1991), Magneto has started reverting to a mutant supremacist stance, and they are enemies once more.[65]

MAGNETO, SUFFERING, AND THE DIFFUSION OF THE HOLOCAUST

The changes Claremont brought to Magneto were of a kind with his work overall; he was more interested in characterization than in action, and this led him to develop the X-Men's personalities in a variety of ways. If not for the intervention of others, Magneto might have become something else entirely in the end. As it stands, his character trajectory under Claremont suggests Americanization, wherein "affirmative" framings of the Holocaust, and a focus on "survivors" and "rescuers" has become prominent.[66] Claremont has said that in thinking about how to make Magneto more three-dimensional, he asked himself:

> What was the most transfiguring event of our century?' In terms that are related to the whole super-concept of the X-Men, of outcasts, and persecution. And I thought, "Okay! It has to be the Holocaust!" [. . .] it allowed me to turn him into a tragic figure, in that his goals were totally admirable. He wants to save his people! His methodology was defined by all that had happened to him. When I can start from the premise that he was a good and decent man at heart, I then have the opportunity over the course of 200 issues to redeem him.[67]

Whether reflecting Claremont's thinking at the time or a reconstruction after the fact, this statement accurately if incompletely represents Magneto's development and echoes a steadily increasing American familiarity with the Holocaust. It also exhibits the American inclination to find redemptive meaning in history, which in Holocaust representation often tends toward individualization, moralization, and universalization. This last aspect is discernible not least in the unrelenting intensity of Magneto's insistence on the protection of mutants—floating signifiers of any Other—rather than Jews or, for that matter, any other group that perished at the hands of the Nazis.

As it fits into Magneto's characterization, the Holocaust appears less as the Nazi regime's systematic murder of six million Jews—the victims are, after all, almost entirely absent in Magneto's redemption and remembrance—than as a sentimentalized personal tragedy which, as a collective rejection coupled with an individual one, deepens a character background and motivates one man's loss of hope, turn to evil, and subsequent return to a righteous path. The comics' version of the Holocaust also addresses the political climate of their time and place, thematically and narratively focusing the tensions that characterize the comics, particularly in the sense that it motivates Magneto's paranoid extremism in terms of a rejection of American values, which in turn fuels much of mankind's fear of mutants.[68] Magneto's survivor characterization, then, partially realizes the potential, inherent in all fictionalized Holocaust accounts, of reshaping actors and events to suit present-day fantasies.[69]

This can be perceived either as trivializing the Holocaust, an accusation sometimes leveled against representational universalization of Auschwitz, the use of tattoos as symbols for victimization, and the generalization of "Never again" as a slogan of moral protest—all of which happens with Magneto—or as an argument for learning from history. At the same time, as if acknowledging the oft-argued unrepresentability of the historical Holocaust, the genocide's appearances are framed as references to the past and warnings of potential futures; the few Holocaust events that do appear are invariably fragmentary and incomplete. Magneto's redemption can then also be interpreted as an attempt to teach a lesson about prevention from memory, especially when one considers that it entailed an embrace of Xavier's dream of coexistence: we must remember, it says, but we cannot let thoughts of retribution lead to parochialism or extremism, nor should anger or despair over what happened prevent affirming life and striving for betterment together.[70]

Evidence suggests that the reception of Magneto's survivor identity has been positive. Simcha Weinstein notes, "In a world where a shocking number of people claim never to have heard of the Auschwitz concentration camp, this can only have a positive effect."[71] Writer and translator Marie-Catherine Caillava writes in revealing terms: "The more Magneto is linked to our world and our history, the more we can learn from him. If he were a generic victim, we could only learn so much. But by making him a Jew, we gain access to a wealth of history, experiences, hopes, mistakes, prejudices, rage and wisdom."[72] This is no doubt true, but one should temper these readings with an understanding that the openness of mutantcy in the X-Men universe, its use to signify any otherness and its invitation for readers to make it their own, leads to a problematic endpoint: by bringing the Holocaust to the mutant comics page, Magneto the survivor invites readers to make the suffering of the Holocaust's victims their own and suggests that whatever feelings of otherness the reader might feel are equivalent to the otherness genocidally inflicted on European Jewry.[73]

One need look no further than comics journalist Peter Sanderson's introduction to a 1982 X-Men companion to find examples of how the Holocaust's presence in X-Men comics was understood that way:

> A number of the X-Men are foreigners who now find themselves living in the United States, an alien land. [. . .] Note the explicit parallel drawn between mutants and persecuted minorities in *X-Men* #150, wherein it is revealed that Magneto, as a child, was an inmate at Auschwitz, and that over the years, as far as he knows, his entire family has been destroyed.

> All of these distinctions reinforce the impression created by the X-Men's identity as mutants. *The word "mutant" can symbolize for the reader any reason for feeling alienated from society*, whether it be sex, race, creed, physical appearance, special talents that are misunderstood or provoke jealousy, or any more personal reason. The power of the mutant concept makes *The X-Men* unique.[74]

Magneto's experience is, to use Rosenfeld's words, "individualized, heroized, moralized, idealized, and universalized," his failed redemption an attempt to make him, as a survivor, a figure of "heroic witness" and a redeemer of the human spirit and of hope, who invites others into the suffering of the Holocaust. For this, and for numerous other reasons,[75] it is important to read Magneto's shifting meanings against time and place, and to thus see him as a representation of the Holocaust and an example of its American reception, but neither as a link to the ethnoracial dimensions of the genocide itself nor as a tool for understanding the Holocaust as a historical reality.

NOTES

1. This chapter is a revised and expanded version of a section that first appeared in my 2013 Lund University PhD dissertation, "Re-thinking the Jewish–Comics Connection." I would like to thank Sean Guynes-Vishniac for his insightful comments on an earlier version of this chapter.

2. Michael Aushenker, "Minority Retort," *Jewish Journal*, April 30, 2003, https://web.archive.org/web/20110408111722/http://www.jewishjournal.com/arts/article/minority_retort_20030501/.

3. Greg Pak and Carmine Di Giandomenico, *X-Men: Magneto Testament* (Marvel Comics, 2009).

4. *Uncanny* was added to the title with #142, February 1981. Claremont's run on *New Mutants* could have been brought into this discussion, but doing so would have added little except further examples of the same processes.

5. See, for example, Lawrence Baron, "X-Men as J Men: The Jewish Subtext of a Comic Book Movie," *Shofar: An Interdisciplinary Journal of Jewish Studies* 22, no. 1 (2003): 44–52; Mary-Catherine Caillava, "Magneto the Jew," in *The Unauthorized X-Men: SF and Comic Writers on Mutants, Prejudice, and Adamantium*, ed. Len Wein, 52 (Smart Pop, 2006); Rivka Jacobs, "The Magneto Is Jewish FAQ," November 9, 1998, http://www.alara.net/opeople/xbooks/magjew.html; Simcha Weinstein, *Up, Up, and Oy Vey! How Jewish History, Culture, and Values Shaped the Comic Book Superhero* (Baltimore: Leviathan Press, 2006).

6. Cf. Martin Lund, *Re-constructing the Man of Steel: Superman 1938–1941, Jewish American History, and the Invention of the Jewish-Comics Connection* (New York: Palgrave Macmillan, 2016), 4–5.

7. Matthew J. Costello, *Secret Identity Crisis: Comic Books and the Unmasking of Cold War America* (New York: Continuum, 2009), 20.

8. In *Uncanny X-Men* #150, reprinted in Claremont et al., *Essential X-Men* Vol. 2, np. Future references to the Essential volumes (2–11) are abbreviated as *EXM*2–11.

9. Jonathan D. Sarna, *American Judaism: A New History* (New Haven: Yale University Press, 2004), 334.

10. Sarna, *American Judaism*, 52–53; Peter Novick, *The Holocaust in American Life* (Boston: Houghton Mifflin Harcourt, 2000), 220–26, 231–38, passim.

11. Novick, *Holocaust in American Life*, 220.

12. See Michael Goodrum and Philip Smith, "'Corpses . . . Coast to Coast!' Trauma, Gender, and Race in 1950s Horror Comics," *Literature Compass* 14, no. 9 (2017): e.12399, for a discussion of the Holocaust in horror comics of the 1940s and 1950s; Marcus Streb, "Early Representations of Concentration Camps in Golden Age Comic Books: Graphic Narratives, American Society, and the Holocaust," *Scandinavian Journal of Comic Art* 3, no. 1 (2016): 29–58.

13. It is difficult to do this process justice here, but a brief recapitulation of major events seems prudent. In the immediate post-WWII years, survivors were discouraged from speaking about their experiences, and Jews were not presented as having been singled out specifically for persecution and genocide. In the late 1940s and throughout the 1950s, little was said about the genocide, in part because of geopolitical realignments: the Russians were now the enemy, and the Germans were no friends, and the Holocaust posed a problem in this respect. Further, the political used references to the Holocaust to oppose German rehabilitation, which stoked fears that the anti-Semitic canard of a particular Jewish affinity with socialism and communism would reappear. Initially in the early 1960s, little was still being said about the Holocaust, and although the 1961 trial of Adolf Eichmann in Israel was widely publicized, and the Holocaust was still also discussed in universal terms and in relation to totalitarianism, it did lead to a greater understanding of the Nazi crimes against Jews. By the late 1960s, however, the term Holocaust was coming into common usage, and interest in the genocide grew among Jewish Americans for a variety of reasons: fears or perceptions of increasing anti-Semitism; the ethnic revival and the realization for many who went looking for their roots that their family trees had been cut off; and the rise of identity politics, among others. Also of crucial importance was the survival of Israel in the 1967 "Six-Day War" and the realization half a decade later, after the war of 1973, that the country's situation was still precarious, which inspired—among other things—a new form of secular Judaism that has been called a "Judaism of Holocaust and Redemption," according to which the Holocaust was a dark chapter that was followed by a brighter one in the founding of the modern state of Israel. All of this, and more, inspired Jewish Americans to learn more, which in turn led to more discussion and more representation that soon crossed over into the American mainstream. (This account is based on Rosenfeld, *End of Holocaust*; Novick, *Holocaust in American Life*; Hilene Flanzbaum, "Introduction: The Americanization of the Holocaust," in *The Americanization of the Holocaust*, ed. Hilene Flanzbaum (Baltimore: Johns Hopkins University Press, 1999), 1–17. The Judaism of Holocaust and Redemption is introduced in Jacob Neusner, *Judaism in Modern Times: An Introduction and Reader* (Oxford: Blackwell, 1995), 206–20.

14. Rosenfeld, *End of Holocaust*; Novick, *Holocaust in American Life*; Hilene Flanzbaum ed., *The Americanization of the Holocaust* (Baltimore: Johns Hopkins University Press, 1999).

15. Flanzbaum, "Introduction," 1–3.

16. Idealized, because the nation's history contains many events that prove that it has historically been far easier to speak of liberty and equality than it has been to deliver them to all: the near-extinction of the indigenous peoples who predated European colonization; the Middle Passage, Jim Crow, and the New Jim Crow of racialized mass incarceration; Chinese Exclusion; Japanese internment; the Red Scares; the long and protean history of American whiteness and its

concomitant marginalization, exclusion, and oppression; the racial profiling and surveillance of Muslims after 9/11; and much more. Rosenfeld, *End of Holocaust*, 59–61; see also Novick, *Holocaust in American Life*, 114.

17. Novick, *Holocaust in American Life*, 213–14; see also Rosenfeld, *End of Holocaust*, 262.

18. Cf. Novick, ch. 3; Rosenfeld, *End of Holocaust*.

19. Cf. Henry Greenspan, "Imagining Survivors: Testimony and the Rise of Holocaust Consciousness," in *The Americanization of the Holocaust*, ed. Hilene Flanzbaum (Baltimore: Johns Hopkins University Press, 1999), 58: "As survival eclipsed adjustment as a primary virtue in American culture at large, our response to these [Holocaust] survivors underwent a transformation. 'Out of the ashes' or 'the darkness' or 'defeat,' we began to look for heroes and victories and the 'joy of survival.'" Quotes in body from pp. 49–50. A second discourse about survivors emerged around the same time, focusing instead on survivors as "archetypal victims, guilty, ghostly, silent, and estranged." See also Rosenfeld, *End of Holocaust*, 76–79.

20. Arie Kaplan, *From Krakow to Krypton: Jews and Comic Books* (Philadelphia: Jewish Publication Society, 2008), 115.

21. Cf. Costello, *Secret Identity Crisis*, 85–161, on the general tendency to psychologize characters in Marvel comics in these years.

22. Claremont, *Uncanny X-Men*, #104; and #112–13 *EXM1*.

23. In *EXM2*. Cf. Costello, *Secret Identity Crisis*, 147–52.

24. Claremont, *Uncanny X-Men*, #150, *EXM3*.

25. Claremont, *Uncanny X-Men*, #150, *EXM3*. Cf. John Fitzgerald Kennedy, "Inaugural Address," Miller Center of Public Affairs, January 20, 1961, http://millercenter.org/president/speeches/detail/3365: "Let every nation know, whether it wishes us well or ill, that we shall pay any price, bear any burden, meet any hardship, support any friend, oppose any foe to assure the survival and the success of liberty."

26. Claremont, *Uncanny X-Men*, #150, *EXM3*.

27. Christopher Lasch, *The Minimal Self: Psychic Survival in Troubled Times* (London: Pan Books, 1985), 111–12. Cf. Hartmut M. Hanauske-Abel, "From Nazi Holocaust to Nuclear Holocaust: A Lesson to Learn?" *The Lancet*, August 2, 1986. Even Elie Wiesel, a Holocaust survivor who has dedicated his life to remembrance, felt in the early 1980s that "the next Holocaust will be nuclear. It will affect all of us" (see Jack Nusan Porter, "Elie Wiesel: Bearing Witness," *New York Times*, November 20, 1983, http://www.nytimes.com/1983/11/20/magazine/l-elie-wiesel-bearing-witness-053226.html; John S. Friedman, "The Art of Fiction LXXIX: Elie Wiesel," *Paris Review*, no. 91 (Spring 1984): 130–78; Gary Libman, "Lest We Forget, Elie Wiesel Remembers: Holocaust Survivor Speaks Out against Arms Race 'Suicide,'" *Los Angeles Times*, May 13, 1987, http://articles.latimes.com/1987-05-13/news/vw-4077_1_elie-wiesel. As Novick, *Holocaust in American Life*, 112, 231, and Rosenfeld, *End of Holocaust*, 33–50, 69–75, show, this tendency to use the Holocaust comparatively predated the 1980s and has survived into the new millennium.

28. Unlabeled "Calligraphy" notebook, box 11, Chris Claremont papers 1973–2011, University Archives, Rare Book & Manuscript Library, Columbia University in the City of New York.

29. John Lewis Gaddis, *The Cold War: A New History* (New York: Penguin Press, 2005), 180.

30. Cf. Gaddis, ch. 5.

31. Claremont, *Uncanny X-Men*, #150 (*EXM1*).

32. Cf. the comment in Rosenfeld, *End of Holocaust*, 84–85, about Spielberg depoliticizing the political aspects of the Holocaust in favor of "raw sadism of an extremely personal kind" in *Schindler's List*.

33. Claremont, *Uncanny X-Men*, #161 (*EXM3*), emphasis added.

34. Claremont, *Uncanny X-Men*, #161 (*EXM3*).

35. Claremont, *Uncanny X-Men*, #161 (*EXM3*). Cf. Rosenfeld, *End of Holocaust*, 62.

36. Greenspan, "Imagining Survivors," 49.

37. Claremont, *God Loves, Man Kills* (*EXM4*).

38. Claremont, *Uncanny X-Men*, #196 (*EXM5*).

39. Kaplan, *From Krakow to Krypton*, 122–23.

40. Cheryl Alexander Malcolm, "Witness, Trauma, and Remembrance: Holocaust Representation and X-Men Comics," in *The Jewish Graphic Novel: Critical Approaches*, ed. Samantha Baskind and Ranen Omer-Sherman, 144–60 (New Brunswick, NJ: Rutgers University Press, 2010), 155–56.

41. Robert G. Weiner and Lynne Fallwell, "Sequential Art Narrative and the Holocaust," in *The Routledge History of the Holocaust*, ed. Jonathan C. Friedman, 464–69 (London: Taylor & Francis, 2010), 466.

42. Claremont, *Uncanny X-Men*, #199 (*EXM6*).

43. Rosenfeld, *End of Holocaust*, 16–25; Novick, *Holocaust in American Life*, 226–27.

44. Rosenfeld, *End of Holocaust*, 62–68; Flanzbaum, "Introduction"; see also Novick, *Holocaust in American Life*, 214–20, 240, 260. A. Roy Eckardt and Alice L. Eckardt, "Travail of a Presidential Commission Confronting the Enigma of the Holocaust," *Encounter* 42, no. 2 (Spring 1981): 103–14, present the difficulties experienced by committee members. James Ingo Freed, "The United States Holocaust Memorial Museum, "*Assemblage*, no. 9 (June 1, 1989): 59–79, does the same from the architect's point of view.

45. Cf. Rosenfeld, *End of Holocaust*, 11, 68–69; Novick, *Holocaust in American Life*, chap. 11.

46. Rosenfeld, *End of Holocaust*, 76–94; Novick, *Holocaust in American Life*, 272–76.

47. Claremont, *Uncanny X-Men*, #199 (*EXM6*).

48. Claremont, *Uncanny X-Men*, #199 (*EXM6*).

49. Claremont, *Uncanny X-Men*, #200 (*EXM6*).

50. Claremont, *Uncanny X-Men*, #200 (*EXM6*).

51. Claremont, *Uncanny X-Men*, #200 (*EXM6*).

52. Roughly a year prior, Reagan had joked into a live microphone that he had "outlawed Russia forever" and that bombing would commence in five minutes, putting the USSR on high alert. By the time this comic was published, however, tension had begun to ease somewhat. See Bruce J. Schulman, *The Seventies: The Great Shift in American Culture, Society, and Politics* (Cambridge: Da Capo, 2002), 227–29; Gaddis, *Cold War*, ch. 6.

53. Claremont, *Uncanny X-Men*, #200 (*EXM6*).

54. Michael Galchinsky, *Jews and Human Rights: Dancing at Three Weddings* (Lanham, MD: Rowman & Littlefield, 2008), 45–50.

55. References to Nazism, the Holocaust, or anti-Semitism were never exclusively connected to Magneto during Claremont's tenure, however. The "Days of Future Past" arc (*Uncanny X-Men*, #141–42, 1981), for example, had featured Holocaust references, and the storylines connected with the island nation Genosha (introduced in *Uncanny X-Men*, #235, 1988)—while focused on allegorizing South African Apartheid—also used symbolic language connected with the Holocaust.

56. Chris Claremont, Dave Cockrum, and Sam Grainger, "The Gentleman's Name Is Magneto," *Classic X-Men* #12 (Marvel Comics, 1987), 6.

57. Chris Claremont, John Byrne, and Kieron Dwyer, "Showdown!" *Classic X-Men* #19 (Marvel Comics, 1988), 10.

58. Chris Claremont and John Bolton, "A Fire in the Night!" *Classic X-Men* #12 (Marvel Comics, 1987), 12.

59. Chris Claremont and John Bolton, "I, Magneto!" *Magneto #0: The Twisting of a Soul* (Marvel Comics, 1993), 17.

60. Cf. Novick, *Holocaust in American Life*, 228–30.

61. Claremont and Bolton, "I, Magneto!," 17. Worth noting is that on this page Magneto also experiences a seizure, the pain of which he describes as "worse than the bite of the Kapo's whip, the murder of my parents and family, the death of a child . . . the loss of a beloved wife." Later in the story he speaks again of his anguish over losing his wife and child.

62. When Isabelle has been killed, "Control" explains to Magneto that they have come after him because he has gone "haring off on [his] own." When Magneto responds that it has never been a problem before, he is told, "[That] was when you were sanctioning *their* Nazis. The other side's. Richter was one of ours. A *very* important asset. [. . .] The *Russians* are the enemy, and we'll work with whoever we have to beat them." Claremont and Bolton, "I, Magneto!," 22.

63. Claremont, *Uncanny X-Men*, #274 (*EXM11*).

64. Claremont, *Uncanny X-Men*, #275 (*EXM11*).

65. Claremont, *X-Men*, #1–3 (Vol. 2) (*EXM11*).

66. Rosenfeld, *End of Holocaust*, 85–86.

67. Quoted in Kaplan, *From Krakow to Krypton*, 120.

68. Claremont, *Uncanny X-Men*, #150 (*EXM3*); Claremont, *Uncanny X-Men*, #196, 20 (*EXM5*); Claremont, *Uncanny X-Men*, #199 (*EXM6*).

69. Rosenfeld, *End of Holocaust*, 30.

70. Cf. Rosenfeld, *End of Holocaust*, 60: "Because Americans are also pragmatic in their approach to history, they are eager to learn what 'lessons' can be drawn from the past in order, as many are quick to say, to prevent the worst excesses 'from ever happening again.' In short, one should take what one can from history and then move on, hopefully to a better day."

71. Weinstein, *Up, Up, and Oy Vey!*, 114.

72. Caillava, "Magneto the Jew," 108–9.

73. Cf. Neil Shyminsky, "Mutant Readers, Reading Mutants: Appropriation, Assimilation, and the X-Men," *International Journal of Comic Art* 8, no. 2 (Fall 2006): 387–405, 388.

74. Sanderson, "Introduction," 10–11; emphasis added.

75. In the years since Magneto's Jewishness was made part of the comics canon, his survivor identity has increasingly become a non sequitur rhetorical bludgeon, to be brought out at the oddest moments, as for example in the 2016 *Inhumans vs. X-Men* crossover. The story deals with a gas that turns humans into so-called Inhumans if they have the genetic potential for it but also causes illness in mutants. When it turns out that this gas is about to dissipate into the atmosphere and blanket the whole planet, Magneto is made to exclaim: "My people will not be *gassed* to death." This betokens a great deal of ignorance on behalf of the writer and a severely lacking understanding of the Holocaust and what is appropriate in its representation—the mere presence of the word "gas" is enough to prompt a Holocaust comparison where there is no way to reasonably motivate one.

WORKS CITED

Aushenker, Michael. "Minority Retort." JewishJournal.com, April 30, 2003. https://web.archive.org/web/20110408111722/http://www.jewishjournal.com/arts/article/minority_retort_20030501/.

Baron, Lawrence. "X-Men as J Men: The Jewish Subtext of a Comic Book Movie." *Shofar: An Interdisciplinary Journal of Jewish Studies* 22, no. 1 (2003): 44–53.

Caillava, Mary-Catherine. "Magneto the Jew." In *The Unauthorized X-Men: SF and Comic Writers on Mutants, Prejudice, and Adamantium*, edited by Len Wein, 52. Smart Pop, 2006.

Claremont, Chris, and John Bolton. "A Fire in the Night!" *Classic X-Men* #12. New York: Marvel Comics, 1987.

Claremont, Chris, and John Bolton. "I, Magneto!" *Magneto #0: The Twisting of a Soul*. New York: Marvel Comics, 1993.

Claremont, Chris, John Byrne, and Kieron Dwyer. "Showdown!" *Classic X-Men* #19. New York: Marvel Comics, 1988.

Claremont, Chris, Dave Cockrum, and Sam Grainger. "The Gentleman's Name Is Magneto." *Classic X-Men* #12. New York: Marvel Comics, 1987.

Claremont, Chris, et al. *Essential X-Men* 2–11. New York: Marvel Comics, 2001–2013.

Costello, Matthew J. *Secret Identity Crisis: Comic Books and the Unmasking of Cold War America*. New York: Continuum, 2009.

Eckardt, A. Roy, and Alice L. Eckardt. "Travail of a Presidential Commission Confronting the Enigma of the Holocaust." *Encounter* 42, no. 2 (Spring 1981): 103–14.

Flanzbaum, Hilene. "Introduction: The Americanization of the Holocaust." In *The Americanization of the Holocaust*, edited by Hilene Flanzbaum, 1–17. Baltimore: Johns Hopkins University Press, 1999.

Flanzbaum, Hilene, ed. *The Americanization of the Holocaust*. Baltimore: Johns Hopkins University Press, 1999.

Freed, James Ingo. "The United States Holocaust Memorial Museum." *Assemblage*, no. 9 (June 1, 1989): 59–79.

Friedman, John S. "The Art of Fiction LXXIX: Elie Wiesel." *Paris Review*, no. 91 (Spring 1984): 130–78.

Gaddis, John Lewis. *The Cold War: A New History*. New York: Penguin Press, 2005.

Galchinsky, Michael. *Jews and Human Rights: Dancing at Three Weddings*. Lanham, MD: Rowman & Littlefield, 2008.

Greenspan, Henry. "Imagining Survivors: Testimony and the Rise of Holocaust Consciousness." In *The Americanization of the Holocaust*, edited by Hilene Flanzbaum, 45–67. Baltimore: Johns Hopkins University Press, 1999.

Hanauske-Abel, Hartmut M. "From Nazi Holocaust to Nuclear Holocaust: A Lesson to Learn?" *The Lancet* 2 (8501) (August 2, 1986): 271–73.

Jacobs, Rivka. "The Magneto Is Jewish FAQ." November 9, 1998. http://www.alara.net/opeople/xbooks/magjew.html.

Kaplan, Arie. *From Krakow to Krypton: Jews and Comic Books*. Philadelphia: Jewish Publication Society, 2008.

Kennedy, John Fitzgerald. "Inaugural Address." Miller Center of Public Affairs, January 20, 1961. http://millercenter.org/president/speeches/detail/3365.

Lasch, Christopher. *The Minimal Self: Psychic Survival in Troubled Times*. London: Pan Macmillan, 1985.

Libman, Gary. "Lest We Forget, Elie Wiesel Remembers: Holocaust Survivor Speaks Out against Arms Race 'Suicide.'" *Los Angeles Times*, May 13, 1987. http://articles.latimes.com/1987-05-13/news/vw-4077_1_elie-wiesel.

Lund, Martin. *Re-constructing the Man of Steel: Superman 1938–1941, Jewish American History, and the Invention of the Jewish-Comics Connection*. New York: Palgrave Macmillan, 2016.

Malcolm, Cheryl Alexander. "Witness, Trauma, and Remembrance: Holocaust Representation and X-Men Comics." In *The Jewish Graphic Novel: Critical Approaches*, edited by Samantha Baskind and Ranen Omer-Sherman, 144–60. New Brunswick, NJ: Rutgers University Press, 2010.

Neusner, Jacob. *Judaism in Modern Times: An Introduction and Reader*. Oxford: Blackwell, 1995.

Novick, Peter. *The Holocaust in American Life*. Boston: Houghton Mifflin Harcourt, 2000.

Pak, Greg, and Carmine Di Giandomenico. *X-Men: Magneto Testament*. New York: Marvel Comics, 2009.

Porter, Jack Nusan. "Elie Wiesel: Bearing Witness." *New York Times*, November 20, 1983. http://www.nytimes.com/1983/11/20/magazine/l-elie-wiesel-bearing-witness-053226.html.

Sanderson, Peter. "Introduction." In *X-Men Companion II*, edited by Peter Sanderson, 7–16. Stamford, CT: Fantagraphics Books, 1982.

Sarna, Jonathan D. *American Judaism: A New History*. New Haven: Yale University Press, 2004.

Schulman, Bruce J. *The Seventies: The Great Shift in American Culture, Society, and Politics*. Cambridge: Da Capo, 2002.

Shyminsky, Neil. "Mutant Readers, Reading Mutants: Appropriation, Assimilation, and the X-Men." *International Journal of Comic Art* 8, no. 2 (Fall 2006): 387–405.

Streb, Marcus. "Early Representations of Concentration Camps in Golden Age Comic Books: Graphic Narratives, American Society, and the Holocaust." *Scandinavian Journal of Comic Art* 3, no. 1 (2016): 29–58.

Weiner, Robert G., and Lynne Fallwell. "Sequential Art Narrative and the Holocaust." In *The Routledge History of the Holocaust*, edited by Jonathan C. Friedman, 464–69. London: Taylor & Francis, 2010.

Weinstein, Simcha. *Up, Up, and Oy Vey! How Jewish History, Culture, and Values Shaped the Comic Book Superhero*. Baltimore: Leviathan Press, 2006.

CHAPTER SEVEN

"HOW WOULD YOU LIKE TO GO BACK THROUGH THE AGES—IN SEARCH OF YOURSELF?"

Time Travel Comics, Internationalism, and the American Century

JORDAN NEWTON

Americans have recently found it more comfortable to see where they have been than to think of where they are going.
—Richard Hofstadter, *The American Political Tradition* (1948), xi

Time travel has proven to be an enduring mechanism for exploring alternate pasts, presents, and futures. It can concern the ability of the individual to effect change, sometimes on a personal level, sometimes nationally, even globally. Through the dialogue it establishes with other periods, time travel can also be a tool for narrating nations.[1] In the confusion of the early Cold War period, superhero comics, like the US, were in a state of flux. It was in this context that the notion of "the American Century," a term popularized by Henry Luce in 1941, began to take root.[2] Although contested from the outset both domestically and internationally, the term, indicating a period of American ascendancy in international affairs, provides a useful model for considering the period.[3] Richard Hofstadter touches on contemporary uncertainty in the foreword to his epoch-defining work, *The American Political Tradition*, but superheroes showed how the past could become a space not just for comforting reflection but for negotiating future direction.[4] Through the actions of their friend, Professor Carter Nichols, Batman and Robin are sent on a series of adventures in time and discover that the past offers a means of finding themselves and, allegorically, the nation; the process of discovery also articulates purpose and rationale, dramatizing and simplifying geopolitics.[5] As Victoria Byard notes, "the timeslip fantasy drama was particularly suited to investigating historical paradigm shifts and the breakdown of metanarratives, such as imperialism, national identity, and the concept of a great tradition," and it was precisely this situation in which the US found itself as it surveyed the ruins not only of Europe, but of nineteenth-century European ideological projects.[6]

Through superhero narratives, a clear picture of the US emerges as a nation intricately imbricated in geopolitical processes; through the privileged model of superheroism offered as allegory for the US, the nation emerges as a leader in this new (old) world.[7] Superhero narratives about time travel at this specific historiocultural moment therefore indicate both uncertainty and confidence, a desire to look to others for guidance, but in carefully crafted ways that privilege desired outcomes, dependent on clear hierarchies of power and heroism that foreground the US. Despite the way in which the narratives and images, and the ideologies with which they are infused, structure responses, comic books were able "to address problems that are usually relegated to 'higher' literary types, or at least to more self-consciously experimental and philosophically oriented ones," engaging with profound questions of precisely what constitutes "America" and what role it should serve in the international arena through the apparently escapist act of sending their protagonists backward in time.[8] This chapter considers the function of antiquity as a destination in the context of the early Cold War, and the role of Batman and Robin as mediators of the messages found there for the modern world.

PAST AND PRESENT—COMIC INTERVENTIONS

In some superhero comic books of the late 1940s, travel to distant pasts is offered as both fantastic adventure and solution to contemporary problems. Travel in time was supported by more conventional international travel, showing how superhero comic books engaged, however obliquely, with notions of critical internationalism, defined by Robert Shaffer as a process of the "interchange of information between Americans and other peoples" and, as such, a project that "existed in creative tension with that of intercultural understanding."[9] This stands in contrast to a more triumphant internationalism interested only in projecting American values, rather than engaging in dialogue.[10] A key difference between critical internationalism in reality and in these fictions, however, is that the places and people met by the superheroes are also, inevitably, American projections through time and space. No matter how dialogue is presented, it is on American terms; dialogue of this nature can therefore be seen as a cover for the inherent superpower politics of narratives, or as an appeal for dialogue as an approach, albeit one within a framework that privileges American superpower engagement as the ultimate means of settling disputes. Interventions in the past therefore become not just explorations for parallels, a sort of "how to" guide for puzzled readers, but also a model for tactical intervention in the present, in terms both of outcomes and acceptable reasons for involvement. As such, these narratives become a sort of "always-already" justification for contemporary actions showing how history has always been leading to this point, something demonstrated through trips to a range of pasts that foreshadow the present and future.

Time travel, however, serves a more general purpose. David Wittenberg states, "Time travel fiction is a 'narratological laboratory,' in which many of the most basic theoretical questions about storytelling, and by extension about the philosophy of temporality, history, and subjectivity, are represented in the form of literal devices and plots, at once both convenient for criticism and fruitfully complex."[11] This can be applied beyond narrative theory. Narratives of travel, whether in time or space, can be seen to function as a laboratory where readers consider the present, its relationship to the past, and its trajectory into the future (in the early Cold War period, both Batman and Wonder Woman, for instance, travel to the year 3000 AD to see how society develops). Time travel stories in particular offer a plurality of potential futures, suggesting unease about the project of the American Century but also the desire to explore it, to enact it, and to find justifications for the future in the past—and to see how the present extends into the future. Creative tensions inherent in the project of critical internationalism are therefore set against projects of empire and set to work in a space distant and yet present.[12]

Time, and mobility within it, is often associated with threat; the attempt to prevent something from occurring through altering past actions, or the eruption of some distant past in the unprepared present—as in the monster attacks prompted by nuclear testing in *Godzilla* (1954), *The Beast from 20,000 Fathoms* (1953), and so on. The presence of nuclear tests and the destructive return of the long gone suggest anxieties regarding the end of all life on Earth but also the primitive reasoning for it: violence. In meddling with the primeval forces of nature, man threatens his own undoing. In the comics under consideration here, the tone is more celebratory, but anxieties still pervade the narratives and images. The very act of looking to the past suggests a certain degree of discomfort in the present, especially when Batman uses his adventures in time to measure himself against past societies in locations with contemporary geopolitical relevance, most notably Greece. Site of a bloody civil war between nationalists and communists in the early Cold War period, Greece is also synonymous with notions of antiquity and, crucially for the Cold War context in which these comics were created and received, democracy. In the years that followed the Second World War, Greece was embroiled in a civil war between Nationalists and Communists; international support for both sides transformed a domestic concern into a global conflict. In looking to the past, the US could position itself as a twentieth-century equivalent to ancient Greece—a pioneering force for democracy (though "democracy" of both was problematic by modern standards). In a story that allows the US to measure itself against ancient Greece and her contemporary European neighbors, *Batman* #48 (1946) sees Batman and Robin thwart a Persian plot to spark civil war in ancient Greece at the first Olympic Games. Geopolitical commentary is an inherent part of the narrative, with Batman's intervention in the past foreshadowing American intervention in the Greek Civil War from 1946 to 1949 by over a year. The Truman Doctrine (1947) and Marshall Plan (1948) provided military and financial aid to Greek nationalists to support them in their confrontation with communism. Essentially, the past and the future, previous issues and current dilemmas, morph into one continuous present. The logical sequence of events seems to be coming apart: Batman intervenes in the present through the past, creating patterns of repetition in the process—as well as the implicit notion that intervention is never wholly successful. It could also be seen as engaging with Cathy Caruth's notion that there is an "inherent latency" in historical experience, that "it is only in and through . . . forgetting that it is first experienced."[13] It is Batman's interventions in the past that create the situations that lead to the need for American intervention in the present, allowing the events "recovered" through cultural representation to be experienced.

In addition to the problem of faith in the nation and its mission, time travel also calls the very notion of time into question. This was made clear in 1960, when Richard E. Sullivan expressed contemporary anxieties as centered on "a loss of faith in time itself."[14] Sullivan argues that, in his account of pre-twentieth-century man's faith in the benevolence of "the long run" as a manifestation of cosmic justice, it was "senseless to joust violently with destiny. The good things came slowly, as many wise men discerned in looking back across the past."[15] With the advent of time travel, Batman and Robin did not just further disrupt belief in this notion in the present; they also did so in the past by accelerating development or resolving disputes in the moment, rather than in the "long run." Confronted with the very real possibility that time, and being, could suddenly end, conventional concepts of structure were subjected to assault. Time became flexible and mutable, something to be explored and manipulated; in so doing, narrative experiments with time attested to its precarity, but also to its continuity. David Seed demonstrates the ways in which postwar science fiction authors looked to history for parallels, as a "script" whose "replay might shed light on the plot of the present," and, by extension, the future.[16] A number of comics took this further by explicitly relocating their protagonist to "a" past in order to explore the present and the relationship between the two. In doing so a range of anxieties were themselves explored: implicitly, the notion of time continuing; geopolitical questions regarding the global role of the US in the developing Cold War and its right to "rule" the "free world" on its own terms; and issues of gender and its representation at a time of significant conflict around gender roles and the patriarchal structure that contained, defined, and relied on them in order to function in and maintain its contemporary form.[17] Batman and Superman travel through time on missions, whereas Lois Lane, on any of her frequent trips through time or space, usually takes finding herself a husband as her first point of business. Clear divisions in roles for men and women are therefore embedded, as is the notion that marriage remains, whatever the year, the overriding concern for women. However, looking to the distant past implies the transferability of actions from one distinct context, the early Cold War, to another entirely unrelated one, suggesting the problem of presupposing something akin to a continuous present and projecting values and ideologies into alien contexts.

Narratives and images contained in early Cold War comics engaged with some of the dramatic possibilities of the inherently dramatic phrase "the American Century." The USA emerged from the Second World War as the most powerful nation on the planet, and its discovery of nuclear power ultimately changed the landscape of war, politics, and, ultimately, life as people knew it. The US had essentially harnessed the power of the gods by the end of the Second World War, and, at least to begin with, it was theirs and theirs alone to do with as they pleased. Nuclear actions have chain reactions. The US, then, was staring into the abyss, into uncharted territory; as such, it is important to remember Nietzsche's statement "He who fights with monsters should be careful lest he thereby become a monster. And if thou gaze long into an abyss, the abyss will also gaze into thee."[18] In fighting the monsters of the Second World War, and particularly in the way the US delivered the final blows of the war in the Pacific, there was some unease as to whether the US had "abdicated its position of moral leadership by employing the tactics of its enemies" through its atomic assault on civilian populations.[19] The treatment of ethnic and linguistic minorities by the US government during and after the war also needs to be taken into account when assessing its monstrosity.[20]

Driven by internationalist notions of spreading democracy (and American business), the US set out to construct a global system on its own terms.[21] In doing so the whole world would be watching, waiting, relying on, and scrutinizing every decision: the US would finally realize John Winthrop's desire of 1630 to become "as a city upon a hill."[22] However, the first test of American resolve and strategy was not long in arriving: the Second World War seemed to have led not to peace, but rather to a cold war, one that directed attention to specific areas and placed strain on conventional faultlines. The US was finding that with great power comes great responsibility; at the start of the American Century, it was America's shoulders on which this responsibility rested.

In a time of such great confusion, then, what if America could take inspiration from the past? What if America could go back through the ages in search of oneself? To not only live the American Century but to project it literally backward and forward in time to create American Centur*ies*. In a present where men seemed dishonorable, paranoia had infected both city and suburb, science threatened the extinction of mankind, and the future looked entirely unclear, it made sense to look to the past for answers. Men had, after all, previously dealt with such issues—albeit on a much smaller scale—and had emerged triumphant. Time travel as a narrative device allowed Americans to escape the present and take solace in the past. This perhaps explains why time travel became a relatively common trope in the immediate aftermath of the Second World War and throughout the long, bitter conflict that would become known as the Cold War.

The past, however naively, is often romanticized as a simpler time for all. Ancient Rome, for example is described in *Batman* #24 (1944) as a "splendid, seething city where gladiators fought on crimson sands and chariots churned at break-neck speeds!'"[23] Likewise, ancient Greece is described as being a place of "glory.'"[24] Similarly, in *Wonder Woman* #9 (1944), antiquity is presented as an era of perfection.[25] Essentially, the past is used as a device to map contemporary issues onto a romanticized era. While Wonder Woman presented the most frequent engagement with the past through the very nature of her character as a relic of this period, Batman was the most frequent traveler through time. With the introduction of Professor Carter Nichols in *Batman* #24 (1944), Batman and Robin embark on a number of adventures to the premodern world, seeing ancient Rome, ancient Greece, and the Vikings, to name just a few. In many of these stories, the issues of the past clearly translate into the modern day.

SAVING THE PRESENT, ONE PAST AT A TIME

One of the major themes that run throughout Batman and Robin's time travel exploits is the depiction of the Dynamic Duo as saviors. In *Batman* #24, #38 (1946), and #52 (1949), Batman is seen to take the place of a less-capable premodern man in order to save the day. In *Batman* #24, the Dynamic Duo thwarts a plot to fix a chariot race by having Batman take the place of Rome's best chariot racer, Gito, who is about to compete in his last race. In *Batman* #38, Batman—an "honorary Athenian citizen" at this point—competes in the first Olympic Games as a last-minute replacement, beating the Herculean Lysis in the pentathlon—arguably the most grueling challenge of the games—with little effort.[26] Furthermore, in *Batman* #52, Batman replaces his Viking doppelgänger so that he may redeem himself in the eyes of his comrades, who regard him as a coward. Mapping contemporary concerns onto the past, the perceived superiority of Batman and Robin, not just as twentieth-century men but as Americans, says a lot about the triumphant internationalism of the period that characterized one approach to American geopolitics. As Dominick LaCapra argues, "there has been an important tendency in modern culture . . . to convert trauma into the occasion for sublimity, to transvalue it into a test of the self or the group," a process clearly in operation in these Batman stories.[27] Interpreting the premodern man as the rest of the world at this point, and viewing Batman and Robin as the enlightened, intellectually and physically superior Americans, illustrates that these narratives were engaging with attempts to construct the present through reference to the past. In the process, they both attest to the "long run," as Sullivan termed it, while also calling it into question: Batman and Robin are not content only to correct issues in their own time; they also travel to the past to intervene in issues that were, in the "long run," largely resolved. In so doing they testify to an investment in the individual over and above impersonal historical forces.[28]It can be argued that America's perceived international superiority carries over into the depiction of science and magic in these time travel stories. As is to be expected with travel to the ancient world, the twentieth-century man's science was viewed as magic by premodern audiences. In *Batman* #36 (1946), Batman and Robin travel to the time of King Arthur and Merlin. The famed wizard is known for his unrivaled knowledge of magic—or at least, that is, until he meets his match in Batman. Essentially, one of the focal points of this story depicts a showdown of sorts between Batman and Merlin, where Batman thwarts the great wizard at every turn because of his scientific understanding. For context, when Merlin seemingly summons thunder and lightning—a trick exclusively reserved for the gods—Batman's superior scientific intellect tells him that this is not the case despite the naive crowd's unquestioning belief but is instead a measly gunpowder concoction—not magic, just simple science. In the light of America's discovery concerning nuclear power, this could be a knowing jab at the rest of the world, a further subtle suggestion that the premodern, superstitious man represented the rest of the world to America's twentieth-century man of science.[29]

Another interpretation is that time travel narratives depict an urge to return to such a state of naïveté. In descriptions that laud the past as perfect or glorious, there is a clear sense of longing, of desire for simpler times. The atomic bomb changed the landscape of life as people knew it, a fact increasingly apparent as elements of Cold War logic and rhetoric became increasingly embedded in American society, culture, politics, and economics. Moreover, the years leading up to the Second World War had dragged America out of the splendid sense of isolation that had underpinned the (apparently) blissful ignorance of interwar isolationism, a decision solidified and made irreversible by the end of the Second World War. If such a concept was possible, time travel would allow Americans to return to a simpler, less terrifying time, a time when modern science did not exist but, ironically, everything seemed to make a lot more sense. Rather than the complexities attendant with peering behind the curtain of creation and destruction, simple solutions could be more comfortably accepted. The difficulties of such an idea are rendered explicit while Merlin performs on stage. In his critique of and contest with Merlin, Batman represents the desire of the audience to peer behind the curtain, to discover the machinery that makes the tricks work, and, as a result, the ideologies those tricks strive to uphold. Modernity, or at least its Cold War aspects, has undermined the ability to accept things at face value according to these stories.

Keeping with this more nostalgic take on the past, the premodern world, for all its visible flaws, is depicted as a time when men respected one another. Evil men still existed. War was still a very real factor. But good always thwarted evil and could always be told apart from bad—at least this is how the past is romanticized here. The same was not true of the world in which Batman and Robin's readers lived. The Second World War was the stage on which atrocities such as the Holocaust and the atomic bombing of Hiroshima and Nagasaki were acted out; the developing Cold War seemed to suggest that there may yet be repeat performances. Not only had the horror of atomic warfare not been expunged by its repeated occurrence, the act of dropping atomic bombs seemed to work toward a world in which other states would not only develop such weapons but might also use them. In looking back, the generation reading these comics viewed honor and respect as courtesies belonging to a bygone era—for there can be no honor and respect in combat when the weapons involved render vast swathes of territory nuclear wastelands.[30] While for most, minor details such as a king wearing his best jewels in honor of his guests in *Batman* #49 (1948), or Batman being knighted for his efforts in *Batman* #36, will be glossed over as insignificant moments in the grander scheme of these fantastical stories, they should nevertheless be seen as significant within the context of a world gone mad. Produced at a time when mankind was heading toward the possibility of nuclear warfare and the potential for atomic annihilation—a fact made more frightening by the apparent absence of honor among men—it should not be considered too great a leap to associate the depiction of these values here with the desire for a chance to live in a less hostile and more honorable world—or at least one where combat was governed by rules and individual skill rather the abstract collective scientific acumen. Kings donning full ceremonial regalia or bestowing honors on visitors should also be seen in the context of Old World diplomacy, a system from which the US was divorced as the result of its modernity and status as a republic. However, in such manifestations of respect for American citizens, it can be seen as a passing of the mantle, with "Old World" being literalized through the element of time travel. Batman and Robin demonstrate that the US was always already willing and able to adopt the mantle of global leadership, eliding past isolationist attitudes and the nation's relative historical weakness.

Time travel clearly captured the imagination of America at the end of the Second World War, but it was far from just a phase. These time travel narratives continued to resonate throughout the Cold War as a way of helping readers to look back in order to move forward at times of great uncertainty.[31] Contemporary science fiction narratives also began to deal more seriously with questions of time travel and potential futures, demonstrating the relevance of the trope behind these superhero narratives. Throughout the Cold War, science fiction posited the idea that inspiration and solace could be found in tales of the past, and not just that, but that the past taken as a whole had led to this moment. To recontextualize Sullivan's remarks about the long run, it might be not so much that people had lost faith in the ability of time to heal all wounds, but rather that they increasingly believed in their own capacity to effect radical change. Apparent advances in civil rights, urban regeneration, and the overwhelming transformation of the American economy in the postwar world certainly suggested that secular miracles were possible. What we know in retrospect is not only that these were not miracles but that they were not even solutions; each contained the genesis of its own failures.

CONCLUSION

The time travel narratives explored here suggest that movement through both time and space offer points of comparison with the present; the differences to be found there are both prospective models for conduct, yet also justificatory ones. The travelers through time or region sometimes begin as uncertain, looking somewhere other than their present reality for guidance, but in doing so largely find justification in their own strength, judgment, and preferred course of action. However, the mutability of time and place that leads to this conclusion has within it the seeds of uncertainty—of a process of becoming rather than being. By positing the past as a source for, as well as of, the future, the past is changed through the hero's intervention, just as the hero is changed by his journey to the past. Even as justification for present policies is found, the process by which it is found cannot help but be transformative of the individual who discovers it. That time travel happens repeatedly in the historical moment of the early Cold War flags the confusion of that time as it also reproduces its conviction: in looking back anxiously at history to find the triumphant ascendancy of American values and strength, the USA, through its superhero proxies, finds precisely what it requires, presupposing ahistorical ideologies that exist unproblematically outside the conditions that give rise to them. The past and present therefore exist simultaneously, pursuing parallel lines of development that intersect and overlap, influencing each other in ongoing processes of mutual construction. As a result, both past and present, through their mediation in comics, emerge as collective constructions that are never, and never can be, fully settled. Such uncertainty suggests disruptive influences that problematize narrative historical accounts. In Kaja Silverman's terms, the atomic bombing of Japan and its literal and geopolitical fallout in the early Cold War can be perceived as a moment of historical trauma. Such occurrences lay bare the dominant fiction, the dynamic narratives that order society in particular ways for the benefit of particular groups, exposing the ideological machinery it needs to perform its usually obscured function; the "reflecting surface" of ideology in which society views itself cracks, calling into question belief in its "natural" status.[32] Batman's adventures both direct attention to this through pointing to disruption and simultaneously attempt to reinstate "natural" orders through their activities—which are undertaken through breaking the natural order of chronological flow. Just as a creative team is responsible for the contents of the comic, the comics themselves are built around a team. Batman might be the focus of their adventures, but he is accompanied by Robin, assisted by Professor Nichols, and dependent on others for the action that drives the narrative. Both creators and created are then dependent on an audience to grant the contents of the comic existence, in the short term by filling in its gaps and, in the long term, by considering its narrative interventions in larger narrations of the nation and the reader (another twin process of becoming that exists in and through dialogue).

Long before Batman's first point of departure for time travel (the assignation of origins, and deployment of correct time-based terminology, for those able to move around in time is a difficult process), Nietzsche theorized the notion of the "untimely," with historical reflections "acting counter to our time and thereby acting on our time . . . for the benefit of a time to come."[33] Batman's politicized time travel adventures are certainly an attempt to represent actions outside the moment of their creation and reception in order to act on that moment; however, while the narratives and images analyzed here both create and repeat versions of the historical past, they themselves become subjects of repetition. In 1967, with Batmania at its height, DC reprinted a number of old adventures in 80 Page Giant format to capitalize on this. As if to ram home the point that these narratives had been sourced from the past for largely financial reasons, *Batman* #187 (1967) reprinted a story from #125 (1959) wherein Batman travels to the seventeenth century to establish the provenance of a painting recently bought at auction. In *Batman* #193 (1967), the story from #52 (1949) is reprinted in which Batman travels back in time to meet some Vikings. After this, the reprint strategy shifted to the origins of major characters in the Batman narrative universe, a sensible move in a time of plummeting circulation and market oversaturation.[34] The traumatic present of the past, the early Cold War, is also reinterpreted through this process as something to be looked back on fondly, the myth of the "good old days" of the Eisenhower administration, in contrast to the present situation; the act of re-presenting the past here is not therefore a straightforward repetition, but rather a repackaging that can itself be repackaged, though always already in relation to the same Cold War anxieties.[35] The Cold War posited the end of repetition; time travel, especially at the behest of market capitalism, forcibly asserts it.

NOTES

This chapter is based on a paper presented at Drawing on the Past: The Pre-modern World in Comics, a conference held at the IHR in London, September 10–11, 2018. That paper was written and researched with Michael Goodrum, and I am grateful to him, the other editors of this volume, and those attending the conference for their helpful comments when writing this chapter.

1. This is clearly demonstrated in Chris Bishop, *Medievalist Comics and the American Century* (Jackson: University Press of Mississippi, 2016).

2. Henry Luce, "The American Century," *Life*, February 17, 1941.

3. For a useful consideration of the history of the term "the American Century," see Tony Smith, "Making the World Safe for Democracy in the American Century," *Diplomatic History* 23, no. 2 (1999): 173–88.

4. Richard Hofstadter, *The American Political Tradition: And the Men Who Made It* (New York: Vintage, 1948).

5. Nichols appeared in nineteen issues of *Batman* between his first appearance in *Batman* #24 (1944) and #127 (1959), eight issues of *World's Finest Comics* between #42 (1949) and #138 (1963), and six issues of *Detective Comics* between #116 (1946) and #295 (1961). Nichols subsequently appears as a supporting character in the four-issue mini-series *America vs. the Justice Society*, discussed by Matthew Costello in this volume.

6. Victoria Byard, "'I Belong to the Future': Timeslip Drama as History Production in *The Georgian House* and *A Traveller in Time*," in *Time Travel in Popular Media: Essays on Film, Television, Literature and Video Games*, ed. Matthew Jones and Joan Ormrod (Jefferson, NC: McFarland, 2015), 151.

7. Michael Goodrum, *Superheroes and American Self Image: From War to Watergate* (London: Ashgate, 2016), passim.

8. David Wittenberg, *Time Travel: The Popular Philosophy of Narrative* (Oxford: Oxford University Press, 2013), 11.

9. Robert Shaffer, "Pearl S. Buck and the East and West Association: The Trajectory and Fate of 'Critical Internationalism,' 1940–1950," *Peace and Change* 28, no. 1 (2003), 4–5.

10. Shaffer, "Pearl S. Buck and the East and West Association," 17.

11. Wittenberg, *Time Travel*, 2.

12. American empire was in a state of flux in the early Cold War period, with formal decolonization of the Philippines in 1946 occurring alongside the process of more-abstract economic and cultural projects of empire. Comics were not completely removed from this process: see Michael Goodrum, "'Friend of the People of Many Lands': Johnny Everyman, 'Critical Internationalism' and Liberal Post-war US Heroism," *Social History* 38, no. 2 (2013): 203–19. Batman's investigation of the appearance of his face in medieval Chinese fireworks also provides an opportunity for American interventions to be presented as peacemaking: the Batman rockets are created as a celebration of the hero ending a war, though his actions restore to him territory claimed by Marco Polo, resonating with notions of empire in Southeast Asia then at play through the Korean War and other colonial conflicts. Bill Finger, Jim Mooney, et al., "The Amazing Adventure of Batman and Marco Polo!" *World's Finest Comics* #42 (DC, 1949). Peacemaking is also presented domestically when Batman helps Captain Lightfoot, a colonial era captain of police, prevent a war between Native Americans and the residents of Gotham in 1753 in Bill Finger, Bob Kane, et al., "The Batman of Yesterday!" *Batman* #79 (DC, 1953). "Peace" is clearly constructed on American terms.

13. Cathy Caruth, *Unclaimed Experience: Trauma, Narrative, and History* (Baltimore: Johns Hopkins University Press, 1996), 17.

14. David Seed, *American Science Fiction and the Cold War* (Edinburgh: Edinburgh University Press, 1998), 40.

15. Richard E. Sullivan, "The End of the 'Long Run,'" *Centennial Review of Arts and Science* 4, no. 3 (1960), 401.

16. Seed, *American Science Fiction*, 40.

17. Wonder Woman, particularly in the Marston/Peter era from 1941 to 1948, is a constant reminder of tensions between the sexes. Similarly, "Lois Lane, Girl Reporter," which ran as a support feature in *Superman* from *Superman* #28 (1944) to #42 (1946), showcased Lois's abilities as a reporter, resonating (albeit belatedly) with the Rosie the Riveter–style empowerment of the Second World War. For more on Lois, and contemporary debates about gender relations and their representation in comics, see Michael Goodrum, "'Superman Believes That a Wife's Place Is IN THE Home': Superman's Girl Friend, Lois Lane, and the Representation of Women," *Gender & History* 30, no. 2 (2018): 442–64. Lois is also a frequent time traveler in the 1950s.

18. Friedrich Nietzsche, *Beyond Good and Evil.*

19. William W. Savage Jr., *Commies, Cowboys and Jungle Queens: Comic Books and America, 1945–1954* (Middletown, CT: Wesleyan University Press, 1998), 12.

20. See, for instance, Ronald Takaki, *A Different Mirror*; Nancy C. Carnevale, "'No Italian Spoken for the Duration of the War': Language, Italian-American Identity, and Cultural Pluralism in the World War II Years," *Journal of American Ethnic History* 22, no. 3 (2003): 3–33; Lauren Rebecca Sklaroff, "Constructing GI Joe Louis: Cultural Solutions to the 'Negro Problem' during World War II,' *Journal of American History* 89, no. 3 (2002): 958–83.

21. For their commitment to establishing the dominance of American finance in particular, see Benn Steil, *The Battle of Bretton Woods: John Maynard Keynes, Harry Dexter White, and the Making of a New World Order* (Princeton: Princeton University Press, 2013).

22. John Winthrop," City upon a Hill," sermon delivered July 2, 1630. Full text available here: https://www.greatamericandocuments.com/speeches/winthrop-city-upon-hill/.

23. Joseph Samachson, Dick Sprang, et al., *Batman* #24 (DC Comics, 1944).

24. Edmond Hamilton and Jim Mooney, et al., *Batman* #38 (DC Comics, 1946).

25. William Moulton Marston and Harry G. Peter, *Wonder Woman* #9 (DC Comics, 1944).

26. Marston and Peter, *Wonder Woman* #9.

27. Dominick LaCapra, *Writing History, Writing Trauma* (Baltimore: Johns Hopkins University Press, 2001), 23.

28. This individualistic approach can also be seen in *Wonder Woman* #39 (DC Comics, 1950), where Wonder Woman strives to prove that no one "in a democracy is unimportant."

29. This interlude also draws on Mark Twain, *A Connecticut Yankee in King Arthur's Court* (1889), a frequent point of inspiration for travel to the past—and one described as "an object-lesson in democracy" by William Dean Howells in *Harper's Magazine* in 1890: http://twain.lib.virginia.edu/yankee/cyharper.html. Another excellent articulation of the same basic principle is *Evil Dead 3: Army of Darkness* (1993), which exaggerates these discussions past the point of parody while also drawing on Cold War science fiction/fantasy special effects by Ray Harryhausen.

30. The terror of nuclear war was represented in *Captain Marvel Adventures* #66 (Fawcett, 1946), when Captain Marvel was the sole survivor of a global nuclear war.

31. We might also think of travel back from the postapocalyptic future in the late Cold War era in story worlds such as the *Terminator* franchise, which suggest that even though the current trajectory of society might be disconcerting, there was always hope for its correction.

32. Kaja Silverman, *Male Subjectivity at the Margins* (London: Routledge, 1992), 24.

33. Friedrich Nietzsche, "On the Uses and Disadvantages of History for Life," in *Untimely Meditations*, trans. R. J. Hollingdale (Cambridge: Cambridge University Press, 1983), 60.

34. This origins strategy was also pursued in reprint form in *World's Finest Comics* #271 (DC, 1981), a series that had earlier reprinted one of its own time travel stories (from #138, 1963) in #206 (1971).

35. The 1950s are represented quite unproblematically in the first two installments of the *Back to the Future* franchise, for instance.

WORKS CITED

Binder, Otto, and C. C. Beck. *Captain Marvel Adventures* #66. Fawcett Publications, 1946.

Bishop, Christopher. *Medievalist Comics and the American Century*. Jackson: University Press of Mississippi, 2016.

Cameron, Don, and Win Mortimer. *Detective Comics* #116. DC, 1946.

Carnevale, Nancy C. "'No Italian Spoken for the Duration of the War': Language, Italian-American Identity, and Cultural Pluralism in the World War II Years." *Journal of American Ethnic History* 22, no. 3 (2003): 3-33.

Caruth, Cathy. *Unclaimed Experience: Trauma, Narrative, and History*. Baltimore: Johns Hopkins University Press, 1996.

Finger, Bill, and Bob Kane. *Batman* #79. DC, 1953.

Finger, Bill, and Sheldon Moldoff. *Detective Comics* #295. DC, 1961.

Finger, Bill, and Jim Mooney. *World's Finest Comics* #42. DC, 1949.

Finger, Bill, and Jim Mooney. *World's Finest Comics* #138. DC, 1963.

Finger, Bill, and Dick Sprang. *Batman*. DC, 1959.

Goodrum, Michael. "'Friend of the People of Many Lands': Johnny Everyman, 'Critical Internationalism' and Liberal Post-War US Heroism." *Social History* 38, no. 2 (2013): 203–19.

Goodrum, Michael. *Superheroes and American Self Image: From War to Watergate*. London: Ashgate, 2016.

Goodrum, Michael. "'Superman Believes That a Wife's Place Is in the Home': Superman's Girl Friend, Lois Lane, and the Representation of Women." *Gender & History* 30, no. 2 (2018): 442–64.

Hamilton, Edmond, and Jim Mooney. *Batman* #38. DC Comics, 1946.

Hofstadter, Richard. *The American Political Tradition: And the Men Who Made It*. New York: Vintage, 1948.

Jones, Matthew, and Joan Ormrod, eds. *Time Travel in Popular Media: Essays on Film, Television, Literature and Video Games*. Jefferson, NC: McFarland, 2015.

LaCapra, Dominick. *Writing History, Writing Trauma*. Baltimore: Johns Hopkins University Press, 2001.

Luce, Henry. "The American Century." *Life*. February 17, 1941.

Marston, William Moulton, and Harry G. Peter. *Wonder Woman* #9. DC, 1944.

Nietzsche, Friedrich. "On the Uses and Disadvantages of History for Life." In *Untimely Meditations*. Translated by R. J. Hollingdale. Cambridge: Cambridge University Press, 1983.

Samachson, Joseph, and Dick Sprang. *Batman* #24. DC Comics, 1944.

Savage, William W., Jr. *Commies, Cowboys and Jungle Queens: Comic Books and America, 1945–1954*. Middletown: Wesleyan University Press, 1998.

Seed, David. *American Science Fiction and the Cold War*. Edinburgh: Edinburgh University Press, 1998.

Shaffer, Robert. "Pearl S. Buck and the East and West Association: The Trajectory and Fate of 'Critical Internationalism,' 1940–1950." *Peace and Change* 28, no. 1 (2003): 1–36.

Silverman, Kaja. *Male Subjectivity at the Margins*. London: Routledge, 1992.

Sklaroff, Lauren Rebecca. "Constructing GI Joe Louis: Cultural Solutions to the 'Negro Problem' during World War II." *Journal of American History* 89 no. 3 (2002): 958–83.

Smith, Tony. "Making the World Safe for Democracy in the American Century." *Diplomatic History* 23, no. 2 (1999): 173–88.

Steil, Benn. *The Battle of Bretton Woods: John Maynard Keynes, Harry Dexter White, and the Making of a New World Order*. Princeton: Princeton University Press, 2013.

Sullivan, Richard E. "The End of the 'Long Run.'" *Centennial Review of Arts and Science* 4, no. 3 (1960): 391–408.

Takaki, Ronald. *A Different Mirror: A History of Multicultural America*. Boston: Little, Brown, 2009.

Twain, Mark. *A Connecticut Yankee in King Arthur's Court*. New York: Charles L. Webster, 1889.

Wittenberg, David. *Time Travel: The Popular Philosophy of Narrative*. Oxford: Oxford University Press, 2013.

MYTHIC HISTORIES

CHAPTER EIGHT

FEDERAL BUREAU OF ILLUSTRATION

Comics Depictions of J. Edgar Hoover

MAX BLEDSTEIN

Cartoonist Rick Geary draws on a rich comics tradition in *J. Edgar Hoover: A Graphic Biography* (2008), tackling the life of the FBI's founder in a medium often used by the man himself (in conjunction with coconspirators) to develop his hagiographic image in the public eye.[1] Hoover's first comics appearances began in newspaper strips such as *War on Crime* (1936–1938) and morphed into cameos in comic book series such as *Dynamic Man*, found in *Mystic Comics* (1940–1945), and *Dale of the FBI*, found in *Daring Mystery Comics* (1940–1942).[2] As Geary notes, many of these comics were written at Hoover's behest to burnish his reputation and that of the FBI in popular media.[3] The comics relied on the idealism of fantasy, linking Hoover with superheroes. The fantastical elements mixed with references to real tactics used by the FBI to inflate the value of the organization and that of its director. The inflation epitomizes uses of superhero comic books to construct an American national identity and rally support for American institutions.

In contrast, Geary's graphic biography critiques such a construction through a satirical approach to depicting Hoover using sardonic visual humor and an honest reckoning with less flattering elements of his life. Such elements have previously been addressed in Anthony Summers's *Official and Confidential: The Secret Life of J. Edgar Hoover*.[4] Throughout the biography Summers refers to famous rumors about Hoover, as exemplified by the description of him and colleague and intimate friend Clyde Tolson as "a Washington legend, one heavy with the innuendo that they were homosexual lovers."[5] Summers's book has since been critiqued as a "homophobic fun-house projection" based on "an appalling lack of substantive evidence."[6] But Geary trades Summers's homophobia for a more nuanced and less problematic critique of Hoover's life. Reading Geary's work in dialogue with previous comic book depictions of Hoover thereby reveals *J. Edgar Hoover* to be an example of how comics art has emerged as what

Charles Hatfield calls "a radically new kind of expressive object," as opposed to its propagandistic past.[7] Geary's use of visual techniques throughout *J. Edgar Hoover* to critique the graphic biography's subject exemplifies developments in modern American cartooning, particularly when read in conjunction with earlier propaganda comics featuring Hoover and the FBI.

COMICS AS AMERICAN PROPAGANDA

Media, and comics specifically, were essential to Hoover's justification of his power and that of the FBI to the American people. Nickie D. Phillips and Staci Strobl describe Hoover as "convinced of the importance of crafting a positive media image of the FBI."[8] As a result of his interest in media, he subscribed to five Washington newspapers and paid particular attention to their comic strips.[9] Along with Tolson, Hoover oversaw the *War on Crime* strip, which depicted the FBI's efforts in comics form.[10] Such strips, along with superhero comic books, radio, film, and television, helped to develop the mythology of the FBI in the American imagination.[11] Richard Gid Powers argues that Hoover's power stemmed more from the impact of these works than from the FBI's achievements.[12] Hoover became seen as an "autonomous symbol of the law," not by fighting crime but through pop culture depictions of his efforts .[13] These depictions disseminated ideas of what Hoover himself described as "America's effort to become free and to incorporate freedom in our institutions," which, he argued, had "to become the basis for our American unity."[14] Comics were among the many media harnessed to spread such ideas.

Although Hoover released propaganda in both comic strips and comic books, I will focus my attention on the latter due to their formal capacities. Joseph Witek notes the two forms' commonalities but also argues that they "diverge so fundamentally as to constitute different literary forms."[15] The concision of comic strips necessitates repetition and narrative concentration, whereas comic books allow for more expansive storytelling.[16] Witek explains that while comic books "can be discursive and oblique in their narrative and thematic connections; comic strips are of necessity concentrated, with each verbal and visual element directed to a single and immediate effect: the termination of a strip becomes its rationale."[17] Accordingly, Pascal Lefèvre suggests that these different forms "even stimulate different manners of consuming."[18] Thus, although Hoover used both for propagandistic purposes, I center my analysis around the use of the storytelling potential of comic books to promote narratives of the strength and validity of Hoover and the FBI amongst the American public.

Hoover's use of comic books exemplifies uses of media for the construction of national identity. The comics exemplify what Lauren Berlant calls the "National

Symbolic," defined as "the order of discursive practices whose reign within a national space produces, and also refers to, the 'law' in which the accident of birth within a geographic/political boundary transforms individuals into subjects of a collectively-held history."[19] In the boundary of the United States, pop culture works such as comics featuring the FBI inform the American people of the individuals and institutions keeping the country safe. Hoover worked to preserve the hegemony of such depictions through the FBI's monitoring of writer Pearl S. Buck, who headed an organization that put its name to comics with liberal messages.[20] This surveillance complemented the work of comics depicting Hoover that, as my close reading shows, promote reverence for the FBI and its director. In spite of the intrinsic arbitrariness of national identity, cultural texts can facilitate the construction of shared national values. Such construction has happened in the United States in part through the prevalence of stories depicting what Jason Dittmer describes as the "nationalist superhero": defined as "superhero narratives in which the hero (or very rarely, the heroine) explicitly identifies himself or herself as representative and defender of a specific nation-state, often through his or her name, uniform, and mission."[21] My chapter shows comics in which such heroes also represent Hoover and the FBI.

These comics demonstrate how the medium has been an especially valuable propagandistic tool. Although Ramzi Fawaz chronicles the reclamation of the superhero for marginalized people, Fawaz also shows the initial connection between superheroes and American nationalist ideology.[22] Fawaz describes how "the superhero's robust masculinity served as metaphor for the strength of the American body politic against the twin evils of organized crime at home and fascism abroad."[23] Superhero comics thereby facilitated the dissemination of a nationalistic and gendered image, an image Hoover sought to exploit for the purposes of his own self-promotion. My reading of this exploitation builds on the work of scholars who have discussed at length the construction of American identity as defined against foreign villains in comics.[24] Their research lays the foundation for my reading of Hoover's attempts to sway American public opinion through comics.

Comics' influence over American culture in the late 1930s to early 1940s stemmed in part from the socioeconomic and political circumstances of the period. Jeffrey K. Johnson speculates that the devastation of economic hardships led to Americans finding comfort in the power and strength of superheroes.[25] In addition to this financial influence, the increase in European war violence in 1940–1941 corresponded with an increase in foreign threats being depicted in American comics.[26] Ferenc Morton Szasz argues that the topical appeal, along with widespread circulation, "allowed the comics to shape public opinion in ways that can hardly be imagined."[27] Hoover and the FBI, as depicted in comics, exemplify this influence.

VENERATING AUTHORITY

Comic books featuring Hoover and the FBI depict both Hoover and the organization as powerful figures fighting enemies of America on its behalf. I focus my analysis on three particular series: *The Shield*, found in *Pep Comics* (1940–); *Dynamic Man*; and *Dale of the FBI*. None of these series name Hoover directly; however, all three feature the FBI prominently, including the organization's director (identified as such and closely resembling Hoover in visage). As Powers points out, Hoover's comics presence frequently revolves around dispatching heroes to their missions and welcoming them back afterward.[28] Powers describes Hoover's position in comic books as "a sort of gray eminence managing a stable of action heroes," allowing him to "be an intermediary between the realms of out-and-out fantasy and newspaper reality."[29] While I do not dispute Powers's comments, I suggest that Powers fails to capture the hegemonic presence of Hoover and the FBI in these comics. My close readings demonstrate the extent to which the comics venerate both the organization and its founder.

Such veneration can be seen in opening captions of *The Shield*, which encourage readers to begin stories featuring the titular hero by first contemplating his patriotism and connection with Hoover. The series' subtitle also serves to establish this connection: "G-Man Extraordinary." Although the text of the comic's opening caption changes, it always features references to the hero's determination to protect the country, and even the relationship between those efforts and the FBI. The series begins with a splash panel showing the Shield breaking through a sheet, as the accompanying text describes his determination to protect "the U.S. government from all enemies."[30] The caption also provides his origin story, in which his alter-ego, Joe Higgins, pursues "an appointment as a G-Man to carry out his avowed purpose" after his father dies at the hand of "foreign spies" during World War I.[31] The text further explains that the only person other than Higgins who knows this story is Hoover, referred to only as "the chief of the FBI."[32] As the series progresses, the opening captions emphasize the imminence of the country's danger, such as in a description of the "great need" for the Shield's help due to "America's dream of peace [being] close to shattering."[33] An image of the Statue of Liberty lies next to the text, reminding the reader of the stakes at hand. The captions eventually become even more explicitly jingoistic, describing the Shield's position "at the helm of his ship of state, the United States of America, as he steers a steady course toward the port of all patriots . . . America for the Americans!"[34] Thus, stories featuring the Shield begin by informing the reader of the hero's patriotic mission and the link between that mission and Hoover through knowledge of the Shield's identity.

In addition to the implication of Hoover's relationship with the Shield, Hoover dispatches him and other heroes to fight for American values, as Powers describes.[35] Following a two-shot featuring Hoover pointing at the Shield while explaining that "the public is clamoring for action" in response to the "reign of terror" being caused by foreign spies, a series of panels depicts their violent attacks against American military targets.[36] Hoover serves a similar function in *Dynamic Man*, recruiting the titular hero to fight a villain murdering bankers.[37] As in *The Shield*, two-shots emphasize the connection between Hoover and the hero by showing them in the same panels, such as when Hoover asks Dynamic Man to fight jewelry store thieves shortly after learning of their crimes.[38] Similarly, soon after Hoover hears of a series of bank robberies in *Dale of the FBI*, he demands that a lackey "send Dale in right away," and subsequently assigns him to the case.[39] In each of these sequences, Hoover responds to attacks against American citizens by summoning superheroes to defend the targets.

Hoover also welcomes the superheroes back after their successes to remind readers of his role in American victories. Following Dale's defeat of bank robbers and kidnappers, Hoover thanks him for his part in the "clean sweep" of the criminals, to which Dale responds by describing the "pleasure" of taking down "that dirty crowd," while a confident grin affirms his happiness.[40] In contrast, Dynamic Man explains that he encounters "a little bit of trouble" in taking out the villainous Dr. Vee, but Hoover's description of apprehending Dr. Vee and extracting a confession suggests the benefit of overcoming the challenges.[41] Hoover also does not work with the heroes in isolation, as he explains when solemnly responding to the Shield's news of his success by telling him, "The entire nation is grateful."[42] In moments such as these, Hoover links his efforts with the interests of the entire country, showing the reader that the achievements of the FBI and those of the US as a whole are intertwined.

Hoover's presence emphasizes his individual strength while also highlighting the power and authority of the FBI as an organization. After the Shield leaves a meeting with Hoover in FBI headquarters, two "sinister figures" follow and attack the hero.[43] Prior to the attack, the two men discuss how the Shield's presence in the office building suggests that he spies on their gang, showing criminals' fear of the FBI.[44] The Shield demonstrates the organization's ethics when he refrains from acting on a hunch: "I can't cause a fuss . . . without being sure of my facts!"[45] Hoover also emphasizes the FBI's duty to respond to threats to the country when he tells the Shield that "it is up to the FBI to discover what happened to" five ships that disappear near Puerto Rico.[46] The Shield's institutional affiliation plays a clear role in his efforts, such as in a scene in which he introduces himself as "Joe Higgins of the FBI" to a senator threatened by foreign villains.[47] When a mother and father discover that their daughter has been kidnapped, he immediately describes the situation as "a case for the FBI"; a portrait of the daughter in the same panel reiterates the cost of the villains' action.[48] In such sequences, the comics show the FBI to be a crucial force for keeping the American people safe.

The authority depicted suggests the legitimacy of invasive espionage tactics. In a *Dynamic Man* story, Hoover explains to the hero that villains' theft of cars "permits us to investigate," without suggesting a need for a warrant or any other legal procedures.[49] When the Shield cannot get into a hotel room where criminals are plotting an attack, he uses a "radio sound detector" to listen in on the conversation.[50] He hears about a plot "to assassinate the Army chiefs" and immediately attacks the villains, suggesting the value of the eavesdropping.[51] In a similar scene, the Shield uses his "electric ear" to hear about an oncoming submarine attack, allowing him to prevent the attack just in time.[52] Following one bombing (showing the willingness of foreign spies to act), the Shield uses the ear to prevent a follow-up attack by identifying the target.[53] These scenes stand out in part due to wiretapping being key amongst a number of tools "which, adopted under the guise of 'wartime necessity' and found to be highly useful shortcuts, became standard, albeit secret, investigative tools of Hoover's FBI."[54] The depictions of a primary example of one of those shortcuts also justify the FBI's invasiveness, since the comics show the productive potential of listening in on enemies' conversations.

As a result of the information gleaned through the espionage, the heroes learn of potential crimes and need to stop their culprits, thereby glorifying extrajudicial arrest. Following one of the Shield's uses of the electric ear, he finds an airplane pilot bound up by two men.[55] The hero undoes the rope tying the victim up and uses it to "securely" bind his attackers.[56] The comic positions the Shield's act as a response to the villains' attack, suggesting it to be justified by the nefarious actions leading to the binding. In this manner the comic suggests the legitimacy of stopping criminals through arrest, legal or not.

Arrest is not always enough to stop the villains, which requires acts of violence from the heroes; however, the comics justify the acts by framing them as responses to other provocations. In one scene an assailant describes the Shield as a "dirty copper" while the other restrains him, emphasizing the nature of the threat to the hero's well-being by saying, "I'll knock your head off!"[57] After the comic establishes the threat of violence against the Shield, he fights back, and emanata next to the villains emphasize the force of his response. The Shield then cries, "Now it's my turn," framing his violent attack as retributive rather than unprovoked.[58] In a similar scene in *Dale of the FBI*, Dale frees himself from being held hostage by punching his kidnappers with "great force" and subsequently gaining control of their car.[59] For Dynamic Man, violence proves to be an effective method of extracting information, as holding up a man by his shirt collar and asking him about the whereabouts of his coconspirators yields a quick and useful response.[60] In these passages, the comics portray violence as an effective, necessary, and justified technique for stopping criminals. The scenes suggest violence to be inextricable from routines of policing.

Some of the actions to which the heroes respond highlight specific crimes, thereby reminding readers of threats from which the FBI (hypothetically) can protect them. Among the crimes depicted, references to bank robbery suggest an especially strong correlation with other ways in which Hoover burnished his public image. As Powers shows, the killing of notorious bank robber John Dillinger was a crucial moment in Hoover's development of the FBI's media persona.[61] Powers describes the death of Dillinger as "Hoover's greatest achievement in shaping a complex, unstructured news event into an incontrovertible FBI triumph."[62] Accordingly, a similar narrativizing of efforts to stop bank robbers can be seen in the comics. For example, an entire *Dynamic Man* story revolves around a villain named "The Hood" murdering bankers and breaking into banks.[63] Dynamic Man swoops in to stop the threat to capitalism, foiling the Hood's plans and revealing his true identity.[64] Likewise, bank robbery is also a dangerous threat in the world of *Dale of the FBI*, as depicted in a dramatic panel showing henchmen terrifying bank tellers and customers with tommy guns. Hoover's shaping of media continues in these comics, which call attention to the prevalence of bank robbery and the terror it embodies for the American people.

This terror prompts readers to volunteer on the country's behalf. The heroes are eager to fight for American needs, such as when the Shield responds to Hoover's congratulations for successful completion of a mission by asking, "What's my next assignment?"[65] Their willingness to keep fighting both encourages readers to take comfort in the heroism on display and induces anxiety through the suggestion of further threats. Characters are also willing to sacrifice themselves for the good of the US, such as in a sequence in which Dale stands on the wing of a plane in flight in order to foil mobsters.[66] Echoing a similar sentiment, a caption describes how the Shield "risks his own life to save the lives of others" after he catches a bomb aimed at American citizens, and the accompanying caption (depicting the bomb's detonation) emphasizes the risk he faces.[67] Throughout the comics, heroes do not only volunteer to fight for the country with excitement but are more than willing to die.

Although these jingoistic comics often depict Hoover, he later would make statements critical of the medium. In June 1950, years after the publication of the comics I have discussed, Hoover testified in Washington to the Special Committee to Investigate Crime in Interstate Commerce, which included an inquiry into the adverse effects of comics on adolescent behavior.[68] Hoover downplayed the role of comics in children committing crimes, but he nonetheless suggested that comics "may influence the susceptible boy or girl who already possesses definite anti-social tendencies."[69] While Hoover distanced himself from such an influence here, his use of comics for propagandistic purposes nonetheless suggested a belief in their powers. He showed a similar belief in his statement in the January 1960 issue of the *FBI Law Enforcement Bulletin*, in which he decried the transmission of "obscene literature across our land through the means of films, decks of playing cards, photographs, 'comic' books, salacious magazines, paperbacked books and other pornographic products."[70] Hoover had faith in the ability of comics to affect the actions of American children, and he sought to direct those actions toward what he saw as the country's (and his own) best interests.

DRAWING TRUTH TO POWER

If propaganda comics about Hoover and the FBI depict an unblemished vision of American power, Geary's work captures a darker view of political history. In two of his recurring series, *A Treasury of Victorian Murder* (1995–2007) and *A Treasury of XXth Century Murder* (2008–), Geary depicts noteworthy true crime stories, ranging from kidnappings to presidential assassinations. Throughout these comics Geary draws the readers' attention to the humanity of the victims and the injustices working against them. Another graphic biography, *Trotsky* (2009), tells the story of someone with vastly different political views from Hoover's.[71] The sardonic critiques of *J. Edgar Hoover* rely on a formal mastery of comics art, which contrasts with Ian Gordon's assessment of Geary's images in *J. Edgar Hoover* as "simply illustrative" drawings that "seldom add anything to the story being told."[72] Instead, Geary's visuals develop a sophisticated mockery of Hoover and the FBI, using a medium once employed for the untarnished construction of his public image.

Geary most fully realizes his radical historiographic depiction in his graphic biography of Hoover, beginning with the book's opening splash page. Beneath a drawing of Hoover menacingly wielding a tommy gun, two captions atop circular inset panels describe him as a "crusader against the menace of Communism" and a "guardian of public morality."[73] In the panel below the former, Geary draws Hoover as a knight wielding a large sword, as well as a shield adorned with stars and stripes (reminiscent of the badge carried by the Shield). In the panel below the latter, Hoover holds a tablet (presumably supposed to be the Ten Commandments) with one hand and pedantically points in the air with the other. Geary's visual allusion to Hoover's propaganda comics reminds the reader of their existence, highlighting the less valiant aspects of Hoover's character. The connection between Hoover's concept of "public morality" and Judeo-Christian values mocks the tenor of Hoover's fervor. Hoover's pointing recalls common depictions of Moses holding the Ten Commandments, further establishing an ironic association with religious conviction. These opening images set up a much less flattering portrayal of Hoover than he receives in the earlier comics.

In addition to satirical caricature, Geary exploits the mixed media of comics to mock Hoover. Geary's humor often relies on what Hatfield calls the "tensions" of comics, in which a "plurality of messages" operate in conflict with one another.[74] Geary makes particular use of Hatfield's first tension, which involves words played against images in order for one "to contradict or complicate or ironize the other."[75] As Hatfield notes, the complexity of these tensions requires the reader to play a significant role in unpacking their meaning.[76] Geary uses this role to ask the reader to think critically about Hoover's actions, in contrast to the lack of critique seen in the propaganda comics.

Geary's exploitation of the tension between text and image can be most clearly seen in his mockery of the FBI's impotence (particularly relative to Hoover's view of the organization). In one exemplary panel, Geary refers to Washington as a "sprawling center of power," then shows a fervent group of Vietnam protestors undermining that power.[77] In another, Geary illustrates text describing Hoover's "unique skills" with an image of him sorting a filing cabinet, a task which one imagines he would not need to be unique to execute.[78] Geary features an even more jarring juxtaposition of word and image in his description of the FBI's "little jurisdiction outside of a small number of interstate crimes," accompanied by an image of Hoover looking out at the Capitol Building.[79] The image of one of the key concentrations of American political power highlights Hoover's relative lack of political clout. Geary's mockery of Hoover's inaction also spreads over several panels, such as in a sequence in which a senator asks Hoover to confirm that he has "never personally apprehended a criminal," to which he struggles to respond, as illustrated by the black circle inside his thought balloon in the following panel.[80] These words and images mock Hoover and the FBI for having little actual control in spite of their delusions of grandeur.

Geary also uses the discrepancy between words and drawings in the graphic biography to poke fun at Hoover's inability to build emotional relationships with the people around him. Although Geary emphasizes Hoover's position as "his mother's protector and breadwinner," the tense looks on their faces as they stand together suggest a lack of familial warmth in their relationship.[81] Geary shows a similar coldness between Hoover and his secretary, Helen Sandy, whom he describes as "a trusted assistant," which contrasts with the accompanying image of the two of them with blank facial expressions, hardly suggesting an abundance of trust in their relationship.[82] Hoover's lack of feelings shared with the people around him follows him to death, as demonstrated by President Richard Nixon's awkward and uncomfortable look as he delivers Hoover's eulogy.[83] Throughout the graphic biography, Geary satirizes Hoover's struggles with developing social ties.

Geary also critiques Hoover by depicting his atavistic (even for his time) racism, which further condemns him in the reader's eyes. Geary describes the "malign influence" Hoover sees in the civil rights movement, in spite of the Kennedy administration's support for it.[84] In the same panel, Geary adds a further level of irony to Hoover's statement by drawing an American flag amidst a group of civil rights protestors, suggesting a patriotism Hoover presumably would have seen as anything but malign.[85] Geary features a similar undermining of Hoover in a panel describing his surveillance of Martin Luther King due to suspicions of Communist activity, in which a group of marchers holds both a sign reading "EQUAL RIGHTS NOW" and another American flag.[86] Geary also uses Hatfield's first tension to mock Hoover's racism, such as in a panel depicting the Lincoln Memorial (drawing on associations between Lincoln and antiracist activism) accompanied by a caption describing Hoover's backward views coming from being "the product of a segregated Southern city."[87] These sequences shame Hoover for his racism, suggesting both his myopia and its negative impact on his professional abilities.

Hoover's ideological preoccupations led to his abuses of power. Geary describes a mass arrest of immigrants in Boston, accompanied by a splash page featuring a close-up on the people's feet, bound together by chains.[88] In addition to the pains of detainment shown in the image, Geary describes the prisoners being "detained in a windowless corridor with no toilet facilities" and leaves this aspect to the reader's imagination.[89] Geary symbolizes Hoover's overreach with an image of his face looming ominously above the FBI headquarters, paired with text describing "his paranoia, his vengefulness, his total control."[90] The panel captures the excessiveness of the menace Hoover brings to the FBI. Unlike the images of Hoover as a stoic defender of justice in the earlier comics, Geary shows him to be a tyrannical madman.

Hoover's overstepping of boundaries includes unwarranted brutality against civilians, which solidifies the graphic biography's critical portrait. In a panel showing a man arrested in a union raid, Geary draws two guards, one of whom carries a nightstick, holding his arms.[91] Although Geary does not show acts of police brutality on the page, the presence of the weapon next to the prisoner suggests the strong possibility of him soon becoming its target. The graphic biography shows state violence much more explicitly in a later splash panel, in which troops clad in riot gear beat anti–Vietnam War protestors.[92] Geary describes Hoover's view of the protestors as "dangerous to the American way of life," but the troops are the only ones in the panel posing physical danger.[93] While the violence in these panels does not differ drastically from that seen in superhero comics, Geary raises moral questions around the use of violence through implying police attacks against civilians.

Geary also calls attention to Hoover's media manipulation, with which, by virtue of its form, Geary's work is intrinsically in dialogue. Geary mentions Hoover's "daily comic strip," *War on Crime*, and draws comic books featuring the FBI.[94] Although Geary does not explicitly call attention to the connection between his own work and the propaganda comics, the image of the propaganda comics within a modern graphic biography facilitates Geary's metacritique. Geary likewise depicts

Hoover's use of media by describing the "series of favorable articles" written by journalist Rex Collier for the *Washington Star*.[95] Here, Geary makes his critique more explicit through the strained expression on the writer's face, suggesting the struggle of writing positively about Hoover. The representation of this challenge captures the labor behind propaganda, labor hidden by the earlier comics.

Geary highlights some of the possible reasons Hoover would want to heavily control his image in the media, most notably rumors about his sexual orientation. Although Powers concludes that there "is no compelling evidence for a definitive judgment" about whether or not Hoover had a sexual relationship with Tolson, Powers does confirm the plethora of gossip surrounding the two men.[96] There were a number of reasons for this gossip, such as the two eating nearly every meal together, and spending weekends and vacations together.[97] As a result of the rumors, Hoover tasked FBI agents with tracking down their sources and pressuring them to deny the allegations.[98] Like Powers, Geary does not confirm whether or not the relationship was sexual, but he does describe it as "so intimate and comfortable that, over time, it embodied the characteristics of a marriage."[99] Geary captures this intimacy through an image of Hoover with his arm around Tolson, smiling with a warmth unseen in the images of him with his mother and secretary.[100] Hoover's display of affection contrasts with the stoicism seen throughout the superhero comics.

Following Geary's repeated satirical and critical depictions, he puts the reader in Hoover's perspective, presenting the discomfort of identification with a figure so heinous. Following Dwight Eisenhower's election as president, Geary depicts him and Attorney General Herbert Brownell greeting Hoover at the White House in a splash panel in which Eisenhower and Brownell extend their arms in front of a sign reading "WELCOME."[101] Geary illustrates the panel from Hoover's point of view, as he is the one being welcomed. Thus, the reader shares Hoover's perspective in this panel, which feels particularly discomforting given the unsavory qualities Geary spends most of the rest of the graphic biography depicting. Not only does Geary critique and mock Hoover, but he asks the reader to experience the ugliness of walking in the shoes of the object of the satire.

The sophistication of Geary's cartooning techniques, as seen in this page and throughout the graphic biography, contrasts with the earlier propaganda comics to capture the evolution of American comics art. As I have demonstrated, Geary's mockery of Hoover through comics shows how modern uses of the medium can undermine the legacy of a historical figure. Although propaganda such as the comics I describe in the first section of my chapter surely have not disappeared, they exist alongside works such as Geary's historiographic critique. In examining these works in dialogue with one another, I have attempted to fulfill Witek's request for scholars "to consider the heritage of fact-based comic books in America and then to ask how such comic books function as narrative media and as embodiments of ideology."[102] Whereas comics featuring Hoover once embodied the ideology of the FBI, Geary's *J. Edgar Hoover* tears down illusions of American jingoism.

NOTES

1. Rick Geary, *J. Edgar Hoover: A Graphic Biography* (New York: Hill and Wang, 2008).

2. David Hajdu, *The Ten-Cent Plague: The Great Comic-Book Scare and How It Changed America* (New York: Picador, 2009), 52.

3. Geary, *J. Edgar Hoover*, 2008.

4. Anthony Summers, *Official and Confidential: The Secret Life of J. Edgar Hoover* (New York: G. P. Putnam's Sons, 1993).

5. Summers, *Official and Confidential*, 80.

6. Charles Morris, "Pink Herring & the Fourth Persona: J. Edgar Hoover's Sex Crime Panic," *Quarterly Journal of Speech* 88, no. 2 (2002): 229.

7. Charles Hatfield, *Alternative Comics: An Emerging Literature* (Jackson: University Press of Mississippi, 2005), 7.

8. Phillips, Nickie D., and Staci Strobl, *Comic Book Crime: Truth, Justice, and the American Way* (New York: New York University Press, 2013), 21.

9. Hajdu, *Ten-Cent Plague*, 62.

10. Hajdu, *Ten-Cent Plague*, 62.

11. Frankie Y. Bailey and Donna C. Hale, "Popular Culture, Crime, and Justice," in *Popular Culture, Crime, and Justice*, ed. Frankie Y. Bailey and Donna C. Hale (Belmont, CA: Wadsworth, 1998), 10.

12. Richard Gid Powers, *G-Men: Hoover's FBI in American Popular Culture* (Carbondale: Southern Illinois University Press, 1983), 51.

13. Richard Gid Powers, "Myth, Ritual, and the Comic Strip *G-Man*," in *Rituals and Ceremonies in Popular Culture*, ed. Ray B. Browne (Bowling Green, OH: Bowling Green University Popular Press, 1980), 210.

14. J. Edgar Hoover, *Masters of Deceit: The Story of Communism in America and How to Fight It* (New York: Holt, 1958), 334.

15. Joseph Witek, *Comic Books as History: The Narrative Art of Jack Jackson, Art Spiegelman, and Harvey Pekar* (Jackson: University Press of Mississippi, 1989), 6.

16. Witek, *Comic Books as History*, 8–9.

17. Witek, *Comic Books as History*, 9.

18. Pascal Lefèvre, "The Importance of Being 'Published': A Comparative Study of Different Comics Formats," in *Comics & Culture: Analytical and Theoretical Approaches to Comics*, ed. Anne Magnussen and Hans-Christian Christiansen (Copenhagen: Museum Tusculanum Press, 2000), 98.

19. Lauren Berlant, *The Anatomy of National Fantasy: Hawthorne, Utopia, and Everyday Life* (Chicago: University of Chicago Press, 1991), 20.

20. Michael Goodrum, "'Friend of the People of Many Lands': Johnny Everyman, 'Critical Internationalism' and Liberal Post-War US Heroism," *Social History* 38, no. 2 (2013): 215.

21. Jason Dittmer, *Captain America and the Nationalist Superhero: Metaphors, Narratives, and Geopolitics* (Philadelphia: Temple University Press, 2013), 7.

22. Ramzi Fawaz, *The New Mutants: Superheroes and the Radical Imagination of American Comics* (New York: New York University Press, 2016), 6.

23. Fawaz, *New Mutants*, 7.

24. Michael Goodrum, *Superheroes and American Self Image: From War to Watergate* (Burlington, VT: Ashgate, 2016); Matthew J. Costello, *Secret Identity Crisis: Comic Books and the Unmasking of Cold War America* (New York: Continuum, 2009).

25. Jeffrey K. Johnson, *Super-History: Comic Book Superheroes and American Society, 1938 to the Present* (Jefferson, NC: McFarland, 2012), 7.

26. Bradford W. Wright, *Comic Book Nation: The Transformation of Youth Culture in America* (Baltimore: Johns Hopkins University Press, 2001), 40.

27. Ferenc Morton Szasz, *Atomic Comics: Cartoonists Confront the Nuclear World* (Reno: University of Nevada Press, 2012), 2.

28. Powers, *G-Men*, 159.

29. Powers, *G-Men*, 156.

30. *Pep Comics* #1 (MLJ Magazines, 1940).

31. *Pep Comics* #1.

32. *Pep Comics* #1.

33. *Pep Comics* #3 (MLJ Magazines, 1940).

34. *Pep Comics* #6 (MLJ Magazines, 1940).

35. Powers, *G-Men*, 159.

36. *Pep Comics* #1.

37. *Mystic Comics* #2 (Timely Comics, 1940).

38. *Mystic Comics* #3 (Timely Comics, 1940).

39. *Daring Mystery Comics* #3 (Timely Comics, 1940).

40. *Daring Mystery Comics* #3.

41. *Mystic Comics* #1 (Timely Comics, 1940).

42. *Pep Comics* #3.

43. *Pep Comics* #1.

44. *Pep Comics* #1.

45. *Pep Comics* #1.

46. *Pep Comics* #2 (MLJ Magazines, 1940).

47. *Pep Comics* #6.

48. *Daring Mystery Comics* #3.

49. *Mystic Comics* #3.

50. *Pep Comics* #3.

51. *Pep Comics* #1.

52. *Pep Comics* #2.

53. *Pep Comics* #4 (MLJ Magazines, 1940).

54. Curt Gentry, *J. Edgar Hoover: The Man and the Secrets* (New York: Norton, 1991), 287.

55. *Pep Comics* #2.

56. *Pep Comics* #2.

57. *Pep Comics* #1.

58. *Pep Comics* #1.

59. *Daring Mystery Comics* #3.

60. *Mystic Comics* #3.

61. Richard Gid Powers, *Secrecy and Power: The Life of J. Edgar Hoover* (New York: Free Press, 1987), 189–93.

62. Powers, *Secrecy and Power*, 189.

63. *Mystic Comics* #2.

64. *Mystic Comics* #2.

65. *Pep Comics* #1.

66. *Daring Mystery Comics* #3.

67. *Pep Comics* #3.

68. Hajdu, *Ten-Cent Plague*, 172.

69. Quoted in Hajdu, *Ten-Cent Plague*, 173.

70. Federal Bureau of Investigation, January 1960, *FBI Law Enforcement Bulletin*, 1960.

71. Rick Geary, *Trotsky: A Graphic Biography* (New York: Hill and Wang, 2009).

72. Ian Gordon, "Let Us Not Call Them Graphic Novels: Comic Books as Biography and History," *Radical History Review* 106 (Winter 2010): 189.

73. Geary, *J. Edgar Hoover*, 3.

74. Hatfield, *Alternative Comics*, 39.

75. Hatfield, *Alternative Comics*, 37.

76. Hatfield, *Alternative Comics*, 39.

77. Geary, *J. Edgar Hoover*, 4.

78. Geary, *J. Edgar Hoover*, 12.

79. Geary, *J. Edgar Hoover*, 17.

80. Geary, *J. Edgar Hoover*, 37.

81. Geary, *J. Edgar Hoover*, 9.

82. Geary, *J. Edgar Hoover*, 10.

83. Geary, *J. Edgar Hoover*, 101.

84. Geary, *J. Edgar Hoover*, 83.

85. Geary, *J. Edgar Hoover*, 83.

86. Geary, *J. Edgar Hoover*, 84.

87. Geary, *J. Edgar Hoover*, 80.

88. Geary, *J. Edgar Hoover*, 15.

89. Geary, *J. Edgar Hoover*, 15.

90. Geary, *J. Edgar Hoover*, 91.

91. Geary, *J. Edgar Hoover*, 14.

92. Geary, *J. Edgar Hoover*, 90.

93. Geary, *J. Edgar Hoover*, 90.

94. Geary, *J. Edgar Hoover*, 41–42.

95. Geary, *J. Edgar Hoover*, 24.

96. Powers, *Secrecy and Power*, 169–73.

97. Gentry, *J. Edgar Hoover*, 190.

98. Powers, *Secrecy and Power*, 171–72.

99. Geary, *J. Edgar Hoover*, 44.

100. Geary, *J. Edgar Hoover*, 44.

101. Geary, *J. Edgar Hoover*, 67.

102. Witek, *Comic Books as History*, 11.

WORKS CITED

All-Star Comics #4. All-American, March–April, 1940.

All-Star Comics #9. All-American, February–March, 1942.

Bailey, Frankey Y., and Donna C. Hale. "Popular Culture, Crime, and Justice." In *Popular Culture, Crime, and Justice*, edited by Frankie Y. Bailey and Donna C. Hale, 1–20. Belmont, CA: Wadsworth, 1998.

Berlant, Lauren. *The Anatomy of National Fantasy: Hawthorne, Utopia, and Everyday Life*. Chicago: University of Chicago Press, 1991.

Costello, Matthew J. *Secret Identity Crisis: Comic Books and the Unmasking of Cold War America*. New York: Continuum, 2009.

Daring Mystery Comics #3. Timely Comics, April 1940.

Dittmer, Jason. *Captain America and the Nationalist Superhero: Metaphors, Narratives, and Geopolitics*. Philadelphia: Temple University Press, 2013.

Fawaz, Ramzi. *The New Mutants: Superheroes and the Radical Imagination of American Comics*. New York: New York University Press, 2016.

Federal Bureau of Investigation. January 1960, *FBI Law Enforcement Bulletin*.

Geary, Rick. *J. Edgar Hoover: A Graphic Biography*. New York: Hill and Wang, 2008.

Geary, Rick. *Trotsky: A Graphic Biography*. New York: Hill and Wang, 2009.

Gentry, Curt. *J. Edgar Hoover: The Man and the Secrets*. New York: Norton, 1991.

Goodrum, Michael. "'Friend of the People of Many Lands': Johnny Everyman, 'Critical Internationalism' and Liberal Post-War US Heroism." *Social History* 38, no. 2 (2013): 203–19.

Goodrum, Michael. *Superheroes and American Self Image: From War to Watergate*. Burlington, VT: Ashgate, 2016.

Gordon, Ian. "Let Us Not Call Them Graphic Novels: Comic Books as Biography and History." *Radical History Review* 106 (Winter 2010): 185–92.

Hajdu, David. *The Ten-Cent Plague: The Great Comic-Book Scare and How It Changed America*. New York: Picador, 2009.

Hatfield, Charles. *Alternative Comics: An Emerging Literature*. Jackson: University Press of Mississippi, 2005.

Hoover, J. Edgar. *Masters of Deceit: The Story of Communism in America and How to Fight It*. New York: Holt, 1958.

Johnson, Jeffrey K. *Super-History: Comic Book Superheroes and American Society, 1938 to the Present*. Jefferson, NC: McFarland, 2012.

Lefèvre, Pascal. "The Importance of Being 'Published': A Comparative Study of Different Comics Formats." In *Comics & Culture: Analytical and Theoretical Approaches to Comics*, edited by Anne Magnussen and Hans-Christian Christiansen, 91–105. Copenhagen: Museum Tusculanum Press, 2000.

Morris, Charles. "Pink Herring & the Fourth Persona: J. Edgar Hoover's Sex Crime Panic." *Quarterly Journal of Speech* 88, no. 2 (2002): 228–44.

Mystic Comics #2. Timely Comics, April 1940.

Mystic Comics #3. Timely Comics, June 1940.

Pep Comics #1. MLJ Magazines, January 1940.

Pep Comics #2. MLJ Magazines, February 1940.

Pep Comics #3. MLJ Magazines, April 1940.

Pep Comics #4. MLJ Magazines, May 1940.

Pep Comics #6. MLJ Magazines, July 1940.

Phillips, Nickie D., and Staci Strobl. *Comic Book Crime: Truth, Justice, and the American Way.* New York: New York University Press, 2013.

Powers, Richard Gid. *G-Men: Hoover's FBI in American Popular Culture.* Carbondale: Southern Illinois University Press, 1983.

Powers, Richard Gid. "Myth, Ritual, and the Comic Strip *G-Man*." In *Rituals and Ceremonies in Popular Culture*, edited by Ray B. Browne, 206–25. Bowling Green, OH: Bowling Green University Popular Press, 1980.

Powers, Richard Gid. *Secrecy and Power: The Life of J. Edgar Hoover.* New York: Free Press, 1987.

Summers, Anthony. *Official and Confidential: The Secret Life of J. Edgar Hoover.* New York: G. P. Putnam's Sons, 1993.

Szasz, Ferenc Morton. *Atomic Comics: Cartoonists Confront the Nuclear World.* Reno: University of Nevada Press, 2012.

Witek, Joseph. *Comic Books as History: The Narrative Art of Jack Jackson, Art Spiegelman, and Harvey Pekar.* Jackson: University Press of Mississippi, 1989.

Wright, Bradford W. *Comic Book Nation: The Transformation of Youth Culture in America.* Baltimore: Johns Hopkins University Press, 2000.

CHAPTER NINE

WHEN HAWKMAN MET TAILGUNNER JOE

How the Justice Society of America Constructs the Fifties as a Usable Past

MATTHEW J. COSTELLO

In the twentieth century, the superhero narrative has helped construct and define American national identity, encouraging global involvement between world wars, triumphing American superpower during the Cold War, and reflecting on the costs of global power after the Cold War.[1] One aspect of this construction has been the treatment of America's past.[2] With the development of narrative continuity as a central feature of the superhero narrative (at least in comics) from the 1970s, the saga of the superheroes has commented on America's history to inform its present. Superhero tales address both what we know of the past and how we know it. Examining different versions of one superhero story retold in different periods can offer insights into how superhero tales construct history as a usable guide to understanding the present.

One such story is "The Defeat of the Justice Society," by Paul Levitz and Joe Staton.[3] In this story, the superhero group the Justice Society of America (JSA) is called to testify before the "Combined Congressional Un-American Activities Committee" in 1951. When the committee demands they reveal their secret identities, the JSA members, led by Chairman Hawkman, refuse. They then disappear from the scene, retiring for over a decade. This story, retold in 1985 and 2005, is set in the 1950s, an era central to ideological discourse in the United States for the last several decades.[4] From *American Graffiti* (1973) to the culture wars of the 1990s, the fifties have been a major trope of discourses of politics and nation in the United States. Some describe an era of economic abundance and social stability, a golden age to be regained. Others portray an era of racism, forced conformity, and social repression, a symbol of a past from which the nation has progressed.[5] Both treat the era as what Jan Assman calls a "figure of memory," a cultural touchstone that informs ideas of nation and proper political action.[6]

Since Van Wyck Brooks called for "the past experience of our people to be placed at the service of the future," historians have examined how constructing a usable past informs the present.[7] Often identified as a Whiggish account of history—reading the past through the lens of the present—such readings are frequently cast as conservative, using the past to justify the present.[8] Others see revisionist accounts of scholars such as Charles Beard as an instrumentalist reading of history—attempting to find in the past a means of challenging the present.[9] This seemed particularly significant during the New Deal, when, as Jones suggests, "the use of the past was largely negative: history represented something to transcend."[10] Warren Susman tried to bridge this divide by suggesting that a usable past needed to be both mythic and historical, where the mythic elements represented a static, fixed past that informed the conservative tendency, and history provided the dynamic, changing, progressive element.[11]

Victoria Hattam finds history an important guide to political agency, going beyond the divides among historians defined above. She identifies three ways history can promote contemporary political agency. By unmasking assumptions about the way things are and always have been, history can denaturalize the present, problematizing that which is taken for granted. By exploring the contingencies of how practices and actions came to be, history also resurrects abandoned alternatives, creating new options for the present. Finally, history informs contemporary action by bringing to light past accommodations and settlements that make the present possible.[12]

This summary suggests that the relation of past to present often hinges on the tense in which the past is cast. The past may be expressed in the perfect tense, as a closed period, separate from the present as it was for the New Deal historians. In this case, past events had occurred but do so no longer; the past is something against which to measure the present or some condition to transcend, but not active and alive, still affecting the present. Similar to the Whiggish historians, the past can also be cast imperfectly, as an ongoing narrative filled with events, ideas, and processes that still affect the contemporary world. As such, history loses some of its definitive quality, for as processes that have been (and may still be) occurring, history becomes more interpretable, more contested. This imperfect past may inform politics, help define positions, but cannot offer as definitive a claim of certainty as the past cast perfectly. Finally, as for Hattam, the past and the present might be informed by the same concerns and issues, or the past might serve as a repository of possible answers to contemporary problems. In this case, the past and the present are coterminous, and the past becomes present, echoing Faulkner's claim that the past is never dead, or even past.

The analysis that follows sets the three tellings of the story of the Justice Society and the senator in their political and cultural contexts to interrogate the relation of past to present. Several elements are explored in each context. The first involves the tense and form given to the past. The past may be offered as a formal history, supported by archival evidence, referencing specific events. The past may also be cast as the memory of participants, less reliable than archives but often more informative. The form in which the past is offered is affected by its tense; perfect past history is often more archival and definitive but frequently more mythic, while the imperfect past may involve fallible and contested memories but may be more mundane. The functional use of the past can be evaluated if the tense and form of history are set in the context of broader trends in the extant political culture, so the analysis must explore the cultural contexts of the stories and relate the tense and form of the past to the moment of their appearance. Thus, the story from 1979 will reflect post-Watergate, post-Vietnam America at the apogee of the New Deal coalition that preceded the Reagan presidency, when Americans sought to put a past behind them, to assure themselves that they were now free of prior wrongs. The mid-1980s story appears amidst the renewed Cold War, the breakdown of that New Deal coalition and the postwar consensus it represented. The new coalitional politics that sought a return to a golden age, represented by Reagan's victory, elicited a different engagement with the past than did the late 1970s. The 2005 story arrived at the end of the culture wars of the 1990s and after the terrorist attacks of 2001, when there was a perceived need to move beyond the bickering of the previous decade to engage with the issues generated by an increasingly globalized world. The continued presence of global threats and the continued problems facing American society suggest a past and present that face similar problems. As these political and cultural contexts change, so too does the relation of past to present in the story of Hawkman and Tailgunner Joe.

THE JSA AND CCUAC

The Justice Society of America (JSA) appeared in comic books from National Periodicals (later DC comics). The JSA roster included, among others, the Flash, Green Lantern, Hourman, Dr. Fate, Hawkman, the Atom, and Johnny Thunder. Appearing for the first time in *All Star Comics* #3 (Winter 1940), the JSA continued to fight crime until 1951, when its comic was cancelled, a victim of the changing tastes of readers who had become more interested in crime and horror comics. When superhero comics returned to favor in the late 1950s (beginning what aficionados call the Silver Age, against the Golden Age, which began with the first appearance of Superman in 1938), it was only a matter of time before the heroes from the 1940s reappeared. This happened in 1961 when the Silver

Age Flash met the Flash of the Golden Age (*Flash* #123). This was followed by several more meetings between the two Flashes and between the Silver Age Justice League of America and the Golden Age Justice Society.

By the 1970s the JSA had again become popular, appearing in new issues of *All Star Comics* and *Adventure Comics*, with Golden Age heroes fighting alongside younger heroes. While the Golden Age stories had followed an episodic structure, with little continuing story over several issues, superhero comics of the 1970s were increasingly presented as one continuous story taking place within the publisher's "universe" of heroes and villains. For comic book fans, maintaining this continuity was one of the joys of reading. As the commitment to continuity became stronger, the earlier stories needed to be incorporated into it.[13] The Justice Society presented a major problem for continuity: Where were these heroes from 1951 until 1961?[14]

1979: "THE MAN WHO DEFEATED THE JUSTICE SOCIETY"

Levitz and Staton answer this question in "The Defeat of the Justice Society." In this initial version, the events set in 1951 involving the "Combined Congressional Un-American Activities Committee" (CCUAC) compose only three pages of a seventeen-page story. The Justice Society thwarts an attempt to destroy them by criminals, whom they promptly turn over to federal authorities. Recognizing one of the captives as a Soviet spy, the federal agents inform the politicians, who subpoena the JSA to testify before Congress about their relationship with the man. The committee orders the members of the JSA to remove their masks. "If you are good Americans, you will show this committee your faces, and then we may *begin* the process of clearing you," one senator states. The members of the JSA display shock, and Chairman Hawkman stands. "We respectfully decline, Senator," he tells the Committee. "Our faces, our names, our lives are our own business. Don't worry, you won't be hearing from us again." At this the JSA vanish from the room in a cloud of smoke, to be neither heard nor seen for eleven years.

The tale is told in flashback, as Huntress, the daughter of Batman, recounts the tale to Powergirl, a young Kryptonian, like Superman. The reader encounters the story secondhand, through the eyes of the younger heroes who had not experienced the Red Scare of the 1950s. Huntress uses images from the JSA's computer archive to illustrate the events, giving the story the semblance of a formal "history"—archival footage supporting the recounting of events. This history, however, is an amalgamation of different institutions and periods. The "Combined Congressional Committee" brings together the House Committee on Un-American Activities (HUAC) and the Senate Subcommittee on the Investigation of the Loyalty of State Department Employees (known as the Tydings

Committee, after subcommittee chair, Millard Tydings). The story features close-ups of two committee members, one who resembles Senator Joseph McCarthy, the central figure of the Tydings Committee from 1950 to 1954, and the other Richard Nixon, who served on HUAC (1946–1949), gaining national fame during the investigation of Alger Hiss in 1948. The fictional history conflates time, space, and identity, rendering the era unified and complete, a mythic age, closed off from the contemporary period, cast in past perfect.

So temporally isolated from the present is the story that Powergirl needs Huntress to parse its moral for her. Powergirl's response to the story is incredulity. "You're kidding! You've got to be kidding!" she exclaims to Huntress. "They just gave up and went away for years?!" Huntress tells her, "It was a different world then, Powergirl—a sick, sad world a few men had twisted out of shape. It was a hard time to be honorable in." Powergirl, still unbelieving, claims it had to have been the work of some supervillain. "Nope, not a supervillain in sight, not even a dishonest man," replies Huntress, "simply a madman who got himself a little power and started to use it to crush people."

Powergirl's inability to comprehend the motives of the JSA suggests that the actions of her heroic forebears have no relevance in 1979, that the past is, in the words of David Lowenthal, "a foreign country." Between the late 1970s and the early years of the Cold War, there is a temporal and cultural chasm. The reference to Nixon (and McCarthy) as a "madman" supports Huntress's claim that the period was aberrant, warped by the actions of a few. The specific identification of Richard Nixon in the post-Watergate seventies suggests to the reader that the people (or the law) have proven superior to "madmen" with power. The world is thus once again safe for men of honor. While the fifties are nostalgia in popular consumer culture (the film version of *Grease* was released in 1978, and *Happy Days* still topped the television ratings), the politics of the period are placed in the past perfect tense, and they no longer affect the lives of Americans. Separated from the contemporary world by a distance so great that the young find the events unbelievable, the past perfect fifties serve merely as a myth of a repressive past to which the present is morally superior. The past is usable, but only as an index against which to measure the value of the present.

1985: "AMERICA VS. THE JUSTICE SOCIETY"

The reinvigorated Cold War of the Reagan administration gave the fifties a new importance. Reagan's aggressively anticommunist rhetoric defined a Manichean conflict between the goodness of America and the "empire of evil."[15] Practically, this was manifest in a massive military expansion, including the stationing of a new generation of intermediate-range nuclear missiles in Europe. This renewed

Cold War conflict recalled the ideas and actions of the fifties, echoing the rhetoric and policies of the Eisenhower administration. The 1984 presidential reelection campaign claimed it was "morning again in America," referring to a mythic fifties, an idealized American society before the tumults of the 1960s and the policies of détente that characterized the 1970s. Popular entertainment rekindled its interest in Cold War narratives as *The Day After* and *Amerika* gave television viewers a chilling view of potential Cold War outcomes, and film viewers saw the Soviets defeated by high school students and boxers in *Red Dawn* and *Rocky 4*. The rebirth of the Cold War in the post-détente world transformed the fifties narrative from the tale of an isolated and closed epoch into the contested terrain of the culture wars.

Decrying big government as the problem while expanding both its size and scope, the Reagan administration contributed to the disjunction between language and reality that was called postmodern in the mid-1980s. The real seemed to fade away, and only competing interpretations remained. History was reduced to ideology, transmitted mainly by memory. Jameson suggests postmodernism was "an attempt to think historically in an age that has forgotten how to think historically in the first place."[16] The historical thinking of the postmodernists, though, exchanged historical narrative for subjectivist interpretation, and historical meaning became a product of political position. Forgoing metanarratives for disruptions in which underlying power structures would be revealed, postmodernism saw everything as sui generis, adopting a universal presentism. "Postmodernism abandons all sense of historical continuity and memory, while simultaneously developing an incredible ability to plunder history and absorb whatever it finds there as some aspect of the present."[17] The superhero comics of the period plundered away, with the seminal works that transformed the genre—*American Flagg!* (1983–89), *Watchmen* (1986–87), and *The Dark Knight Returns* (1986)—offering alternative histories and Cold War futures as they deconstructed the superhero and American superpower. When ketchup was a vegetable and nuclear missiles were peacekeepers, it was difficult to find objective truth or objective history.

In the midst of political transformation and cultural contestation, Roy Thomas, Rafael Kayana, Mike Hernandez, and Alfredo Alcala retold the story of the JSA and HUAC in *America vs. the Justice Society*. This four-issue miniseries was conceived by Thomas, an aficionado of Golden Age superhero comics, as placing all JSA stories from the forties to the seventies in chronological sequence. The story of the JSA before HUAC occurs on one page in issue 3. Still, the earlier story permeates this one. In this tale the JSA must defend itself before a joint session of Congress when accused of treason during World War II. Their accuser is the late Batman, who had become highly critical of the JSA in his later years as police commissioner of Gotham City. Batman left a diary to be released after his death, in which he claimed the JSA had collaborated with Hitler. This situation is orchestrated by a millionaire named O'Fallon, who blames the JSA for the death of his father several years earlier. His father had been Senator O'Fallon, identified as the man who led the investigation into the JSA in 1951. The structure of the story follows the earlier one (JSA accused by government must defend itself against a charge of treason), and is also linked narratively (the events are set in motion by the actions in the previous story).

Where "The Defeat of the Justice Society" was presented as objectively recounting a historical event, *America vs. the Justice Society* renders the past only subjectively, as competing memories. Clark Kent reads Batman's diary, noting that it presents facts but questioning its interpretations. Batman's memory as recorded in his diary is contrasted with a recollection of events by Jay Garrick, the Flash, and later with the entire JSA membership as they recount the events of their careers. Even as these memories are presented as evidence before the Congressional Committee, the validity of memory is questioned throughout the story. A core element of the plot involves the death of Batman in a previous tale. Having come out of retirement to save the JSA, Batman was revealed at the time to be Bruce Wayne. The mystical superhero Dr. Fate had cast a spell altering memories such that everyone remembers that both Bruce Wayne and Batman died in the incident, but believe they were two different people. When Powergirl crashes the hearings to defend the JSA, she describes the separate deaths of Batman and Bruce Wayne. Dick Grayson (Batman's former sidekick, Robin, now counsel for the Committee) thinks, "Powergirl's telling the truth, bless her. Dr. Fate warped all memories, even the JSAers'."[18] The memories of the heroes, the key element of contest, are able to be warped. Memory, unlike the objective facts of history, is fallible.

The contest between memory and history within the narrative is also fought by the narrative itself. This series consciously attempts to define a history. Much of the story is a chronological enumeration of the JSA's adventures from the 1940s to the present, replete with footnotes, presented on the front and back inside covers, referencing the specific issues in which stories originally appeared. These trappings of history (the attempt by Thomas to create a definitive chronology for the JSA) permeate the narrative of competing memories, forcing a confrontation between history and memory and between different memories.

These contests are waged both in front of and through the younger generation of heroes. The children of the 1940s heroes watch the hearings on television, having been told by their parents to stay out of the conflict. More directly involved are the younger heroes associated with Batman, Huntress, and Robin. The Huntress, Helena Wayne, is the daughter of Batman and counsel for the JSA. Younger than Robin and less tied to her crime-fighting father (she was raised by her mother), Huntress is unwilling to believe the accusation and ready to reveal Batman's secret identity if it will clear the JSA. Robin—Dick Grayson, Bruce Wayne's ward and Batman's partner for many years—does not believe the accusation against the JSA, but gives it credence because of its source; he is more concerned with protecting Batman's honor than is Huntress. The two represent opposing relations to the past. Huntress would jeopardize the memory of Batman for the sake of the present, while Robin seeks to maintain the integrity of that past, even at the cost of the JSA. He is unwilling to reject *his* memory of the past and seeks to reconcile what he sees as two opposing truths—that the JSA members are not traitors and that Batman was not a liar. Robin's involvement in the actions of both the JSA and Batman, and his stronger commitment to remembering the events, gives him greater insight into the present situation. This insight leads him to uncover the plot against the JSA by O'Fallon and longtime JSA foe and time traveler Per Degaton. Robin's discovery clears the JSA of the treason charge and reveals Batman's accusation as a stratagem to protect the JSA from Degaton even after his death.

The tense of the story has changed from 1979. With current events set in motion by the previous story (the death of O'Fallon's father), and relying on active (if imperfect) memory, the actions portrayed here are not completed but ongoing. No longer closed off from the present, the past informs the debates between actors and defines their political positions. The present constructs the past as contested terrain, and navigating that terrain becomes a political act. Robin's success in uncovering Degaton's plot is not achieved by finding a real history but by negotiating a space between the competing memories of Batman and the Flash, both of whom retain the aura of mythic virtue. It is this political skill that the past can teach the young, because no "authentic" history exists to guide them, as the facts of the JSA are clouded by the interpretations informed by memory.

2005: JSA/JSA

The myth of a fifties suburban idyll reached its zenith in the 1990s. The first President Bush remembered a "kinder, gentler" era. The 1996 Republican presidential nominee Robert Dole wanted to build a bridge to the past, a time of "tranquility, faith and confidence in action." Former Speaker of the House Newt Gingrich remembered it as an era when there was a clear sense of what it meant to be an American.[19] Used as a major trope in the polarized cultural politics of the decade, the fifties became a subject of academic concern. Scholars sought to explain the use of the fifties in discourse but also to discover the historic fifties behind the myth.[20] This new historiography emphasized a range of issues, such as the intellectual history of the period, the emergence of the national security state, and the treatment of traditionally marginalized groups such as women, youth, and

Black Americans. It then moved beyond the location of those elements as things "in the past" by exploring the impact of this history on contemporary politics.[21]

Having weathered the culture wars of the 1990s, and awash in a sea of globalization that swept American jobs overseas, terrorist attacks onto US shores, and US soldiers into Iraq and Afghanistan, Americans remained divided over fundamental ideological issues. Battles over national security and civil liberties played out daily in the newspapers and, unsurprisingly, found their way into superhero comics in what became the most politicized era for the medium since the early 1970s. Marvel heroes fought a civil war in an allegorical story about the USA PATRIOT ACT.[22] DC heroes were revealed to be altering the memories of villains and heroes to achieve greater security.[23] Even for these heroes, right action had become obscured, and the very identity of the hero was in question.

Into this context of polarized politics and unclear national identity, Geoff Johns engages history, myth, and memory in "JSA/JSA."[24] Here the younger heroes of the current JSA, most prominently the teen-aged Stargirl, travel to 1951, to the day after the JSA resign, to convince them to redon their masks to foil an attempt by (again) Degaton to assassinate President Truman. Johns displaces the myth of the 1950s onto the myth of the Golden Age heroes. As the Golden Age heroes are mythic paragons of virtue, so the fifties as a suburban idyll in which the nation is whole, pure, and purposeful is equally mythic. The myth of the Golden Age heroes, however, offers insufficient guidance to young Stargirl and her compatriots. Only after they have acquired a clearer vision of the heroes' reality can they draw a guiding lesson. So, too, only when the myth of the fifties is complemented with an authentic history can the past offer useful guidance into the future.

The story begins with Stargirl at her parents' breakfast table after a night of fighting villains, thinking about her reasons for being a hero. Her musings about the older superheroes frame the story as a reevaluation of the fixity of the past and its relevance for the modern world. She notes that an older JSA member, Wildcat, told her that the older heroes had their own problems to work through and were not always unwavering paragons of virtue. "It's kind of hard to think that now . . . You can't imagine them ever being novices, heroes that made mistakes, that had problems. You can't imagine them being—like us."[25] The conclusion that Powergirl drew from the story Stargirl is about to encounter—that the previous heroes were nothing like her—becomes the starting point for Stargirl. Both younger heroes mythologize their predecessors, much as Americans have mythologized the fifties. As Stargirl reconsiders her predecessors in light of her experiences, the reader is forced to reconsider the myth of the fifties.

As Stargirl sits down to eat breakfast, a group of masked men appear and kill her family, including her infant cousin. Striking back in anger, she kills her assailants and is pulled from the scene by time traveler Rip Hunter, who is assembling the younger members of the JSA to return to 1951 to stop Degaton's assassination plot. Returned to the fifties, the young heroes find their predecessors in a variety of situations that reflect the problems of the moment. The younger heroes recognize that those they mythologized have foibles and messy lives of their own, forcing them to reconsider their idols and their definitions of heroism. "JSA/JSA" is the first version to offer a view of the past beyond the political. In fact, it is the messy private lives of the humans who wear masks in 1951 that drive the members of the JSA to disband. They are people, not just icons, as the younger heroes discover.

The stories of the present-day hero facing his/her predecessor compose the bulk of the narrative and demonstrate how the present and past face each other. Stargirl, who questions her own contributions to the JSA, confronts the original Starman, who has been driven insane by his guilt over helping develop the atomic bomb. The current Mr. Terrific, a Black American, is forced to confront the racism of the age. He must ride in a Jim Crow car and is assaulted by the KKK. He discovers that his (white) namesake/predecessor adopted a mixed-race child—his illegitimate nephew—the offspring of his brother and a Black madame from New Orleans. Most telling is the story of young hero Atom Smasher, who in a previous story allied himself with a former JSA enemy to seek revenge against the murderer of his mother. That enemy (Black Adam) now rules the fictional country of Kandhaq and maintains stability by mercilessly killing all associates of the former corrupt regime. By joining him Atom Smasher had become morally questionable, his choice of unjust means to achieve moral ends rendering him too ambiguous for membership in the JSA, so much so that Stargirl rages that he is a criminal when she finds him on the trip to the fifties. Now returned to the fifties to convince the Atom, the man who inspired him to be a hero, to stay the course, he finds that the Atom is informing on his friends for the FBI, which has threatened to arrest Atom's fiancée and her family. "I thought I'd see the original Atom witness just how much I failed his legacy," Atom Smasher thinks, "but am I just repeating it?"[26] As the Atom refuses to inform at the last minute, Atom Smasher begins to reconceive his notion of justice and morality.

Beyond such direct political commentary, the story also challenges the myth of the white, middle-class suburban idyll. The wealthy Dr. McNider (Dr. Midnight) lives a life of comfort, but even his world has perils. To his dismay, his fiancée lights a cigarette. "They're like chewing gum," she responds blissfully, twelve years before the surgeon general links them to cancer.[27] Hourman is sacrificing his white, suburban family utopia for his addiction to Miraclo, the drug that gives him his power.

While Roy Thomas used footnotes to give his annals of the JSA authenticity, Geoff Johns relies on direct quotations from Senator McCarthy, properly identifies the House Committee, and deploys other historically accurate elements to lend credence to his presentation of the 1950s.[28] This attempt to offer an "authentic" fifties corresponds with the changed notion of time that is being presented. The past was unfathomable in 1979 for Powergirl, who had only her myths to guide her, and available only through subjective memories for Robin in 1985. For Stargirl, the past is current, available to her as a direct experience. The sense of authenticity is achieved by replacing flashback and memory with the time travel, in which the present and past are brought into a single moment. The time travel narrative creates a unique perspective on time, giving the past an "enduring presence," as Kelley Wagers notes in her study of Octavia Butler's *Kindred.*[29] Atom Smasher, Mr. Terrific, and Stargirl need not rely on the memories or records of their predecessors—time travel permits them to have the same experiences. The past and the present become one. Bringing the past and present together gives to all involved a temporal perspective that helps define right action; the enduring presence of the past offers direction and meaning to the younger heroes. The actions of the heroes are a legacy for the next generation. Stargirl tells Starman, "Your life continues past today, 'kay? Your accomplishments, your sacrifices. You'll be an inspiration for generations to come. Like me."[30] The narrative stretches into the future as Stargirl is twice aided by the time-traveling Starwoman, revealed as her infant cousin grown to adulthood. Stargirl has become to her cousin what Starman is to Stargirl; Starman's legacy becomes Stargirl's destiny. She learns that her heroes are not without flaw, and that the past is not perfect, or truly past, and thus acquires more ways to encounter her present, developing a less rigid moral vision. Having initially attacked Atom Smasher's presence because he failed to live up to her rigid notions of virtue (derived from her weak understanding of the past), Stargirl accepts him by the end.

In contrast Degaton represents historical nihilism. Degaton and his minions travel through time, altering it at will. Degaton has weaponized time travel, using it to erase the memories and history that define the heroic identity, undermining the motives and power of the heroes. Holding the Golden Age Hourman hostage, Degaton sends his agents back in time to murder those who would be Hourman's childhood friends and future family, leaving him bereft of any real identity. By deleting the past, Degaton removes any meaning for the present. After ordering the death of one childhood friend, Jason Huntington, Degaton asks Hourman, "I wonder if you even remember Jason anymore? Or do you just recall the loneliness? The empty void during your school years. Stretching out each day."[31] Having lost the past that defined him, Hourman screams in anguish. Absent any meaningful connection with the past, Degaton has no moral codes to guide his present. Before ordering the death of Walker Gabriel, a time traveler who opposes him, Degaton chides him, "You're . . . one of a dozen travelers. Believing they have to set things right. But what you fail to realize, my friend, is that there is no right."[32]

"JSA/JSA" suggests that history is neither closed from the present nor a mere influence on it, but the same as the present. "Glad ta know there's heroes still in the future," Johnny Thunder tells the future Jakeem Thunder. "Days like these, a guy gets to wondering, y'know?"[33] To identify true moral action—to be usable—the past and present must be joined, not merely navigated. Signaling this point, neither Johnny nor Jakeem Thunder can call on the mystical Thunderbolt by uttering their magic phrase. Only when they discover that they must say the phrases simultaneously—when the present and past are combined in mutual understanding—does the Thunderbolt appear, ending the threat of Degaton.

Having saved President Truman from Degaton, the young heroes of the JSA return to the present. Stargirl returns to find her family alive and well, and she faces the future with an understanding that the past is not dead, but something filled with and made by people who are much like her, and that understanding that past in a nuanced and sophisticated way can help her understand the present more clearly. In the final panel of the story, she looks to her infant sister, who she knows will be a hero in her own right, and recognizes that Wildcat was right: "you never stop learning to be a hero."

CONCLUSION

The story of Hawkman and Tailgunner Joe reveals a changing encounter with the fifties in specific and the past in general. Portrayed as past perfect era of mythic repression in 1979, the tale reinforces the belief that Americans have blocked a threat to the virtue of their system in Watergate. It is a story of democratic triumph over tyranny. As those myths enter the imperfect tense to become competing memories by 1985, they support the value of ideological transformation and political and cultural debate. As the fifties moved from consumer culture to battleground for the culture wars, the relation of past and present became ever more important, spawning a renewed historical interest in the period. In "JSA/JSA" the present and past are brought together through time travel, and the fifties and the twenty-first century are seen as coterminous, with actors confronting the same issues, but now with an expanded repertoire of responses, giving them a more aware and effective sense of agency to address new concerns of a nation emerging from the culture wars and increased globalization. In each era a usable past was created, but they did not all look the same. Different types—and tenses—of history perform different functions, but all are ways in which history becomes a usable past.

NOTES

1. An earlier version of this paper was presented at the first Conference of the Superhero Project, Mansfield College, Oxford, September 2015. I would like to thank Annika Hagley, Richard Reynolds, Randy Duncan, Nelson Hathcock, and Eleanor Willging, as well as the editors of this volume, for valuable comments, although all errors and flaws herein remain, of course, mine.

2. There is a growing literature on the superhero and national identity. Significant works include Jason Dittmer, "'America Is Safe While Its Boys and Girls Believe in Creeds!': Captain America and American Identity prior to World War 2," *Environment and Planning D: Society and Space* 25 (2007): 401–23; Marc DiPaolo, *War, Politics and Superheroes: Ethics and Propaganda in Politics and Film* (Jefferson, NC: McFarland, 2011); Jeffrey Johnson, *Super-History: Comic Book Superheroes and American Society, 1938–the Present* (Jefferson, NC: McFarland, 2012); Matthew Costello, "Super-Powered Americans and American Superpower," in *The Cambridge Companion to American Science Fiction*, ed. Eric Carl Link and Gerry Canavan (London: Cambridge University Press, 2015), 125–39; Michael Goodrum, *Superheroes and American Self Image: From War to Watergate* (London: Routledge, 2017); Chris Gavaler, *Superhero Comics* (New York: Bloomsbury, 2017).

3. Paul Levitz and Joe Staton, "The Defeat of the Justice Society," *Adventure Comics* #466, 1979.

4. It is retold again in 2010 on three pages of issue #2 of the ten-issue series *DCU: Legacies* (Wein and Kubert). This series is a chronology of significant events in DC continuity. While part of the narrative, the story is treated only briefly and lacks the narrative elements that give the three versions discussed here their comparability. In particular, the 2010 version does not set the tale in the context of younger heroes who need to be educated about being heroes, rendering it void of ideological content.

5. Comic book fandom developed its own myth of the fifties. Perceived as contributing to juvenile delinquency, comic books came under attack in the late 1940s, with public crusades that led to Senate hearings and mass burnings of books. Fueled by the pseudoscience of psychologist Fredric Wertham, whose anti–comic book polemic *Seduction of the Innocent* became a best seller, the crusade was revitalized in the early 1950s with more book burnings and Senate hearings. In the wake of these hearings, major publishers formed the Comic Magazine Authority, imposing the most stringent code of self-censorship in American media. While the code did not produce industry decline (it was already in decline), it hastened it. Comic creators and fans thus see their industry as a victim of the censorious politics of the 1950s and tend to emphasize the repression of the period. This does not necessarily imply ideological position, as defending free speech fits well with both sides of the US political divide. A large literature treating these events exists. The best scholarly treatment remains Amy Kiste Nyberg, *Seal of Approval: The History of the Comics Code* (Jackson: University Press of Mississippi, 1998). Tending more to the mythical is the very readable David Hadju, *The Ten-Cent Plague: The Great Comic Book Scare and How It Changed America* (New York: Farrar, Straus and Giroux, 2008). Michael Goodrum discusses this period in *Superheroes and American Self Image*, 66–73. Bart Beaty offers a reevaluation of the criticism of Wertham in the context of the evolution of the academic study of communications in *Fredric Wertham and the Critique of Mass Culture* (Jackson: University Press of Mississippi, 2005). For a solid analytical review of industry trends and the effect of the code, see Jean-Paul Gabilliet, *Of Comics and Men: A Cultural History of American Comic Books*, trans. Bart Beaty and Nick Nguyen (Jackson: University Press of Mississippi, 2010), 29–55.

6. Jan Assman, "Collective Memory and Cultural Identity," trans. John Czaplicka, *New German Critique* 65 (1995): 127.

7. Van Wyck Brooks, "On Creating a Usable Past," *The Dial* 44 (April 1918): 340.

8. Jean. V. Matthews, "'Whig History': The New England Whigs and a Usable Past," *New England Quarterly* 51 (June 1978): 193–208; Colin Gordon, "Crafting a Usable Past: Consensus, Ideology, and Historians of the American Revolution," *William and Mary Quarterly* 46 (October 1989): 671–95. David Lowenthal offers this as a common, but not exclusive, use of the past in *The Past Is a Foreign Country* (London: Cambridge University Press, 1985), 41.

9. J. R. Pole, "The American Past: Is It Still Usable?" *Journal of American Studies* 1 (April 1967): 63–78.

10. Alfred Haworth Jones, "The Search for a Usable American Past in the New Deal Era," *American Quarterly* 23 (December 1971): 710–24.

11. Warren Susman, "History and the American Intellectual: Uses of a Usable Past," *American Quarterly* 16, pt. 2, supplement (Summer 1964): 243–63.

12. Victoria Hattam, "History, Agency and Political Change," *Polity* 32 (Spring 2000): 333–38.

13. Revising fictional histories to alter the meaning of previous events is known as "retroactive continuity," or "retconning," a term often attributed to Roy Thomas.

14. Because it recreated Golden Age heroes with new costumes and histories in the 1950s and 1960s, DC had a problem creating a continuity retroactive to the 1940s. They resolved this problem by positing that there were multiple Earths; the Golden Age heroes lived on Earth 2, while the Silver Age heroes lived on Earth 1. To simplify this continuity, in the 1985 *Crisis on Infinite Earths*, all the Earths were collapsed into one with a single continuity that begins in the mid-1980s. Thus, the JSA stories from 1979 and 1985 take place on Earth 2, while the 2005 story takes place on the only Earth left. The 2010 series, *Final Crisis*, recreated the "multiverse" of pre-crisis DC but did not populate it as before. Confused? Me, too.

15. See Ronald Reagan, "Address to the National Association of Evangelicals," March 8, 1983, Orlando, Florida, accessed April 2, 2008, http://www.reagan.utexas.edu/archives/speeches/public papers.html.

16. Fredric Jameson, *Postmodernism, or the Cultural Logic of Late Capitalism* (Durham, NC: Duke University Press, 1992), ix.

17. David Harvey, *The Postmodern Condition: An Enquiry into the Origins of Cultural Change* (London: Wiley-Blackwell, 1991), 54.

18. Roy Thomas and Dann Thomas, *America vs. Justice Society* #4 (DC Comics, 1985), 20.

19. George H. W. Bush, "1988 Republican National Convention Speech, 18 August 1988," accessed May 10, 2012, http://www.americanrhetoric.com/speeches/georgehbush1988rnc.htm; Robert Dole, "Republican National Convention Speech, 15 August 1996," accessed May 10, 2012, http://www.4president.org/speeches/dolekemp1996convention.htm; Newt Gingrich, *To Renew America* (New York: Harper Collins, 1999), 7.

20. Mary Caputi, *A Kinder, Gentler America: Melancholia and the Mythical 1950s* (Minneapolis: University of Minnesota Press, 2005); Daniel Marcus, *Happy Days and Wonder Years: The Fifties and the Sixties in Contemporary Cultural Politics* (New Brunswick, NJ: Rutgers University Press, 2004).

21. Paul Boyer, *By the Bomb's Early Light: American Thought and Culture at the Dawn of the Atomic Age* (Chapel Hill: University of North Carolina Press, 1985); Aaron Friedberg, *In the Shadow of the Garrison State: America's Anti-Statism and Its Cold War Grand Strategy* (Princeton: Princeton University Press, 2000); Elaine May, *Homeward Bound: American Families in the Cold*

War Era, rev. ed. (New York: Basic Books, 1999); James Gilbert, *Cycle of Outrage* (New York: Oxford University Press, 1985); Mary Dudziak, *Cold War Civil Rights: Race and the Image of American Democracy* (Princeton: Princeton University Press, 2000). This literature is vast. Stephen Whitfield offers an overview of politics and culture in *The Culture of the Cold War*, 2nd ed. (Baltimore: Johns Hopkins University Press, 1996), and John Kenneth White explores the legacy of Cold War politics for contemporary America in *Still Seeing Red: How the Cold War Shapes the New American Politics* (Boulder, CO: Westview Press, 1988). Bart Beaty reconsiders the work of Fredric Wertham in *Fredric Wertham and the Critique of Mass Culture* (Jackson: University Press of Mississippi, 2005). Useful edited collections include Lary May, ed., *Recasting America* (Chicago: University of Chicago Press, 1988), and Joel Foreman, ed., *The Other Fifties: Interrogating Midcentury Icons* (Urbana: University of Illinois Press, 1997).

22. Mark Millar and Steve McNiven, *Civil War* (New York: Marvel Comics, 2007).

23. Brian Meltzer and Rags Morales, *Identity Crisis* (New York: DC Comics, 2004).

24. Geoff Johns, Dan Kramer, and Keith Champagne, "JSA/JSA," *JSA* #68–72, DC Comics, 2005.

25. Johns, Kramer, and Champagne, *JSA* #68, 2.

26. Johns, Kramer, and Champagne, *JSA* #70, 10.

27. Johns, Kramer, and Champagne, *JSA* #70, 17.

28. The line between actual events and media events, however, is sometimes stretched. When challenged by the KKK to tell them "what do they call you up North, boy," Mr. Terrific paraphrases Sidney Poitier from *In the Heat of the Night*: "They call me Mr. Terrific!" Johns, Kramer, and Champagne, *JSA* #70.

29. Kelly Wagers, "Seeing 'from the Far Side of the Hill': Narrative, History, and Understanding in *Kindred* and *The Chaneysville Incident*," *MELUS* 34, no. 1 (Spring 2009): 23–45; see also Lowenthal, *Past Is a Foreign Country*, 26–28.

30. Johns, Kramer, and Champagne, *JSA* #71, 13.

31. Johns, Kramer, and Champagne, *JSA* #71, 9.

32. Johns, Kramer, and Champagne, *JSA* #69, 18.

33. Johns, Kramer, and Champagne, *JSA* #71, 17.

WORKS CITED

Assman, Jan. "Collective Memory and Cultural Identity." Translated by John Czaplicka. *New German Critique* 65 (1995): 125–33.

Beaty, Bart. *Fredric Wertham and the Critique of Mass Culture*. Jackson: University Press of Mississippi, 2005.

Boyer, Paul. *By the Bomb's Early Light: American Thought and Culture at the Dawn of the Atomic Age*. Chapel Hill: University of North Carolina Press, 1985.

Brooks, Van Wyck. "On Creating a Usable Past." *The Dial* 44 (April 1918): 340.

Bush, George H.W. "1988 Republican National Convention Speech, 18 August 1988." http://www.americanrhetoric.com/speeches/georgehbush1988rnc.htm. Accessed on May 10, 2012.

Caputi, Mary. *A Kinder, Gentler America: Melancholia and the Mythical 1950s*. Minneapolis: University of Minnesota Press, 2005.

Costello, Matthew. "Super-Powered Americans and American Superpower." In *The Cambridge Companion to American Science Fiction*, edited by Eric Carl Link and Gerry Canavan, 125–39. London: Cambridge University Press, 2015.

DiPaolo, Marc. *War, Politics and Superheroes: Ethics and Propaganda in Politics and Film*. Jefferson, NC: McFarland, 2011.

Dittmer, Jason. "'America Is Safe While Its Boys and Girls Believe in Creeds!': Captain America and American Identity prior to World War 2." *Environment and Planning D: Society and Space* 25 (2007): 401–23.

Dole, Robert. "Republican National Convention Speech, 15 August 1996." http://www.4president.org/speeches/dolekemp1996convention.htm. Accessed on May 10, 2012.

Dudziak, Mary. *Cold War Civil Rights: Race and the Image of American Democracy*. Princeton: Princeton University Press, 2000.

Foreman, Joel, ed. *The Other Fifties: Interrogating Midcentury Icons*. Urbana: University of Illinois Press, 1997.

Friedberg, Aaron. *In the Shadow of the Garrison State: America's Anti-Statism and Its Cold War Grand Strategy*. Princeton: Princeton University Press, 2000.

Gabilliet, Jean-Paul. *Of Comics and Men: A Cultural History of American Comic Books*. Translated by Bart Beaty and Nick Nguyen. Jackson: University Press of Mississippi, 2010.

Gavaler, Chris. *Superhero Comics*. New York: Bloomsbury, 2017.

Gilbert, James. *Cycle of Outrage*. New York: Oxford University Press, 1985.

Gingrich, Newt. *To Renew America*. New York: Harper Collins, 1999.

Goodrum, Michael. *Superheroes and American Self Image: From War to Watergate*. London: Routledge, 2017.

Gordon, Colin. "Crafting a Usable Past: Consensus, Ideology, and Historians of the American Revolution." *William and Mary Quarterly* 46 (October 1989): 671–95.

Hadju, David. *The Ten-Cent Plague: The Great Comic Book Scare and How It Changed America*. New York: Farrar, Straus and Giroux, 2008.

Harvey, David. *The Postmodern Condition: An Enquiry into the Origins of Cultural Change*. London: Wiley-Blackwell, 1991.

Hattam, Victoria. "History, Agency and Political Change." *Polity* 32 (Spring 2000): 333–38.

Jameson, Fredric. *Postmodernism, or the Cultural Logic of Late Capitalism*. Durham, NC: Duke University Press, 1992.

Johns, Geoff, Dan Kramer, and Keith Champagne. "JSA/JSA." *JSA* #68–72 (DC Comics, 2005).

Johnson, Jeffrey. *Super-History: Comic Book Superheroes and American Society, 1938–the Present*. Jefferson, NC: McFarland, 2012.

Levitz, Paul, and Joe Staton. "The Defeat of the Justice Society." *Adventure Comics* #466. New York: DC Comics, 1979.

Lowenthal, David. *The Past Is a Foreign Country*. London: Cambridge University Press, 1985.

Marcus, Daniel. *Happy Days and Wonder Years: The Fifties and the Sixties in Contemporary Cultural Politics*. New Brunswick, NJ: Rutgers University Press, 2004.

Matthews, Jean V. "'Whig History': The New England Whigs and a Usable Past." *New England Quarterly* 51 (June 1978): 193–208.

May, Elaine. *Homeward Bound: American Families in the Cold War Era*. Rev. ed. New York: Basic Books, 1999.

May, Lary, ed. *Recasting America*. Chicago: University of Chicago Press, 1988.

Meltzer, Brian, and Rags Morales. *Identity Crisis*. New York: DC Comics, 2004.

Millar, Mark, and Steve McNiven. *Civil War*. New York: Marvel Comics, 2007.

Nyberg, Amy Kiste. *Seal of Approval: The History of the Comics Code*. Jackson: University Press of Mississippi, 1998.

Pole, J. R. "The American Past: Is It Still Usable?" *Journal of American Studies* 1 (April 1967): 63–78.

Reagan, Ronald. "Address to the National Association of Evangelicals." March 8, 1983, Orlando, Florida. http://www.reagan.utexas.edu/archives/speeches/publicpapers.html, Accessed April 2, 2008.

Susman, Warren. "History and the American Intellectual: Uses of a Usable Past." *American Quarterly* 16 (Summer 1964): 243–63.

Thomas, Roy, and Dann Thomas. *America vs. Justice Society* #4 (DC Comics, 1985).

Wagers, Kelly. "Seeing 'from the Far Side of the Hill': Narrative, History, and Understanding in *Kindred* and *The Chaneysville Incident*." *MELUS* 34, no. 1 (Spring 2009): 23–45.

White, John Kenneth. *Still Seeing Red: How the Cold War Shapes the New American Politics*. Boulder, CO: Westview Press, 1988.

Whitfield, Stephen. *The Culture of the Cold War*. 2nd ed. Baltimore: Johns Hopkins University Press, 1996.

CHAPTER TEN

AFTERSHOCK'S *ROUGH RIDERS* AND REIFICATION OF RACE REIMAGINED

CHRISTINA M. KNOPF

American culture depends on the establishment and standardization of whiteness through the conflation of citizenship and race.[1] Whiteness is assumed to be invisible and is the standard by which those deemed nonwhite are understood.[2] But, in moments when white hegemony is challenged, Raka Shome argues, it positions itself as an Other through visible markings of whiteness.[3] Such a moment of challenge occurred with the election of Barack Obama—America's first Black, and first biracial, president.[4] This transitional moment laid the groundwork for the 2016 presidential campaign where changing racial demographics highlighted the effects of the white patriarchy on American politics.[5] So influential was white identity in the election that *Salon*'s Andrew O'Hehir called Donald Trump "America's first white president"—the first successful presidential candidate to define his campaign by whiteness in "a yearning to return to an era when the president was always going to be a white guy."[6] An editorial in the *New York Times* declared, "The election of 2016 marked a turning point in white identity" when "to see yourself as white has fundamentally changed, from unmarked default to racially marked."[7]

The politics of whiteness shapes the public's understanding of the American presidency, described by Shome as "the ultimate site of white masculinity and the ultimate site where whiteness, masculinity, and nationhood are fused."[8] Similarly, the superhero genre was historically "a white-male-dominated power fantasy [. . .] based in ideas around physical performance and power in relation to the negotiation of identity."[9] Emerging out of pulp fiction during the Great Depression and coming of age amidst the propaganda of World War II, superheroes have long served as a proxy for American geopolitical identity. The superhero is typically a singular, usually white and masculine, embodiment of the nation, embedded within "racialized understandings of the nation-state," wherein white heroes fight against minority villains or with minority sidekicks, establishing a dialectic of minority inferiority.[10] In such narratives, white protagonists serve as stand-ins for American idealism as the good whites defending diversity and modeling inclusion against those who would divide the country or undermine its fragile multiculturism.[11] Ramona Liera-Schwichtenberg observes a similar trend in films depicting troubled presidencies and notes that marking racism as an individual flaw rather than a systemic problem is a strategy of contemporary whiteness.[12]

These two figures of white Americanism—the president and the superhero—merge in comic books that cast superheroes as presidents and those that reimagine presidents as superheroes. This analysis is concerned with the latter category, in which three titles particularly stand out, the parodic *Time Lincoln* and *Steampunk Palin* from Antarctic Press, and, the focus here, the speculative *Rough Riders* from AfterShock Comics. These comics are notable in that they not only reimagine past presidents as superheroes but do so through the steampunk aesthetic.

Steampunk is a consideration of historical legacy in light of contemporary attitudes.[13] It speculates through "what if" scenarios at significant moments in history. Stories of steampunked superheroic presidents therefore provide avenues for understanding the historical legacies of nationalism and the presidency in relation to current political attitudes. Though alternate histories challenge historical record and the accepted limits of both the physical and social worlds, recognizing the influence of determinist theories in history, this chapter argues that there are racial limits to the experiment when they depend on particular generic and aesthetic traits.[14] Steampunk's blending of reality and fantasy creates a spectral aesthetic that lives in the past, present, and future.[15] It also makes the familiar exotic, constructing the self as Other and, thus, aspects of white, masculine, heteronormative, middle-class Victorian culture are both mythologized and reified.[16] Steampunk's alternative history is "knotted through temporal loops and folds."[17] For Slavoj Žižek, a temporal loop of subjective experience suggests that "by progressing forward, we return to where we always already were."[18] Indeed, while steampunk is premised on the idea of the "Victorian period as simultaneously other to and identical with our contemporary moment," the similarities between the Victorian and present ages are, arguably, what compromise steampunk's critical stance.[19] As Michel Foucault observed, "For a long time, the story goes, we supported a Victorian regime, and we continue to be dominated by it even today," relying on the same strategies of suppression when confronted by chaos.[20] In the 2016 debut of *Rough Riders*, Theodore Roosevelt recruits an elite team of up-and-coming legends—magician Harry Houdini, boxer Jack Johnson, cowgirl Annie Oakley, and inventor Thomas Edison—in a race to acquire alien technology left at the scene of the attack on the USS *Maine* in Cuba in 1898—the event that started the Spanish-American-Cuban-Filipino War. The series was followed by the one-shot *Rough Riders Nation* #1, which claimed to contain the declassified documents proving the existence and legacy of Roosevelt's incredible team. *Rough Riders Volume II* was released in 2017, with the team investigating a conspiracy behind the assassination of William McKinley. In a third volume, released in 2018, Houdini summons Roosevelt to fight an ancient evil from another realm.

As the political parties named their nominees for America's 2016 presidential election, a *Time* editorial noted that despite the divisive politics of the moment, Theodore Roosevelt was held up as a model of strong leadership by each party. *Forbes* contributor Theodore Roosevelt Malloch even went so far as to claim Donald Trump as a modern version of Roosevelt. Though the former essay's author, Kermit Roosevelt III, was dubious about such a claim, he argued that "in some ways [Roosevelt's] story parallels America's—and shows us how we can use the past to understand the present," noting that both Roosevelt and America transformed and strengthened their identities through struggle and suffering.[21] It is the questions of image, identity, and present-day parallels that are of interest in this consideration of AfterShock's *Rough Riders*. Accepting Joseph Good's claim that "the historical personages or literary characters appearing in steampunk form a hermeneutic chain, an intertextuality that links one work to another," I approach the first two volumes of *Rough Riders* through intertextual criticism informed by critical hermeneutics.[22] Like intertextualities, critical hermeneutics acknowledges the integrative nature of analysis, wherein the critic recognizes the significance and relationships of noted elements and applies critical insights regarding power and the (mis)uses of language to the inquiry.[23] At the forefront of this analysis is attention to how history is engaged through allusions or alterations, while also considering the interplays of superhero and steampunk motifs and of presidential mythology and superhero mythos, while examining the implicit assumptions about power and race.

NATIONAL LEGENDS AND CONQUERING HEROES

John Shelton Lawrence and Robert Jewett trace the emergence of the superheroic presidency, a unification of "physical heroism and moral perfection," to the same era that gave rise to the American superhero genre—the Axial decade of economic hardship and worldwide war.[24] The rhetorical performance of the presidency suggests who Americans are as people and how they are constituted as a community.[25] Likewise, superheroes act as proxy for particular geopolitical identities, civic virtues, and community beliefs.[26] Steampunk, too, can be linked to performances of a national identity, foregrounding a type of Britishness, and its fascination with a visual aesthetic makes it a natural fit for the comics.[27]

Ronald B. Tobias argues that "Roosevelt was the first major political figure to recognize and embrace the power and reach of film to shape public opinion.

[. . .] He actively courted the camera" as both military man and politician.[28] The photographic archive indicates that Roosevelt crafted and practiced his poses diligently, and with apparent success as the historical understanding of Roosevelt "cannot, and should not, be separated from his cinematic image."[29] According to Tobias, he became a national icon, embodying a belief in the superiority of character, as the base side of Roosevelt the warrior was forgotten in the written and visual narratives that played out as the American public seized upon the image of a bold, brave warrior, unflinching in his duty to his nation and to the downtrodden of other nations.[30]

His continued popularity in contemporary politics, invoked by both liberals and conservatives in their considerations of American identity, marks him as a figure of continued interest and import.[31] With his natural intellect and brawn augmented with advanced (steam-powered) technology, the fictional Roosevelt of *Rough Riders* is tasked by a shadowy cabal of magnates known as the Four Horsemen with missions against perceived threats to the free world. It is a narrative common to the nationalist superhero genre—a white protagonist leading a diverse team to defend freedom and equality against those who would oppress and divide peoples.[32] This type of storyline engages a strategy of contemporary whiteness by suggesting the corruption of whiteness is separate, individualistic, and even anomalous to specified villainous whites.[33] In the case of the *Rough Riders*' Cuban adventure, these villains not only were the Spanish oppressing the Cuban natives but were also aliens threatening to oppress the entire world, and the undead imperial agitator Grigori Rasputin (in a surreal twist nodding to both the imperial undertones of the Spanish-American-Cuban-Filipino War, to a history of the US and Russia as enemies, and to the supernatural myths of war as depicted in Mike Mignola's *Hellboy*).

Rough Riders presents a complex political narrative. Roosevelt opposes the robber baron industrialists in America and vilified regimes abroad and yet is hero of the American establishment with colonial tendencies. Colonialism is found in Roosevelt's actual historical record and in the steampunk aesthetic of *Rough Riders*; Jenny Sundén reads the steampunked body as one that is restrained and mechanized through accoutrements of corsets and cogs, suggesting power and spatial dominance, much as colonialism exerts physical control and geographical dominance.[34] Supporting this reading, steampunks-of-color report being sensitive to the paradox they face when they don the trappings of Victorian culture that exploited and prospered from their ancestors.[35]

Such colonial and exploitative imagery and attitudes appear in *Rough Riders* when Roosevelt, covered head to toe in mechanical armor—symbol of power, wealth, and privilege—perched above a group of Black Buffalo Soldiers, promises that it is by *following him* that they can take their place in history. In truth, the Buffalo Soldiers, with the Ninth and Tenth Cavalries, rushed *ahead* of Roosevelt's

Rough Riders on San Juan Hill, thereby helping Roosevelt to establish his own historical legacy.[36] Roosevelt's arrogant use of the Buffalo Soldiers in *Rough Riders* is reflective of his real-life record on racial matters. Though he frequently promoted the idea of equal opportunity for all, regardless of race, he also perceived Black people as being closer to savagery than civilization in evolutionary progress.[37]

Central to most superhero stories is a dual or alternate identity exemplified in an iconic costume, which typically expresses biography or character, superior abilities and/or technology, and origins.[38] In both real life and in the *Rough Riders* comics, Roosevelt was skilled at crafting and personifying the facets of his public persona. John F. Kasson notes, "Crucial to Roosevelt's success was his ability to turn prized characteristics of manliness into spectacle, literally to embody them."[39] Roosevelt's autobiography "carefully balanced" images of Roosevelt the politician with Roosevelt the game hunter and Roosevelt the military man, executive with rugged images of himself, highlighting both his executive and rugged personas.[40]

In *Rough Riders,* Roosevelt is recruited for adventure not because of "the stuff everyone knows—big-game hunter, cowboy and politician" but because he also has a mysterious "other life...... the fights, the wars, the nights hanging in the shadows and rooftops of the city, helping the down-trodden . . ."[41] His costuming befits his alter-roles. Roosevelt-the-politician-né-businessman wears a suit, differentiating him from Roosevelt-the-steampunk-adventurer who wears his legendary custom-tailored Brooks Brothers military uniform, mechanized for combat.[42] His steam-powered armor features iron plates and brass gears, night-vision goggles perched atop a pith helmet, and rapid-fire gun mounted on his right arm. Such costuming makes the fantastical seem feasible through its historical and technological origins.[43] It also runs contrary to the historical record; in truth, when Roosevelt fought in Cuba, it was the Spanish who had superior weaponry. They fought with 7mm Mauser rifles with repeating bolt action and high-velocity cartridges. The American troops, meanwhile, carried smaller and more outdated rifles and carbines.[44]

That Roosevelt's steampunked armor includes a pith helmet, strongly associated with the British Empire, further hints at a sense of colonialism. Roosevelt was an "enthusiast for empire" and "avowed Anglophile" who desired to forge an alliance with Great Britain.[45] This aspect of history is, however, downplayed in the comic. In *Volume II*, Roosevelt and his Riders uncover a British plot to overthrow the American government, with a fleet of the Royal Navy hidden behind Niagara Falls. The cover of the climactic final issue features a bare-chested Roosevelt wrapped in an American flag striding away from a burning British vessel—an epitome of the rugged, independent American male, heroically celebrating America's own ability to conquer.[46]

MANLINESS AND MACHINES

Steampunk is about the relationship between humans and machines. As Rebecca Onion asserts, "the similarity of steampunk machines to the individual human body is central to the steampunk philosophy."[47] The second volume of *Rough Riders* tackles the entanglement of man/machine and humanity/technology when Thomas Edison uses alien technology to bring Annie Oakley back from the dead, leading the team to argue amongst themselves as to whether such use of technology on a human being made Oakley a "freak" or made her "better."[48] Roosevelt too gets superheroic abilities through technology. His body nearly disappears into a mechanized battle suit. His cyborg-esque gunmetal form is strikingly and significantly similar to the original gray appearance of Marvel's Iron Man. In his dramatistic reading of Iron Man, Ronald C. Thomas Jr. describes him as "a character that represented the unadulterated goodness of the American way of life"—a weapons manufacturer for the US government who became a living weapon, highlighting patriotic ideals of national defense and technology.[49] The same can be said of the steampunk Roosevelt—a militarized embodiment of patriotic ideals of nationhood, manliness, and technology.

In American contexts, steampunk's consideration of man and machine, where technology is a curse and a blessing, often engages the Old West—a space where anything seemed possible as civilization traversed, and scarred, the frontier through railroad tracks and telegraph lines. Roosevelt crafted his persona in this same wild space; born frail and asthmatic to a wealthy family, he embraced the photograph and the pen to reinvent himself as a cowboy. He was one of several elite urban easterners who turned west "to find a cure for their insufficient manhood."[50] In this way the myth of the cowboy may be read as a critique of the new urban industrial America.[51] Cynthia Miller and Bowdoin Van Riper remark, "Heroic figures of the classic Western frequently found themselves balancing their allegiance to the spirit [and environment] of the West [. . .] and their moral commitment" to civilize it.[52] It has likewise been noted that Roosevelt struggled to reconcile his political need to protect nature with his personal drive to conquer it.[53] Such tensions between wilderness/wildness and control, or manliness and mechanics, play out through *Rough Riders*, particularly in its depictions of race.

Whiteness is defined by its relation to imaginary, racialized Others.[54] For example, white imaginaries of Blackness as physical—violent, hypersexual, athletic—simultaneously establish whiteness as intellectual, clerical, and intangible.[55] Though Roosevelt himself was very concerned with athleticism, believing that Americanism was intimately connected to physical development, *Rough Riders* tends to reflect the hegemonic dichotomy of the white mind compared to the Black body.[56] This contrast reflects the real social concerns at the turn of the century about immigrants and people of color outnumbering Americans and undermining white superiority, especially as the frontier days passed and the nation's cowboys gave way to city-slickers.[57]

The steampunk Rough Riders include just one Black person, the pugilist Jack Johnson. Though equipped with steampunk technology, it is Johnson's natural physical ability that is emphasized—typical of the representations of Black figures in popular culture.[58] Such representation is also consistent with Roosevelt's own attitudes that Americaness depended on physical ability, disregarding "nonwhites and immigrants who he believed were not physically or morally capable of being Americans."[59] Johnson's first appearance in *Rough Riders* is in a boxing match; he is shown smiling with blood-stained teeth right before delivering a bloody knock-out blow to the jaw of his opponent.

Roosevelt, when recruiting Johnson for his team, goads him by saying, "You're not that smart," before acknowledging the social injustices of the time and offering Johnson a way to bypass them, though not suggesting that they be corrected.[60] By contrast, his recruitment of Harry Houdini proclaims, "Magic is . . . what the eyes see . . . the ears hear . . . and *the mind* believes [emphasis added],"[61] and Thomas Edison is described as "a man of letters, not action."[62] The contrast between the physicality of Johnson and mentality of Houdini is significant not only because it perpetuates the stereotype of the Black body as supernatural but also because it counters Houdini's cultural legacy of physical prowess. Houdini was "known for some of the most audacious displays of the male body in his time," his escape artistry premised on physical "themes of risk and control.""[63]

The verbal sparring of Johnson and Houdini in *Rough Riders* is therefore symbolic of the cultural fear that Johnson's defeat of white champions Tommy Burns in 1908 and Jim Jeffries in 1910 indicated the decline of white superiority. Amidst the ensuing protests and race riots, a slew of white contenders—"Great White Hopes"—challenged Johnson in an effort to reclaim and reaffirm the dominance of white masculinity.[64] Houdini, epitome of control over the (white) body is pitted against Johnson, symbolizing a physical disruption to the presumed racial order. Their antagonism in the comics thereby represents racial hostilities of their actual era as related to masculinity and dominance.

While men like Houdini reaffirmed the superiority of the white male body in the face of changes and challenges that might weaken or impede it, "popular spectacles of the female body in this period usually revolved around issues of subordination and transgression."[65] The superiority of white masculinity is an undercurrent throughout *Rough Riders*. Annie Oakley's membership on the team is premised on her ability to shoot, just as Johnson's presence is due to his ability to box. As Laura Browder notes, guns are "a charged symbol of women's access to full citizenship, of women's capacity for violence, and of women's sexuality."[66] In reality, too, Oakley rose to fame because of her ability to adapt to, embody, and balance Victorian femininity with the ideals of rugged white masculinity.[67] She sewed her own deliberately girlish costumes and openly opposed women's suffrage. "Oakley's whiteness and ladylike behavior clearly set her apart from the less savory [more racialized] examples of armed women that were floating around popular culture," including contemporaries like Calamity Jane and Lillian Smith.[68] This feminine respectability is echoed in *Rough Riders* when Oakley, the lone female member of the team, twice risks her own life, once for Roosevelt in Volume I and once for Edison in Volume II, believing her role to be less important than those of her white male teammates.

THE RACE-TIME CONTINUATION

Whether the comics' use of steampunk contributes to the rhetoric of whiteness or draws attention to it depends on whether one accepts the cultural legitimation or cultural criticism perspective of comic book content.[69] *Rough Riders* celebrates the historical contributions of women and Black people, even while marginalizing their roles in the comics. "The superhero is an indelibly American invention connoting ideal citizenship through white muscular force," and within superhero narratives whiteness occupies a position of power and triumph, supported and maintained by ethnicity's vulnerability.[70] This is reflected in the actual and steampunked histories when Roosevelt is celebrated for taking San Juan Hill through the sacrifices of his Black Buffalo Soldiers.

Situated at the turn of the century, the Riders face a changing world. Such instability is central to the steampunk aesthetic through the playful displacement of persons, events, or objects and through critical social consciousness relevant to technology, environment, and humanity.[71] As a critical aesthetic, steampunk uses alternate histories that speak to the events of the past and the insecurity of the present to offer an indictment of contemporary times.[72] In this way *Rough Riders* may be read as cultural criticism. *Volume II* comments on contemporary racial tensions through reimagined events of 1901. Edison complained about an America that was "overrun by immigrants and undesirables" and argued that anarchy would "*return* it to greatness," reminiscent of Trump's campaign promise to "make American great again." Johnson challenged "greatness" by asking, "You mean 'whiteness?'"[73]

Despite the critique that steampunk provides in the stories, the use of the superhero formula in these comics still preferences whiteness. Danny Fingeroth argues that the superhero genre is a response to the immigrant experience and the struggle to adapt to a new American (and thus white) identity.[74] This is similar to Roosevelt's own historical perspective of race. His embodiment of white American masculinity was consistent with his perspective on "true Americanism" that argued for the "Americanizing of the newcomers to our shores [. . .] in speech, in political ideas and principles," welcoming the immigrant "who becomes an American" by abandoning the vestiges of their native ancestry.[75] (Similarly, Donald Trump's stance on immigration advocates for assimilation because "we want those coming into the country [. . .] to love our country and the values it stands for."[76]) The narrative of the assimilation struggle is found in *Rough Riders* through the character of Ehrich "Harry" Houdini—a Jewish immigrant who joins the team in order to prove his patriotism.[77] In real life Houdini entertained Roosevelt on a transatlantic voyage in 1914 and then capitalized on the encounter by distributing hundreds of copies of a photograph of their meeting.[78]

Despite Houdini's fervent desire to prove his patriotism through association with Roosevelt, *Rough Riders* highlights his nonwhiteness by frequently partnering him with Johnson, often separating them in the narrative from the white Roosevelt, Edison, and Oakley. Thus, while *Rough Riders* overtly calls out racism, as when various racial slurs are used by their enemies against Johnson, it may also be reinforcing it through repetition and the steampunk trappings of colonial Victoriana.

TRUE AMERICANS

While steampunk has engendered much discussion surrounding gender, class, religion, and war, race is a trickier matter.[79] Despite what some see as alternate history's potential to explore the possibilities of African diaspora, Jaymee Goh noted that there is little room in mainstream steampunk for "nuanced discussions about cultural appropriation, microagressions or unconscious prejudices made manifest."[80] Karen Hellekson argued that alternate histories "revolve around the basic premise that some event in the past did not occur as we know it did, and thus the present has changed."[81] *Rough Riders* differs in that it reimagines the past in line with the present as it is, asking not what if a different history happened but instead what if history happened differently. Thus, rather than challenging assumptions of race, gender, class, and power, the steampunk presidency reinforces a mythic ideal of white masculinity and patriarchy. Despite alternate histories' purpose of presenting counterfactual narratives, *Rough Riders* assumes determinist forces of power and privilege as fixed aspects of the record, even while demonstrating the injustice of them. This is consistent with J. Tillapaugh's observation that as film "returned to the Rough Rider story often during both peace and war, it is interesting that caricature on occasion resulted while *revisionism never did* [emphasis added]."[82]

Lifting the presidency to the status of superhero merges the symbol of nationhood with the embodiment of national identity. The fact that both the American president and the American superhero have historically been white males allows for mutual reinforcement of the hegemony of American white masculinity. This is underscored by the use of Roosevelt, a figure still invoked today as a model of strong leadership, American idealism, and the national story, as the series' hero (despite any shortcomings or criticisms indicated in the text). He is supported by a cast of sidekicks who highlight both his diegetic and historical image of white masculinity. The steampunk context, with its utopic time travel and fetishized colonial industry, further reinforces white masculinity and resituates the dominant, white male of the past to redefine the present and shape the future.

NOTES

1. Laura C. Prividera and John W. Howard III, "Masculinity, Whiteness, and the Warrior Hero: Perpetuating the Strategic Rhetoric of U.S. Nationalism and the Marginalization of Women," *Women and Language* 29, no. 2 (2006): 29–37.

2. For example, Thomas K. Nakayama and Robert L. Krizek, "Whiteness: A Strategic Rhetoric," *Quarterly Journal of Speech* 81 (1995): 291–309.

3. Raka Shome, "Outing Whiteness," *Critical Studies in Media Communication* 17, no. 3 (2000): 366–71.

4. Lisa M. Corrigan, "Whiteness, Economic Precarity, and Presidential Politics," *Spectra* (September/November 2016): 27–31.

5. For example, Brenda Major, Alison Blodorn, and Gregory Major Blascovich, "The Threat of Increasing Diversity: Why Many White Americans Support Trump in the 2016 Presidential Election," *Group Processes & Intergroup Relations* 21, no. 6 (2018): 1–10.

6. Andrew O'Hehir, "America's First White President," *Salon*, December 10, 2016, accessed January 24, 2017, http://www.salon.com/2016/12/10/americas-first-white-president/.

7. Nell Irvin Painter, "What Whiteness Means in the Trump Era," *New York Times*, November 12, 2016, accessed January 24, 1017, https://www.nytimes.com/2016/11/13/opinion/what-whiteness-means-in-the-trump-era.html.

8. Shome, "Outing Whiteness," 369; also see Corrigan, "Whiteness, Economic Precarity."

9. Frances Gateward and John Jennings, "Introduction: The Sweeter the Christmas," in *The Blacker the Ink: Constructions of Black Identity in Comics and Sequential Art*, ed. Frances Gateward, loc. 87–421 (New Brunswick, NJ: Rutgers University Press, 2015), Kindle e-book, loc. 170.

10. Jason Dittmer, *Captain America and the Nationalist Superhero: Metaphors, Narratives, and Geopolitics* (Philadelphia: Temple University Press, 2013), 49; also see Sheena C. Howard and Ronald L. Jackson II, "Introduction," in *Black Comics: Politics of Race and Representation*, ed. Sheena C. Howard and Ronald L. Jackson II, loc. 1–9 (New York: Bloomsbury, 2013), Kindle e-book.

11. Dittmer, *Captain America*.

12. Ramona Liera-Schwichtenberg, "Passing or Whiteness on the Edge of Town," *Critical Studies in Media Communication* 17, no. 3 (2000): 371–74.

13. For example, see Joseph Good, "'God Save the Queen, for Someone Must!': *Sebastian O* and the Steampunk Aesthetic," *Neo-Victorian Studies* 3, no. 1 (2010): 208–15.

14. Karen Hellekson, *The Alternate History: Refiguring Historical Time* (Kent, OH: Kent State University Press, 2011), Kindle e-book; Niall Ferguson, ed., *Virtual History: Alternatives and Counterfactuals* (New York: Basic Books, 1997), Kindle e-book.

15. Brigid Cherry and Maria Mellins, "Negotiating the Punk in Steampunk: Subculture, Fashion, and Performative Identity," *Punk & Post Punk* 1, no. 1 (2011): 5–25.

16. René Ménil, "Concerning Colonial Exoticism," in *Refusal of the Shadow: Surrealism and the Caribbean*, ed. Michael Richardson, trans. Krzysztof Fijalkowski (New York: Verso, 1996), 176–81.

17. Jenny Sundén, "Corporeal Anachronisms: Notes on Affect, Relationality, and Power in Steampunk," *Somatechnics* 3, no. 2 (2013): 370.

18. Slavoj Žižek, *The Metastases of Enjoyment: Six Essays on Woman and Causality* (New York: Verso, 1994), 32.

19. Jason B. Jones, "Betrayed by Time: Steampunk & the Neo-Victorian in Alan Moore's *Lost Girls* and *The League of Extraordinary Gentlemen*," *Neo-Victorian Studies* 3, no. 1 (2010): 102.

20. Michel Foucault, *The History of Sexuality: An Introduction, Volume I*, trans. Robert Hurley (New York: Vintage Books, 1978/1990), 3.

21. Kermit Roosevelt III, "Theodore Roosevelt's Lessons for Today's Politics," *Time*, July 25, 2016, accessed February 9, 2018, http://time.com/4421539/theodore-roosevelt-lessons/.

22. Good, "God Save the Queen," 212.

23. Ronald Bontekoe, *Dimensions of the Hermeneutic Circle* (Atlantic Highlands, NJ: Humanities Press, 1996); Elizabeth Anne Kinsella, "Hermeneutics and Critical Hermeneutics: Exploring Possibilities with the Art of Interpretation," *Forum Qualitative Sozialforschung / Forum: Qualitative Social Research* 7, no. 3 (2006): art. 19, http://nbn-resolving.de/urn:nbn:de:0114-fqs0603190.

24. John Shelton Lawrence and Robert Jewett, *The Myth of the American Superhero* (Grand Rapids, MI: William B. Eerdmans, 2002), 128.

25. Mary E. Stuckey, *The President as Interpreter-in-Chief* (Chatham, NJ: Chatham House, 1991).

26. Dittmer, *Captain America*.

27. Cherry and Mellins, "Negotiating the Punk"; Jones, "Betrayed by Time"; Good, "God Save the Queen."

28. Ronald B. Tobias, *Film and the American Moral Vision of Nature: Theodore Roosevelt to Walt Disney* (East Lansing: Michigan State University Press, 2011), 49.

29. J. Tillapaugh, "Theodore Roosevelt and the Rough Riders: A Century of Leadership," in *Hollywood's White House: The American Presidency in Film and History*, ed. Peter C. Rollins and John E. O'Connor (Lexington: University Press of Kentucky, 2005), 97.

30. Tobias, *Film and the American Moral Vision*, 58.

31. Leroy G. Dorsey, *We Are All Americans, Pure and Simple: Theodore Roosevelt and the Myth of Americanism* (Tuscaloosa: University of Alabama Press, 2007).

32. Dittmer, *Captain America*.

33. Liera-Schwichtenberg, "Passing."

34. Jenny Sundén, "Clockwork Corsets: Pressed against the Past," *International Journal of Cultural Studies* 18, no. 3 (2015): 379–83; Sundén, "Corporeal Anachronisms."

35. Jenny, Sundén. "Steampunk Practices: Time, Tactility, and a Racial Politics of Touch," *Ada: A Journal of Gender, New Media, and Technology*, no. 5 (2014), http://adanewmedia.org/2014/07/issue5-sunden/.

36. Jerome Tuccille, *The Roughest Riders: The Untold Story of the Black Soldiers in the Spanish-American War* (Chicago: Chicago Press Review, 2015), Kindle e-book.

37. Thomas G. Dyer, *Theodore Roosevelt and the Idea of Race* (Baton Rouge: Louisiana State University Press, 1980).

38. Peter Coogan, "The Hero Defines the Genre, the Genre Defines the Hero," in *What Is a Superhero?*, ed. Robin S. Rosenberg and Peter Coogan (New York: Oxford University Press, 2013), Kindle e-book, loc. 257–62.

39. John F. Kasson, *Houdini, Tarzan, and the Perfect Man: The White Male Body and the Challenge of Modernity in America* (New York: Hill and Wang, 2001), Kindle e-book, loc. 49.

40. Kasson, *Houdini, Tarzan, and the Perfect Man*, loc. 49.

41. Adam Glass, "The Big Stick," *Rough Riders* #1, AfterShock Comics, 2016.

42. Tobias (*Film and the American Moral Vision*) notes that the real Roosevelt also used clothing to establish public identities. He chose the uniforms of his Rough Riders carefully to craft a public image of a cowboy cavalry, with slouch hats, blue flannel shirts, and handkerchiefs around their necks.

43. Barbara Brownie and Danny Graydon, *The Superhero Costume: Identity and Disguise in Fact and Fiction* (New York: Bloomsbury, 2015), Kindle e-book, 45.

44. Tuccille, *Roughest Riders*.

45. George C. Herring, *From Colony to Superpower: U.S. Foreign Relations since 1776* (New York: Oxford University Press, 2008), 337.

46. Adam Glass and Patrick Olliffe, "Strange Days," *Rough Riders: Riders on the Storm* #6, AfterShock Comics, 2017.

47. Rebecca Onion, "Reclaiming the Machine: An Introductory Look at Steampunk in Everyday Practice," *Neo-Victorian Studies* 1, no. 1 (2008): 145.

48. Adam Glass and Patrick Olliffe, "Into This World We Are Thrown," *Rough Riders: Riders on the Storm* #2, AfterShock Comics, 2017.

49. Ronald C. Thomas Jr., "Hero of the Military-Industrial Complex: Reading Iron Man through Burke's Dramatism," in *Heroes of Film, Comics and American Culture: Essays on Real and Fictional Defenders of Home*, ed. Lisa M. Detora (Jefferson, NC: McFarland, 2009), Kindle e-book, loc. 2020.

50. Michael S. Kimmel, *The History of Men: Essays on the History of American and British Masculinities* (Albany: State University of New York Press, 2005), 53.

51. Paul Cohen, "Cowboys Die Hard: Real Men and Businessmen in the Reagan-Era Blockbuster," *Film & History: An Interdisciplinary Journal* 41, no. 1 (2011): 71–81.

52. Cynthia J. Miller and A. Bowdoin Van Riper, "Blending Genres, Bending Time: Steampunk on the Western Frontier," *Journal of Popular Film and Television* 39, no. 2 (2011): 86.

53. Tobias, *Film and the American Moral Vision*, 65.

54. Anoop Nayak, "Critical Whiteness Studies," *Sociology Compass* 1/2 (November 2007): 737–55.

55. Nayak, "Critical Whiteness Studies."

56. Kasson, *Houdini*.

57. Kasson, *Houdini*.

58. See, for example, Gateward and Jennings, "Introduction." This stereotype extends beyond fiction to popular discourse, especially surrounding sports, as demonstrated in Matthew Hutson, "Whites See Blacks as Superhuman," *Slate*, November 14, 2014, accessed February 9, 2018, http://www.slate.com/articles/health_and_science/science/2014/11/whites_see_blacks_as_superhuman_strength_speed_pain_tolerance_and_the_magical.html.

59. Dorsey, *We Are All Americans*, 2.

60. Glass, "Big Stick."

61. Adam Glass, "Bully for You," *Rough Riders* #2 (AfterShock Comics, 2016).

62. Glass, "Bully for You."

63. Kasson, *Houdini*, loc. 97 and 1045.

64. Graeme Kent, *Great White Hopes: The Quest to Defeat Jack Johnson* (Gloucestershire: History Press, 2005), Kindle e-book.

65. Kasson, *Houdini*, loc. 116.

66. Laura Browder, *Her Best Shot: Women and Guns in America* (Chapel Hill: University of North Carolina Press, 2006), 230.

67. Lisa Bernd, "Annie Oakley and the Disruption of Victorian Expectations," *Theatre Symposium* 20 (2012): 39–48.

68. Browder, *Her Best Shot*.

69. Matthew Paul McAllister, "Cultural Argument and Organizational Constraint in the Comic Book Industry," *Journal of Communication* 40, no. 1 (1990): 55–71.

70. Rebecca Wanzo, "The Superhero: Meditations on Surveillance, Salvation, and Desire," *Communication and Critical/Cultural Studies* 6, no. 1 (2009): 93.

71. Mike Perschon, "Finding Nemo: Verne's Antihero as Original Steampunk," *Verniana* 2 (2010): 179–93.

72. Sundén, "Corporeal Anachronisms"; Jones, "Betrayed by Time."

73. Adam Glass and Patrick Olliffe, "Maiden of the Mist," *Rough Riders: Riders on the Storm* #5 (AfterShock Comics), 2017.

74. Danny Fingeroth, *Disguised as Clark Kent: Jews, Comics, and the Creation of the Superhero* (New York: Continuum, 2008).

75. Theodore Roosevelt, "True Americanism," *Forum Magazine*, April 1894, accessed January 21, 2018, http://teachingamericanhistory.org/library/document/true-americanism-the-forum-magazine/.

76. Donald J. Trump, "Statement from President Donald J. Trump—Immigration," *White House*, September 5, 2017, accessed January 21, 2018, https://www.whitehouse.gov/briefings-statements/statement-president-donald-j-trump-7/.

77. Glass, "Give Them Hell," np.

78. Kasson, *Houdini*.

79. Sundén, "Steampunk Practices."

80. Jaymee Goh, "On Race and Steampunk: A Quick Primer," *SteamPunk Magazine*, no. 7 (2010): 19.

81. Hellekson, *Alternate History*, loc. 85.

82. Tillapaugh, "Theodore Roosevelt and the Rough Riders," 111.

WORKS CITED

Bernd, Lisa. "Annie Oakley and the Disruption of Victorian Expectations." *Theatre Symposium* 20 (2012): 39–48.

Bontekoe, Ronald. *Dimensions of the Hermeneutic Circle*. Atlantic Highlands, NJ: Humanities Press, 1996.

Brooks, Dwight E., and James A. Rada. "Constructing Race in Black and Whiteness: Media Coverage of Public Support for President Clinton." *Journalism & Communication Monographs* 4, no. 3 (2002): 114–56.

Browder, Laura. *Her Best Shot: Women and Guns in America*. Chapel Hill: University of North Carolina Press, 2006.

Brownie, Barbara, and Danny Graydon. *The Superhero Costume: Identity and Disguise in Fact and Fiction*. New York: Bloomsbury, 2015. Kindle e-book.

Carrott, James H., and Brian David Johnson. *Vintage Tomorrows*. Sebastopol, CA: Maker Media, 2013. Kindle e-book.

Cherry, Brigid, and Maria Mellins. "Negotiating the Punk in Steampunk: Subculture, Fashion, and Performative Identity." *Punk & Post Punk* 1, no. 1 (2011): 5–25.

Cohen, Paul. "Cowboys Die Hard: Real Men and Businessmen in the Reagan-Era Blockbuster." *Film & History: An Interdisciplinary Journal* 41, no. 1 (2011): 71–81.

Coogan, Peter. "The Hero Defines the Genre, the Genre Defines the Hero." In *What Is a Superhero?*, edited by Robin S. Rosenberg and Peter Coogan, loc. 243–434. New York: Oxford University Press, 2013. Kindle e-book.

Corrigan, Lisa M. "Whiteness, Economic Precarity, and Presidential Politics." *Spectra* September/November (2016): 27–31.

Dittmer, Jason. *Captain America and the Nationalist Superhero: Metaphors, Narratives, and Geopolitics*. Philadelphia: Temple University Press, 2013.

Dorsey, Leroy G. *We Are All Americans, Pure and Simple: Theodore Roosevelt and the Myth of Americanism*. Tuscaloosa: University of Alabama Press, 2007.

Dyer, Thomas G. *Theodore Roosevelt and the Idea of Race*. Baton Rouge: Louisiana State University Press, 1980.

Ferguson, Niall, ed. *Virtual History: Alternatives and Counterfactuals*. New York: Basic Books, 1997. Kindle e-book.

Fingeroth, Danny. *Disguised as Clark Kent: Jews, Comics, and the Creation of the Superhero*. New York: Continuum, 2008.

Foucault, Michel. *The History of Sexuality: An Introduction, Vol. I*. Translated by Robert Hurley. New York: Vintage Books, 1978/1990.

Gateward, Frances, and John Jennings. "Introduction: The Sweeter the Christmas." In *The Blacker the Ink: Constructions of Black Identity in Comics and Sequential Art*, edited by Frances Gateward, loc. 87–421. New Brunswick, NJ: Rutgers University Press, 2015. Kindle e-book.

Glass, Adam. "The Big Stick." *Rough Riders* #1. Sherman Oaks, CA: AfterShock Comics, April 2016.

Glass, Adam. "Bully for You." *Rough Riders* #2. Sherman Oaks, CA: AfterShock Comics, May 2016.

Glass, Adam, and Patrick Olliffe. "Into This World We Are Thrown." *Rough Riders: Riders on the Storm* #2. Sherman Oaks, CA: AfterShock Comics, March 2017.

Glass, Adam, and Patrick Olliffe. "Maiden of the Mist." *Rough Riders: Riders on the Storm* #5. Sherman Oaks, CA: AfterShock Comics, July 2017.

Glass, Adam, and Patrick Olliffe. "Strange Days." *Rough Riders: Riders on the Storm* #6. Sherman Oaks, CA: AfterShock Comics, September 2017.

Goh, Jaymee. "On Race and Steampunk: A Quick Primer." *SteamPunk Magazine no.* 7 (2010): 16–21.

Good, Joseph. "'God Save the Queen, for Someone Must!': *Sebastian O* and the Steampunk Aesthetic." *Neo-Victorian Studies* 3, no. 1 (2010): 208–15.

Hellekson, Karen. *The Alternate History: Refiguring Historical Time*. Kent, OH: Kent State University Press, 2011. Kindle e-book.

Howard, Sheena C., and Ronald L. Jackson II. "Introduction." In *Black Comics: Politics of Race and Representation*, ed. Sheena C. Howard and Ronald L. Jackson II, 1–9. New York: Bloomsbury, 2013. Kindle e-book.

Hutson, Matthew. "Whites See Blacks as Superhuman." *Slate*. November 14, 2014. Accessed February 9, 2018. http://www.slate.com/articles/health_and_science/science/2014/11/whites_see_blacks_as_superhuman_strength_speed_pain_tolerance_and_the_magical.html.

Jones, Jason B. "Betrayed by Time: Steampunk & the Neo-Victorian in Alan Moore's *Lost Girls* and *The League of Extraordinary Gentlemen*." *Neo-Victorian Studies* 3, no. 1 (2010): 99–126.

Kent, Graeme. *Great White Hopes: The Quest to Defeat Jack Johnson*. Gloucestershire: History Press, 2005. Kindle e-book.

Kimmel, Michael S. *The History of Men: Essays on the History of American and British Masculinities*. Albany: State University of New York Press, 2005.

Kinsella, Elizabeth Anne. "Hermeneutics and Critical Hermeneutics: Exploring Possibilities with the Art of Interpretation." *Forum Qualitative Sozialforschung / Forum: Qualitative Social Research* 7, no. 3 (2006): article 19. Accessed February 22, 2017. http://nbn-resolving.de/urn:nbn:de:0114-fqs0603190.

Lawrence, John Shelton, and Robert Jewett. *The Myth of the American Superhero*. Grand Rapids, MI: William B. Eerdmans, 2002.

Liera-Schwichtenberg, Ramona. "Passing or Whiteness on the Edge of Town." *Critical Studies in Media Communication* 17, no. 3 (2000): 371–74.

Major, Brenda, Alison Blodorn, and Gregory Major Blascovich. "The Threat of Increasing Diversity: Why Many White Americans Support Trump in the 2016 Presidential Election." *Group Processes & Intergroup Relations* 21, no. 6 (2018): 1–10.

McAllister, Matthew Paul. "Cultural Argument and Organizational Constraint in the Comic Book Industry." *Journal of Communication* 40, no. 1 (1990): 55–71.

Ménil, René. "Concerning Colonial Exoticism." In *Refusal of the Shadow: Surrealism and the Caribbean*, edited by Michael Richardson, translated by Krzysztof Fijalkowski, 176–81. New York: Verso, 1996.

Miller, Cynthia J., and A. Bowdoin Van Riper. "Blending Genres, Bending Time: Steampunk on the Western Frontier." *Journal of Popular Film and Television* 39, no. 2 (2011): 84–92.

Nakayama, Thomas K., and Robert L. Krizek. "Whiteness: A Strategic Rhetoric." *Quarterly Journal of Speech* 81, no. 3 (1995): 291–309.

Nayak, Anoop. "Critical Whiteness Studies." *Sociology Compass* 1, no. 2 (2007): 737–55.

Nevins, Jess. *A Blazing World: The Unofficial Companion to* The League of Extraordinary Gentlemen, *vol. 2*. Austin: Monkeybrain, 2004.

O'Hehir, Andrew. "America's First White President." *Salon*. December 10, 2016. Accessed January 24, 2017. http://www.salon.com/2016/12/10/americas-first-white-president/.

Onion, Rebecca. "Reclaiming the Machine: An Introductory Look at Steampunk in Everyday Practice." *Neo-Victorian Studies* 1, no. 1 (2008): 138–63.

Painter, Nell Irvin. "What Whiteness Means in the Trump Era." *New York Times*. November 12, 2016, accessed January 24, 2017, https://www.nytimes.com/2016/11/13/opinion/what-whiteness-means-in-the-trump-era.html.

Perschon, Mike. "Finding Nemo: Verne's Antihero as Original Steampunk." *Verniana* 2 (2010): 179–93.

Prividera, Laura C., and John W. Howard III. "Masculinity, Whiteness, and the Warrior Hero: Perpetuating the Strategic Rhetoric of U.S. Nationalism and the Marginalization of Women." *Women and Language* 29, no. 2 (2006.): 29–37.

Roosevelt, Kermit III. "Theodore Roosevelt's Lessons for Today's Politics." *Time*, July 25, 2016, accessed February 9, 2018, http://time.com/4421539/theodore-roosevelt-lessons/.

Roosevelt, Theodore. "True Americanism." *Forum Magazine*, April 1894. Online at http://teachingamericanhistory.org/library/document/true-americanism-the-forum-magazine, accessed January 21, 2018.

Shome, Raka. "Outing Whiteness." *Critical Studies in Media Communication* 17, no. 3 (2000): 366–71.

Stuckey, Mary E. *The President as Interpreter-in-Chief.* Chatham, NJ: Chatham House, 1991.

Sundén, Jenny. "Corporeal Anachronisms: Notes on Affect, Relationality, and Power in Steampunk." *Somatechnics* 3, no. 2 (2013): 369–86.

Sundén, Jenny. "Steampunk Practices: Time, Tactility, and a Racial Politics of Touch." *Ada: A Journal of Gender, New Media, and Technology*, no. 5 (2014), http://adanewmedia.org/2014/07/issue5-sunden/.

Sundén, Jenny. "Clockwork Corsets: Pressed against the Past." *International Journal of Cultural Studies* 18, no. 3 (2015): 379–83.

Thomas, Ronald C., Jr. "Hero of the Military-Industrial Complex: Reading Iron Man through Burke's Dramatism." In *Heroes of Film, Comics and American Culture: Essays on Real and Fictional Defenders of Home*, edited by Lisa M. Detora, loc. 2014–2229. Jefferson, NC: McFarland, 2009. Kindle e-book.

Tillapaugh, J. "Theodore Roosevelt and the Rough Riders: A Century of Leadership." In *Hollywood's White House: The American Presidency in Film and History*, edited by Peter C. Rollins and John E. O'Connor, 96–114. Lexington: University Press of Kentucky, 2005.

Tobias, Ronald B. *Film and the American Moral Vision of Nature: Theodore Roosevelt to Walt Disney*. East Lansing: Michigan State University Press, 2011.

Trump, Donald J. "Statement from President Donald J. Trump—Immigration." *White House*, September 5, 2017, accessed January 21, 2018, https://www.whitehouse.gov/briefings-statements/statement-president-donald-j-trump-7/.

Tuccille, Jerome. *The Roughest Riders: The Untold Story of the Black Soldiers in the Spanish-American War.* Chicago: Chicago Press Review, 2015. Kindle e-book.

Wanzo, Rebecca. "The Superhero: Meditations on Surveillance, Salvation, and Desire." *Communication and Critical/Cultural Studies* 6, no. 1 (2009): 93–97.

Žižek, Slavoj. *The Metastases of Enjoyment: Six Essays on Woman and Causality*. New York: Verso, 1994.

CHAPTER ELEVEN

"OUT THERE HUNTING MONSTERS"

Manifest Destiny, the Monstrosity of the American West, and the Gothic Character of American History

MICHAEL FUCHS AND STEFAN RABITSCH

Following the meandering courses of rivers, ragged mountain ranges, and, where available, ancient "Indian trails," the journals of the Lewis and Clark Expedition are full of twists and turns as well as encounters and decisions (each of which could have had a decisive impact on the success or failure of their venture). One such decision point came on June 3, 1805, when, upon reaching a fork in the Missouri River, the captains had to determine which stream to ascend in order to achieve one of their expedition's goals: finding the headwaters of the "Big Muddy." They knew that they had to find the Great Falls of the Missouri, their only reliable reference point, in order to be certain of their course. Ascending the wrong stream would have likely kept them from reaching the Pacific Ocean, since they would not have had enough time to clear the Rocky Mountains before the first snow in the fall.

The water of the northern stream was brownish, silty, and turbid, and thus like the river they had followed, while the southern fork discharged water that was clear and brisk "like most rivers issuing from a mountainous country." The expedition was within sight of the Rocky Mountains, and the Missouri's headwaters were purportedly there. Weighing all information available to them, and conducting observations in the vicinity over the next few days, the captains settled on the south fork to "proceed on."[1] While they based their decision on largely rational, albeit still circumstantial, evidence, the rest of the party was quick to correlate that which they had come to know over the previous months with their gut instincts: their men maintained that the northern stream must be the true Missouri. The captains' decision was vindicated a few days later when they reached the Great Falls.

The Lewis and Clark Expedition, which sought to find a navigable waterway to the Pacific Ocean, is a great success story of the American Enlightenment, yet the decision over which stream to ascend—one clear, the other muddy—is symbolic of what Albert Furtwangler has identified as the "lingering eccentricities" that reverberate both in the explorers' observations, conduct, and sensibilities and the American narrative of westward expansion.[2] While frequent, these "eccentricities" appear mostly in the margins of the journals, in moments of introspection and reflection, as the explorers (Lewis more so than Clark) negotiate between Enlightenment rationalism and the awe-inspiring sense of the sublime tampered by tinges of the occult. These "eccentricities," we would argue, provide access to the Gothic anxieties and monstrosities that undergird not only the "epic" conquest of the West but also (the dominant version of) American history at large. After all, American history and the notion of westward progress have always been intricately intertwined. As Frederick Jackson Turner famously put it in 1893, "up to our own day American history has been in a large degree the history of the colonization of the Great West. The existence of an area of free land, its continuous recession, and the advance of American settlement westward, *explain* American development."[3]

Image Comics' aptly titled *Manifest Destiny* (2013–) effectively rewrites and redraws the Lewis and Clark journals by amplifying these "eccentricities." The comic revises the historical journals as well as the historiography of the Lewis and Clark Expedition by emphasizing those aspects that are usually purged from history. In this way the comic series achieves a twofold effect. First, it problematizes the epic character of the journals, exposing how historiographic power and privilege have been applied to the journals with tireless editorial and scholarly abandon. Second, it reveals the haunted character of a purportedly future-oriented nation by allowing for the visual manifestation of the ghosts of the American imperial enterprise, which have plagued American history. By tapping into and literalizing the Gothic undercurrent spectrally present in the journals and the American psyche of the early nineteenth century, *Manifest Destiny* gives concrete, albeit fantastic, shape to the monstrous that undergirds the imperial march of American civilization. By juxtaposing passages from the journals (and historiographical commentary by Lewis and Clark scholars) with *Manifest Destiny*, we will argue that the comic inverts the promise of the ideal(ized) American individual and the American nation that would emerge from the frontier experience, encapsulated in the transformative encounter between civilization and the wilderness. Indeed, the comic re-image-ines American nature as a force that infects back, consumes back, and claims back superiority over the invading agents of American nation-building. American nature brings the explorers face-to-face with their own gruesome selves and the monstrosity of imperial practices. Consequently, (American) readers are confronted with their own and their nation's inner darkness.

CREATING AN AMERICAN EPIC

Today, the Corps of Discovery's iconic journey across the North American continent is considered one of the founding pillars of the American nation-building project. In *Finding the West*, James P. Ronda accordingly observes that "Lewis and Clark are celebrated as pioneer naturalists, cartographers, diplomats, and students of Indian cultures." "And some," Ronda continues, "seem bent on making the Lewis and Clark story into an American epic filled with manly courage and triumphant nationalism."[4] Tellingly, Larry McMurtry hails the expedition as "the first" and also "only American epic" in his review of the "definitive edition" of the Lewis and Clark journals edited by Gary E. Moulton.[5] In so doing McMurtry echoes, and participates in, the tradition of epic-making, which has made the unwieldy corpus of the journals manageable, accessible, and, arguably, enjoyable ever since the first editions became available shortly after the expedition's return. This epic framing became particularly pertinent in the twentieth century, as Bernard DeVoto (1953) and Frank Bergon (1989) published popular editions of the journals that continued to hold sway until an onslaught of new editions was released surrounding the expedition's bicentennial in the early twenty-first century.

To be sure, "epic" is "a word frequently and loosely applied to the expedition itself—the historic act of exploration—with respect to its magnitude."[6] More importantly, "'epic' immediately suggests an affirmation of essential cultural values."[7] Tellingly, Attorney-General Levi Lincoln considered the Lewis and Clark Expedition an "enterprise of national consequence," while Jefferson's secretary of the Treasury, Albert Gallatin, was certain that "the future destinies of the Missouri country are of vast importance to the United States."[8] The principal architect of the expedition, President Jefferson, was convinced that it was a "work . . . done for posterity," as it served to "delineate with correctness the great arteries of this great country."[9] Since then, "the expedition has become the preeminent symbol of a nation heading west," a nation on the brink of achieving greatness.[10] After all, if one believes in the grandiose tales and mythic achievements projected onto the expedition, one might think that Lewis and Clark had accomplished nothing less than laying the groundwork for "the future path of civilization."[11]

These "epic" dimensions of the Lewis and Clark Expedition notwithstanding, an epic becomes an epic only through the practice of retelling; in fact, one might argue that epics have their future repetition (with difference) inbuilt. In his preface to the 1893 edition of the Lewis and Clark journals, Elliott Coues revealingly describes the journals as "our national epic of exploration, conceived by Thomas Jefferson, wrought out by Lewis and Clark, and given to the world by Nicholas Biddle," a statement indicative of the place the expedition was coming to occupy in national myth.[12] Consciously or not, Coues here acknowledges Biddle's influence on shaping America's (and the world's) understanding of the Lewis and Clark Expedition. As the first editor of the journals, Biddle not only compiled the material produced during the expedition but also selected letters and journal entries, added information, and created a narrative—Biddle manufactured history in that he created "a *usable past* from the historic Lewis and Clark expedition."[13]

The expedition was tasked by President Jefferson to compile detailed geographic, geological, meteorological, mineralogical, botanical, zoological, and ethnographic observations on the journey; its journals amount to a log of scientific notes. First and foremost, the journals were intended for the eyes of the president, the intelligentsia who were stirring with national fervor at the time, and politicians in favor of westward expansion. Consequently, Lewis and Clark did not employ a narrative discourse. Similar to ships' logs, the journals contain lengthy and repetitive recollections largely devoid of high drama and conflict. Mundane drudgery, toil, the exigencies of daily survival, and pages upon pages of descriptions constitute the main bulk of the journals. In and of themselves, the journals lack narrative thrust.

Yet, paradoxically perhaps, the journals demand to be made into an epic. Indeed, Albert Furtwangler has suggested that they are an "implied epic of discovery."[14] Consequently, a storyteller was needed to bring an "integrative comprehension" to the journals' "ambiguity of form and formlessness."[15] Since the turn of the twentieth century, editors, and increasingly editor-scholars, together with creators of ancillary texts (e.g., biographies, romance novels, children's books, cookbooks, travel guides, etc.), have taken up this task and recast the journals into an epic mold. On the one hand, they all tell the same story; on the other, the wealth of the source text allows for significant variation and differences in emphasis.

Three sample texts help exemplify the journals' transformation into epic form. Prior to the completion of Moulton's *The Definitive Journals of Lewis and Clark* in 2002, Bernard DeVoto's *Journals of Lewis and Clark* and Frank Bergon's *The Journals of Lewis and Clark* were the most popular editions of the journals. While DeVoto highlights the significance of political geography and thus traces the politics and the economics that drove westward expansion, a quick peek at Bergon's table of contents shows that natural sights (including encounters with Native peoples) function as the main structuring devices.[16] On the other hand, in *Lewis and Clark among the Indians*, Ronda organizes the narrative around encounters with the Other.[17] What these various editions have in common is that they "tell a coherent story by weaving together the highlights of single entries; make steady chronological progress across the continent and back; relegate technical observations to occasional notes or appendixes."[18]

(RE)WRITING HISTORY IN *MANIFEST DESTINY*

Consisting of five collected volumes to date (volume 6 is announced for May 2018), *Manifest Destiny*'s plot follows the trail of the historical expedition from its point of departure in St. Louis, Missouri, to the Pacific Northwest and its presumed return. Offering the "veiled"—and thus alternate—version of the expedition, the comic series embellishes history with supernatural horrors as the explorers encounter creatures ranging from hybrid beasts and insectoid specters to ghoulish entities and shrub zombies. *Manifest Destiny* features a recognizable cast that includes, next to Lewis and Clark, the latter's slave, York, the French Canadian trader and interpreter Toussaint Charbonneau and his teenage wife Sacagawea, the expedition's noncommissioned officers Sergeants Ordway, Gass, and Floyd, and Private Whitehouse—who also kept journals—all the way down to Lewis's Newfoundland dog, Seaman. The comic series adds fictional characters, such as a contingent of convicts who were shanghaied for the expedition in exchange for the promise of freedom (not to say ready-made cannon fodder) and a band of female settlers who survived a deadly plague in a remote French settlement. The comics also rewrite popularly known episodes of the expedition, such as the fate of Sgt. Charles Floyd, the only expedition member to die. While, historically, his death was likely caused by a ruptured appendix, in the comic, he transmutes into a zombie—and he is far from the only one who perishes.

Manifest Destiny thematizes the epic-making strategies editors and scholars have employed over the decades. Indeed, as early as page 3, Lewis concludes that the "[b]iggest obstacle so far is boredom."[19] The comic avoids these long periods of tedium, monotony, and dullness in four ways. First, *Manifest Destiny* employs a tried-and-true formula in storytelling—ellipses. For example, the second collected volume concludes with the party encountering Native Americans on August 2, 1804. Lewis's next entry in the comic is dated August 15. This elliptic character mirrors the structure of most abridged editions of the journals. In the comic series, these temporal jumps create the illusion of a constant flow of action, as (long) periods of nothing exciting happening in the diegetic world are simply omitted.

Second, flashbacks bridge periods of little action, not only providing background information on the characters and the expedition but also offering glimpses into the past of the land and its various civilizations. When the party's youngest member, Private Collins, for example, crawls into a monster's lair, a flashback elucidates his inferiority complex: Throughout his life, it seems, everyone has trampled on him, thereby seriously damaging his sense of self-esteem. As a result, other people constantly mispronounce his name or even call him by different names altogether. However, Collins is not alone looking for the monster; Dawhogg, a so-called Fezron (a birdlike creature that speaks and presents a creative appropriation of the Thunderbird archetype found in numerous Native American cultures), is by his side. When Collins slips, Dawhogg remarks, "Try to stay not dead during the climb. Be more careful, Collins." "It's Collins," the young man responds, expecting the creature not to recognize his identity, marked by his name. However, the Fezron quickly points out, "That's what I said!"[20] Here, two marginalized beings come to accept each other for what they are. This brief moment of mutual recognition highlights the significance of the Fezron storyline's conclusion, in which the explorers wipe out the creatures, culminating in Collins's murder of Dawhogg. As Dragoş Manea has correctly pointed out, Dawhogg "looks particularly human-like here, and the perpetrator's understanding of the moral ambiguity of his action is reinforced by the fact that Collins looks him right in the face, recognizes this humanity and shoots him anyway; twice saying that he is sorry."[21] Consequently, the murder of the Fezron represents the genocide of Native American peoples committed by those who followed in the wake of the expedition. Although the explorers acknowledge Fezron culture, and although they share moments of mutual understanding with the creatures, the thrust of westward progress requires the white settlers to extinguish everything incompatible with their worldview. Indeed, even the most marginal(ized) member of the invading culture triumphs over the nonhuman Other. The flashbacks to Collins's childhood underline his position in two different, yet overlapping, networks of power, as he is simultaneously powerless and powerful.

Third, the comic features drama on the character level. This strategy includes the creation of tensions between members of the party (repeatedly caused by their ennui) but also within particular characters, as their repressed drives and suppressed desires constantly seem to be on the verge of erupting. When Miss Lebrun, one of the women the party picks up at the monster-infested camp at La Charrette, asks Corporal Hardy, a fictional expedition member, whether she may accompany him into the woods, as she "feel[s] safest with [him]," Hardy (mis) interprets her suggestion as sexual innuendos. Once the two have advanced far enough into the forest that no one else can hear them, Hardy remarks, "You beg to come with me. For a stroll away from the others. It's okay to speak your mind now. We have privacy." Miss Lebrun slaps him across the face, stating, "I was scared to be alone, you idiot!" However, Hardy becomes irate, telling her that she "can't make a fool out of [him]" before trying to force himself upon her.[22] The natural environment is quick to punish this would-be transgression, though, as a giant insect forces itself upon him, penetrates his body, and symbolically impregnates Hardy with its offspring.

Most importantly, however, *Manifest Destiny* self-consciously utilizes the serial character of comics and the journey's episodic character to full effect by oscillating between moments of (relative) calmness and climactic events—encounters with various creatures. Arches, which at first appear to be randomly placed in

Whenever Lewis and Clark's party discovers an arch, the action heats up.

the wilderness, visually signpost these narrative highpoints. These arches occupy a liminal position, as their material nature (or, in fact, natural material, as they consist of basic natural resources such as wicker and vines, dung, egg-infested riverweeds, or rock) aligns them with the "uncivilized" world, while their shape and intricate construction speaks to an unknown, possibly supernatural, nonhuman intelligence that must have created them. For readers who fail to understand the pattern the first two times Lewis and Clark's band confronts beasts of the wild, the comic metatextually draws attention to this narrative strategy when convict-turned-explorer Jensen wonders, "Every time we see one of these arches, we're supposed to stand around it and wait to get killed?" after the party has discovered arch number three.[23] After finding the fourth arch (a destroyed one), Clark likewise remarks, "Those things usually accompany those creatures."[24]

Since the party has to kill the monsters encountered in the vicinity of the arches in order to proceed with their adventure (to, quite literally, progress), the comic's episodic structure calls to mind video games. This intermedial reference is reinforced by the fact that members of the Lewis and Clark Expedition repeatedly try different strategies until they find a way to dispose of their foes. For example, their party narrowly escapes an ambush by a small band of bison-centaur hybrids, finding temporary shelter at the fortified, albeit strangely deserted, settlement La Charrette. There they square off with fauna that the local flora seem to have turned into zombie-like and highly contagious husks. The party quickly learns, albeit not without incurring casualties, that firing their rifles, the most sophisticated weapons available in the US at the time, proves utterly ineffective. While fighting the zombie-like things with knives, sabers, and bayonets in hand-to-hand combat is more successful, this strategy would inevitably mean that the expedition would come into direct contact with the plant zombies' all-consuming excretions. Finally, Clark concludes, "after bullets and blades, there's only one avenue left . . . one thing that is never a friend to flora is fire."[25] As humanity's first true piece of technology, fire—in its raw rather than "refined" form—succeeds in taming the forces of wilderness.

Similar to earlier editions of the Lewis and Clark journals, *Manifest Destiny*'s adaptation thus becomes more action-packed than the original text; but unlike most abridged editions of the journals, the comic draws attention to its mode of telling and to the power wielded by its teller (in the case of the comics, primarily Lewis). Besides intensifying the action, speeding up the journey, and increasing the rate in which Lewis and Clark make (more or less) groundbreaking discoveries, every single edition of the journals produced new historical facts. The inclusion of commentaries, publication of (semi-)fictional versions, and uncovering of new journal entries (and additional journals) has resulted in the incessant creation of new historical realities, which—at least partially—have overwritten earlier versions of history. This proliferation of histories results in

Lewis writes and erases history in one fell swoop.

what Paul Ricœur has identified as the uncanny nature of history: "the presence of the absent encountered previously."[26] History, as Sigmund Freud might say, thus becomes strangely familiar, as each new writer seeks to efface earlier versions of the Lewis and Clark narrative. Like a palimpsest, however, these previous narratives remain latently present—prone to resurface.

Manifest Destiny exposes these processes as early as page 4 of the initial issue. After Clark has killed a heron, Lewis starts wondering whether they will encounter creatures other than "birds, small game and Indians" on their journey. He then begins writing in his journal, "Beginning to worry that my president has either been bamboozled by French tall tales or has taken leave of his senses and created such mythology in his own mind," only to cross out the passage and transform it into "Men are braced for action. Surely we will encounter the creatures spoken of by President Jefferson when he wisely commissioned this mission." When Clark asks whether Lewis is "working on the journal," the latter explains, "I'm finishing up the . . . classified document. Then I will enter our feathered friend here into the congressional version."[27]

These panels showcase the ways in which Lewis consciously shapes the journal following Jefferson's directions and thus suggest that the explorers kept multiple journals. In a sense this is of course true, as Lewis and Clark kept their individual journals, frequently copying and amending each other's entries; so did Sergeants.

Ordway, Gass, and Floyd, and Private Whitehouse, the noncommissioned supernumeraries who constituted the second hierarchical tier in the Corps of Discovery. Narratively, Lewis's entry (which he erases from historical record as soon as he adds it) anticipates a flashback that occurs sometime later in the comic. In this flashback scene, set back in Monticello, Virginia, Jefferson orders Lewis to "clear [the Louisiana territory] of creatures" such as the cyclops whose skull the president presents to his soon-to-be-captain.[28] Jefferson tellingly founds his belief in these creatures' existence upon recovered bones. *Manifest Destiny* here plays on what might have been one of the secret agendas behind the Journey of Discovery: Jefferson's hope of finding mastodons roaming in the West (or dispelling their fabled existence once and for all).

As Paul Semonin convincingly demonstrates in *American Monster* (2000), by the time of the American Revolution, the mastodon had emerged as an icon of American nationalism. Soon thereafter the prehistoric animal became a heated topic of contention between Jefferson and French naturalist Georges-Louis Leclerc, Comte de Buffon, who (in)famously postulated that American mammals were inherently inferior to their European counterparts.[29] After a Dutch farmer had discovered a mastodon tooth in Claverack, New York, in 1705, and first bones had been collected in Kentucky in 1739, more and more fossils appeared as settlers slowly began to move westward in the second half of the eighteenth century. Since the notion of extinction began to take shape only in the late eighteenth century, Jefferson was of the firm belief that if "the bones exist . . . the animal has existed"; and if "this animal has once existed, it is probable . . . that he still exists."[30] Owing to his infatuation with mastodons, the long-extinct mammal is the first animal species Jefferson mentions in chapter 6 of *Notes on the State of Virginia* (1785), stressing that "the Mammoth . . . still exists in the northern parts of America."[31] This idea echoes in the president's instructions to Lewis to record "the remains & accounts of any [animals] which may be deemed rare or extinct."[32]

Accordingly, *Manifest Destiny* does, in fact, *not* turn the Lewis and Clark Expedition into a fantastic tale featuring man-beasts, giant carnivorous plants, and other freaks of nature; rather, the comic series exposes the fantastic character built right into the expedition and the Lewis and Clark journals (and the American national character, for that matter). Whereas President "Jefferson wanted . . . an interrelated ensemble of facts, because the culture of science . . . saw nature . . . composed of related facts governed by natural laws," the explorers' enlightened worldview repeatedly reached its limits during their journey across the continent.[33]

THE SUBLIME AND THE LIMITS OF HUMAN UNDERSTANDING

While the historical journals are replete with examples of the explorers reaching their physical limits, transgressions of their intellectual capacities and aesthetic sensibilities are mostly found in moments where they encounter the sublime of western landscapes and/or the many terrifying, nearly fatal encounters with wildlife. One of the many encounters with the sublime occurred on June 13, 1805, when Lewis and an advance party found the Great Falls of the Missouri. Upon realizing what he had found, he noted in his journal: "I hurryed down the hill which was about 200 feet high and difficult of access, to gaze on this sublimely grand specticle." What follows is a lengthy description of minute details that together form the first of multiple cascades. He concludes his observations, however, on a note of frustration and inadequacy:

> [A]fter wrighting this imperfect discription I again viewed the falls and was so much disgusted with the imperfect idea which it conveyed of the scene that I determined to draw my pen across it and begin agin, but then reflected that I could not perhaps succeed better than pening the first impressions of the mind; I wished for the pencil of Salvator Rosa or the pen of Thompson, that I might be enabled to give to the enlightened world some just idea of this truly magnifficent and sublimely grand object, which has from the commencement of time been concealed from the view of civilized man. . . . I hope still to give to the world some faint idea of an object which at this moment fills me with such pleasure and astonishment.[34]

Even though he relates his geological and hydrographic descriptions in great detail, Lewis cannot help but be overwhelmed and indeed frustrated by a feeling of inadequacy. While he wishes for the skills of more refined artists, not least because he wants to adequately relate his discovery to a "civilized" Enlightenment audience, the waterfalls elude rationalism. They are sublime. Accordingly, in order to even come close to understanding them, one has to embrace one's baser human instincts. Lewis's entry apparently draws on Edmund Burke's elaborations on the sublime. Burke famously suggested that nature was the most sublime object. "The passion caused by . . . sublime . . . nature," Burke argued, "is Astonishment." Astonishment implies the enjoyment of beauty but also "some degree of horror." Most importantly, however, in sublime moments, "the mind is so entirely filled with its [sublime] object, that it cannot . . . reason."[35] In this way, these sublime encounters brought the explorers face-to-face with a lack, or rather an inadequacy, of human comprehension and agency, producing a sense of powerlessness and insignificance.

Edward Hicks, *The Peaceable Kingdom of the Branch* (c. 1824–25).

Witnessing such sublime scenery, Lewis expressly wished for the skills and services of a painter, suggesting that the sublime is best captured and rendered visually. He thus in a sense anticipated the rise of a distinctively national tradition of American Romantic landscape painting. In the decades after the expedition's return, painters of the Hudson River and later the Rocky Mountain Schools drew on the evocative power of America's wild spaces to create a visual mythos that celebrated national expansion and dazzled—both with the size of their canvases and their subject matter—domestic and international audiences. Edward Hicks's *Peaceable Kingdom of the Branch* (c. 1824–1825) anticipated this tradition and serves as an intertext to *Manifest Destiny*, as the painting speaks to the utopian aspirations of the new nation that grew out of, and simultaneously were projected onto, American nature.

Furtwangler has contended that Hicks "joins sublime action with sublime scenery, putting a characteristic American deed"—that is, William Penn's treaty with the local natives—"in an outstanding American setting as a background to [national] childhood peaceably emerging among colorful lions and leopards."[36] However, the painting bears a Gothic imprint. As American deeds play out on the left (i.e., the *western* side of the painting), where the William Penn treaty council may easily be replaced by the many councils Lewis and Clark had with native nations, the innocent child-nation is visually destabilized by a potentially dark specter in the shape of a dead, or at least dying, tree. The paratext, suggesting that the "child shall lead [the beasts]," is thus endowed with a second, darker, reading, that points at man's destruction of nature.

By more explicitly inverting the triumphalism presumed to be inherent in westward expansion, *Manifest Destiny* serves as both critique of and corrective to the visual narrative Lewis desperately wishes for in his historical journal entry, and which successive generations of painters shaped into an awe-inspiring national mythos. The frequent encounters between the expedition and the sublime not only betray (proto-)Romantic sensibilities but also provide access to the Gothic undercurrent found in the journals, American wilderness, and American history at large—an undercurrent that is retrieved from the liminal spaces and perception of American history and brought to broad daylight in *Manifest Destiny*.

WRITING NATURE INTO AMERICAN HISTORY

The sublime that Lewis and Clark encountered and struggled with also impinged on their notions of human agency and control, which form the basis for any imperial enterprise. By the end of the nineteenth century, Frederick Jackson Turner used the presupposed expectation to convert and cultivate—and ultimately commercialize—American nature to explain and legitimize the American character (individual and national). Indeed, imperial aspirations lay at the heart of the expedition, which Lewis and Clark articulated in the Enlightenment discourse of understanding the world through scientific inquiry. Even so, encounters with wildlife, especially apex predators, repeatedly reminded the explorers of the uncomfortable limits of the tools of civilization and the presumed agency they afforded them. Their frequent run-ins with grizzly bears in the spring of 1805 arguably provided the template for the fictional explorers' encounters with monstrous creatures in the comic. Not only do these confrontations with bears call into question the American imperial project, but the forces of American nature also counter, resist, and (momentarily) triumph over the invaders and were subsequently amplified in the comic. Consequently, these moments of nature striking back unmask the inadequacy of the tools of empirical control and imperial domination that already come to the fore in the journals.

Lewis's near-fatal encounter with a grizzly on June 14, 1805, was but one of many that, according to the journals, provided the Corps of Discovery with frustration and ample opportunity for introspection. After he narrowly escaped that "large white, or reather brown bear," sighted an enigmatic "tyger cat," and almost became the victim of a buffalo stampede all within only one day, he concluded that "all the beasts of the neighbourhood had made a league to destroy me."[37] Natives had informed the explorers about the formidable ferocity of the yellow bear farther downstream. As the grizzly was largely unknown (not to say mysterious) to science in the early nineteenth century, the expedition initially dismissed these reports as tall tales. On April 29, 1805, Lewis recorded the first encounter with two grizzlies, one of which they killed: "I] was a male not fully grown . . . it is a much more furious and formidable anamal, and will frequently pursue the hunter when wounded. it is asstonishing to see the wounds they will bear before they can be put to death." At first Lewis made a series of predictably confident and outright hubristic comments: "The Indians may well fear this anamal equiped as they generally are with their bows and arrows or indifferent fuzees, but in the hands of skillfull riflemen they are by no means as formidable or dangerous as they have been represented."[38] After multiple bear encounters over the next few weeks, each of which could have easily ended in the loss of human life, Lewis noted: "I find that the curiossity of our party is pretty well satisfyed with rispect to this anamal, the formidable appearance of the male bear killed on the 5th added to the difficulty with which they die when even shot through the vital parts, has staggered the resolution several of them."[39]

Manifest Destiny redraws such encounters in fantastic shades and monstrous shapes, thereby calling into question the presumed imperial power to control and dominate nature given to the explorers through the use of empirical discourse and the tools of civilization (journal keeping, instruments, weapons, etc.). While Lewis and Clark were students and practitioners of Linnaean taxonomy, their imperial mindset drew from self-legitimizing euro- and anthropocentric traditions of the times. However, the comics expose and shatter the hubris derived from white man's presumed position of superiority. By fighting back, the local flora and fauna resist the explorers' attempts at defining and controlling them.

The first encounter with "demons" in the comics specifically recalls Lewis and Clark's skirmishes with grizzlies. A creature that may best be described as a bison-centaur hybrid charges a shore party. The explorers kill the monster with great difficulty. Lewis performs an autopsy and concludes, "This beast is, whatever it is, is only a child."[40] Struggling to agree on a designation, Lewis confides in Clark that he does not know what he should call the creature, as if naming the creature would make it knowable and thus controllable. They settle on employing the misnomer "minotaur" for the benefit of the expedition, suggesting that taxonomic classification "is a fictitious grid we place on nature" in order to perpetuate human exceptionalism and the attendant illusions of human dominance over the natural environment.[41]

The violence of Lewis and Clark's expedition becomes visually manifest when they kill monsters.

However, giving the creature a name does little to alleviate the men's fears. A similar struggle frames the classification of an amphibian creature that at first is compared to "a Japanese demon," the "'filth licker,' which appears to be a cross between a man and a frog." Facing the same conundrum as earlier, Lewis "resort[s] to a more Linnaean classification"—*ranidea*—a "true frog."[42] In a direct confrontation with the creature, Lewis loses his composure, goes berserk, and stabs it to death. Upon retrieving the carcass, Clark observes: "Twenty-nine stab wounds? A bit indulgent no?"[43] Being exposed to, and, in a sense, being infected by the ferociousness of America's wild nature all but negates the explorers' equally aggressive mission to classify and ultimately dominate, which is thinly veiled by the mantle of civilization.

To be sure, the Black American writer and social critic James Baldwin diagnosed that "[v]iolence has been the American daily bread since we have heard of America. This violence . . . appears to be admired and lusted after, and [is] the key to the American imagination."[44] Similarly, Richard Slotkin has famously demonstrated that one of America's dominant myths sees the nation regenerate through violence performed against outside aggressors—from native peoples to radical Muslims.[45] Not stopping at the enemy from without, Slotkin also mapped the West as a "*Fatal Environment* continuous with that of *Regeneration*," where the violent (re)generation of American civilization brought to bear on American nature through tools of cultivation, consumption, and commercialization.[46] Having access to the wealth of an "entire" continent, so his argument goes, allowed the United States to rapidly ascend as a corporate, industrial superpower. Accordingly, in *Manifest Destiny*, Lewis's excessive violence attests to the birth of a "violent empire" incessantly trying to extend its sphere of influence.

A HAUNTED NATION

Carroll Smith-Rosenberg has argued that the key component in America's emerging national identity was the fear of difference. Difference was "perceived as dangerous, disdained as polluting, [and] demand[ed] expulsion."[47] National identities, in general, "guarantee an unchanging 'oneness' or cultural belongingness." They provide citizens with a sense of "common origin or shared characteristics," Stuart Hall has explained.[48] However, the United States was "an uncertain amalgam of diverse peoples, religions, cultures, and languages. No common history, no governmental infrastructure, no shared culture bound them together."[49] Despite the attempts to define its difference from England, the newborn nation inherited the desire to "inhabite and reforme so barbarous a nation" from the British.[50] In particular, "the hierarchical division between civilization and wildness" became a founding pillar of America, as human groups incompatible with the white ideal were aligned with animals and nature.[51]

This binary served (and, in fact, to this day serves) as a discursive anchor to distinguish between various opposites, from the individual to the national level. *Manifest Destiny* makes explicit how the national fear of difference affected individuals by socially implementing repression, which "makes us distinctly human, capable of directing our own lives and co-existing with others," as Robin Wood puts it in one of his seminal essays on American horror.[52] When President Jefferson tasks Lewis to lead an expedition into the West, the explorer is reluctant at first. However, when Jefferson threatens to make Lewis's excesses public ("drunkenly challenging men to duels . . . playing poker with money you don't have, and . . . seducing other men's wives, daughters, and sons") or perhaps even "injur[ing] or worse" Lewis's male lovers, the soldier accepts.[53] There is no room for Lewis's excesses in the formation of the American national identity, as the threats of impurification are expulsed and projected onto marginalized Others.

The comic hence reimagines and amplifies Jefferson's reflections on the reasons for Lewis committing suicide in 1809, which he shared in a letter to Paul Allen in 1813. Jefferson acknowledged that "hypocondriac affections" had afflicted the Lewis family, and while Lewis worked as the president's secretary, he exhibited "at times sensible depressions of mind"; Jefferson surmised that while the expedition "suspended these distressing affections," they "returned upon him with redoubled vigor" once he had returned and taken up the governorship of the Louisiana Territory. Jefferson blamed "a paroxysm of one of these [affections]" for Lewis's suicide.[54] On the other hand, a natural space sui generis, the West was imagined to produce national uniqueness, cohesion, and thus unity. By experiencing the transformative power of the frontier (which failed to affect the historical Lewis), one would become a "real" American, while the nation itself transformed into a democratic ideal destined to not simply achieve greatness but reach a utopian state.

However, the West was hardly a realm of inclusion. The specters created by the "*frontier of exclusion*" continue to haunt the prairies, the mountains and valleys, and the deserts of the West.[55] These ghosts take many shapes and forms, produced by state-sponsored massacres, forced relocations, the destruction caused by extractive industries, measures against (il)legal immigration, and the extermination of Native peoples and nonhuman species. Tellingly, Jacques Derrida has asserted, "Haunting belongs to the structure of every hegemony."[56] Likewise, Homi K. Bhabha has diagnosed that the "comfort of social belonging" is intricately intertwined with "the *unheimlich* terror of the space or race of the Other."[57] Both Derrida and Bhabha thus suggest not only that the dominance of one group over another (or humans over the natural environment, for that matter) is based on the construction of ghosts, but also that the power, created in discourse, is spectral and imaginary. Since the story of the West is the story of the American nation, and vice versa, the West is one of the preeminent locations of America's "national ghosts."[58]

Manifest Destiny focuses on two interrelated tools of power in the context of the Lewis and Clark Expedition: storytelling and scientific discourse. As the comic series demonstrates, these control mechanisms create spectral presences lurking just beneath the surface and along the margins, constantly on the verge of (re)surfacing and (re)intruding. Accordingly, *Manifest Destiny* repeatedly undermines Lewis and Clark's role as vanguards of westward expansion, as explorers of "unconquered" territory. For example, when the expedition discovers the first arch, Lewis is convinced that no "savage could design and execute the construction on [*sic*] a structure such as this."[59] Similarly, as they advance farther westward, the party effectively treads in the footsteps of not only American explorers who had died in the area four years prior but also a small (fictitious) division of the Narváez expedition, which had made its way toward the northwest. These are but two instances in which *Manifest Destiny* not only investigates America's manifest destiny to freely develop the continent, to draw on a phrase in John O'Sullivan's essay "Annexation," but also questions American history.[60] After all, while we have arrived at a point in history in which the presence of Native peoples prior to white settlement in the region is a problem-laden fact, earlier European and Euro-American explorers in the West continue to be relegated to the margins of the Anglo-American success story.

Even though O'Sullivan proclaimed the United States "*the great nation* of futurity," where nature would serve as regenerative antidote to the corruptive effects of "corporate powers and privilege," the natural environment here merely serves as a rhetorical figure.[61] Indeed, in the mythos of the American West, the natural environment occupies the position of yet another "Other" that needs to be subjugated and controlled. In his second essay on manifest destiny, O'Sullivan proclaimed America's "manifest destiny to . . . possess the whole of the continent."[62] The political writer tellingly invoked divine design. Implicitly, he thus drew on the book of Genesis—on the sixth day of creation, "God said, 'Let Us make man in Our image, according to Our likeness; and let them rule over the fish of the sea and over the birds of the sky and over the cattle and over all the earth, and over every creeping thing that creeps on the earth.'"[63] However, *Manifest Destiny* vividly demonstrates that dominion over nature through industrial-scientific means of control has always been a presumptuous illusion.

In the end, the comic symbolically condenses its counternarrative by inverting a potent and arguably pretentious monument to the "success" of westward expansion—the Gateway Arch. Located a few miles south of Camp River Dubois, the expedition's winter camp in 1803–4 before they set out, the Gateway Arch is the centerpiece of the Jefferson National Expansion Memorial commemorating the nation's triumphant westward march (arguably) inaugurated by Lewis and Clark. *Manifest Destiny* cleverly mocks the narrative of westward expansion by redrawing and inverting, indeed subverting, it. Not only is the Gateway Arch multiplied in order to point out that someone/-thing was already "out there," but these arches are constructed out of nature, signaling that the specters of westward expansion readily leap out of the oppressed and suppressed margins of history ready to infect back, consume back, and claim back superiority over American civilization.

NOTES

1. Meriwether Lewis, "June 3, 1805," in *Journals of the Lewis and Clark Expedition*, ed. Gary Moulton, accessed November 15, 2017, https://lewisandclarkjournals.unl.edu/item/lc.jrn.1805-06-03#lc.jrn.1805-06-03.01; we have adopted all quotations from the journals verbatim and will not "[*sic*]" their eccentric orthography, unconventional capitalization, antiquated terminology, etc. At times, *Manifest Destiny* inherits these stylistic eccentricities, which we have also adopted without additional commentary.

2. Albert Furtwangler, *Acts of Discovery: Visions of America in the Lewis and Clark Journals* (Urbana: University of Illinois Press, 1993), 139.

3. Frederick Jackson Turner, *The Frontier in American History* (New York: Henry Holt, 1920), 1, emphasis added.

4. James P. Ronda, *Finding the West: Explorations with Lewis and Clark* (Albuquerque: University of New Mexico Press, 2001), 117.

5. Larry McMurtry, "The First American Epic," *New York Review of Books* (February 8, 2001): 39.

6. Frank Bergon, "Wilderness Aesthetics," in *Lewis & Clark: Legacies, Memories, and New Perspectives*, ed. Kris Fresonke and Mark Spence (Berkeley: University of California Press, 2004), 38.

7. John P. McWilliams Jr., *The American Epic: Transforming a Genre, 1770–1860* (Cambridge: Cambridge University Press, 1989), 3.

8. Levi Lincoln, "Levi Lincoln to Jefferson, 17 April 1803," in *Letters of the Lewis and Clark Expedition with Related Documents, 1783–1854*, 2nd ed., ed. Donald Dean Jackson (Urbana: University of Illinois Press, 1978), 35; Albert Gallatin, "Albert Gallatin to Jefferson, 13 April 1803," in *Letters of the Lewis and Clark Expedition with Related Documents, 1783–1854*, 2nd ed., ed. Donald Dean Jackson (Urbana: University of Illinois Press, 1978), 32–33.

9. Thomas Jefferson, "Thomas Jefferson to William Dunbar; May 25, 1805," *Thomas Jefferson and Early Western Explorers*, edited and transcribed by Gerard W. Gawalt, Manuscript Division, Library of Congress, accessed February 15, 2018, http://www.loc.gov/resource/mtj1.033_0554_0557.

10. Ronda, *Finding the West*, 117.

11. Nicholas Biddle, "The Nicholas Biddle Prospectus," in *Letters of the Lewis and Clark Expedition with Related Documents, 1783–1854*, 2nd ed., ed. Donald Dean Jackson (Urbana: University of Illinois Press, 1978), 547.

12. Elliott Coues, "Preface to the New Edition," in *History of the Expedition under the Command of Lewis and Clark: To the Sources of the Missouri River, Thence across the Rocky Mountains and down the Columbia River to the Pacific Ocean, Performed during the Years 1804–5–6 by Order of the Government of the United States*, ed. Elliott Coues (New York: Francis P. Harper, 1893), v.

13. Heinz Tschachler, "Ken Burns's 1997 *Lewis and Clark* Television Documentary: American History in Detox," *Revista española de estudios norteamericanos* 19–20 (2002): 166; italics in original.

14. Furtwangler, *Acts of Discovery*, 202.

15. Furtwangler, *Acts of Discovery*, 201–2.

16. Bernard DeVoto, ed. *The Journals of Lewis and Clark* (New York: Penguin, 1997).

17. James P. Ronda, *Lewis & Clark among the Indians* (Lincoln: University of Nebraska Press, 2002).

18. Furtwangler, *Acts of Discovery*, 203.

19. Chris Dingess, Matthew Roberts, and Owen Gieni, *Manifest Destiny, Volume 1: Flora & Fauna* (Portland, OR: Image Comics, 2014), 3. We should note here that the comic is, as is often the case with comics, not paginated. To facilitate cross-referencing, we thus simply counted the pages, not including the title and copyright pages.

20. Chris Dingess, Matthew Roberts, and Owen Gieni, *Manifest Destiny, Volume 3: Chiroptera & Carniformaves* (Portland, OR: Image Comics, 2016), 82.

21. Dragoş Manea, "Western Nightmares: *Manifest Destiny* and the Representation of Genocide in Weird Fiction," *Studies in Comics* 8, no. 2 (2017): 166.

22. Chris Dingess, Matthew Roberts, and Owen Gieni, *Manifest Destiny, Volume 2: Amphibia & Insecta* (Portland, OR: Image Comics, 2015), 37.

23. Dingess, Roberts, and Gieni, *Manifest Destiny, Volume 3*, 12.

24. Chris Dingess, Matthew Roberts, and Owen Gieni, *Manifest Destiny, Volume 4: Sasquatch* (Portland, OR: Image Comics, 2016), 35.

25. Dingess, Roberts, and Gieni, *Manifest Destiny, Volume 1*, 54.

26. Paul Ricœur, *Memory, History, Forgetting*, trans. Kathleen Blamey and David Pellauer (Chicago: University of Chicago Press, 2004), 39.

27. Dingess, Roberts, and Gieni, *Manifest Destiny, Volume 1*, 2–4; ellipses in original.

28. Dingess, Roberts, and Gieni, *Manifest Destiny, Volume 2*, 115.

29. Paul Semonin, *American Monster: How the Nation's First Prehistoric Creature Became a Symbol of National Identity* (New York: New York University Press, 2000); Georges-Louis Leclerc de Buffon, Œuvres *complètes de Buffon, tome premier: Théorie de la terre—histoire générale des animaux*, ed. Marie Jean Pierre Flourens (Paris: Garnier Frères, 1853), 677–78.

30. Thomas Jefferson, "A Memoir on the Discovery of Certain Bones of a Quadruped of the Clawed Kind in the Western Parts of Virginia," *Transactions of the American Philosophical Society* 4 (1799): 255–56.

31. Thomas Jefferson, "Notes on the State of Virginia," in *Thomas Jefferson: Writings*, ed. Merrill D. Peterson (New York: Library of America, 1984), loc. 2688.

32. Thomas Jefferson, "Jefferson's Instructions to Lewis," in *Letters of the Lewis and Clark Expedition with Related Documents, 1783–1854*, 2nd ed., ed. Donald Jackson (Urbana: University of Illinois Press, 1978), 63.

33. William H. Goetzmann, "Culture of Science: The Long Good-bye of the Twentieth Century," in *Making America: The Society & Culture of the United States*, ed. Luther S. Luedtke (Chapel Hill: University of North Carolina Press, 1992), 417.

34. Meriwether Lewis, "June 13, 1805," in *Journals of the Lewis & Clark Expedition*, ed. Gary Moulton, accessed November 15, 2017, https://lewisandclarkjournals.unl.edu/item/lc.jrn.1805-06-13#lc.jrn.1805-06-13.01.

35. Edmund Burke, *A Philosophical Enquiry into the Origin of Our Ideas of the Sublime and Beautiful* (London: Dodsley, 1757), 42; capitalization in original.

36. Furtwangler, *Acts of Discovery*, 48–50.

37. Meriwether Lewis, "June 14, 1805," in *Journals of the Lewis and Clark Expedition*, ed. Gary Moulton, accessed November 15, 2017, https://lewisandclarkjournals.unl.edu/item/lc.jrn.1805-06-14#lc.jrn.1805-06-14.01.

38. Meriwether Lewis, "April 29, 1805," in *Journals of the Lewis and Clark Expedition*, ed. Gary Moulton, accessed November 15, 2017, https://lewisandclarkjournals.unl.edu/item/lc.jrn.1805-04-29#lc.jrn.1805-04-29.01.

39. Meriwether Lewis, "May 6th, 1805," in *Journals of the Lewis and Clark Expedition*, ed. Gary Moulton, accessed November 15, 2017, https://lewisandclarkjournals.unl.edu/item/lc.jrn.1805-05-06#lc.jrn.1805-05-06.01.

40. Dingess, Roberts, and Gieni, *Manifest Destiny, Volume 1*, 24–25.

41. Marc Ereshefsky, "Darwin's Solution to the Species Problem," *Synthese* 175, no. 3 (2010): 422.

42. Dingess, Roberts, and Gieni, *Manifest Destiny, Volume 2*, 30–31.

43. Dingess, Roberts, and Gieni, *Manifest Destiny, Volume 2*, 97.

44. James Baldwin, "Freaks and the American Ideal of Manhood," in *James Baldwin: Collected Essays*, ed. Toni Morrison (New York: Library of America, 1998), 815.

45. Richard Slotkin, *Regeneration through Violence: The Mythology of the American Frontier, 1600–1860*, new ed. (Norman: University of Oklahoma Press, 2000).

46. Richard Slotkin, *The Fatal Environment: The Myth of the Frontier in the Age of Industrialization, 1800–1890* (Norman: University of Oklahoma Press, 1994), xvi; italics in original.

47. Carroll Smith-Rosenberg, *This Violent Empire: The Birth of an American National Identity* (Chapel Hill: University of North Carolina Press, 2010), x.

48. Stuart Hall, "Introduction: Who Needs 'Identity'?" in *Questions of Cultural Identity*, ed. Stuart Hall and Paul du Gay (London: Sage, 1996), 4, 2.

49. Smith-Rosenberg, *Violent Empire*, x.

50. Thomas Smith quoted in Nicholas P. Canny, "The Ideology of English Colonization: From Ireland to America," *William and Mary Quarterly* 30, no. 4 (1973): 588.

51. Ronald Takaki, "*The Tempest* in the Wilderness: The Racialization of Savagery," *Journal of American History* 79, no. 3 (1992): 899.

52. Robin Wood, *Hollywood from Vietnam to Reagan . . . and Beyond*, rev. ed. (New York: Columbia University Press, 2003), 64.

53. Dingess, Roberts, and Gieni, *Manifest Destiny, Volume 2*, 114.

54. Thomas Jefferson, "Thomas Jefferson to Paul Allen," in *The Papers of Thomas Jefferson, Retirement Series, Volume 6*, ed. J. Jefferson Looney (Princeton: Princeton University Press, 2009), 423–24.

55. Robert V. Hine and John Mack Faragher, *Frontiers: A Short History of the American West* (New Haven: Yale University Press, 2007), 23; italics in original.

56. Jacques Derrida, *Specters of Marx: The State of the Debt, the Work of Mourning, and the New International*, trans. Peggy Kamuf (New York: Routledge, 1994), 37.

57. Homi K. Bhabha, "Introduction: Narrating the Nation," in *Nation and Narration*, ed. Homi K. Bhabha (London: Routledge, 1990), 2.

58. Renée L. Bergland, *The National Uncanny: Indian Ghosts and American Subjects* (Hanover, NH: University Press of New England, 2000), 17.

59. Dingess, Roberts, and Gieni, *Manifest Destiny, Volume 1*, 8.

60. John L. O'Sullivan, "Annexation," *United States Magazine and Democratic Review* 17, no. 1 (1845): 6.

61. John L. O'Sullivan, "The Great Nation of Futurity," *United States Democratic Review* 6, no. 23 (1839): 426, 429.

62. John L. O'Sullivan, "The True Title," *New York Morning News* (December 27, 1845): 12.

63. Gen. 1:26 NASB.

WORKS CITED

Baldwin, James. "Freaks and the American Ideal of Manhood." In *James Baldwin: Collected Essays*, edited by Toni Morrison, 814–30. New York: Library of America, 1998.

Bergland, Renée L. *The National Uncanny: Indian Ghosts and American Subjects*. Hanover, NH: University Press of New England, 2000.

Bergon, Frank. "Wilderness Aesthetics." In *Lewis & Clark: Legacies, Memories, and New Perspectives*, edited by Kris Fresonke and Mark Spence, 37–69. Berkeley: University of California Press, 2004.

Bhabha, Homi K. "Introduction: Narrating the Nation." In *Nation and Narration*, edited by Homi K. Bhabha, 1–7. London: Routledge, 1990.

Biddle, Nicholas. "The Nicholas Biddle Prospectus." In *Letters of the Lewis and Clark Expedition with Related Documents, 1783–1854*, 2nd ed., edited by Donald Jackson, 546–48. Urbana: University of Illinois Press, 1978.

Buffon, Georges-Louis Leclerc de. *Œuvres complètes de Buffon, Tome Premier: Théorie de la terre—histoire générale des animaux*, edited by Marie Jean Pierre Flourens. Paris: Garnier Frères, 1853.

Burke, Edmund. *A Philosophical Enquiry into the Origin of Our Ideas of the Sublime and Beautiful*. London: Dodsley, 1757.

Canny, Nicholas P. "The Ideology of English Colonization: From Ireland to America." *William and Mary Quarterly* 30, no. 4 (1973): 575–98.

Coues, Elliott. "Preface to the New Edition." In *History of the Expedition under the Command of Lewis and Clark: To the Sources of the Missouri River, Thence across the Rocky Mountains and down the Columbia River to the Pacific Ocean, Performed during the Years 1804–5–6 by Order of the Government of the United States*, edited by Elliott Coues, v–x. New York: Francis P. Harper, 1893.

Derrida, Jacques. *Specters of Marx: The State of the Debts, the Work of Mourning, and the New International*. Translated by Peggy Kamuf. New York: Routledge, 1994.

DeVoto, Bernard, ed. *The Journals of Lewis and Clark*. New York: Penguin, 1997.

Dingess, Chris, Matthew Roberts, and Owen Gieni. *Manifest Destiny, vol. 1: Flora & Fauna*. Portland, OR: Image Comics, 2014.

Dingess, Chris, Matthew Roberts, and Owen Gieni. *Manifest Destiny, vol. 2: Amphibia & Insecta*. Portland, OR: Image Comics, 2015.

Dingess, Chris, Matthew Roberts, and Owen Gieni. *Manifest Destiny, vol. 3: Chiroptera & Carniformaves*. Portland, OR: Image Comics, 2015.

Dingess, Chris, Matthew Roberts, and Owen Gieni. *Manifest Destiny, vol. 4: Sasquatch*. Portland, OR: Image Comics, 2016.

Ereshefsky, Marc. "Darwin's Solution to the Species Problem." *Synthese* 175, no. 3 (2010): 405–25.

Furtwangler, Albert. *Acts of Discovery: Visions of America in the Lewis and Clark Journals*. Urbana: University of Illinois Press, 1993.

Gallatin, Albert. "Albert Gallatin to Jefferson, 13 April 1803." In *Letters of the Lewis and Clark Expedition with Related Documents, 1783–1854*, 2nd ed., edited by Donald Dean Jackson, 32–34. Urbana: University of Illinois Press, 1978.

Goetzmann, William H. "Culture of Science: The Long Good-bye of the Twentieth Century." In *Making America: The Society & Culture of the United States*, edited by Luther S. Luedtke, 413–31. Chapel Hill: University of North Carolina Press, 1992.

Hall, Stuart. "Introduction: Who Needs 'Identity'?" In *Questions of Cultural Identity*, edited by Stuart Hall and Paul du Gay, 1–16. London: Sage, 1996.

Hine, Robert V., and John Mack Faragher. *Frontiers: A Short History of the American West*. New Haven: Yale University Press, 2007.

Jefferson, Thomas. "Jefferson's Instructions to Lewis." In *Letters of the Lewis and Clark Expedition with Related Documents, 1783–1854*, 2nd ed., edited by Donald Jackson, 61–65. Urbana: University of Illinois Press, 1978.

Jefferson, Thomas. "A Memoir on the Discovery of Certain Bones of a Quadruped of the Clawed Kind in the Western Parts of Virginia." *Transactions of the American Philosophical Society* 4 (1799): 246–60.

Jefferson, Thomas. "Notes on the State of Virginia." In *Thomas Jefferson: Writings*, edited by Merrill D. Peterson. New York: Library of America, 1984. Kindle edition.

Jefferson, Thomas. "Thomas Jefferson to William Dunbar; May 25, 1805." *Thomas Jefferson and Early Western Explorers*, edited and transcribed by Gerard W. Gawalt. Manuscript Division, Library of Congress. http://www.loc.gov/resource/mtj1.033_0554_0557. Accessed February 15, 2018.

Jefferson, Thomas. "Thomas Jefferson to Paul Allen." in *The Papers of Thomas Jefferson, Retirement Series, vol. 6*, edited by J. Jefferson Looney, 423–24. Princeton: Princeton University Press, 2009.

Leclerc de Buffon, Georges-Louis. *Œuvres complètes de Buffon, Tome Premier: Théorie de la terre—histoire générale des animaux*. Edited by Marie Jean Pierre Flourens. Paris: Garnier Frères, 1853.

Lewis, Meriwether. "April 29, 1805." In *Journals of the Lewis and Clark Expedition*, edited by Gary Moulton. Accessed November 15, 2017. https://lewisandclarkjournals.unl.edu/item/lc.jrn.1805-04-29#lc.jrn.1805-04-29.01.

Lewis, Meriwether. "May 6th, 1805." In *Journals of the Lewis and Clark Expedition*, edited by Gary Moulton. Accessed November 15, 2017. https://lewisandclarkjournals.unl.edu/item/lc.jrn.1805-05-06#lc.jrn.1805-05-06.01.

Lewis, Meriwether. "June 3, 1805." In *Journals of the Lewis and Clark Expedition*, edited by Gary Moulton. Accessed November 15, 2017. https://lewisandclarkjournals.unl.edu/item/lc.jrn.1805-06-03#lc.jrn.1805-06-03.01.

Lewis, Meriwether. "June 13, 1805." In *Journals of the Lewis & Clark Expedition*, edited by Gary Moulton. Accessed November 15, 2017. https://lewisandclarkjournals.unl.edu/item/lc.jrn.1805-06-13#lc.jrn.1805-06-13.01.

Lincoln, Levi. "Levi Lincoln to Jefferson, 17 April 1803." In *Letters of the Lewis and Clark Expedition with Related Documents, 1783–1854*, 2nd ed., edited by Donald Dean Jackson, 34–36. Urbana: University of Illinois Press, 1978.

Manea, Dragoş. "Western Nightmares: *Manifest Destiny* and the Representation of Genocide in Weird Fiction." *Studies in Comics* 8, no. 2 (2017): 157–70.

McMurtry, Larry. "The First American Epic." *New York Review of Books* (February 8, 2001): 39–42.

McWilliams, John P., Jr. *The American Epic: Transforming a Genre, 1770–1860*. Cambridge: Cambridge University Press, 1989.

O'Sullivan, John L. "Annexation." *United States Magazine and Democratic Review* 17, no. 1 (1845): 5–10.

O'Sullivan, John L. "The Great Nation of Futurity." *United States Magazine and Democratic Review* 6, no. 23 (1839): 426–30.

O'Sullivan, John L. "The True Title." *New York Morning News* (December 27, 1845): 12.

Ricœur, Paul. *Memory, History, Forgetting*. Translated by Kathleen Blamey and David Pellauer. Chicago: University of Chicago Press, 2004.

Ronda, James P. *Finding the West: Explorations with Lewis and Clark*. Albuquerque: University of New Mexico Press, 2001.

Ronda, James P. *Lewis & Clark among the Indians*. Lincoln: University of Nebraska Press, 2002.

Semonin, Paul. *American Monster: How the Nation's First Prehistoric Creature Became a Symbol of National Identity*. New York: New York University Press, 2000.

Slotkin, Richard. *The Fatal Environment: The Myth of the Frontier in the Age of Industrialization, 1800–1890*. Norman: University of Oklahoma Press, 1994.

Slotkin, Richard. *Regeneration through Violence: The Mythology of the American Frontier, 1600–1860*. New ed. Norman: University of Oklahoma Press, 2000.

Smith-Rosenberg, Carroll. *This Violent Empire: The Birth of an American National Identity*. Chapel Hill: University of North Carolina Press, 2010.

Takaki, Ronald. "*The Tempest* in the Wilderness: The Racialization of Savagery." *Journal of American History* 79, no. 3 (1992): 892–912.

Tschachler, Heinz. "Ken Burns's 1997 *Lewis and Clark* Television Documentary: American History in Detox." *Revista española de estudios norteamericanos* 19–20 (2002): 165–75.

Turner, Frederick Jackson. *The Frontier in American History*. New York: Henry Holt, 1920.

Wood, Robin. *Hollywood from Vietnam to Reagan . . . and Beyond*. Rev. ed. New York: Columbia University Press, 2003.

CONTRIBUTORS

LAWRENCE ABRAMS is a PhD candidate at the University of California, Davis, specializing in modern British history, focusing on Scottish ethnic, national, and imperial history. His dissertation explores ideas of union and changing modes for the expression of Scottish identity in political, military, and cultural arenas. He is also working on a project investigating the relationship between comics and national identity in an international and postcolonial context in the activist comic years since 1970. He is the coeditor of *Historians without Borders: New Studies in Multidisciplinary History*, a collected volume developed from a conference he founded together with Kaleb Knoblauch.

DORIAN L. ALEXANDER is a PhD candidate at the University of Washington. Currently, their work focuses on the relationship between revolutionary ideology and fantastical literature, with an emphasis on queerness and historical representation. They also specialize in trans and comic studies and teach history at Seattle Central College. Their work can be found in the *Journal of Graphic Novels and Comics*, the book *Gender and the Superhero Narrative* (University Press of Mississippi, 2018), and the comics journalism magazine *The Nib*.

PETER CULLEN BRYAN received his PhD in American studies at Penn State University. His areas of study include American studies, intercultural communication, and twenty-first-century American culture, emphasizing comic art and fan communities. His research has appeared in the *Journal of Fandom Studies*, the *Journal of American Culture*, and *Popular Culture Studies Journal*, exploring the intersections of creative activism and fan identities in adaptational and transnational spaces. He hopes to one day trace the journeys of Scrooge McDuck himself, and to see how reality stacks up to the legend.

MAX BLEDSTEIN is a PhD student in film studies at the University of New South Wales. He has taught courses on comics and composition at the University of Winnipeg and Brandon University. His work has appeared in *Inks*, *Overland*, *The New Americanist*, and *Jeunesse*. He won the 2021 Graduate Essay Award from the Transnational Cinemas Scholarly Interest Group of the Society for Cinema and Media Studies.

STEPHEN CONNOR holds a BA from the University of Windsor, and an MA and a PhD from Wilfrid Laurier University. He is currently assistant professor of history and associate director of the Centre for Study of War, Atrocity, and Genocide at Nipissing University (North Bay, Canada). Dr. Connor's current research agenda focuses on popular culture, war comic books, collective memory, and representations of conflict.

MATTHEW J. COSTELLO is professor of political science at Saint Xavier University. His work examines the construction of America's global role in the twentieth-century popular political culture, principally film and comic books. His published work includes *Secret Identity Crisis: Comics Books and the Unmasking of Cold War America* (Continuum, 2009) and "US Superpower and Superpowered Americans in Science Fiction and Comic Books," in the *Cambridge Companion to American Science Fiction*, edited by Eric Carl Link and Gerry Canavan (2015).

MARTIN FLANAGAN coauthored *The Marvel Studios Phenomenon: Inside a Transmedia Universe* (2016, Bloomsbury), the first full-length scholarly study of the production entity. His doctoral thesis (Sheffield) was concerned with the cinematic relevance of Bakhtinian theories and was published as *Bakhtin and the Movies: New Ways of Understanding Hollywood Film* in 2009 with Palgrave Macmillan. Publishing regularly on comic book, superheroic and general contemporary Hollywood themes (*Authorship, New Review of Film and Television Studies, IXQUIC, Reconstruction,* and *Closure* journals), Flanagan leads the BA program in film studies at University of Salford, UK.

MICHAEL FUCHS is a postdoc in the project "Fiction Meets Science" at the University of Oldenburg in Germany. He has coedited six books, including *Fantastic Cities: American Urban Spaces in Science Fiction, Fantasy, and Horror* (University Press of Mississippi, 2021), *Intermedia Games—Games Inter Media: Video Games and Intermediality* (Bloomsbury, 2019), and *ConFiguring America: Iconic Figures, Visuality, and the American Identity* (Intellect, 2013), and authored and coauthored more than sixty journal articles and book chapters on various aspects of popular culture and American literature. He is the managing editor of the open-access journal *JAAAS: Journal of the Austrian Association for American Studies*. For more on his past and ongoing work, see www.michael-fuchs.info.

MICHAEL GOODRUM is senior lecturer in modern history at Canterbury Christ Church University, and the coconvenor of the TORCH Oxford Comics

Network. He is the author of *Superheroes and American Self Image: From War to Watergate* (Ashgate, 2016), and coauthor, with Philip Smith, of *Printing Terror: American Horror Comics as Cold War Commentary and Critique* (Manchester UP, 2021). His work has appeared in journals such as *Gender & History*, *Studies in Comics*, *Social History*, and *Literature Compass*. Goodrum is the coeditor of *Firefly Revisited: Essays on Joss Whedon's Classic Series* (Rowman & Littlefield, 2015) and *Gender and the Superhero Narrative* (University Press of Mississippi, 2018), and he has chapters in a number of other edited collections.

BRIDGET KEOWN is a PhD candidate at Northeastern University (Boston), who received her BA from Smith College and her MA in imperial and commonwealth history from King's College London. Her work focuses on the experience and treatment of war trauma among British and Irish women during the First World War. She has been awarded the Larkin Research Fellowship in Irish Studies from the American Conference for Irish Studies to continue this research and was named a Dean's Graduate Fellow in the Humanities Center at Northeastern University for 2018–19. She is currently a contributing writer to Nursing Clio.

KALEB KNOBLAUCH is a PhD candidate in modern European history at the University of California, Davis, specializing in France in the nineteenth century, with a focus on Breton and Celtic history, mass culture, gender, and identity formation. His scholarly interest in comics grew out of this project, studying the influence of the Bécassine *bandes déssinées* on Breton identity, and is also developing methods on using comics in the history classroom and examining the relationship between comics, historical representation, visual literacy, and student writing. He is the coeditor with Lawrence Abrams of *Historians without Borders: New Studies in Multidisciplinary History.*

CHRISTINA M. KNOPF is associate professor in communication and media studies at the State University of New York (SUNY), Cortland. She holds a PhD in sociology/communication from the University at Albany. Dr. Knopf is the author of *Politics in the Gutters: American Politicians and Elections in Comic Book Media* (University Press of Mississippi, 2021) and *The Comic Art of War: A Critical Study of Military Cartoons, 1805–2014* (McFarland, 2015), along with numerous essays on pop culture, politics, and the military. She is a Distinguished Research Fellow of the Eastern Communication Association.

MARTIN LUND is senior lecturer in religious studies in the Department of Society, Culture and Identity, Malmö University. His main research interests concern the intersections of comics and religious studies, comics and space, and comics and identity formation. Recent and forthcoming major publications include the monograph *Re-constructing the Man of Steel: Superman 1938–1941, Jewish American History, and the Invention of the Jewish–Comics Connection* (Palgrave, 2016) and the edited volumes *Muslim Superheroes: Comics, Islam, and Representation* (with A. David Lewis; Ilex Foundation/Harvard University Press, 2017) and *Unstable Masks: Whiteness and American Superhero Comics* (with Sean Guynes Vishniac; Ohio State University Press, 2020.

JORDAN NEWTON has an MA by research in history from Canterbury Christ Church University. He has a first-class honors degree in history from the same institution. Newton's MA thesis investigates themes of movement—international, interplanetary, and interchronal—in American popular culture of the early Cold War era.

STEFAN "STEVE" RABITSCH serves as a visiting professor in American studies with the American Studies Center at the University of Warsaw and is an affiliated postdoctoral scholar with the Center for Inter-American Studies at the University of Graz. A self-declared "Academic Trekkie," he is the author of *Star Trek and the British Age of Sail* (McFarland 2019), coeditor of *Set Phasers to Teach! Star Trek in Research and Teaching* (Springer 2018), and coeditor of the forthcoming *Routledge Handbook to Star Trek*. His professorial thesis project, i.e., his second book—*"A Cowboy Needs A Hat": A Cultural History of Cowboy Hats*—received not only the 2019 Fulbright Visiting Scholar Grant in American Studies, which allowed him to work at the Center for the Study of the American West (West Texas A&M University), but also the 2020/21 Henry Belin du Pont fellowship by the Hagley Museum and Library.

MARYANNE RHETT is associate professor of history at Monmouth University (West Long Branch, New Jersey). A world historian who emphasizes Middle Eastern/ Islamic history, nationalism/ imperialism, and comics studies, her scholarly work reflects these directions, for example: *A Global History of the Balfour Declaration* (Routledge, 2015), "The Mask or the Veil" in *The Middle Ground Journal* (2013), and "Orientalism and Graphic Novels" in *Graphic History* (2012). She is currently finishing *Islam in U.S. Comics at the Turn of the 20th Century*, contracted with Bloomsbury.

PHILIP SMITH earned his doctoral degree at Loughborough University. He is coeditor of *Firefly Revisited* (Rowman & Littlefield, 2105), *Gender and the Superhero Narrative* (University Press of Mississippi, 2015), and *The Search for Understanding: Elie Wiesel's Literary Works* (SUNY Press, 2019), and author of *Reading Art Spiegelman* and *Shakespeare in Singapore* (both Routledge 2016 and 2020). He coauthored *Printing Terror: American Horror Comics as Cold War*

Commentary and Critique (Manchester UP, 2021) with Michael Goodrum. He served as codirector of the Shakespeare Behind Bars program at the Correctional Facility at Fox Hill, Nassau, Bahamas. He is associate chair of liberal arts at Savannah College of Art and Design.

INDEX

<to come>

CPSIA information can be obtained
at www.ICGtesting.com
Printed in the USA
BVHW051515051021
618172BV00004B/35